Attuneme

Attunement
Architectural Meaning after the Crisis
of Modern Science

Alberto Pérez-Gómez

The MIT Press
Cambridge, Massachusetts
London, England

© 2016 Massachusetts Institute of Technology

All rights reserved. No part of this book may be reproduced in any form by any electronic or mechanical means (including photocopying, recording, or information storage and retrieval) without permission in writing from the publisher.

This book was set in Sabon by the MIT Press. Printed and bound in the United States of America.

Library of Congress Cataloging-in-Publication Data
Names: Perez Gomez, Alberto, 1949- author.
Title: Attunement : architectural meaning after the crisis of modern science / Alberto Perez Gomez.
Description: Cambridge, MA : The MIT Press, 2016. | Includes bibliographical references and index.
Identifiers: LCCN 2015038400 | ISBN 9780262528641 (pbk. : alk. paper)
Subjects: LCSH: Architecture--Philosophy. | Architecture--Psychological aspects.
Classification: LCC NA2500 .P454 2016 | DDC 720.1--dc23 LC record available at http://lccn.loc.gov/2015038400

10 9 8 7 6 5 4 3 2 1

For Dalibor Vesely
in memoriam

Contents

Acknowledgments xi

Introduction: The Role of Architecture and Urban Design in Psychosomatic Health 1

Chapter 1: Atmospheres and Moods 13

Urban hygiene in modern planning: questions for psychosomatic health. The colloquial use of "atmosphere" and its recovery in recent architectural aesthetics. The phenomenological root of moods and their intersubjective manifestations. Moods and their relationship to the body's expressiveness.

Chapter 2: Architecture as Communicative Setting 1: Premodern Musical Atmospheres 31

The integrated origins of architectural value in the European tradition. Pythagorean harmony and temperance in Vitruvian theory. Understanding musical analogy in architecture beyond formalistic extrapolations. Musical atmospheres in medieval practice and Renaissance theory. Transformations of traditional concepts in view of the baroque musicalization of the world. The unraveling of synesthesia as a cultural commonplace in the late seventeenth century and its consequences for architecture.

Chapter 3: Architecture as Communicative Setting 2: Modern Poetic Atmospheres 71

From Enlightenment Character Theory to Le Camus de Mézières. The place in-between characterized in words. Romantic Gemüt *and* Stimmung. Stimmung *in philosophy: concordant discord and* opening toward death; the place where a fundamental relation to language arises. The articulation of "constructed" emotional space in the novel. The critical dimension of Stimmung: attunement with a hostile world. The theoretical project as alternative manifestation of "character" and Stimmung, from Piranesi and Boullée to Hejduk. Architecture's expanded field: the arts, ephemeral structures, film, and the media. Continuities between romantic philosophy and surrealism: consequences in modern architecture. Case study: Kiesler's Endless House.

Chapter 4: Architecture as an Unveiling of Place   107

The primacy of place (cosmic and cultural tópos). The relationship between narrative and place: from myth to ritual, to narrative program connecting habits to place. The progressive displacement of narrative by scientific space in the eighteenth century. Lambert: perspective as truth granted by God's generalized geometric space. From Newton's space in Boullée as "limited" infinity, the ultimate "cosmic" sacred architecture as coincidence of opposites, to Laplace's atheistic infinity and the cultural acceptance of Cartesian space as factual (subjectivity). Durand and the denial of the imperative of expression in architecture. Hedonism versus Stimmung. The automatic generation of signs in the Cartesian space of descriptive geometry: functionalism. The space of modernity and the concealment of place, from Schmarsow to Husserl and Merleau-Ponty. The return of place through space. From optical cinematic space to embodied depth in Le Corbusier. The role of poetic writing in Hejduk's Victims. The poetic image and atmosphere.

Chapter 5: *Stimmung*, Phenomenology, and Enactive Cognitive Theory: From Habit to Language   139

Mind, body, and consciousness from Descartes to phenomenology. Developments in "third-generation" enactive cognitive science and neurophenomenology. The primacy of synesthesia (intermodality): the central and indispensable condition for architecture's traditional harmony and modern Stimmung. Visual experience is not picturelike. The nature of lived time—the structure of the living present. Intersubjective place, emerging from empathy. The issue of "presence" in architecture: objects and events. Intertwinings with *hermeneutic aesthetics: beauty as meaning in presence (*aisthésis*) and representation. Intersubjectivity, habit, gesture, and emerging language, and the flesh of the world.* Stimmung *as articulation between embodiment (habits) and language (between biological life,* zoon, *and human life,* logon*).*

Chapter 6: The Linguistic Dimension of Architecture: Attunement and the Poetic Word   165

*I. The Voices (*Stimme*) of Architecture. "Everything" is language. The phenomenology of language. The complementarity of mathematical and rhetorical language in classical theory (Vitruvian* dispositio *and* décor *contributing to communicative settings), in contrast with the antagonism between algorithmic and "emerging" natural languages characteristic of late modernity. The limitations of geometries in generating meaning after Durand, coupled with the imperative of aesthetic experimental innovation in modern architecture. Self-referentiality and its limitations. II. The Voice of the Architect. The linguistic basis of the imagination. The concept of "narrative model." Productive fiction and the central role of metaphor to bring moods to presence. Representing architecture through poetic narrative:* prefiguration *or site,* configuration *or atmosphere,* refiguration *or program. The nature of "plot" in architecture, analogies to the novel (dramatic) and poetry (lyric): atmospheres for events articulated discursively and poetically. Architectural form: housing habits and enabling new sensorimotor skills and understandings: the ethical function of architecture.*

Chapter 7: Representation and the Linguistic Imagination   197

The limitations and promises of digital software and media, in view of the primary linguistic imagination. The technical image: Flusser and Poncelet. "Picturing" forms of representation (digital and hybrid) and their modes of presence: perceptual experience is not pictorial, so architecture should not be identified with a mental picture. The propositional use of form in models and images, bringing together program and expression in architectural design. Three examples of metaphorical modeling: Piranesi, Ledoux, and Hejduk. The "virtual" understood through Merleau-Ponty. Possibilities and limitations of the digital simulation of moods and atmospheres.

Chapter 8: Architecture and *Spiritus* in the Twenty-First Century 215

Architecture and the arts. Prereflective transformative atmospheres (atmos) and reflective poetic images. Atman (Sanskrit for "soul") and atmosphere. Architecture in a secularized world for individuals (modern free subjects) defined by their biology (homo sacer). The temptations of "life for life's sake" resulting from the teleology of biological life. "Architecture" as psychotropic drug from Durand to Houellebecq versus architecture as spiritual environment. Romanticism and the "return" of the gods in aisthésis. Attuned environments: a comprehensive alternative to merely ecological and sustainable cities. The possibility of atmospheres conducive to moods appropriate for focal practices that may foreground the enigmatic present temporality of human consciousness.

Notes 235
Index 265

Acknowledgments

While the issues central to this work have been lifelong concerns, the particulars of this book came together slowly and as the result of numerous interactions with colleagues and students. I owe to Dalibor Vesely the recommendation to study the extraordinary philological work of Leo Spitzer on the concept of *Stimmung*, which, together with my expertise in the history of European architectural theories, contributed to the central historical narrative of this volume. This conjunction disclosed important insights, in particular casting new light on the long-standing analogy between architecture and music.

Lian Chang, a former Ph.D. student at McGill, encouraged me to read third-generation cognitive theory, once putting me on the spot by organizing a seminar on the topic during a visit of mine at Harvard. Subsequently, Juhani Pallasmaa and Sarah Robinson piqued my interest even further by inviting me to serve as respondent at a conference on architecture and neuroscience at Taliesin West. The overlaps between romantic philosophy, phenomenology, and cognitive science gradually became clearer in my mind, as did the important connections between primary synesthetic experience and enactive cognition, *Stimmung* and the contemporary understanding of atmosphere.

Jeff Malpas's insights on the relationship between place and emerging language in his philosophical works became the next piece of the puzzle. Jeff was kind enough to ask me to write about the relationships between place and architectural space, adding a crucial dimension to the historical narrative of the problem at hand.

The role of natural language in architecture, understood through hermeneutics, has also been a constant interest of mine. It has been further intensified during the last few years as I have had the pleasure of interacting with a group of brilliant doctoral students at McGill studying specific aspects of this question. Paul Holmquist and Zubin Singh have been writing on Ledoux and Hejduk, respectively, perhaps the most significant modern architects working with literary language as a tool of architectural representation. Angeliki Sioli shares a similar passion for literature and the modern city. This concern prompted us to write a collaborative paper on Edward Casey's work on mapping, which became important for the present chapter on architectural representation; it also led to other projects through a grant to study "Architecture's Literary Context," awarded by the Social Sciences and Humanities Research Council of Canada. These activities, including our presence at a number of topical conferences, were crucial for the structuring of the chapter on language and metaphor in the present volume.

Jason Crow, another former doctoral student and now at Louisiana State University, was a source for all issues related to digital media. His insightful knowledge of history and philosophy, combined with his expertise in all digital matters, were essential in contemplating how the theoretical possibilities explored in this book could become implemented in contemporary architectural practices.

My colleague and former student Lawrence Bird, from the University of Manitoba, read the manuscript and edited it with great care, raising penetrating questions. His own work on architectural representation and media as well as his deep knowledge of my previous books proved invaluable in the process.

I wish to express my profound gratitude to the staff at the MIT Press, most especially to Roger Conover, for enduring support and dialogue over a lifetime, and to the production editor, Matthew Abbate, for his care and dedication. I am also particularly grateful to Jane Friedman, the manuscript editor, for her rigorous editing and inspiring suggestions.

Last but not least, my wife and colleague, Louise Pelletier, carefully considered all my questions at mealtimes and kindly read selected pieces as needed, providing vital dialogue throughout years of research and writing.

Introduction: The Role of Architecture and Urban Design in Psychosomatic Health

How do you feel today? Are you optimistic about your life and work, happy about its apparent purpose, or are you discouraged, sad, perhaps even depressed? We commonly attribute such feelings to either the nature of our activities, to their factual and *objective* character, or to our own *subjective* brain chemistry. What we probably fail to realize is that while either of these attributions may be partially true, our feelings always coemerge with the rest of our bodily consciousness in perception. Our feelings are therefore *located*, bound to a particular *place* with its specific temporality and qualitative character.

Furthermore, feelings are not merely secondary aspects of consciousness, annoying or pleasurable sensations that act as obstacles to our proper lucid functioning. They are important both because they obviously affect us emotionally but also because, as recent neuroscience has shown, *they actually enable our intellectual understanding*, our rational faculties.[1] As explained succinctly by neuropsychologist Douglas Watt (1998): emotion is "a prototype whole brain event." It is a global state of the brain that recruits and holds together activities in many regions, and thus cannot have simple neural correlates; and it is a prototypical whole-organism event, for it mobilizes and coordinates virtually every aspect of the organism.[2]

Sections of this book will be dedicated to elaborating on these observations, drawing on an array of disciplines from philosophy and sociology to neurobiology, and contextualizing their importance for architecture and urban design. I will be arguing that the environment *matters* in ways that perhaps we have not fully fathomed. It matters not only as a material ecology that must obviously be kept alive for the survival of our species, but also because it is nothing less than *a constituent part of our consciousness*. This is a simple claim, yet one that needs to be addressed fully. While the role of architecture designed by professionals may be debatable today for a number of reasons, it is clear that the physical places where we act are of the utmost importance for our well-being.

The question that opens this book, *How do you feel today?*, would be commonplace if uttered by a physician; it has medical overtones. And yet, as we use it in everyday language to greet a dear friend, we should recognize that it is a particularly modern question as well. The awareness of a feeling subjectivity developed in early modernity as a paradoxical consequence of the objectification of the thinking subject in modern (Cartesian) philosophy; it was already understood in the eighteenth century as an alternative to egocentric reason, and finally crystallized as a reaction to positivistic rationality in early-nineteenth-century Europe. It is thus interesting to note that the self-consciously sensitive individual, prone to psychological and psychoanalytic disturbances and traumas, is also the free subject protected by universal rights and freedoms granted by mere biological existence, in contrast to the status of the common man in older monarchic, theocratic, or imperial political systems.

Foregrounding the significance of feeling for consciousness makes it easier for us to grasp the importance of the environment. Yet—and this will be crucial as I recount in the following chapters the historical roots of certain key concepts—the primordial association of feeling with existence, an inner feeling "like a touch," was already put forward by Aristotle in his treatise *On the Soul*,[3] and the connection of medical interests with architecture is as enduring as our Western theoretical tradition.

Indeed, reflecting a much older Greek understanding of these issues, Vitruvius, the first Roman commentator on architecture, wrote about this relationship in the first of his *Ten Books on Architecture* (ca. 25 BCE).[4] Our era of specialized knowledge tends to gloss over such relationships, misunderstanding their import. Vitruvius believed that the main purpose of a well-designed city, one laid out according to the cardinal orientation of the heavens and with respect to the direction of the winds, was to make possible a healthy life; that a balanced environment (*temperies*), the climate or "atmosphere," was fundamental to a balance (*temperance*) of the humors of the body, resulting in a wholesome psychosomatic existence. The role of architecture, particularly the city's orientation and its buildings' properly proportioned configuration, was to mediate between man and nature, the living cosmos, and thereby contribute fundamentally to the maintaining of such balance, allowing humans to live harmonious lives. In fact, the careful ordering of the city according to the heavenly directions and its geometry was a primary, foundational condition for Vitruvius, one that preceded and enabled the design and proper functioning of specific buildings, like theaters and temples. In other words, it is clear that for Vitruvius *the beautiful and the good, qualities of excellent architecture, constituted a single value.*[5] We could then state that architecture, in this expanded sense, made *dwelling* possible, as the German philosopher Martin Heidegger was later to phrase it. For such is the nature of poetically inhabiting the world.[6]

Under normal circumstances we feel well when we are at home, regardless of whether our house has been designed by an architect or a developer. No one would deny that modern houses designed by architects can offer profound and instructive experiences, but the historical role of architects has generally had little to do with the domestic side of things. In our domestic milieus, regardless of whether we own our house or rent it, we manage to fashion places that resonate positively with our aims; we transform even buildings that may in essence be no better than parking garages into cozy corners and appropriate environments, dressed with our memories and hopes. However, as soon as we venture out into our "developing" or postindustrial cities, or we jump in the car for a commute, our emotional state changes. The change will depend on our particular situation, and there are obviously exceptions to the generalities I list below. Historically, however, it was the architect's job to make you feel at home in the city, to intensify your sense of purpose and belonging in public, through the institutions that framed daily life. Indeed, this was the part of life that truly mattered, as it involved our social body, our being with others that reflected back a sense of purpose through our actions.

Our own very different, generally less positive, attitude toward the public realm seems to have its origins in the changing urban milieu of nineteenth-century Europe.[7] Our feelings when we leave home are less certain, for we cherish the privacy that we believe is of the essence; we may even say that most typical urban environments tend to alienate us. The public realm has become a space of transit, or one where we go for voyeuristic thrills, and particularly to consume—when we believe negotiating our needs through the Internet is not possible or desirable.

Regardless, the public realm is inevitably the space where we appear for others as embodied consciousness, and for this reason, as I will further elaborate in this book, it is crucial to our self-understanding. Since the public realm resists its traditional roles, however, we easily reduce it to a GPS map, or try to ignore it by checking our electronic screens until we get to our points of destination or to meet a prearranged online date. It is symptomatic that, in general, modern cities disregard the importance of walking as do modern city dwellers, for whom it is merely an inefficient mode of transit. Yet walking is emblematic as a primary mode of perception, not only because it provides a space of recollection and meditation, but also because it represents our universal human journey; as Antonio Machado's famous poem declares: "wanderer, there is no road, the road is made by walking." Today, this disclosure that puts its emphasis not on the destination but on the action itself no longer seems to matter.

* * *

I have often written about how historical architecture managed to express order. That order was enhancing and profoundly eloquent for human beings in specific times and places, and rooted in their distinct cultures.[8] Despite our present distrust of languages and artifacts as constructs motivated by power and political control, we can recognize how historical architecture managed to orient human action largely by implementing in form and space a symbolic geometry outfitted with articulate ornament. Such architecture operated by giving place to our embodied consciousness; it achieved this both emotionally, by moving us in an appropriate way toward our actions, and intellectually, by reflecting mimetically the picture of a purposeful universe. Indeed, all of this is not difficult to imagine in a time when architecture functioned primarily to frame religious life—one that was lived and felt as religious through and through—revealing cosmic and transcendental meanings in material form and space.

Experienced not through some detached, voyeuristic observation, but by individuals engaged in actions, affected by emotions, and exercising their intellectual, linguistic skills, the order expressed by architecture could be grasped by all members of society. Architecture and the living stories that articulated people's lives—what we often term their identity—resonated harmoniously. Whether the initial concept for a particular structure arose out of the dreams of a medieval monk, the aspirations of a Dutch merchant, or the scientific reveries of a baroque philosopher, the resulting built environment seemed to emerge from the bottom up, precisely like the languages of everyday life, not imposed by any one (genius) in particular, but growing out of the culture itself.

In the traditional cultural worlds that I evoke, both Western and non-Western, political institutions drew their legitimacy from assumed transcendental principles. The architecture and urban configurations that made visible such institutions functioned to house a significant public life that today we may find suspect, and its exploitative means of construction even abhorrent. Yet it was a public life that prioritized the social body as a primary experience, as opposed to the Cartesian ego-consciousness of modernity that culminates in our urban lives as solitary consumers. In other words, architecture was responsible for circumscribing social life and establishing *limits* within which one could *place* oneself. While it sometimes worked in tandem with historical political systems that challenged our democratic values, such architecture in fact also enabled human freedoms.

The epistemological and political revolutions of late-eighteenth-century Europe ultimately transformed all this, foregrounding the sovereign subject that had been developing as a philosophical concept for nearly two hundred years. The individual came to be understood as the unquestionable, autonomous origin of consciousness, endowed with inherent rights and freedoms, to the detriment of the understanding of the primacy of the social body. As Michel Foucault and his followers have stressed, buildings and urban environments thereafter became primary instruments of surveillance and control in the service of the new policed nation-states, necessary mechanisms for coping with the potential excesses of the newly free citizens. This modern confluence of control and self-conscious free will meant that, flourishing in a technological world in which growth and progress were imagined as inevitable, buildings and cities began to enact limits merely following the dictates of political power and setting administrative boundaries, shunning entirely their primary, time-honored function in the furtherance of collective psychosomatic health.

It is plainly obvious that, amid these changed circumstances, some of architecture's long-standing cultural roles could no longer be fulfilled. The important transformations undergone by the profession since the early nineteenth century have been well documented by historians. I have offered my own diagnosis of the scope of the changes that usher in modernity in *Architecture and the Crisis of Modern Science* (1983). City planners prevailed over architects and urban designers, adopting the values of engineers in the service of political power and economic expediency; reason, utility, and efficiency became the determinants of a physical environment that progressively became more sanitized, and, together with the rise of scientific medicine (now truly founded upon the new sciences of chemistry and biology), resulted in an increased life expectancy, most evident nowadays in all so-called developed nations. While one may always argue that a long life is not necessarily a good life, particularly at the expense of others and of the very survival of our humanity, this quantitative gain has comprised one of the most powerful and unquestioned arguments on behalf of the superiority of our technological ways. Other than through a quest for hygienic shelter, architects seemed incapable of playing their traditional role, contributing to the psychosomatic health of society.

Confronted by the inability of traditional forms and processes to express modern values and utilize new materials, architects had no other option but to "experiment," aligning their discipline with the fine arts and deploying creative processes to arrive at novel, emotionally charged forms. Like other artistic disciplines engaged in poetic making—a making that attempts not imposition but disclosure, the revelation of something that is "already there" and is thus familiar to a culture while also being new—architecture during the last two centuries has suffered the limitations of potential solipsism and near nonsense. This is the syndrome of architecture made for architects, particularly, as I will argue in this book, when detached from language and not framed through appropriate critical questions. This has prolonged the crisis—even, some would claim, the agony—of the discipline. Yet the fundamental existential condition to which architecture perennially responded remains as pressing as always: the profound need for humans to inhabit a resonant world they may call home, a healthy world for both mind and body, even when separated by global technological civilization from an innate sense of place.

Eminent thinkers like Martin Heidegger, Hans-Georg Gadamer, and Octavio Paz have demonstrated the vital role the arts must play in a modern and contemporary society, particularly after the loss or weakening of traditional political and religious structures. Architecture shares with the arts a fundamental task: nothing less than a possible unveiling of truths—in a sense that is unlike that of mathematical algorithms and closer to a disclosure of human purpose in the face of mortality, through specific contexts and actions. This task is crucial, and it unfolds into architecture's primary calling to bring about beauty and justice in the world, superseding political ideologies and mere pragmatic considerations. Architecture's central role continues to be to provide a home, ultimately a place of fruition and completeness analogous to erotic experience, a place for dwelling and not merely a shelter for our physical bodies. When most fully realized, architecture offers the gift of psychosomatic completeness, true health and well-being for the social body, a space of appearance consonant with its actions and habits.

So it is regrettable that the central concerns of mainstream contemporary architectural practice seem to be increasingly efficient techniques of fabrication and the commonplaces of sustainable development, as if appropriate meanings would emerge automatically from the process itself. The so-called architectural avant-garde, on the other hand, continues to discuss the relative merits of form generation capable of bypassing language, misunderstood and suspect for its potential (Foucauldian) associations with power. This obsession can be found most recently in the use of algorithmic parameters to design structures supposedly responsive to certain programmatic aims or site conditions. But these merely result in top-down impositions, short-lived novelties that ignore the potential meanings of places, the poetics of materials, and cultural values. Hubert Dreyfus and Sean Kelly have shown how postindustrial environments that inherently express nothing but efficiency accentuate our societies' nihilistic tendencies, reinforced by our dominant rationality.[9] Likewise, environments valorized in terms of the economic payoff their novel monuments may yield, tend to conceal autochthonous values, natural beauty, and biological purpose.

Arguably, even more serious pathologies would plague our world civilization were these tendencies to prevail unchecked. In a future where we finally become eternal through cloning, inhabit indistinct spaces where we remain mostly fixed to computer terminals, live isolated lives protected from disruptive desires while exchanging memories of previous lives with others to pass the time in a pleasurable daze, we would effectively exist out of human time and place. This is the dream/nightmare scenario that, as evoked by Jean Baudrillard, in some ways could appear to be just around the corner. Yet significantly, this future can be articulated only as fiction: an important question to which we shall return in the last chapter.[10]

Human consciousness, one that is not merely in the brain but is fully embodied, needs an external environment pregnant with meanings and emotions for its self-awareness. It is futile to try to hypothesize what might happen if the environment was simply "smooth" and opposed no resistance, like a perfectly "comfortable" place or a drug-induced hallucination. Despite our present enthusiasm for digital communications, for the commodification of sex and violence and their universal availability, our consciousness can't actually exist as a brain in a vat, in the absence of dialogue or exchange of expressive bodies in the bittersweet lived space of the passions that characterize human *love*. This condition, ultimately rooted in our sexual, animal being, brings about the greatest pleasures, yet also pain and great suffering. And our psychosomatic health depends on it. Neurobiologist Semir Zeki has made a similar point describing what he called, paraphrasing Balzac, the "splendors and miseries of the brain." Examining through artistic expressions the organ that has always represented our human evolutionary triumph, Zeki has demonstrated how the human brain is fundamentally determined by an innate concept he calls "unity in love"; the brain itself could simply not function without a lack, the pain and pleasure of desire.[11]

All of this suggests two major paths for architecture in the twenty-first century. It may enhance our human values and capacities, which we might also term our spirituality. Or it may continue eliminating spaces of expressive bodily communication and desire by producing ever more "intelligent" environments, i.e., efficient but ultimately unfulfilling, however sustainable or formally dazzling they may be. This book is aimed at clarifying how architecture can contribute to the former and avoid the pitfalls of the latter.

***

Leaving aside all arguments among dogmatic religions, discredited by their claims to an absolute and exclusive truth, and acknowledging the disenchantment of the human environment brought about by a rational proclamation of the death of God, there are numerous occasions when all of us, regardless of what we believe, feel beyond doubt that life is worth living. *This is the core of aesthetic experience when properly understood,* the capacity of "that which appears" to reveal a sense of purposefulness—be it the smiling face of a child, a poem about love by Sharon Olds, a calm sea, a glorious sunset behind the mountains, or an "unfinished" slave by Michelangelo. This is our proper encounter with beauty, truly a synonym of "meaning." It is not reducible to a polarity between the pretty and the ugly, nor merely the opposite of the sublime, but rather, as Gadamer suggests, the one and only unquestionable value that "simply" appears, that may be shared by many in a particular time and place, and is inseparable from its particular linguistic articulations. It may be found in manmade artifacts and in the natural world, returning us to an insight that is fundamental to our animal life: the biological homeostasis that drives every single cell of our body and is the ultimate engine of evolution built upon purposefulness. Beauty, thus properly understood, is life-affirming, a gift of meaning central to our psychosomatic health, to a sense of attunement with our environment. Offering such attunement through the human actions to which it *gives place* is perhaps architecture's most durable contribution to humanity through the ages.

While it is tempting to follow these thoughts with an analogy to animal architecture, to a wondrous and efficient nest a bird may build to be at home in nature, for example, the issue is far from simple for humans.[12] This mimetic intuition has been present since the beginning of architectural writing, discussed by Vitruvius in relation to the origins of human dwelling in his second book,[13] yet the problem of generating architecture on such exemplary homeostatic models must necessarily operate through language. Aristotle articulated his famous distinction between *zoe* (biological life) and *bios* (linguistic, properly human or political life) in the fourth century BCE. It is obvious that for humans eating is not merely about subsistence, nor sex exclusively for reproduction. The deep awareness of the continuities and differences between animal and human consciousness brought about by human language is always a subtext in discussions concerning architectural meaning in the treatises that make up the Western corpus. Thus, the central concern with harmony as a fundamental element of architectural design since the outset of classical architectural theory is always expressed in manifold ways; it is expected to be both *felt* emotionally and *understood* intellectually, while acknowledging that in the case of humans the outcome of a harmonious, well-tempered environment for action would also enhance a *desire for desire* itself, a paradox for animal homeostasis. In his search for genuine aesthetic meaning in surrealism, André Breton would express this succinctly as the "convulsive" coincidence of desire and fulfillment.

***

In order to better grasp the possibilities for a meaningful architecture responsive to contemporary cultures and their complex interrelations, a task that has largely remained elusive during the last two centuries, it is important to bracket its most obvious objective and formal properties: those that seem evident to us given our scientific and aesthetic preconceptions, such as clever and innovative "composition," stylistic "coherence," good resolution of details, impressive massing, balanced dimensions, structural virtuosity, and "contextual" integration. I will instead turn my attention to the concepts of mood and atmosphere, outlining the recent interest in these notions and articulating their philosophical implications, connections to habits (understood through phenomenology), and potential to carry meaning beyond tectonic and stylistic specificity. I will then draw on the association of atmosphere with the key German concept of *Stimmung*, one that had its modern origins in the philosophy of romanticism. Drawing from Leo Spitzer's remarkable philological study of the word itself, I will elaborate on the roots of *Stimmung* in Western ideas of harmony and temperance (i.e., proportion), concepts that were themselves central in the articulation of meaning in traditional architectural theory. This historical section will demonstrate the depth and importance of the topic, concentrating on how the concept shifted as a result of the epistemological and scientific revolutions that ushered in modernity and then speculating on how it may be possible for us to comprehend fully and grapple with mood and atmosphere today.

A subsequent chapter will follow an alternative historical route to discuss the primary tradition of architecture as an unveiling of place, recognizing the ontological primacy of place and its connections to language. This section will include a discussion of traditional articulations of place and architectural space, and an account of the progressive displacement of narrative by scientific space in the eighteenth century. It will expand on the moment in which the problem of volitional architectural expression was declared fallacious and natural language was intentionally excluded from the processes of instrumental and Beaux-Arts architectural design during the early nineteenth century. These historical accounts will already point to the importance of emerging, poetic, narrative language as a key element in the generation of architecture that will be useful for further discussion.

Deploying arguments from the fields of phenomenology and recent neuroscience, I will then explore the primacy of synesthesia in human consciousness and the nature of human perception as action. Understanding these relationships is key to grasping how *Stimmung* might be put to use today and thus realizing architecture's contemporary potential for attunement. This will prepare the ground for a discussion of the inextricable connections between a primordial synesthetic perception and emerging language, in the sense of Heidegger and philosophical hermeneutics: language as primarily poetic (metaphoric) and at odds with the more prevalent understanding of human languages as constructed, more or less arbitrary codes. Building upon romanticism's insights into the importance of narrative and fiction, I will address the significance of engaging poetic language in design. Taking as a point of departure relevant writings from Maurice Merleau-Ponty, Octavio Paz, and Paul Ricoeur, among others, I will show how natural languages are part of the flesh of the world, how there is a continuity between the expressivity of the body, gesture and language, leading to the crucial role of language in the architectural imagination, one that seeks to accept responsibility for both its authorial voice and the cultures which it serves, ultimately avoiding the arbitrariness and banality of form. I will conclude by returning to the book's initial questions: facing the difficulties concerning the place of spirituality in a nondualistic reality, and highlighting its importance for the well-being and sustainability of human cultures, one in which architecture should play its inveterate, crucial role.

1
Atmospheres and Moods

For hundreds of years the European city remained a theater of complex and diverse atmospheres, sharply characterized for all our senses and perceived as appropriate to many varied public actions. As a place and as a world it created moods that could variously appear or recede into the background of activities, but that rarely assumed the neutral, homogeneous and isotropic quality that we associate with geometric space. In the late eighteenth century this started to change, seemingly driven by a simple quest for public hygiene, and in diverse degrees and with varying speeds resulted in a fundamental transformation of cities into the urban conditions that we encounter today. This was just one of many changes that coincided with the end of the ancien régime and the birth of the modern national states, but that nonetheless had a profound impact on our environment today, robbing *place* of crucial qualitative elements. The space of the city began to be perceived in analogy to the geometric emptiness that could be inferred from a set of Cartesian coordinates: the space of modern planning.

Pierre Patte was perhaps the first late-eighteenth-century French writer to conceptualize the city in terms of "circulation," a metaphor that soon became dominant among planners and that remains unquestioned even today as we think of the metropolis in terms of flux and networks, linking institutional, commercial, and private spaces.[1] While the city had been understood up until this point as a hierarchical assemblage of places for focal action—traditionally, political and religious activities and rituals, and, in the eighteenth century, social and theatrical public functions—Patte believed that better cities called for different priorities, namely an efficient infrastructure for the circulation of goods, vehicles, people, air, and water. Patte was obsessed with clean air, since he, like his contemporaries, assumed that bad smells were causes of disease. He therefore proposed that cemeteries be relocated outside of the city walls (certainly away from the centers, and particularly the precincts of churches), thereby removing the "memory" of death that had always functioned as the foundation of the city for the living. Conversely, Patte's contemporary Jean-Rodolphe Perronet became famous for designing many of the beautiful bridges we can admire today over the Seine in Paris. Perronet insisted on the removal of all ancillary structures that had previously characterized bridges as places, and the lowering of arches so that they could remain almost level with the roads, a development on behalf of improving the efficiency of vehicular traffic. Patte showed how a good city was also defined by effective sewer systems. Water, like air, had to circulate. Ivan Illich has explained how at this juncture water itself transformed in the modern European collective consciousness from a mythical and poetic element, a repository of memory and ultimate substance of purification (one of the four elements of nature customarily cited by Aristotle), into H_2O: a liquid made up of gases that would only fulfill its hygienic function by circulating.[2]

Throughout the following centuries, these changes took hold. While during the eighteenth century strong smell was identified with good health and warm baths with sin and sensual pleasure, during the nineteenth century this equation was largely reversed.[3] Cities became increasingly odorless. The material world could now be conceptualized by the new science of chemistry in terms of the recently developed periodic table of the elements: differences accounted for by quantitative distinctions between atoms. Let me emphasize the importance of this conceptual shift: since *perception is action* (rather than a mere passive reception of sensations—a notion I will elaborate later in this book) and depends on our skills, including those of a conceptual nature, what this meant in actuality was that modern European men and women could no longer easily perceive the poetic qualities and polysemic symbolic potential of water—or any other material, for that matter. The qualities that had always characterized *place* went into hiding. Cities were designed through the "calculation" of rational planners, who naturally ascribed little importance to the atmosphere of public spaces, concentrating instead on urban networks that might efficiently accommodate traffic, spaces that could be surveyed and controlled better for being neutral in character. This surveyability was in line with the ethos of the Baudelairian *flâneur*, who, by definition, was captivated by purely visual phenomena, by the phantasmagoria of the city. Nowadays, even more enlightened planners who argue on behalf of pedestrian cities and struggle to eliminate cars from public spaces tend to use purely quantitative methods and data to further their cause. Such objectives certainly improve the quality of life in places like Copenhagen or Manhattan, for example, but they leave the premises themselves unaltered.

Of course, it is possible to accept and even celebrate the universality of homogeneous, more or less neutral space ("no place") for its associations with the accomplishments of modern life, or to claim that our electronic gadgets may fulfill the role of better tuning the environments we inhabit to our particular needs.[4] Yet most of us are still disturbed by the nearly identical "qualities" shared by car parks and housing blocks, or by airports and corporate hotels, mainly inviting transit and never lingering. We can obviously burn a little incense and light some candles if we wish to cultivate a mood for a romantic evening in our room—on the condition that the smoke detector is not activated and the motion detector doesn't turn on the lights if we move too passionately. While most technologically induced environments do indeed become stages of our daily tragicomedies, it is no overstatement to assert that the moods they inspire are rather negative, generally making us anxious and emotionally disturbed. While the origins of both human happiness and psychopathologies remain a complex and hotly debated issue, there is a malaise and disenchantment clearly linked with our "advanced" consumer societies. Daniel Heller-Roazen speculates that our contemporary inability to mourn (with roots in nineteenth-century mental pathologies) may indeed be an actualization of the Cartesian unfeeling mind that asserts thinking as a condition of existence, practically obliterating (or at least concealing) the Aristotelian "I feel (inwardly), therefore I am."[5] The respective physical environment in both cases, the classical polis and the modern metropolis, I will continue to argue, is an integral part of such consciousness.

Perhaps surprisingly, the impoverishment of the qualitative and emotive living environment in cities was an important motivation behind the late-eighteenth-century recognition of character and atmosphere as visual aesthetic categories, and also, more radically, for the identification of *Stimmung*—"tone or mood"—as essential for artistic communication in romantic philosophy and architectural theory. This second recognition is far more important for the purposes of my argument in this book. I will endeavor to show its origins and significance in earlier architectural treatises, going back to Vitruvius and his equating of good "tempered" architecture (and good cities) with human well-being (both "physical" and "spiritual"). The former, however, has resulted in a more or less continued interest in atmosphere in the visual arts and architecture, one that is positive yet manifold, sometimes superficial as it is associated with aesthetic effects in presentation drawings, buildings, and installations, or even misleading for its problematic psychological and philosophical assumptions. A brief discussion of these concerns will be useful in laying the groundwork for my handling of this topic.

***

In an insightful essay published in one of the last issues of *Daidalos*, the scholarly Berlin architectural journal that appeared between 1981 and 1998, Mark Wigley stated succinctly that atmosphere may well be "the central objective of the architect,"[6] yet, in his own words, one rather impossible "to nail down." The term is used colloquially to denote perceived qualities of space—for example, the "joyful atmosphere" of a sunny summer day, or the "tense atmosphere" in a courthouse prior to the handing out of a verdict. In English we may also use as a synonym the French word *ambiance*, describing the rooms where our activities take place with a full range of adjectives from "cheerful" to "melancholy," "light" to "oppressive." Gernot Böhme, who has devoted major scholarly works to the study of atmosphere in aesthetics, characterizes it as the prototypical "between" phenomenon, for which reason it is easier to grasp in Eastern than in Western ontology,[7] the former being generally at odds with Western dichotomies of idealism and realism, objectivism and subjectivism. Böhme elaborates a concept formulated by German phenomenologist Hermann Schmitz, who argues that feelings do not originate "inside" the self, but are given to experience as "unlocalized, poured forth atmospheres ... which visit (haunt) the body which receives them ... affectively, which takes the form of ... emotion."[8] For Schmitz, atmospheres are "affective powers of feeling, spatial bearers of moods." In Böhme's view, such atmospheres constitute the "space of feeling" or "mood" (*Gefühlsraum*).[9] Recovering important insights from Aristotelian ontology, Böhme concludes that atmospheres are neither something objective, mere qualities that things possess, nor something subjective, mere psychic states. They are "thing-like," in that they make possible the qualitative presence of things, and also "subject-like," in that they are sensed in bodily presence by human beings, and this sensing is at the same time a bodily state of being of subjects in space.[10]

Böhme rightly points to the meteorological origin of atmosphere as a quality of air and climate, and to the fact that it immediately shifts attention away from judgment (what is represented) to sensory perception (how something is present). It thus restores to "aesthetic" its original meaning, suggesting the primacy of perception for human understanding. In his remarkable first book, *The Spell of the Senses*, David Abram reveals the subtle but radical dependence of human cognition on the natural environment, even while affected by technologies that have severed our ancient reciprocity with the natural world.[11] He devotes a chapter to *air*, that "most pervasive presence," that envelops, caresses, and embraces us, inside and out, while being utterly invisible: an unseen enigma that enables life to live.[12] Indeed, air intertwines us with the environment as it nourishes us, and joins us to others through speech, the medium of thought: "its ineffability seems akin to the ineffability of awareness itself."[13] Air, Abram writes, is "the very mystery of the living present, it is that most intimate absence from whence the present presences, and thus a key to the forgotten presence of the earth."[14] Not surprisingly, many peoples understand—and premodern Europeans understood—awareness or mind not as a power residing inside their heads, but rather as a quality that they themselves are inside of, one that is both emotional and cognitive. Buddhist meditation calls for a concentration on breathing precisely to recognize this awareness, while the prereflective and the reflective body align through our attention to the rhythms of respiration, revealing through focused examination the true nature of perception and its primacy in cognition. This is no place for a detailed analysis of the foundational role of this basic, intercultural human characteristic; suffice it to recall the complex meanings of ancient Greek and Latin terms such as *psyche*, *pneuma*, and *anima*: the state of being alive, breath, and consciousness, all rolled into one. For our purposes, this connection of atmosphere in architecture to *air* is already a clue to its relevance in the discussion of architectural meaning.

I will later stress the importance of recovering the original (ancient Greek) sense of *aisthésis*, referring not only to visual perception but to apprehension by all the senses, enabling an understanding through nonrepresentative concepts of that which is perceived by embodied consciousness.[15] It is important to emphasize that atmospheres are spatial phenomena, but always intertwined with temporality; they are never "outside" time. Thus they challenge the present-day ubiquity of telecommunications and its supposedly public spaces by focusing attention on locality and physical presence. This is crucial, as we will consider the possibilities of architectural meaning in a world increasingly consumed by its obsessions for iPhones and computer screens.

Modern architects have debated the merits and limitations of an interest in atmosphere in design, a debate that can be traced back to the early nineteenth century, when Jean-Nicolas-Louis Durand forcefully rejected (for the first time in a text on architectural theory) all uses of watercolor in architectural drawing, manifesting his desire for all architects' plans, sections, and elevations to be drafted with fine, precise lines.[16] This prohibition of atmospheric drawing is congruent with Durand's functionalist position, one recommending that architects ignore any impulse for expressivity and merely "solve the problem" of space planning for buildings in an efficient manner. It coincided with his distancing from his teacher's theoretical projects, the famous drawings of Étienne-Louis Boullée, with their explicit *caractère* that comprised the very agenda of *architecture parlante*: emotive and intellectual communication resulting from the emulation of atmospheres found in nature and articulated in Boullée's poetic texts.[17]

Much later, Le Corbusier reiterated Durand's position in his teachings to young architects, asking students to use a grid and precise ink drawings, explicitly avoiding atmospheric effects in their designs, while Frank Lloyd Wright took an opposite position, often "craving utility and a beautiful atmosphere" in his work.[18] Atmosphere is particularly problematic for modern architects since it is impossible to objectify. This problem had already emerged in the nineteenth century, with some romantic architects attempting to recover the expressive techniques that had been excluded by Durand; the result was carefully rendered presentation drawings of the selfsame functional buildings, but hardly an opening up of the design process to *Stimmung*. Architects that embrace atmosphere find it impossible to approach it directly, to "nail it down," as it were, particularly if the standard tools of representation are taken for granted, with their explicit or implicit dismissal of the temporality of presence as a dimension of perception. As I will discuss later, this stance is implicit in the writings of poststructuralist theoreticians in the lineage of Jacques Derrida (like Mark Wigley), and one taken for granted in many discussions concerning the aesthetic merits of contemporary "starchitecture."

One of the most significant attempts to engage atmosphere at the level of urban design in twentieth-century Europe came from the situationists, who reacted against the neutrality of the modern planned city and referred to "architecture as pure atmospheres." For Guy Debord this meant deemphasizing building in favor of décor, one capable of producing "distinct psychic atmospheres" that might be differentiated in cities.[19] Again, given the ambiguity of the concept, and arguing from his political and sociological standpoint, Debord soon rejected Constant Nieuwenhuys's architectural vision of New Babylon, the machinelike city producing discrete and mutating atmospheres. He regarded the configuration of appropriate atmospheres as a project of a revolutionary society, capable of molding its own décor from the bottom up.

Nevertheless, the visions articulated by Constant (among others) during the last century seem to have inspired a widespread trend, buttressed today by digital media and favored in recent parametric and biomorphic architecture. In these, all senses of a spectator—usually assumed to be a passive "recipient" of sensations—are engaged through electronics, light, and sound in order to produce emotions and "affect." For their explicit objective of engaging all the senses, such multimedia works have been generally understood as quintessentially atmospheric architecture. A notable early example is the Philips Pavilion designed by Le Corbusier for the 1958 Brussels world's fair (whose experiential space was designed mostly by Iannis Xenakis), and, much more recently, the H_2O Pavilion on the island of Neeltje Jans (in Holland) by NOX/Lars Spuybroeck.[20] The multisensory experience in the Philips Pavilion was driven by behaviorist psychology in an attempt to evoke atmospheres through a collage of perceptual stimuli, producing a "forced" synesthesia. The H_2O Pavilion is meant to create proprioceptive (internal bodily) stimuli, related to the movement and position of the "recipient," who interacts with the building though sensors and "interfaces" with data transmitted to a computer from a weather station monitoring wind speeds and water levels. The result is a constant modification in the light and sound that accompanies the visitor, supposedly revealing something of the essence of water.

The deliberate engagement of synesthesia in such projects is certainly interesting and in itself not problematic. On the contrary, a full understanding of perception as primordially synesthetic, and of the stakes implied by that fact, is intrinsic to the design of good architecture. Architectural meanings emerge in "performance" as events; they are not primarily intended for a voyeuristic, objectifying, or touristic gaze. Yet coupled with a misunderstanding of perception's true nature and its relationship to cognition, and given the present-day identification of the brain (understood as the sole organ of consciousness) with the computer, to pay lip service to synesthesia leads to numerous failures, among them the confusion of knowledge with information and of digitalized interactivity with intersubjective embodied dialogue. It also perpetuates the fallacious divide between the aesthetics of emotion and that of judgment. For this reason, the architecture that results often borders on hallucination, such as the emotive architecture that "bleeds, exhausts, that turns and even breaks ... that pricks," articulated by Coop Himmelb(l)au,[21] or the living architecture described by J. G. Ballard in his works of science fiction: "psychotropic" houses that respond to the inhabitants' emotions by moving, shifting and even committing murder.[22] Such misunderstandings are also behind the nightmare of so-called "intelligent" architecture that ostensibly reproduces (and improves) the logical patterns of human reasoning as it interfaces with its inhabitants.

***

Among contemporary architects engaged with the issue of atmosphere, Peter Zumthor stands out as exemplary. His buildings create atmospheres so as to reveal qualities of *place* that appear as autochthonous, resonant with the activities to which rooms and spaces in his projects are particularly dedicated. His manner of working is reminiscent of that of Adolf Loos, who wrote that the great architect, a true artist, must first "identify a feeling for the effect he wants to create."[23] Appropriate effects such as "fear and terror in a dungeon, divine awe in a church, or gaiety in a tavern" must be clearly identified, and yet, Loos insists, "they originate in the material used and the form."[24] Indeed, only in this way can architectural atmospheres expect to become poetic images, acquiring permanence and staying power.

In his own writing Zumthor explicitly relates the concept of atmosphere to architectural quality, explaining, "quality architecture to me is when a building manages to move me."[25] Zumthor relates the experience of atmosphere to the importance of "first impressions," valorizing the prereflective knowledge of the embodied mind as it acts in perception. "I enter a building, see a room, and—in the fraction of a second—have this feeling about it. We perceive atmosphere through our emotional sensibility—a form of perception that works incredibly quickly."[26] Providing a lyrical description of a square in early spring while sitting at a café, in view of its flower market, the right number of people, a wonderful range of noises, temperature pleasantly fresh and warm, and its architecture in the background, he asks himself what is so moving about the experience: "I remove the square and my feelings disappear. I could never have had those feelings without the atmosphere of the square."[27] And yet, how can an architect achieve atmospheres with such intensities, capable of sustaining such resonant moods? Like many architects, Zumthor has a tendency to identify such moods in paintings and photographs; his book *Atmospheres* is replete with such examples. In fact, the volume's epigraph is by John Turner, who in 1844 famously stated in a conversation with John Ruskin: "Atmosphere is my style." All the same, designing "objects for use," as any architect must, Zumthor recognizes the complexity of that goal: seemingly appearing in between objective qualities and subjective expectations.[28] While the distinct and emotive "moods" of paintings and photographs can offer important insights to the architect, the nature of architecture as space for framing human actions is altogether different. Are there clues in the tradition of our discipline that point to strategies for embracing modes of understanding, perception, and representation other than the pictorial image? This is indeed the question I wish to pursue.

One crucial lesson we can already extract from this cursory account of the valorization of aesthetic atmospheres in modernity is the fact that architectural quality understood in this way has very little to do with "formal style," whether connoting the identifying traits of an architect's work, a fashion, or a historical category. Issues such as formal coherence or semantic expression of any kind (regional difference, cultural identity, gender, ideology, marketing, and the like) may or may not contribute to such quality, but they can never fully subsume it. In other words, architectural meaning does not simply obey the rules of semiotics and its signifying pairs—its relationship to language will be shown to be of a different order. Not that these categories of communication are unimportant in themselves, but they must be understood as subsidiary. Architectural quality likewise is hardly the result of the formal novelty that secures the inclusion of projects and buildings in the latest journals or websites. Since architectural quality is distinct from the particularities of style, it also precludes its reduction to formal categories such as simplicity versus complexity, frequently used today to justify computer-generated formal fashions. In other words, Antoni Gaudí and Le Corbusier, Ludwig Mies van der Rohe and Frederick Kiesler, John Hejduk and Sigurd Lewerentz, Steven Holl and Peter Zumthor, have all produced works that are, while physically and tectonically very different, conducive to the creation of appropriately tuned moods for human situations, revealing affective purpose in and through the human actions they frame. Not all the works of a given architect accomplish this feat, but when they do, it is of the greatest cultural and life-enhancing value.

In the introduction to an anthology entitled *Paradoxes of Appearing* (2009), Michael Asgaard Andersen and Henrik Oxvig set out to explore the importance of moods and atmospheres in architecture.[29] This collection of essays extends the interest discussed thus far in the fleeting emotional reality that characterizes the spaces we occupy, a reality so essential to architectural meaning. Andersen and Oxvig rightly argue that such awareness has escaped traditional philosophy until relatively recently, quoting Merleau-Ponty, Böhme, and Gilles Deleuze. The result, for them, has been an objectifying aesthetics that misses what is essential in architecture.

Similar concerns drive a number of even more recent publications on the subject, which came to light during this book's preparation. *Architectural Atmospheres: On the Experience and Politics of Architecture* (2014), edited by Christian Borch, is a collection of essays by Gernot Böhme, Juhani Pallasmaa, the artist Olafur Eliasson, and the editor, first presented in a 2011 conference on the topic.[30] Both Böhme and Pallasmaa insist on the limitations of reducing architecture to images, stressing instead the importance of multisensory experience for grasping the full potential of architectural and urban spaces. Borch enjoins the reader to consider as well the political connotations of atmospheres, capable of inducing particular behaviors. In a succinct and brilliant essay published in 2015, David Leatherbarrow entered the conversation with a brief summary of the importance of the concept as it developed during the nineteenth century, followed by a sharp discussion of the foibles of understanding atmosphere as a mere "orchestration of effects."[31] While acknowledging the significance of the notion as it relates to habits and embodiment, Leatherbarrow warns against its reification apart from the tectonic qualities of a building.

Indeed, the challenge remains to comprehend fully how atmospheres may convey not only fleeting sensations or emotions but also cognitive meanings through settings of events. This is indeed a central issue for architecture when placed squarely beyond eighteenth-century aesthetics, a discipline that reduced primary aesthetic cognition to a *gnoseologia inferioris*, or a "secondary class of judgment."

* * *

Atmosphere clearly matters for humans in multiple ways and is related to our emotions and moods. Yet, given our propensity to fall back into Cartesian object-subject dichotomies, it is crucial to emphasize that we don't "project" our own interior mood on the natural or cultural landscape; our perception is not "merely" subjective. Rather, moods are primarily mimetic of natural places and manmade spaces. David Abram describes how our various "interior" moods were originally borrowed from the earth, itself moody and capricious.[32] Thus, "anger and livid rage" derive, at least in part, from "our ancestral, animal experience" of violent thunder and lightning. Similarly, the "emotional release" fed by the flow of tears can be seen as coming from rain, clarity of mind from transparent air and a blue sky, and inward confusion from the experience of being enveloped in fog. "Our conceptualization of the emotional mood or 'feel' of things is unavoidably entwined with metaphors of 'atmospheres,' 'airs' and 'climates.'" As such, we may conclude that the environments in which we live, with primary reference to nature itself, have their own "feeling-tone" that can be revealed to different cultures through poetic language.[33]

Abram further notes that prior to the dissolution of the Aristotelian cosmos amid the scientific revolution of seventeenth-century Europe, the earth and sky felt like an interior shared by mankind, of varying dimensions and qualities in diverse cultures and times. This space might have been associated with a vast tent, a body, or a temple, but it was always protected and intimate. Not surprisingly, human architecture and cities were always mimetic of this cosmos, not only its perceived figure, articulation, and intelligibility, particularly in the Western tradition after Plato, but also its atmospheric moods. The questioning of this autochthonous interior by the new concepts of space in classical physics in the aftermath of Copernicus and Galileo coincided with a turn inward in the philosophy of Descartes, the birth of modern subjectivity. I have previously written about the grave architectural consequences of the dissolution of the Aristotelian cosmos as a primary referent, and will consider its impact on the issue of atmosphere in the next chapters.[34]

For the moment it is important to note that, despite our modern, often-egotistical self-understanding, we cannot have emotions without the external prompts of the environment. I hinted above at the crucial argument by Antonio Damasio, who demonstrates that emotions are crucial for cognition; they have a life-enhancing, evolutionary origin and are borne out of the body's engagement in the world. In this light, good architecture should be primarily concerned with creating the moods appropriate to positive emotions that support ethical human action, articulated in the form of a narrative program, inevitably enhancing a wholesome (*whole* and *holy*) and healthy life; more on this later. Even if the ordered, intersubjective cosmos is gone, metaphoricity is at work everywhere in human experience, as is the central metaphor: *the inner is the outer*. Thus, proper architecture can be expected to reveal that we belong (and experience purpose), that we may be "at home" *in* the earth: on the earth, under the sky. And for mankind, *home* is not merely an isolated house; it must necessarily be a social space for embodied communication. Moods, as we will see, are eminently communicative; they have a bearing on *habits* that themselves are at the root of perceptual cognition and are central to the primacy of our social reality.[35]

***

Modern architects, from Durand onward, have often argued for the self-referentiality of the discipline. Perhaps most famously, Peter Eisenman has insisted over the years that the problems of architectural design are strictly formal and syntactic; "program" should be of no concern, since the building, once it is realized and exists in the public realm, can be used differently. As recently as 2014, he criticized Rem Koolhaas's curatorial project for the Venice Biennale on architectural "elements" and their historical transformations for its disregard of syntax as the only crucial issue for architectural meaning—since, according to Eisenman, "a window is always a window," now or in antiquity.[36] For such a position, it

[margin note: NARRATIVE PROGRAM]

appears obvious that architecture's intentional aesthetic values must not depend on the contingencies of history or program, for who can deny that a Greek temple, for example, preserves its architectural values even if it is used today as a tourist attraction. This stance constitutes a license to design "architecture for architects," to experiment with all manner of form generation desperately vying for novelty. And yet, despite the apparent logic of the argument, the problem is far from simple when we attempt to determine appropriate and responsible tactics for architectural and urban design.

The dream of self-referentiality is a long-standing one among modern and contemporary artists, architects, and writers, struggling since the nineteenth century to free themselves of the tyranny of signs, of the expectation that their works should convey unambiguous messages to attain the same legitimacy accorded by society to the language of scientific prose and applied science. And yet, even if a poem is crafted with words "about words" rather than being "about the world" (as in the case of Stéphane Mallarmé), the imperative of speaking about something "other" remains. Works in any discipline that don't recognize the importance of their cultural (historical) or natural worlds often appear irrelevant or make little sense. It is significant that Eisenman himself for a brief period in the early 1980s seemed able to understand the limitations of his position. It is worth quoting in full:

> I am no longer interested in semiology: I am interested in poetics, and I think they are very different concerns. Equally, I am no longer interested in philosophy, but rather fiction. I think fiction is much more philosophical than philosophy. I do not have much relationship today with my earlier work dealing with syntax. I do not reject or deny it. It merely is something else. ... It is the poetic aspect of architecture which now interests me. No matter how many syntactically correct architectural sentences we might make, they may not contain poetry.[37]

The consideration of moods and atmospheres is an important step to overcoming these contradictions and apparent dead ends in modern and contemporary architecture. Hubert Dreyfus has been an articulate proponent of this position, discussing in a recent paper the distinction between the mood *in* a room and the mood *of* the room.[38] Our actions can indeed change the mood in a room; we can joke, scream, or dance in a baroque church, or use it for events that, while distant from a Jesuit liturgy, retain something kindred with it, perhaps the performance of a Bach concerto. Such actions can range from being receptive and in the spirit of dialogue with the perceived qualities of a place to being frankly critical and challenging. As we noted, the mood of a neutral modern room can be manipulated through incense or lighting or even artificial acoustics. All of this is to say that, in fact, the user "transforms" the space through his or her actions, exactly as a poem is renewed and changed every time a reader returns to it—even without turning the page. This goes to the heart of our matter and will be discussed in later chapters: the difficult-to-grasp yet crucial temporal dimension of architectural meaning. Nevertheless, without the atmosphere provided in the first instance by the baroque architect for a specific meaningful human action in the vivid present, no later significant interpretations would be possible. Architects must thus be capable of infusing spaces with particular tones resonant with focal actions: cheerful, sad, oppressive, quiet, familiar or strange, agitated or quiet. One could argue that such moods are "built in," like those in a work of poetry; one could imagine a neutral space, intentionally open to all moods (like Miesian architecture, a favorite ideal of modernity), or a collection of rooms with specific moods. There might even be the option of designing rooms that support and encourage a specific range of moods appropriate to an intended use. At best, the outcome is an environment that "makes sense" for a particular action and reveals, whenever architecture "occurs," purposefulness and limits.

The design of appropriate moods and atmospheres for human actions is a central topic of this book. I will be gathering evidence to unpack the fundamental nature of this concern for architectural meaning, trying to propose some concrete strategies with firm philosophical and historical foundations. For the contemporary architect, all problems become issues of representation: how can we "represent" intended moods in design once these are identified? While digital technologies keep developing and opening possibilities, mostly through software that is not dedicated to architectural design,[39] it generally remains true that "in the virtual world the mood of the background space cannot come to resemble the mood of a similar space in the real world and so give guidance to the architect."[40] I shall expand on this problem in a later chapter on representation, but first I must attempt an introductory approximation to the issue of moods in relation to lived experience. My aim here will be to contextualize the questions that frame the historical interpretations in the following three chapters.

***

As observed above, moods are not "merely" subjective but, rather, are primary in perceptual experience, intertwined with *place*, setting the tone for cognition, action, and thought. Besides Hubert Dreyfus, a number of important modern philosophers, such as Gilbert Ryle, Martin Heidegger, Maurice Merleau-Ponty, and more recently Nick Crossley and Alva Noë, have concerned themselves with this problem.[41] Their point of departure is an overcoming of the Cartesian (dualistic) understanding of reality; the Cartesian model fails to explain the way moods are normally shared in the everyday world, where our bodies spontaneously express our moods and others pick up on them and respond to them.[42] Merleau-Ponty calls this "intercorporeality" and writes: "It is as if the other person's intention inhabited my body and mine his."[43] Recent neuroscience has found an explanation for this phenomenon through the identification of "mirror neurons," firing in our brains whether we make a determinate motion or merely see another person moving in a similar way (the same theory that is currently accepted for the phantom limb syndrome). Yet this explanation should not return us to the assumption that all is resolved in the brain. In fact, as Crossley points out, much more is at stake, namely, the primacy of intersubjectivity or the "social body" (the notion that we are mindful and embodied agencies and not objective minds and bodies) over the Cartesian construction of the ego-centered individual, with its identity residing inside the skull.[44]

We think of moods and emotions as inner occurrences, generated by our subjectivity, mainly because of the language of feelings we use to refer to them. When we say that we feel "scared" or "moved," for example, these words may refer to the experience of a number of bodily sensations. Such emotions, however, are always contextual; the same inner bodily sensation could evoke a diverse feeling in a different context.[45] Merleau-Ponty has put this succinctly: for human consciousness there is a coincidence of the inner and the outer; my sadness is the melancholy of a rainy day. Beyond this, emotions are articulated by natural languages and must be learned (like jealousy, for instance), and they are heterogeneous, since they may also involve personal inclinations (such as introversion). In sum, emotions do not refer to various bodily sensations or to "ghostly, inner mental states" but, instead, render specific configurations of sensation, behavior, and disposition intelligible by relating them to an environment, to architecture.[46] Giving place to appropriate emotions, architecture may bring about the meaningful articulation of bodily activity in a worldly social context.

Emotions are ways of being in the world—*attunements*, as Heidegger called them—bodily transformations that operate at a prereflective level. Like sleep, emotions "come over you." One can invite them, and architecture can be instrumental in doing so, but they come from the outside, like the Greek divinities in epic literature and drama. Both Merleau-Ponty and Heidegger agree that our existence is always "mooded."[47] Heidegger writes: "Attunements ... in advance determine our being with one another. It seems as though an attunement is in each case already there, so to speak, like an atmosphere in which we first immerse ourselves ... and which then attunes us through and through."[48] Like an atmosphere, a mood is shared and is contagious (like laughter and yawning), as used to happen in traditional ritual activities and still may today in dramatic, sports, or political events.

Moods are also ambivalent, an ambivalence mirrored in the architecture that gives them place. On the one hand they are our fundamental manner of being with one another, for affect is always present in consciousness, even when seemingly neutral or cold. They even influence our thinking; emotions are crucial for cognition, as I observed above, citing Damasio. As such, the moods or emotions infiltrating our being so as to underlie all our experiences, even without necessarily being recognized, are potentially those that compel us beyond all others. Thus Heidegger can write: "those attunements which attune us in such a way that we feel as though there is no attunement there at all ... these attunements are the most powerful."[49] Yet on the other hand, since they come from outside and take us over, they can also be very noticeable; Sartre understood emotional outbursts as magical transformations that bring new levels of meaning into situations.[50] In this sense, they seem to stand outside of us. The Greek epics show precisely this situation: Helen was taken over by Eros and famously caused the Trojan War, but on her return her husband Menelaus did not blame *her*. As we will see later on, Nicolas Le Camus de Mézières, the first architect ever to deem it crucial to verbally articulate the mood of rooms for architectural meaning, still identified these with Greek divinities. Whether a mood so fills us as to erase the distinction between us and the world, or is perceived as a separate being coming to us from without, our attunement to a situation makes things relevant to us (Homer certainly thought so): we feel more complete and become participants; our lives matter. Supporting this experience may be architecture's humble yet vital (and difficult to accomplish) achievement in a secular age. The challenge is to grasp exactly how this possibility stems from a deep and genuine architectural tradition and its cultural roots, and how it may be implemented.

Dreyfus observes that Heidegger, after discerning the foundational importance of attunement, evokes the possibility of dwelling in spaces built around "focal practices" that draw a group together in a shared mood so that the action may be experienced as purposeful. This is precisely what occurred in the Greek theater during the spring festivals in classical Athens, an experience described by Aristotle as *catharsis*, a form of emotional and intellectual cognition that oriented the spectators of Greek tragedies to their place in the cosmos, destiny, and politics, and perhaps happens still to some degree in Hans Scharoun's Berlin Philharmonic Hall during musical performances, to give one recent example. Mood "can bring us in touch with a power that we cannot control and that calls forth and rewards our efforts—a power that we, therefore, (may) recognize as sacred."[51] The sense that a mood is shared is constitutive of the excitement; every individual perceives himself or herself as part of a larger whole, even though the recognition of spiritual wholeness may not be corroborated by intellectual understanding (as in contemporary sports events, for instance, obviously not equivalent to the sense of orientation granted by a Greek tragedy or a contemporary work of art). Moods are truly gifts that come from the outside and are out of our control. These events are often represented in film and literature as "reconciliatory," like a meal that may start in discord and eventually brings everyone together. These are the moments in which architecture manifests itself most clearly, as it differentiates itself from the lived environment and its generalized affect, and yet is significant only as it responds to the tacit emotional tone of cultural existence.

Emotionality is always present in human experience and is related to sexual desire. In his *Phenomenology of Perception*, Merleau-Ponty explains how we are fundamentally driven by sexual desire, how erotic perception is not an intellectual representation but occurs as a bodily aim for another body in the world; this is what matters to us, but unlike in animals, this is no fixed instinct resulting in set behaviors.[52] Sexuality is a dimension of our being-in-the-world shaped by other dimensions of our social life, but "our perceptual and motor life is sexually structured."[53] Eros, the divine and human creative force that joins and separates, is the basic human emotion, at the root of love, our greatest gift, as philosopher Jean-Luc Marion has characterized it.[54] According to Merleau-Ponty, the other distinctly human desire is a "desire for desire, or desire for recognition," which stems from our discovery of the Other's consciousness in childhood.[55] Thus we develop self-consciousness, and interdependence arises. This desire, stresses Crossley, is central to the constitution of the social world (Alexandre Kojève, Merleau-Ponty's teacher, famously stated that human history is the history of desired Desires).[56] A desire for recognition is precisely what motivates Hannah Arendt's "space of appearance," the fundamental characteristic of public space and the kernel of architecture.

Emotionality is a constant aspect of our milieu because things matter to us, not merely for their use value, but because they are symbols of the desire for the Other.[57] Excellent architecture, one that may reveal life as purposeful, accommodates the space of desire without trying to foreclose it (through mere comfort—or by hiding its openness to death, the horizon bounding our lives). It accommodates and furthers the appropriate moods for focal actions (unfortunately not always appreciated in our era of distraction and electronic gadgets) that allow humans the possibility of being present. These are as varied as a meal in common, an engaged conversation, or making love: actions that become habitual and crystallize into a social contract.

2
Architecture as Communicative Setting 1: Premodern Musical Atmospheres

I have suggested that the communicative function of architecture, at once emotional and intellectual, operates primarily through the *atmospheres* that qualify humanity's space of desire, giving place to focal actions, ultimately to significant events. I evoked the affinities of atmosphere with air, the breath of climate, and of air with speech: these alone suggest architecture's capacity to speak intersubjectively, revealing *places* endowed with moods or qualities, constituting the receptacles of consciousness. All of this also starts to illuminate architecture's true, yet often ignored or misunderstood, unique aptitude to imitate our natural habitat between the earth and the sky, acknowledging its priority for human dwelling as our sole and *finite* home. As I will explain later, this true *mimetic* capacity is poetic, and therefore not reducible to platitudes from sustainable development or mathematical and geometrical architectures based on imported concepts from instrumental science (such as biomorphism or biomimetism). It is obvious that multiple factors contribute to the creation of atmospheres, among them forms and their geometries, the dimensions and proportions so familiar to architects. But equally and often more important are colors and textures of surfaces, the weight and origin of materials, the care or lack of detailed execution, and the characteristics of varying sorts of light: their evenness or flickering quality, relative permanence, or rate and nature of change. The qualities of diverse sounds, acoustic reverberation or absorbency, olfactory qualities and their combinations, and so on contribute just as much to the creation of atmospheres. The difficulty is that while it is easy to generate a list such as this, and some of these characteristics are relatively easy to control through instrumental design operations, our embodied experience where meaning actually appears is always *primarily* synesthetic and enactive. In other words, it is never possible to simply add one characteristic to another as a factor in an equation, or as if it were a question of information that might be reduced to 0s and 1s. The experience of a whole is primary and not differentiated among the sensory modalities, and it always hinges as well upon *invisible* availabilities present to perception in particular circumstances, such as the properties of a site, and what may be accessible "behind the walls."

It is encouraging to see that many modern and contemporary artists and architects have become concerned with atmospheres, mostly aiming for the "in-between" of a reality so often presupposed as dualistic (subject/object). Yet, in many cases, the production and reception of such works assume perception to operate *partes extra partes*, through autonomous sensory mechanisms, as the conveyance of "information" to the brain. Regardless of very diverse formal preferences ranging from orthogonal to organic shapes, crystalline to folded, simple or complex "tectonics," the aim is mostly that of effect. Recognizing the imperative role of participation in the conveying of aesthetic emotions, multimedia artists and architects often engage changing atmospheres as a means of interactivity. This may involve the spectators or inhabitants, but more often than not it simply demands awareness through technologically produced effects. As such, it is crucial to emphasize that the real issue is not some seductive interactivity, flashy effect, or "changing liquid quality." While it initially emerged in the context of artistic practices by romantic writers and artists, the concept of *Stimmung* was not merely borne of the reification of a subjective observer. Rather, as I will argue in chapter 3, to properly understand its scope in modern artistic practices after romanticism, one must understand the concept of atmosphere in light of the full linguistic range that the German word *Stimmung* possessed at its inception. But in this chapter I will first show how the concept itself has deep roots in the mainstream architectural tradition, in its European theories and practices. These considerations will better equip us to grasp its full potential.

* * *

It will no doubt surprise most readers to learn that the concept of *Stimmung*, at the root of the present interest in *qualitative* architectural atmospheres, often associated with the ephemeral and "subjective," has its origins in the Pythagorean notion of world harmony and its "objective" mathematical ratios, formalized by Plato in his dialogue *Timaeus*. This seeming paradox is fundamental to the arguments in this book. Plato's work is central to the architectural theories in the Western corpus from Vitruvius to early modernity; it is a key to their understanding of beauty and meaning, particularly in terms of the concepts of harmony and proportion. The simple story from *Timaeus* is as follows: the Demiurge (a figure eventually assimilated with the Judeo-Christian Creator) made the cosmos with an eye to mathematical perfection, the "music of the spheres" evident to the naked eye in the workings of the luminaries in the superlunary world; and the architect emulates this operation in the creation of his buildings, giving order to the human world.

Plato's articulation of the "music of the spheres" led architectural writers, from the time of Vitruvius to the end of the seventeenth century, to emphasize the centrality of a musical analogy to the creation of meaningful architecture. This analogy has captured the imagination of architects, and countless books, projects, and essays continue to be devoted to its decryption. Goethe famously suggested that architecture is "frozen music," but what does that mean, exactly? The tendency has been to conflate the issues of harmony and proportion with questions of formal composition: the "correspondence" of parts of buildings among themselves as constituting a perfect whole, from which nothing can be added or taken away. This has often defined architectural beauty as perfect syntax, regardless of the particularities of its elements or even its historical period—a definition that remained operational even after the paradigms of classical architecture were questioned in modernity. I will argue that this seemingly obvious interpretation of the musical analogy is profoundly flawed. We seem to have missed the most vital issue, which is not formal refinement, but the creation of atmospheres. Yes, the musical analogy that is set forth in relation to architecture does concern beauty, the experience of harmony, but its crucial dimension is a deeply felt psychosomatic health. The creation and inhabitation of such an architecture is an experience that is present through human action, through a lived, good life; its aim is not a detached "aesthetic," critical, or disinterested contemplation.

To grasp the cognitive value of musical or harmonic atmospheres and the confluence of the qualitative and the quantitative implied in *Stimmung*'s linguistic origins, it is imperative to keep in mind throughout these pages a proper understanding of Plato's articulation of reality. This is particularly true in regard to the delicate problem of the appearance of *ideas in* the place/space (*chóra*) of human experience (*aisthésis*). It is crucial that we resist reducing such articulation to the (misunderstood) dualistic Platonism of a modern technological culture that regards *ideas*, particularly mathematical entities, as external to lived experience. Such is the position of ideas evidenced universally through the top-down instrumentalization of science.[1] The present chapter will conclude precisely at that moment when Plato is misunderstood in the architectural writings of Claude Perrault, who was profoundly influenced by René Descartes's dualistic (mis)interpretation of *ideas*.

***

This chapter is guided by Leo Spitzer's masterful philological study of *Stimmung*.[2] As Spitzer reveals, the range of the German word is astounding, capable of denoting both fugitive emotionalism and an objective apprehension of the world. Moreover, there appears to be a constant, unrelenting musical connotation attached to the term, a potential musicality present in the word's family, along with its intellectual connotation of environmental unity and the feelings prompted by it.[3] Spitzer explains that the German word seems uniquely modern in that it gained currency after the Enlightenment, yet is fundamentally indebted to the all-embracing Greco-Roman and Christian traditions at the root of all European languages—what Edmund Husserl liked to call the "spiritual history of Europe." In its current German meaning of "changing mood of the moment," *Stimmung* translates easily into "mood" or "atmosphere," "humor" or "temper." Its more prevalent early European sense as the "unity of environment and man," however, finds no full equivalent in common modern usage and translations. In fact, the word originally did not suggest a changing, temporary condition but rather a stable "tunedness" of the mind, *the attunement of embodied consciousness*.

Indeed, according to Spitzer *Stimmung* partakes of two semantic threads interwoven in ancient and medieval thought: the ideas of the "well-tempered mixture" and the "harmonious consonance." Through an exhaustive analysis of textual evidence from philosophy, theology, literature, and music theory in Western cultures, Spitzer concludes that the two concepts, κεράννυμι (*keránymi*, in Greek), which translates as *temperare* (in Latin), meaning "to mix or combine in the right proportions" (as in the combination of water and wine to make a tempered drink), and αρμονία (Greek), translated as *concentus* or *consonantia* (Latin) and meaning "harmony and concert" (of musical sounds or forms), cannot be fully grasped apart from each other. As Spitzer explains, both semantic threads were integrated in European culture and separated only during the seventeenth and eighteenth centuries. Only after the Enlightenment, he concludes, did European thought come to question the central feeling of musicality at the core of all meaning. It is important to stress that the modern German *Stimmung* nevertheless retains these two etymons, sometimes reflecting one, sometimes the other; this is particularly visible in some translations of the word, as in the French *accord* or the English *temper*.

In the following pages I will examine some selected instances from the history of architecture and its theories, most of them well known, to remind the reader of the central role both concepts and their constellations of related ideas played in the articulation of architectural meaning. Under the new light shed on these concepts and with the help of brief allusions to the history of music theory, however, the connotations of such architectural theories will appear different from their conventional understanding, typically framed by a retroactive imposition of notions of architectural value and meaning drawn from eighteenth-century aesthetics. Tracing the persistence and transformations of both concepts through time until the late eighteenth century will already suggest some options that open up in early modernity and that are perceived and handed down to us by romantic philosophy (a story to be continued in the following chapter). But first let us further unpack the two word families associated with *Stimmung*.

***

On the side of the "well-tempered mixture" (like all those necessary to make bricks, concrete, paint, or glass, for example), we have the Greek verb κεράννυμι.[4] The cognate κρᾶσις (*krásis*) denotes "the right mixture," or "equilibrium." In Latin it is translated as *temperatus*, meaning "temperate," "moderate," or "in balance," as in, for example, the desired climate—atmosphere, ecology—of a city that may lead to a healthy and well-balanced life. The *temperies*, or "right proportional mix" of the four (Aristotelian) elements constituting the environment (water, air, fire, water), with their dynamic qualities (of heat, cold, moisture, dryness), are reciprocated by the four bodily humors for good health; in sheltering these, architecture must contend with the *intemperies*, the outdoors, identified as "adverse or intemperate weather, temperature or climate."

During the first century BCE Cicero further associated *temperans*, "temperance," with *sóphrona*, "prudence," implying that what is temperate (like a person's character) is also appropriately ordered and wise; conversely, *distemperantia*, "distemper," is both "disorder" and "illness" (in Greek, δυσκρασία, *diskrasía*).[5] So *temperare, temperantia* refer to both moral and psychic harmony and to climate, demonstrating the reciprocity of the inner and outer realms of consciousness and evoking psychosomatic health.

The Greek term εὐκρασία (*eukrasía*)—"health," "harmony," "balance"—epitomizes the central objectives of architecture as set out in its theories from Vitruvius to the baroque. Its Latin equivalent, *temperatus*, yields *tempus*, "segment of time" (Greek καιρός, *kairós*), the etymological origin of the word *time* in modern European languages. Being etymologically related to *temperance*, it means not *any* time in some mathematical continuum of seconds, but "the right or convenient time for action" and "the right measure." This definition, along with its sense of "a cut-off section," can be spatial as well as temporal: thus, it is the root of *templum* (Greek τέμενος, *témenos*), "temple," that which is "set apart" from ordinary space and time. *Templum* becomes the archetype of architecture, both as a temple building and by its designation of the ordering focus of the ancient city, the location where a gnomon was placed to translate the cardinal order of the heavens onto the land and determine the orientation of the city fabric, where *cardo* and *decumanus* cross. Given its associations with time, *temperare* (to temper) would denote an "intervention at the right time and in the right measure," effected by a wise σώφρον (*sóphron*), perhaps an architect who "adjusts, adapts, and mixes," seeking to harden or soften materials or effects. According to Spitzer, the Greek notion of measure and order inherent in σωφροσύνη (*sophrosíni*) pertains even to the most menial, everyday utensils, and eventually underscores a musician's need to "temper" the strings of an instrument for its proper tuning.

The second word family composing *Stimmung* has its origins in the Greek term αρμονία (*armonía*). This term is clearly significant for the present study since *harmony* became a key term in architectural treatises from Vitruvius to the eighteenth century, as they sought to clarify the nature of architectural meaning or beauty: of that value which is unquestionably "given in appearance." It is important to note that *armonía* was initially a quality of embodiment, of perfect adjustment and articulation, stemming from a deep-seated preoccupation of Greek culture straddling the preclassical and classical eras, which projected this concern at all levels: language, anatomy, the figurative arts, music, artifacts (including the *daídala*—objects and buildings—made by the *architektón*), and military and political orders.[6] *Armonía* originally meant "joining," "agreement," even a "well-crafted joint"; only later did it signify a concordance of sounds and the more general "combination or adaptation of parts, elements or related things, so as to form a consistent and orderly whole,"[7] with more explicit reference to mathematics. Conversely, συμφονία (*symphonía*) works "in reverse" as it imparts its musical order to situations and listeners.

In Latin the two Greek terms, *armonía* and *symphonía*, may be respectively translated as *consonantia* and *concentus* (the modern term "concert" renders both *symphonía* and *concentus*). Spitzer also notes the close affinity between the Latin *concentus* and *temperantia* (from the first word group under discussion).[8] Notably, *concentus* is also in *concinnitas*, perhaps the most crucial term in Leon Battista Alberti's theory of Renaissance aesthetics, summarizing his concerns with proportional harmony and metaphorical signification in architecture. In the first chapter I suggested that architecture frames focal actions (ritual, political, or familial) that lead to "concord." *Concord* and *accord* are complex cognates of the musical Latin terms, usually deployed in regard to fulfilling human situations, situations that make us whole and reflect purposefulness. *Concordare* refers to both the "tuning and harmony of hearts" (*cor, cordis*) and "chords" (χορδή, *chordí*): a duality that reveals the reciprocity of psychological and environmental harmony. Finally, the Latin verb *concertare* means "to fight" and "to emulate," rendering words from Greek that contain both φίλια and ἔρις, denoting "harmony within strife." For Heraclitus, *strife* (the arrow) can easily turn into the lute, both attributes of Apollo.[9] The name of the bow (βιός) is "life" (βίος) and its work, "death." The Greek mind was able to perceive harmony in discord, the triumph of "symphony" over discordant voices, the potential for unity while acknowledging the "bittersweet" space of desire that characterizes the human condition.[10] *Con-certare* implies the idea of a world harmony to which one must strive to adjust oneself; music and architecture are privileged means to this end. The Romans inherited the concept of "discordant concord," or *concordia discors*, as Pliny writes. Posidonius, the brilliant Stoic philosopher most likely to have influenced Vitruvius, conceived of this notion as a cosmic principle of world cohesion.

* * *

Underlying European spiritual history, which culminates in our world technological civilization, is an appreciation for the fundamental role of music as a carrier of intellectual and emotional knowledge. We ultimately owe this heritage to the centrality of music in Greek thought, an interest that was passed on both to Christianity (through the Fathers of the Greek and Latin churches) and to Islam (through the Arabic translations of Greek texts). Music's centrality is underscored in Plato's *Republic*, in which musical innovation is forbidden because altering the laws of music is seen as potentially endangering the state's foundations.[11] The *poietís*, Creator, is a poet and a composer, ultimately driven by external forces (divinities). In this the *poietís* differs greatly from the *dimiurgós* (sculptor), who is more properly a craftsman and closer to a *vánausos* (technician). *Techné-poiésis*, "architectural creations," were soon recognized as possible outcome of both modes of endeavor. This duality reflects the complexities of architecture's status, intertwined with the order of religious and political institutions, and throughout Western history relating in varying fashions to both the mechanical and the liberal arts.

Democritus states that the essence of human happiness consists in "harmony"; playing the flute, he writes, is the remedy for most ills of the flesh.[12] To arithmetic, astronomy, and geometry he added music, completing the group of perfect mathematical disciplines that comprised the enduring *quadrivium* of the classical liberal arts. However, the connection between these disciplines and the physical environment of lived, everyday experience was never taken for granted. In general, ancient thinkers recognized that ideal perfection belonged in the human mind (and in the superlunary realms of the planetary motions), and not in the world of existing beings on earth. It followed that human artifacts could only approximate such perfection via imitation, particularly via the crafts that prioritized harmony, such as music and architecture. In other words, a geometrical discipline such as Euclid's does not identify "Euclidean space" as a realm where humans dwell; ancient thinkers never believed that humans actually existed in Euclidean space. Yet the perfection of geometry did evoke the possibility of human places as harmonious atmospheres. In fact,

Democritus prefers to emphasize the attainment of harmony through the proper proportion, or *temperance*, of the four elements. Not surprisingly, he is mentioned by Vitruvius at the outset of the latter's discussion of architectural materials, all conceived as dynamic mixtures of the four Aristotelian elements.[13]

In its earliest form, the musical concert—or harmonious, temperate, and moving environment—was not a performance on a narrow stage for spectators in search of entertainment. Rather, it was a song articulated every day and night by a fittingly ordered nature, eventually echoed by the human community. The "concert of the stars" is no mere metaphor originating in musical performance as we might think today; it was initially the night itself that gave the concert, Plato's awe-inspiring "star dance" that enthralled and seduced humans as they turned to face the sky; this was the event recalled in *Timaeus* as the origin of philosophy and the arts.[14] Harmony is given to man's understanding in the contemplation of the heavens, a synesthetic experience that encompassed all the senses, not only for enjoyment, or for the thrill of effects, as we may easily imagine today, but as an ally of the soul in search of order. Plato equated the world soul with light, emanating from the luminaries in the sky and reciprocated by our eyes to enable vision, and with the good (*agathón*). He therefore aligned it with world harmony, not the harmony Democritus identified in the physical elements, but an incorporeal harmony, a mathematical harmony present in the regular heavenly motions that would eventually enter Neoplatonism and Christianity as an aspect of God. Archytas of Tarentum, a Pythagorean friend of Plato, had set out what he thought were the precise physical laws of musical harmony in proportions—the relationship between the length of strings and the pitch of tones (2:1, octave; 3:2, fifth; 4:3, fourth, etc.). For him, mathematics and music were "sister disciplines."[15] In *Timaeus*, Plato uses the exact same ratios to set forth a new cosmogony, a story about the origins and the order of the cosmos and its contents brought about by a musically (and mathematically) inspired Demiurge. This story, of a vastly different nature than Hesiod's seventh-century BCE divine genealogies, applies these ratios to located resonances between the divine world soul, the regulation of the cosmos (*physis*, the environment), and the human mind (*psyché*).[16]

The tetrachord—number four in Pythagorean cosmology—was perceived as crucial, the foundation of the "sacred tetractys." The well-tempered state of the soul, the body, and the universe depended on the harmonious combination of the four elements and their dynamic forms as qualities of heat, cold, moisture, and dryness.[17] These four basic qualities of Heraclitus, when mixed, constituted the human body and the climate. For this reason, temper and temperature, personal health and climate, are imbued with the moral connotation of temperance, *eukrasía*. *Krásis*, or *temperantia*, denotes the aim of reconciling opposing forces—Empedocles's "strife and love"—in line with Greek teaching on the temperaments which became most explicit in Hippocratic and Galenic medicine (humoral pathology). *Eukrasía*, the "quality of the world soul," was identified with the sun in Cicero's *Dream of Scipio*, the text that introduced the Pythagorean theory of the harmony of the spheres to Christians. As I have suggested, the Romans used a number of terms to express harmony: *temperans, concentus (concinere), convenientia,* and *consensus (consentiens)*, the last of which often also related to anthropomorphic terminology.[18]

***

Vitruvius wrote his architectural treatise around 25 BCE, several years after the death of Cicero. The text is famous for being the unique extant classical source setting out architectural theory, Vitruvius's own acknowledgment of multiple precedents notwithstanding. Regardless of the author's degree of intellectual sophistication, which has been a source of debate, the book reveals *armonía* and *temperantia* to be the ultimate objectives of architecture, objectives that characterize its meaning and value for human society and its role as a communicative setting for framing significant actions.[19] Among those he cites as precedents are Pythagorean teachings, the writings of Heraclitus, Democritus, and Epicurus, in addition to the works of Plato and Hippocrates. He was also influenced by Cicero and probably more immediately by the Stoic interpretations of Greek philosophy, which tended to reduce the distance between the ideal mathematical disciplines and their applications. Geminus of Rhodes, writing circa 73–67 BCE, for example, believed in the existence of two kinds of mathematics, intelligible and perceptible. Among the latter, those potentially present to experience, he lists disciplines evidently ruled by geometries, like astronomy and optics, while including practices kindred to music and architecture, such as canonics, geodesy, and mechanics.[20]

A careful examination of book 1 reveals important insights that support our interpretation of Vitruvius's position. His treatise is not about efficient technical production, formal composition, or innovation. Instead, his use of *ratio*, or discourse, partakes of the principles of Greek *theoría* (Lat. *contemplatio*), acknowledging the ontological priority of cosmic harmony (in his *corpus* Vitruvius includes an entire book [book 9] on astrology and the means to translate the geometric order of the heavens onto the earth by means of sundials). In book 1, describing the nature of the architect's knowledge, Vitruvius emphasizes the importance of the mathematical and grammatical disciplines (the liberal arts, from Cicero) necessary to realizing the communicative potential of the architect's work. Theory serves as a means for the architect to align his work with what matters, to create works that respond to the given order of nature; Vitruvius insists that theory is the same for a doctor or an architect, for example, since it has to do with knowledge to orient action. It is "contemplative" in nature, crucial for an architect, who, like the Platonic Demiurge in *Timaeus*, keeps an eye on perfection to bring about his work in imitation of the cosmos. The aim of such theory is *sophía*, also called "theoretical wisdom," a combination of *nous*, "the ability to discern reality," and *epistéme*, a type of knowledge that is logically built up, and teachable, and that would be eventually equated with science. It concerns universal truths, such as the mathematical basis of harmony (proportions) in design. Such theory, however, is neither a prescriptive technique nor an applied science; the actual practice of architecture was never understood as the "application" of such theory. Rather, *faber* and *techné* (making and technics) issued from both talent and acquired skills, becoming an irreducible knowledge of the body that was moderated by a specific *practical knowledge*, also deemed to be different from *theoría*.

Indeed, this latter form of discourse corresponds more closely to Aristotle's "practical philosophy," constituting a way to articulate *phrónesis*, "practical wisdom" or "wisdom in action," through the telling of stories. Practical knowledge leading to *phrónesis* also involves a capability for prudent rational thinking to consider actions that can deliver desired effects. Aristotle states that *phrónesis* is not simply a skill (*techné*), since it involves the ability to both achieve a certain end as well as to reflect upon and determine positive ends consistent with the overall aims of a good life: the stability involved in good politics. This constitutes the ethical dimension of action.

In chapter 2 of book 1, Vitruvius describes the crucial terms and operations for good architecture. He reiterates the Greeks' conviction that architecture must imitate the harmonious articulation of the superlunary cosmos. Human existence occurs in the sublunary world, in a universe of perpetual generation and corruption. It is only through the realizations of arts and crafts (*techné-poiésis*), and specifically through *mímesis*, that this world can embody the mathematical/musical harmony of the superlunary world. This is the role of the expressive and constructive arts like music and poetry, and particularly architecture: they reveal, in this realm of finite existence, an order analogous to that of the heavens by imitating the "heavenly star dance." Thus, Vitruvius insists on the importance of order, *dispositio* (the Greek *táxis*), on the basis of proportions, using terms like "commensurability" (the Greek *symmetría*) and "eurhythmy" to describe how well-adjusted parts can contribute to the experience of harmony.[21] In the same section, he immediately alludes to the difficulties of actualizing such harmonies in the physical world: *sollertia*, a "cunning, practical intelligence" (the Greek *métis*), is crucial to make all adjustments necessary for works to convey such intended perfect harmonies, particularly in view of the specific nature of works and the weakness associated with human vision, prone to distortions due to site conditions, the location of perceived elements, and the like.

Next, and directly following this important clarification, Vitruvius describes the "species of design" that today we associate with the standard forms of architectural representation, particularly the plan and the elevation. But he understands these as footprints and physical traces, rather than as sections or projections: the forms of representation with which we are now familiar. While I have discussed issues of representation elsewhere,[22] I should emphasize here that Vitruvius is not speaking of drawings as we might think. However these *idéai* (Greek) might have been externalized, the ultimate aim for the architect was performative. That is, the architect was ultimately responsible for creating the setting for communication, particularly the public "space of appearance," in the form of appropriate atmospheres for the different focal actions that constituted cultural life. Vitruvius concludes this section with a long discussion on "correctness," décor, decorum, related to ornament, the dress that architecture must wear to actually function in public. In this section his discourse shifts to the telling of stories drawn from traditions, a form of practical philosophy deploying *phrónesis* and applied to important issues of meaning and buildings' appropriateness to natural sites and cultural situations (focal actions as programs)—such as the appropriate ornament on columns in temples according to their tutelary divinities, and so on. It is important to note that, though on the surface these considerations are rendered as formal issues and for us may appear even arbitrary, the numbers involved in the proportions as well as the words that compose these stories act in concert. Both elaborate how precisely architecture communicates, how it can be mimetic of the cosmos through the architect's cultivation of *sophía*, seeking harmony. They together contribute to architecture's engagement of our emotions in view of a specific location and particular program, one made temperate through *phrónesis*.

Indeed, for Vitruvius harmony is the fundamental quality of beauty (*venustas*), literally sexual attraction: an arrangement of parts that seduces the user/observer and creates a significant, "well-tuned" space for human activities, *the right atmosphere*, in turn, leading to a wholesome, healthy, and meaningful life. Thus, it is inconceivable to interpret the other two famous qualities of architecture identified in chapter 3 of his treatise—"solidity," or "soundness," and "commodity," or "utility"—as independent values related to building engineering or planning.[23] Instead, they are all aspects of meaning, contributing to the experience of harmony. We have established that the Latin verb *concertare* is both "to fight" and "to emulate"; it contains the two Greek terms *phília* and *éris*, "harmony within strife," signifying the possibility of unity while acknowledging the bittersweet space of desire.[24]

In this chapter, Vitruvius also enumerates the three kinds of artifacts that qualify as architecture—buildings, machines, and gnomons—a combination that appears enigmatic only when we see them as modern objects. A machine in the context of a living *physis* (as opposed to a modern machine in a natural world, itself conceived as a physical mechanism) is also liable, not unlike a building, to reveal the harmonious workings of the celestial luminaries, governed by *mathémata*. And finally, the gnomon is crucial in connecting the task of the architect to the earth, precisely by literally grounding the order of the heavenly star dance.

The gnomon is in fact key to explaining the transition to the next and final chapters in the foundational first book, which deal with cities. On the surface this would appear to be an abrupt shift in scale, going directly from the education of the architect and basic architectural principles to questions of urban design, yet the sequence makes perfect sense in view of our considerations. For Vitruvius, the central concern is to first ensure that the right order is in place for all building operations, so that life may be healthy, beautiful, and just. Thus the *templum* (the high ground at the center of the *urbs*) of architecture must be established, at which the gnomon, or "shadow tracer," establishes the connection between the harmony in the sky, particularly the four cardinal directions (north, south, east, and west), and the order of urban space, the place for humans. Once this order is established, the *cardo* and *decumanus* may be traced, limits named, doors located, and corners firmly marked—and building can proceed. The musical order drawn from heaven's star dance is evidently symbolic of cosmic *armonía*, but it is equally connected to the experience of nature, namely the experience of air, *atmosphere*. It is linked with the invisible winds (breath, spirit) that bring about changing qualities, both positive and negative, to urban dwellers: *temperantia*.

This last issue is of great concern to Vitruvius, for whom understanding and consideration of the directions of the winds is fundamental, since they actualize the mixtures of heat, cold, moisture, and dryness. Drawing from Greek humoral medicine and its belief that all illness comes from the outside, from the *intemperies*, he declares that atmospheric *temperance* (today what we might call "ecological stability" or "biological homeostasis") is fundamental to ensuring good life, and that the architecture of the city must achieve this objective. We should also recall that in Pythagorean medicine, music was believed to be the best cure for ailments, since the issue was the proper attunement of body and soul, a concept that was revived in the Renaissance by Marsilio Ficino, among others.[25] Regardless of the stylistic and symbolic specificity of classical architecture which obviously responded to the distinct nature of habits and values in Rome, in contrast to our post–French Revolution individual rights and freedoms, we can recognize in this concern deeply resonant interests; and this is indeed the issue I would like to emphasize. It is perhaps not surprising that an early German rendition of Vitruvius in Rivius's *Baukunst* of 1547, uses the formulation *concent der Stimmung* in relation to book

2, chapter 2 of the treatise. According to Spitzer, this phrase refers to the "temperament" of music brought about by tuning, and is identified with the "harmony of symmetry," stressing the musical possibilities of Vitruvius's term *commodulatio*.[26] We will explore the importance of an increased musicality evident in late Renaissance and baroque architectural theory after a brief detour through the Middle Ages.

***

While acknowledging the self-evident ontological priority of the heavens, Aristotle was skeptical about Plato's harmonious world soul. Nevertheless, he thought of friendship as a musical performance emerging from the tuning of two souls. This concept of *philia* was adopted by the Church Fathers.[27] For the Christians, a central issue related to well-being and eventual salvation in the afterlife is the feeling of *caritas*, also built upon an analogy between music and Christian love, which is, indeed, the nature of cosmic order.[28] Writing in the fourth century, Ambrose described the third day of Creation in *Hexameron*, incorporating the Greek concept of world harmony, with enthusiasm for the beautiful and good world as leading toward the transcendental God.[29] According to Spitzer, Ambrose must be credited with the invention of Christian hymns—a response in sounds and thoughts to divine grace, humanity contributing pious songs to nature's singing waves, both of them sacred.[30] This is nothing less than an *incarnation* of the music about which the Greeks speculated—world harmony itself—an important accomplishment continued in later European musical traditions.[31] The Christians replaced the star dance of the heavens with the dances of angels, and thus the Greek Fathers introduced *choreia*, ritual dances, in the church.[32]

In contrast to Ambrose, his near-contemporary Augustine of Hippo turned the problem of harmony "inward." As understood by Augustine, only man's self-consciousness, resting on temporal-rhythmical grounds, could lead to an intuition of world harmony and God. Drawing from Plato, Augustine associated the Judeo-Christian God with the Demiurge, yet in his cosmology He was the *Archimusicus* as well as the *Architectus*, capable of creating the world *ex nihilo*. His cithara is a monochord, and his harmony a sequence in time ruled by number; the perception is temporal, rather than the spatial fullness of Ambrose's performances.[33] In our present purgatorial stage, waiting for what then appeared to be the imminent second coming of Christ, Augustine stresses inner-worldliness, closer, as I will show in the next chapter, to romantic *Stimmung*, deployed in view of *unpoetic* immediate surroundings. Amid the chaos immediately following the wake of the Roman Empire, Boethius wrote in the fifth century that music, *musica humana*, is so naturally united with us that we cannot be free of it, even if we so desired.

We should recall the medieval ambivalence concerning architecture and human works reflected in Augustine's two cities, the Purgatorial City of Man and the perfectly cubic, crystalline, and harmonious City of God as described by John of Patmos in the Apocalypse (Rev. 21–22:5): the diaphanous city descending from heaven at the end of time. The highly skilled master mason is always a tool of God *architectus*, communicating His intentions through the Bishop or the Abbot, and his work is based on geometrical procedures, not numbers. While with its cubic and circular perfection the ideal City of God, described in poetic words, could be visualized, drawn, and desired, the cathedral—the Christian *urbs* or *ecclesia*—is always unfinished.

The idea of world harmony, in which music symbolizes the totality of the world, was ever-present in the Middle Ages. Yet it is important to emphasize music's affinity with *arithmetic* in the *quadrivium*, a grouping consolidated by Boethius in the fifth century. The Pythagorean tradition insists on relating music to "multitudes," to the four first discrete (natural) numbers (Greek *arithmós*), as opposed to "magnitudes," the continuous and irrational measurements of *geometry* that have direct applications to the world of men. This supposition remained unquestioned until the mathematical work of Nicolas Oresme in the fourteenth century and the musical experiments of Vincenzo Galilei in the sixteenth, eventually allowing for a modern scientific conception of precise music intervals between the twelve semitones of an octave in a pentatonic scale measured through frequencies.[34] This account reveals the insurmountable distance that was assumed to exist between the perfect superlunary world and the corruptible sublunary sphere in medieval Christian/Aristotelian cosmology. Divine providence had mixed the tones so that music, though rational, was mysterious: becoming an objective reminder of (Christian) truths ultimately inaccessible to the human mind.[35] Even Pythagoras, according to Boethius in his telling of the story about the ancient sage discovering musical harmony while visiting a forge, recognized a "fifth hammer" in the ensemble that emitted "a single consonance from differing sounds," yet it was a hammer in utter discordance with all, one that had no proportionate mass to the others and could not be reduced to any of the first four natural numbers that divided the monochord, and was thus discarded by the sage.[36] Medieval musical practice remained attached to the monochord—a succession of tones ruled by intervals among the first four natural numbers. Nevertheless, by the ninth century John Scotus Erigena could define the music of the *organum* as polyphonic and compare it to the concept of "discord in concord" in the whole creation. Erigena's theodicy is based on world harmony, on the musical proportions that are rooted in man's inner sense, a transcendental sensitivity that makes us feel the sweetness of harmony.[37]

The great Gothic abbey churches and cathedrals of the twelfth and thirteenth centuries, emerging as a unique architectural synthesis in contrast with previous elaborations of older Roman forms, are already a manifestation of European humanity's greater confidence giving material form to the unfinished City of God. The imminence of apocalypse abated, and amid the growth of urban culture, universities, and new monastic orders, the Christian belief in the potential perfectibility of God's creation by men and their works took on new meaning. This is evident, for example, in the writings of Hugh of St. Victor, who emphatically valorized the crafts for human salvation.[38] Creating positively miraculous environments filled with dim, gemlike luminosity, soaring inexplicably and flaunting the coherence of their structures, the great Gothic churches are striking in comparison to their Romanesque predecessors. The Neoplatonic origin of Gothic light metaphysics (by association with the writings of Pseudo-Dionysus) has been often pointed out.[39] Still assuming the ultimate supraluminous and incomprehensible darkness of God (and His music), the material support provided by architecture—its stonework, furnishings, windows, and religious artifacts such as bejeweled relics and reliquaries—became indispensable to the ascent of the human soul to an encounter with God.

This is clear in Abbot Suger's writing on the renovation of his abbey church at St. Denis, the first building where Gothic architecture was implemented in full: a remarkable achievement that has been studied from many angles, from the political to the aesthetic.[40] Suger writes eloquently about the anagogical power of the crafted materials toward Christian illumination.[41] More recently, Jason Crow has stressed the importance of the crafting of stone itself in this accomplishment, analogous to the transmutation of a base *prima materia*.[42] This is an *ars* (*techné-poiésis*) conducted through geometrical and alchemical processes that *tempered* terrestrial materials through "cutting, shaping, forging, molding, filing and polishing to approach the ineffable matter of the heavens." In his two documents on the administration and consecration of the church, Suger describes the completion of his "perfect stone." Crow speculates that craft operates in analogy of God's creation of Christ—the exemplar of the dual being with a single nature—in terrestrial matter, transforming his domain into a glowing gem.[43]

Gothic cathedrals, true centers of medieval urban life, were key to physical and spiritual health, encompassing all knowledge deemed necessary for salvation, like the Scriptures themselves in the form of *Biblia pauperum*, and capable of resonating with the musicality of the human soul. And yet it must be emphasized that it was only through ritual action that heavenly harmonies became fully evident. This is most explicit in Suger's passage on the consecration of his church, where he first evokes the disorder of crowds in the cramped, old building he had inherited: bodies pressing up against each other, mixing and moving in a violent and turbulent manner. During the consecration, however, all participants were assigned specific locations and followed a set choreography. Suger created a veritable *choreia*, a cosmological dance during his dedication ceremony:

> You might have seen—and those present did see not without great devotion—how so great a chorus of such great pontiffs, dressed in white vestments, splendidly arrayed in pontifical mitres and precious orphreys embellished by circular ornaments, held the crosiers in their hands, walked round and round the vessel and invoked the name of God by way of exorcism; how so glorious and admirable men celebrated the wedding of the Eternal Bridegroom so piously that the King and the attending nobility believed themselves to behold a chorus celestial rather than terrestrial, a ceremony divine rather than human.[44]

For Hugh of St. Victor, this consecration offered an epiphany second only to the incarnation of God in Christ.[45] Disordered medieval habits could be tempered through well-crafted buildings, but only during rituals like this would the celestial chorus meet the human, and *armonia/concentus* become plainly evident in the human world. The well-documented role of ritual mystery plays in reorienting and attuning medieval urban life during recurring liturgical festivals in cities, typically associated with Easter and Christmas, is further evidence of this fact.[46]

***

During the Renaissance, architecture undertook the task of building a more permanent and all-encompassing harmonious environment for human life on earth. Unlike classical antiquity, Renaissance culture, with its Christian component, consolidated the belief in a world created by a rational and omnipotent God for human use (*propter nos*); the notion supported the presumed affinity between the human and divine minds both to understand God's creation (a rational and musical cosmos, as hypothesized by Copernicus and Kepler), and to construct a resonant human world through the role of architecture and the arts in the configuration of cities. Architecture and painting, governed respectively by numerical proportions and the proportionality of *perspectiva artificialis*, were expected to constitute an auspicious setting for human life, a sacred gift of incarnation yet always in the hands of fate (*Fortuna*), aligning free will with the divine order of the heavens. Acquiring the same status as the original seven liberal arts, architecture became a primary vehicle for self-understanding, allowing humans to partake of divine light and music. Even public spaces could be conceptualized as external rooms, with their facades as pictures: as seen, for example, in the main square in Pienza in the fifteenth century, or Michelangelo's Roman Campidoglio in the sixteenth.

While Renaissance texts on architecture are heterogeneous in their interests and forms, ranging from discursive theory to fictional narratives and more didactic texts, all authors are in agreement on the privileged standing of architecture capable of contributing harmonious settings for human action. Leon Battista Alberti, recovering and "correcting" the Vitruvian theoretical corpus through his humanist interests in *De re aedificatoria* (1452), recognized the possibility of translating the experience of beauty in God's natural world into the built world. In his terms, the *musica mundana*, as embodied in the colors of nature's flowers or the graceful form of a youthful body, was to be carried into the act of design through *lineamenta*, literally meaning "drawing lines in the mind's eye," the idea or geometric outline composing the face of a building. In analogy to the human face, facades epitomized the expressive force of the building and were to be proportioned harmoniously, employing the four first natural (Pythagorean) numbers. He writes: "Beauty is a harmony of all the parts in whatever subject it appears, fitted together with such proportion and connection that nothing could be added, diminished or altered but for the worse."[47] Alberti understood harmony as governed by number (Greek *arithmós*), comprising "all the music" of a building, number that unfolds into three conditions: *numerus* (the qualitative perfect number in the mind), *finitio* (the "real measurement" in the physical world), and *collocatio* (in-placement, evoking "correction" or *temperance*, to account for the site and other particular conditions).[48] Echoing Vitruvius on décor, Alberti added ornament *(ornamentum)* to beauty *(pulchritudo)* as a component of architectural meaning, conceptualized as a beautiful body's "dress," necessary for its appearance in public.[49] *Ornamentum* is articulated by classical columns and their particular detailing, elements—which are also ruled by proportions—that are bearers of *moods*, ranging from *gravitas* (Doric) to *festivitas* (Corinthian or Composite), contributing appropriate settings for human actions congruent with the stories that the buildings tell. Words are as crucial as numbers in this objective, and together they allow beauty to "shine" through, thus attaining *concinnitas*, "congruity," the perfection of beauty revealed in nature through metaphor, ultimately contributing to *concentum*, a "concert," like that of the stars.[50]

More obviously inspired by Marsilio Ficino's Neoplatonism, the hero of the *Hypnerotomachia Poliphili* (1499) reveals the primarily synesthetic understanding of perception prevailing in the Renaissance, which is, as I have suggested and will explain further, a condition for grasping the full possibilities and communicative potential of *Stimmung*; one that allows harmonies to be visible as well as audible, *touching* the fullness of bodily consciousness. In one episode of his narrative, Poliphilo experiences a quasi-erotic completeness in the presence of a beautiful, sensuous frontispiece, the gateway of one of the fragments of classical architecture he encounters during his pilgrimage in search of his beloved Polia.[51] Only after describing the emotional and cognitive experience of harmony, produced by the surrounding music, the sensuous materials, their textures and colors, and the stories about good and bad fortune (*concordia discors*) displayed in the iconology of the gate, does he decide to go and measure the building; he learns that the facade is governed by proportions generated by the first four natural numbers, and notes the discovery as a lesson for future architects. Architecture thus promotes well-being; a stabilizing catharsis, a good life in view of the uncertainties of destiny and the bittersweetness of human experience, always driven and often torn by desire.

While admitting that bodies had to be prepared through "proportion, arrangement, and aspect" to receive the splendor of beauty, Ficino also argues elsewhere that proportions in themselves are unable to account for beauty in simple things. In his words, "the eye sees nothing else except the light of the sun, for the shapes and colors of bodies are never seen unless they are illuminated with light. ... The eyes, with the help of a certain ray of their own, perceive the light thus imprinted: the light itself cannot be a body, since it fills the whole world instantaneously from east to west, penetrates the whole body of air and water everywhere without obstruction." Music and light share this important quality; they are like "the third face of God," which is the beauty of the world, presenting itself as "incorporeal to the eyes through the incorporeal light of the sun."[52]

Furthermore, Ficino thought that man could improve his life, make it healthier physically and spiritually, and attune his soul to the astrological influences of the universe, surrounding himself with correspondingly favorable forms, materials, colors, and music.[53] This deliberate search for attunement of personal embodied consciousness (which Ficino conceived of as the immortal Christian soul—he is actually responsible for consolidating this concept *in opposition* to a mortal body, in Christian dogma) is an early precursor of the romantic project we will be discussing in the next chapter. Particularly in the case of sickness or disharmony, music would be the best therapy. According to Ficino, just as the harp communicates the vibration of one plucked string to others, the stars can communicate their musical (luminous) pulse to stones, plants, and human characters.[54] This desire to live human life "according to the stars," a human existence that starting in the Renaissance became increasingly perceived as having more value than a passing stage toward eternal life and thus acquired greater inherent dignity,[55] led to an increased interest in music and architecture for everyday life, particularly evident during the sixteenth and seventeenth centuries.

Indeed, it is only after the invention of counterpoint in the fourteenth century, with the possibility of distinguishing parallel consonances and dissonances, that the nature of musical performance gave priority to simultaneous, i.e., vertical harmonies over successive intervals (as was the structure of Greek modal music); in this way, music became generally more sensuous.[56] While in the Middle Ages artistic music and the music of nature were conceptualized as analogous, so that a bird was thought to sing like a learned organist, the idea of concordance of voices, so consistent with the notion of Christian world harmony, did not lead to simultaneously apperceived polyphony before the fifteenth century.[57] This is evident in the new *a cappella* singing of the times, which, developing from the canon, introduced four voices entering one after the other, each imitating the preceding one; such is also in evidence later in the fifteenth century with the beginnings of polyphonic instrumental accompaniment. It is no coincidence that painters of the period began concerning themselves with the harmonic proportionality of space as a setting of a depicted figure. In *Della pittura* (1435–1436) Alberti emphasizes that, while a painter should always tell a story, as previously, this goal is not enough; he should also be engaged with the proportionality of depth as it appears on the surface of the work, attainable through one-point perspective (*perspectiva artificialis*). This method enabled artists to deploy mathematics to produce a harmonious setting for a scene, revealing a musical structure that was kindred to the divine mind, while familiar from experience.

In the chapters on architecture of his *Divina proportione* (1507), Luca Pacioli, a disciple of Piero della Francesca, relates the mathematics of painting to an understanding of the law of proportional triangles.[58] Luca assumed the Platonic order of a harmonic cosmos, and postulated the ordering of the world according to a Christian divine proportion (the so-called "continuous" irrational proportion that rules the Golden Section, 1:0.618, which he believed had deep affinities with the Christian Trinity).[59] Grasping full well the fact that painters and architects were concerned with "magnitudes" rather than "multitudes," Pacioli—a brilliant mathematician credited with the introduction of Arabic numerals into accounting practices—sought a geometric rather than arithmetic approach to the problem of pictorial and architectural harmony. Unlike Alberti, he claimed that geometry was superior to arithmetic (or to proportions applied to plans and elevations as mental images), because of its practical applications; it enabled one to draw lines and surfaces even if their proportions are not "rational," definable through natural (whole) numbers. Like his contemporaries he insisted that painting and architecture should take their place among other liberal disciplines, more specifically in the mathematical *quadrivium*. But for Pacioli, resonant with older medieval assumptions, music becomes manifest in the human environment through the crafts of stonecutting and construction, emulating

God's continuous harmony present in the world through the Incarnation of Christ. Meaning in architecture appears by means of "very finely carved stone" capable of demonstrating through embodied experience (*palpabiliter*) the "squaring of the circle"—the *concert*, or "coincidence of opposites," that we recognize in musical and architectural atmospheres well tuned for human life, but that remains an unsolvable aporia in mathematics.[60]

Renaissance polyphony culminated in Giovanni Pierluigi da Palestrina's expansive music, which, according to a biographer, evokes space over time, possessing "a certain quality of indefiniteness," creating "an atmosphere on which the spirit floats."[61] Around the same time, Andrea Palladio imagined the possibility of applying relationships of ratios, such as 4:2::2:1, to the harmony of volumes. This constituted a *proportionalità* capable of encompassing the design of lived space, framing a good life, and now including its three directions: breadth, depth, and height. Indeed, this concept of a sequence of proportions (as opposed to a simple ratio) implied either time (as in music) or volume; it was made familiar to him by his acquaintances and patrons, among them the mathematician Sylvio Belli and the Venetian patrician Daniele Barbaro, who thought of *proportionalità* as the ultimate secret of arts seeking to draw from the "necessary truths" of mathematics. Barbaro conveyed this emphasis in his annotations to the sections on music (book 5, on the theater) in his own translation of Vitruvius's *Ten Books* (1556 in Italian; 1567 in Latin), for which Palladio provided the illustrations.[62]

Palladio's own treatise, his popular *Quattro libri* (1570), is a concise text written in Italian that, in contrast to the writings of Vitruvius and Alberti, reveals no interest in articulating issues of decorum through stories. Thus the emphasis is on *theoría*, still independent of technical knowledge, but leaving aside Aristotle's practical philosophy; he eliminates all the anecdotal material so as to concentrate on the all-important "musicality" of classical architecture. (It is hardly surprising that Palladio has often been singled out by twentieth-century architects and writers as the originator of modern "formalism" and linked to Le Corbusier, for example, by critics like Colin Rowe, though this unfortunately misrepresents central aspects of the Renaissance architect's intentionality.)[63] Palladio notates with numbers the modular dimensions in plans, sections, and elevations, indicating their *proportionalità*. These notations reveal his desire to render domestic and civic everyday life as harmonious experiences, and are reconciled in his projects with a great sensitivity for *commoditas*, issues that today we would associate with utility, as well as a respect for cultural precedents and habits in the framing of a good and healthy life. It is important to emphasize that the plans of his own villas, included in the treatise, are not like modern working drawings; rather, they are "ideas" to be executed through *sollertia* in view of the specific conditions of a given project, which never result in precise proportions in reality but, instead, are always "tempered." Akin to his predecessors, Palladio understood the possibility of revealing the ideal in the original sense of Plato, appearing through his art *in* the imperfect world of man, never as a totalizing (top-down) planning operation (like in modernity), but as a carefully considered adjustment of harmonic proportions in his designs, responsive to the natural and historical conditions of particular sites. His "renovation" of the basilica in Vicenza is a wonderful case in point. Palladio respected the existing medieval buildings with all their geometric and constructive imperfections and multifarious uses. At the same time he imbued the structure with the harmonic perfection of his architectural idea, as precisely rendered on the pages of the *Quattro libri*,[64] fully conveyed to the citizen in the experiences of everyday life. The result is so successful that even today the uninformed visitor usually assumes that the building is indeed perfectly orthogonal and thoroughly regular. For Palladio, harmony was inextricably associated with temperance, crucial for a healthy life in its full psychosomatic meaning, recognizing the spiritual wholeness necessary for man, whose existence had acquired a newly sacred dimension; this emphasis was in accordance with Christian dogma and its recently acquired Neoplatonic and hermetic associations—reflected most notably in his famous use of temple fronts as facades for secular dwellings. He related harmony and temperance in a concise but important paragraph in the preface to his fourth book, exalting the wonders of the *machina*, or the world, praising its ornaments (the heavenly luminaries) and the heavens, which by their "continual revolutions" change the seasons as required by nature, their motion preserving "itself by the sweetest harmony of temperature."[65]

In providing specific instructions and describing the nature of mathematical relationships as threefold—arithmetic (based on addition and subtraction), geometric (based on multiplication and division), and harmonic (a combination of both)—Palladio reiterates the importance of the basic natural Pythagorean numbers as the basis for proportionality, but also includes the number five.[66] This addition may be a nod to Gioseffo Zarlino's *Harmonic Institutions* (1558). Also a native of the republic of Venice, Zarlino was a chapel master in St. Mark's basilica and arguably the most important writer in the development of music theory since Boethius.[67] His work plays a part in our story, because, while he tries to do justice to the innovations of musical practice in his time and thus expands the range of numbers to include five and six (beyond the first four natural numbers), he still argues, like Palladio, on behalf of an all-encompassing Pythagorean theory of harmony based on numbers and proportions, and accounting for the entirety of the cosmos. According to this theory, a single arithmetic ratio can be found for each consonance, and the beauty of intervals is that of harmonic numbers sounding together. Despite the imperfection of the physical world, it could partake of the ideal, since in music and architecture physical occurrences could be led back to ratios of essences.

* * *

The first author to question the bonds tying musical sounds to immutable arithmetical ratios was Vincenzo Galilei, who did so in a critique of Zarlino's work published in Florence in 1589.[68] His contribution today seems relatively minor—he merely proved that the inequalities required for the production of intervals in strings are not the same as those required for intervals in mass (as among the percussive hammers in Pythagoras's story).[69] However, the implications of this realization were far-reaching, for they disproved that the harmonic intervals of music were the result of unchanging mathematical ratios. Ancient and medieval Aristotelian cosmologies were vertical; the sonorous numbers were associated with the eternal spheres whose mathematical motions placed them at the summit of the scale of Being. Consonances by numbers were generally not applicable to physical beings. Aristotle had insisted that the living natural world, *physis*, save some exceptions like optics and anatomy, was not capable of being understood through mathematics. Music affected a conjunction between the lower and the higher regions, one that architecture emulated. Vincenzo's discovery coincided with a major shift in European epistemology, leading to the horizontal, homogeneous universe of modern science, and eventually to an understanding of numbers as merely formal, operational signs, unhinged from definite and discrete things; numbers could become fractional, algebraic, negative, or irrational (as John Wallis might put it in the seventeenth century), and geometry could be rendered through algebraic equations (like in Descartes's analytic geometry), challenging the long-held distinction between the two mathematical disciplines of "multitudes" and "magnitudes."

It is important to emphasize that, despite such transformations, the belief in the harmonic and musical order of Christian creation was not questioned; on the contrary, it became dogmatic, fueling the desire to put forward scientific hypotheses in order to better grasp the invisible order of the cosmos as God had created it, in ways that might not be readily accessible to our senses. That such hypothetical knowledge might attain a claim to truth first became possible in the second half of the thirteenth century, as a result of theological debates concerning the limitations of Aristotelian *theoría*—aimed exclusively at "saving the phenomena" given to human perception in a world presumed finite and unique.[70] This Aristotelian worldview did not allow for the omnipotence of a Christian God who might have created the universe "otherwise" and in ways invisible to our senses, and its contestation was at the origins of modern cosmology as articulated by Copernicus and Kepler. Indeed, as Amos Funkenstein has thoroughly demonstrated, the early modern scientists of the sixteenth and seventeenth centuries treated all theological topics in their works, making traditional modes of theologizing obsolete; their theology was inseparable from their science and philosophy, and was secular in the sense that it was oriented toward the world.[71] The Christian belief in the divinity of the mind also drove the possibility of misinterpreting Plato and turning Platonism into its modern incarnation, favoring the rational intellect and its instrumental capacities over the emotional senses and eventually leading to the postulates of modern philosophy in the works of René Descartes.

Perhaps not surprisingly, it was Vincenzo Galilei's famous son, Galileo Galilei (1564–1642), who conceived of the initial unification of celestial and terrestrial physics. He began with an imaginary experiment (the consideration of motion in a vacuum—a condition impossible to actualize in sublunary reality) that led him to revise the very concept of physical movement and base it on the principle of inertia, thus putting an end to the hierarchical Aristotelian cosmos of antiquity and the Middle Ages and its anthropomorphic and animistic explanations of motion. Geometric (Euclidean) space, having been previously understood as the realization of supralunary contemplation and therefore considered a mental reality, became universalized and was assumed to be present also in the places of our sublunary worldly existence, lending its mathematical explanatory structure to all aspects of physical experience. Correspondingly, also in opposition to place-bound Aristotelian physics, motion became a "state" that did not affect the essence of moving objects, which could be represented not by inextricable intrinsic and contextual qualities but by mathematical properties and a set of coordinates. As a result, the effective presence of mathematical relationships in a physical world now conceptualized as a machine at multiple scales, had to be proven to our intellect though quantitative experiments; the priority became to *understand* intellectually the presence of a divine harmony in the world of man.

Johannes Kepler, a self-avowed disciple of Pythagoras and follower of Copernicus,[72] shared Galileo's belief in the world as the artifact of a "geometricizing God." Contrary to the Greek philosopher and his Renaissance followers, however, he revealed that the fundamental elements of the cosmos that underscore its harmony, are geometrical and not arithmetical, for numbers are "nothing … but the expressible part of geometry."[73] His *Harmonice mundi* (1619) presents a complete theory of music based on polygons inscribed in circles that define musical consonances, succeeding in a way that the Pythagorean numbers did not. His conception of harmony is fundamentally a cognitive activity that nevertheless fully explains elliptical planetary motion. He famously stated that, given our earth's eccentric position in the solar system, we could not "experience" the music of the spheres, but could merely understand it through a distant perspective; such was the Christian's God gift to our rational mind, kindred to His. The alignment of the six planetary orbits in cadential unison probably takes place only once in the creation, yet man's sublunary "counterpoint," the artificial symphony of several voices (polyphony), is performed "in a brief portion of an hour," recalling the "perpetuity of the whole duration of the world."[74] Despite his appreciation of the poetics of the cosmos, Kepler's scientific conception of harmony contributed to the instrumentalization of music theory, linking it to compositional issues, a tendency that would finally come to fruition in Jean-Philippe Rameau's eighteenth-century theories of tonal composition. Humans would therefore have to act upon the world to prove such divinely inspired truths, appearing as mathematical data through experiments, or through sensuous experience in geometrically generated artifacts. The cultural importance of music actually increased during the baroque period, amid the efforts to align human with divine will, while in architecture the connections with music would start to be examined, rejecting the older Pythagorean assumptions. Emphasis would be placed upon the geometrization of the environment, to be inscribed with the language of nature itself, in baroque cities, secular and religious buildings and gardens.

Between the late sixteenth and the early seventeenth centuries, scientists and mathematicians like Galileo, Giovanni Battista Benedetti, and Isaac Beckman would recognize that for sound to be understood mathematically, it had to be correlated to the vibrations of strings and not to their length as expressed in rational, natural numbers.[75] Ratios could again notate the properties of sounding bodies, but these were exclusively acoustical properties (empirical—in the sense of modern experimental science—and related to the physical reality and morphology of instruments), and the numbers in question could not in themselves distinguish harmonic intervals from other sounds. As Heller-Roazen explains, such modern ciphers were symbols of any quantities whatsoever, be they discrete or continuous.[76]

During the Renaissance, synesthesia explained the sensuous by reference to a Pythagorean theoretical speculation on number harmony. In contrast, baroque synesthesia, which generally outlived Descartes's devastating critique well into the eighteenth century, as I will explain below, emphasized the evident multisensory reality of the individual sensations and sensuousness, as, for example, in the works of Robert Fludd and Athanasius Kircher. The latter's *Musurgia universalis* is arguably the first theory to connect musical performance with nature's sounds and emotions, as well as *musica theorica* and *musica prattica*.[77] He defines music's ability to agitate the human heart as its "magnetic attraction," while consonance in the chimes between liver and heart (a perfect octave) is literally a manifestation of good health.[78] Baroque music often emphasized its analogies with poetry and painting as well, primarily based on bodily affect.[79] Marin Mersenne, the well-known correspondent of the greatest minds of his time, wrote two treatises on the analogies between music and the world,[80] not in the old hermetic tradition like Kircher and Fludd, but based on the assumption that sound was a physical object related to mechanical motion. He posited analogies between intervals and measurements, between seven colors and seven consonant intervals, between tastes and specific consonances (for example, the octave is sweetness; the perfect fourth, saltiness), and even between geometric figures and specific musical phenomena. Thus, a line connected to strings and monophonic chant, a plane related to metal sheets or simple counterpoint, and a solid to resonating bodies and pieces for several voices.[81]

The musicality of the starry heavens was often expressed in literature; Kepler himself compared the sound emanating from its source to the rays from the stars.[82] The great cosmic machine played a concert associated with Christian grace, in the tradition of Dante's morning hymn in the tenth canto of *Paradiso*, sung not by an Ambrosian congregation but by a clock; Augustine's numbers were embodied in the motions of an engine that symbolized all the cosmic laws of interdependency, well-temperedness, and beauty.[83] This symbolic quality of mechanical devices was explicit during the seventeenth century, as they often became mimetic of the universe and revealed God's presence through light, sound, and magnetism, as is particularly evident in Kircher's speculations. Based on the same scientific, musical, and philosophical assumptions, the pronounced geometrization of nature that characterizes baroque gardens sought the creation of attuned atmospheres for mankind. Their perspectival vistas and their awe-inspiring, playful fountains and automata comprised an appropriate theater for political rituals. This baroque synesthesia is obviously at work in the very successful Jesuit sacred spaces with their new emphasis on the image, as manifested in their churches' *quadrattura* frescoes and in the ephemeral architecture of the *theatrum sacrum*, where the geometric perspective disclosing infinity to human experience is associated with the light, music, and flavor of God.[84]

Baroque architects arrived at innovations in design through geometric operations in plans and elevations; baroque architecture synthesizes geometry with sensuous experience, creating spaces in which qualitative place appears due to the agency of geometric combinations, enabling the contemplation of the luminous divine presence. Through such operations it offers to vision an intimation of infinity, like in the Jesuit *quadrattura* frescoes or French gardens with their unlimited vistas. Though totally opposed to such representations of infinity, geometric operations are also at the center of Guarino Guarini's treatise, his *Architettura civile* (published posthumously in 1737).

The structure of Guarini's treatise is strikingly different from that of previous works on architecture. The table of contents has the appearance of a technical book, and its emphasis is on the arts of making: the trades employed in building. Divided into five parts, or individual treatises, it describes building as a virtual construction of orthogonal projections. The text begins with a general section on architecture, including definitions and elementary geometry, followed by sections on plan (*ichnographia*), elevation "raised upward from the plan" (*orthographia elevata*), and "thrown orthography" (*ortografia gettata*). This last section is his addition to the traditional Vitruvian tools of representation, concerning itself with issues of parallel projection in the vertical dimension—"casting bodies which are suspended above back down into the plan in order to extend their surfaces"—both for symbolic and technical purposes, like stonecutting. The last section is on *geodesia* (surveying, mensuration, and the shape of the earth). At the very outset of the treatise, he writes: "Architecture depends on geometry, but it is nevertheless a flattering art that should never displease the senses by the use of reason."[85]

In his philosophical treatise *Placita philosophica*, written in Paris in 1665, Guarini, like many of his contemporaries, claims that the foundation of reasoning is mathematical, and that mathematical knowledge is equivalent to divine knowledge. Nevertheless, spiritual entities must necessarily be evident to our senses.[86] As seen in his works on cosmology, his scientific theorizing never begins with hypotheses (à la Copernicus), but aims at "saving the phenomena"; grounded in the experiential world, it gives priority to embodied perception in the tradition of classical *theoría*.[87] Mathematical rationality is never in contradiction to sensuous experience as a source of true knowledge; in his explicit valorization of the senses he opposes contemporary philosophers like Descartes and Malebranche. Guarini believed that a thorough synthesis was possible: indeed, this comprises the main article of faith of baroque art and architecture.

Guarini shared with other baroque artists, architects, and scholars a belief in geometry as a universal *language*, a true *clavis universalis* for knowledge.[88] He reiterated Vitruvius's fundamental categories for good architecture while interpreting them through this new understanding: buildings have to accommodate the customs (habits) of cultures, places, and people, displaying profound respect for a given site and using inexpensive, local materials; moreover, they must be seductive (beautiful) and well built.[89] Yet their encompassing meaning, allowing for eloquent communication, is wholly dependent on the use of geometry as a tool of design. The treatise for the most part is a description of geometric operations, *know-how* (previously an autonomous *techné* in old classical theories) that had acquired special status as real knowledge through its association with the operations of God's creation. These technical operations, such as surveying, measurement of surfaces and volumes, and stereotomy, are all conducive to the expression of meaning in one's synesthetic experience of architecture, as it frames significant rituals.

Guarini's geometry is strictly Euclidean and not projective (not a "perspectival geometry") in the modern sense. In fact, he always emphasizes the disconnections between optics and geometry, criticizing in his *Placita philosophica* the confusions brought on by perspectival illusionism (as in the Jesuit *quadrattura* techniques). Geometry is concerned with the truth, i.e., parallel lines (and the light of God), while perspective deceives our senses and is the cause of error.[90] He is therefore totally at odds with Descartes's understanding of perspective as a paradigm of truth. On the contrary, since perspective suggests that parallel lines converge at a point at infinity, this creates a lie, as this point is nonexistent on the surface of the earth. This lie heralds the "end of appearance" and threatens our capacity to "see things in God." Images are like reflections without opacity, "making the surface of the body appear," and perspective distorts real experience because it reveals "too much, too quickly," thus violating human tactility and temporality.[91]

While emphasizing architecture's dependence on a divine, geometric language, obviously recognizing the priority of continuous magnitudes over numbers (*artithmós*), Guarini declares that the rules of classical authors were not to be venerated. Ignoring the inveterate analogies of proportion and music that had now become unhinged from cosmic or absolute meanings, he states unambiguously that the old rules of proportion in Vitruvius's and other Renaissance treatises could be adjusted and changed, always with the aim of finding balance and avoiding excess. Indeed, measurement simply aids the ensuring of *concordance*, still posited as a fundamental value but based upon sensuous experience.[92] Even the orders could be modified with rhetorical intent, made more sober or richer and more graceful, in order to suit the expressive demands of a project and resulting in free inventions and naturalistic ornament. Acknowledging a desire for something new in architecture, Guarini claims that it is important to break the rules precisely because the senses tend to err, and as the goal of architecture is to please, adjustments are crucial. Thus, he valorizes the importance of traditional optical corrections, congruent with his understanding of perspectival vision as limited and inferior to our full synesthetic consciousness.

Guarini's mimetic architecture comes about through an instrumental use of geometry, believed to comprise the generative characters of God's nature. This art opens up possibilities for the invention of form and space that are also resonant and thoroughly integrated with ornament, whose communicative potential was granted by culture. Furthermore, Guarini was clearly respectful of cultural habits and Catholic rituals, conceiving architecture in the context of a genealogy that could account for the overlapping of tradition and innovation.[93] Architecture becomes geometry, generated out of simple elements and releasing internal spaces (usually domed), to manifest the luminescence of God. Guarini understood this luminescence as His light granted onto us, rather than its effect as a picture, as was common in Jesuit illusionistic frescoes. Geometric figures are combined and thus believed to reflect the structure of the natural world, its full synesthetic meaning—texture, light, smell—construing complex and truly novel buildings, and giving place to atmospheres appropriate to the diverse programs of Guarini's projects. Thus his masterpiece, the chapel of the Holy Shroud in Turin (housing that most sacred of Christian relics with the imprint of Christ's dead body prior to his resurrection), creates an atmosphere of *vaghezza* (his term, which he defines as "beauty, sensuousness, and desire"), a space of desire for God, while recalling the atmosphere of Christ's crucifixion, the eclipse that signaled his death on Calvary.[94] Through its "diaphanous" materiality woven with stone and light, the chapel makes present the absent body of Christ (like the relic it contains), creating a mysterious penumbra that becomes brighter toward its summit, yet is never too bright, and never "infinite."

***

While Pythagorean assumptions and musical analogies started to unravel in seventeenth-century architectural theories, it should be remembered that both opera and the modern instrumental concert are baroque inventions (ca. 1600), reflecting a particular cosmic feeling of world harmony. Opera both revived the Greek musical dramas (*triune choreia*) and medieval musical drama, *musica mundana,* the *sacra rappresentazione*, or *lauda*.[95] It is interesting to note that early operas are about music itself, as with the many versions of the Orpheus and Eurydice story, where the Greek musician-god is brought back to life to prove in person, on the stage, the magical power of music, which, when deployed in the service of love, can master nature and even conquer hell. This tradition would culminate in the eighteenth century with Mozart's *Magic Flute* (premiered in 1791), one of the most popular operas ever written, where music is associated with love and the Enlightenment's geometric rationality as represented by Freemasonry, making it possible to render "the Earth a heavenly kingdom, and mortals like the gods."[96]

Furthermore, Isaac Newton's natural philosophy and its "empirical" law of universal gravitation—regarded as an absolutely truthful, mathematical expression of the divine order of the cosmos—vindicated the aural experience of musical harmonies as potentially universal as well, an experience of beauty rooted in nature and human biology, shared by all. Newton, in fact, had presumed an association between "natural" (absolute, geometric) space and time, and God, a necessary (if often concealed) hypothesis that allowed his physical theories to operate, but his "empirical truths" were accepted by all and extrapolated into many disciplines.[97] Furthermore, in his *Optiks* he drew an analogy between the seven tones of the diatonic scale and the seven colors of the rainbow contained in white light, evoking the possibility of an understanding of harmony that included both vision and hearing. Later in the eighteenth century, the famous composer and theoretician Jean-Philippe Rameau stressed the importance of our innate ability to hear consonance even without any intellectual knowledge of musical harmony, leading him to argue for the primacy of music as the truly empirical origin of all *mathemata* upon which the very rationality of the sciences was founded. In a similar vein, architects like Charles-Étienne Briseux, following in the footsteps of other late-seventeenth-century collaborations between theoreticians of music and architecture such as that of René Ouvrard and François Blondel, could extrapolate this thinking back into architecture, expecting proportional relationships (generated geometrically) to convey emotion and character (meaning) in buildings the same way that modes or tonalities operated in music.[98]

As we have established, during the seventeenth and eighteenth centuries, architecture and garden and urban design shifted their preferences from arithmetic to geometry as a primary tool for designing environments as expressive settings, always mindful of their particular rhetorical tasks. The scope of this change was enormous: whole cities like Rome were transformed; gardens in the French and English styles either flaunted the laws of perspective in the former case, or engaged geometrical operations to create the very artifice of picturesque nature in the latter; while innovative buildings by architects like Francesco Borromini and Guarini were designed through geometric combinations. Arithmetic proportions were deemed important in some cases, often associated with musical intervals that could be rendered as graphic dimensions, but their role had to be justified empirically, not in relation to any cosmic determinacy. The analogies between music and architecture became a subject of debate and were usually argued with reference to the scientific theories of Descartes, Galileo, Kepler, Kircher, and Newton, who in diverse ways assumed that light functioned and, in some instances, even moved very much like sound.

While the arguments behind architectural theories shifted from deduction in the seventeenth century (Cartesianism) to induction in the eighteenth (Newtonianism), instrumental concerns began to dominate, leading to a top-down, rational approach to design, collapsing the old contemplative *theoría* with technical knowledge. This reduction of theory to technique in architectural design was tempered in the seventeenth century by an Aristotelian concept of nature and the still-unquestioned synesthetic nature of perception, as well as by the inveterate associations of discourse with rhetoric, genealogies, and iconology. During the eighteenth century it was modulated through character theory's concerns with expression and decorum, most famously in the *Essai* of Marc-Antoine Laugier (1751), where metaphysical issues were again foregrounded. Yet the emergence and increasing prevalence of instrumentality as a theoretical impulse in design would have important consequences, contributing to the undermining of centrality of musical attunement for architecture's communicative function.

***

As is well known, René Descartes (1596–1650) declared for the first time ever the "thinking substance," or *ego* (the subject or "soul," today a brain-centered consciousness), as a totally autonomous constituent of a dualistic reality. This mind was capable of understanding itself in relation to an "extended substance" (the object, a mechanical nature deployed in isotropic, geometric space) by virtue of the mathematical rationality of its divine innate ideas. Unlike Aristotle, for whom our first evidence of existence is an inner feeling that is experienced in analogy to touch, and for whom reality is given undividedly to our situated bodily consciousness that shares much with animals, in Descartes's new philosophy the human being is truly set apart from both animate and inanimate beings by his/her logical thinking. Furthermore, there is an assumed breach between the body, its emotions, sensations, and feelings, often fueling the imagination (and sin), and the dispassionate, godly logical mind. Soul and body were believed to be fundamentally at odds with each other, and this became a central belief for modernity, still present today at a popular level, even if the soul is identified with the material brain. In the Cartesian model the body as a mechanism is understood as driven by an incorporeal soul (akin to a computer driving a machine). Meanings are not truly *experienced*, but are arrived at through associations of information in the brain. These Cartesian assumptions that radically underscore modern and contemporary thought, and that today are disproved by phenomenology and neuroscience (as I will explain in chapter 5), are key to understanding how architecture was led to abandon its inveterate capacity to bring about cultural and natural attunement.

Descartes thought of the five senses as discrete mechanisms for passive perception, each one autonomous from the other, conduits of subjective sensations that should therefore be distrusted. This represented a fundamental critique of the primacy of experience and perceptual synesthesia (the integrated sensory modalities) as the very condition for our apprehension of the truth of reality: an epistemological revolution that eventually led to what Spitzer called the breaking apart, during the seventeenth and eighteenth centuries, of the one integrated field encompassed by world harmony and well-temperedness, *concentus* (harmony) and *temperare* (temperance, appropriateness). This coincided (as Novalis would later put it)[99] with the questioning of the Christian *musica mundana* by the modern mechanistic spirit. Eventually, music would indeed lose its central position in European culture as a paradigm of attunement, one that could work its magic propagating psychosomatic health and understanding throughout the different orders of being, from the material to the spiritual.

There are several aspects of this shift that can be grasped separately in the history of music.[100] On the one hand, we have observed that the practice but especially the theory of music in the premodern era was an integral part of *scientia*, or philosophy. Music was at the center of all articulations of worldview and cosmology. By the eighteenth century its standing shifted (despite Rameau's previously cited exceptional and highly controversial arguments), and music slowly became a social pursuit and a sign of taste and status. While musical performance was part of a healthy life, accompanying focal actions such as rituals, banquets, political functions, and battles, it eventually acquired the character of the new "distant" aesthetic objects, culminating in the rise of "concert" or "pure" music as we know it, which began to take hold in the nineteenth century: music meant to be experienced in the absolute silence and darkness of the concert hall, a curiously trying experience to which we have somewhat become accustomed. Spitzer concludes: "At the end of the eighteenth century *Stimmung* was crystallized—robbed of its blossoming life."[101] As I will show in the next chapter, this is precisely where the romantic critique starts, and the sequels, so familiar to us, frequently become problematic misunderstandings, underscored more often than not by a latent Cartesianism (the imperative of subjectivity). Today, these include the remnants of twentieth-century psychology and early cognitive science, with its analogy of the brain and the computer, and the presumption of understanding as the processing of data, a notion that makes it impossible to grasp *Stimmung*'s full potential for architecture.

* * *

Descartes's philosophical revolution and its resultant undermining of the musical analogy in architecture are best represented by the architectural theories of Claude Perrault. His understanding of architectural meaning, as expressed in his writings on architecture and scientific topics,[102] will provide a fitting conclusion to this chapter.[103] Perrault was a doctor, biologist, and architect, close to the court of Louis XIV, mainly through the agency of his famous brother, the writer Charles Perrault, who was a close advisor of Jean-Baptiste Colbert. Perrault was among a group of scientists, associated with the new Académie Royale des Sciences, who could conceptualize a distinction between truths in science (and architecture was among these) and truths of religion. Thus, unlike Johannes Kepler—for whom, in the early seventeenth century, the discovery of a "six-cornered snowflake" that fell on his coat as he crossed an icy bridge appeared as God's geometric "formative quality" at work throughout the universe—Perrault could perceive geometry as merely an expedient tool and mathematics as simply data expressed by experiments.

Writing toward the end of the seventeenth century, Perrault echoed Guarini's interest in putting forward an instrumental theory of architecture and in questioning the analogy between proportions in architecture and music. The latter was a point of contention explicit in his polemic with François Blondel, the founder and head of the French Académie Royale d'Architecture, in whose view this analogy constituted the proof of the connection between proportions and positive beauty, i.e., architectural meaning.[104] Perrault went much further than other baroque architects, however, particularly in his demystification of mathematics and his belief in the superiority of the moderns when compared to ancients' accomplishments in all disciplines, including both music and architecture. In a short treatise on the music of the ancients, part of his *Essais de physique*, Perrault questions what he sees as his contemporaries' unjustifiedly high regard for ancient music. He likens this to ancient painting, which he contends is only good at pleasing the senses and flattering the heart but ignores judgment, unaware of the principles of *perspectiva artificialis*, which since Descartes had stood for the true relationship between the mind and the world.[105] He asserts the superiority of modern polyphony, which, similar to painting, flatters the intellect through its complex mathematical structures.

Perrault still concedes that in music, mathematical ratios could be understood as a source of positive (natural) beauty; this was demonstrated through the auditory experience of harmonies and dissonance. Such was not the case for architecture, however, a discipline that also depended on mathematical dimensions but that was addressed to vision. In architecture such proportions could not be proven to "cause" the feeling of harmony or beauty.[106] In other words, adjustments could be made within a certain range without much consequence. While in his view historical change affected all the arts, in the case of architecture this meant that proportions could only account for "arbitrary beauty" as opposed to positive or natural beauty. Their presumed aesthetic quality would only manifest itself in conjunction with other evident characteristics of aesthetic value, such as a building's richness of materials, excellent execution, and bilateral symmetry.[107]

Furthermore, music is addressed to hearing while architecture is oriented toward vision. For Perrault the discreteness of the two senses meant that they could not be conflated. In both art forms numerical ratios have nothing to do with the old cosmic numbers or the music of the spheres. In architecture the use of numerical proportion is nothing but an instrument to simplify the design of the five classical orders and systematize their relative dimensions, making design more efficient.[108] He grants that ratios of dimensions are crucial to understanding physical phenomena, or geometry when it expresses forces as vectors, as in mechanics (statics and dynamics), but that they are certainly not central to architectural meaning (beauty). In this and other important issues, particularly his faith in progress—placing architectural theory on the same footing as other sciences that were increasingly intended to approximate truth in the future—Perrault anticipates the early-nineteenth-century theories of Durand and Rondelet. He shows himself already unable to grasp traditional architecture's communicative function through attunement.

Strikingly, for Perrault humans actually "see" in perspective, and thus the old technique of "optical correction," fundamental for all earlier writers on architecture as a device for making buildings appear as harmonious as possible to synesthetic perception (always affected by the limitations of human vision), became useless. He characterizes this fundamental aspect of the architect's practical wisdom (*sollertia*) as either an excuse for the failures of most previous theories on the classical orders and their complex and imprecise prescriptions that were useless for practical applications, or as a rationale for mediocre craftsmanship that could not actualize precise designs. In his view the rules should be applied with precision, one-to-one and without ambiguity, in terms of a relationship between language, mathematical proportions, and action no different from the way a computer "talks" to the milling machine today.

Perrault's theories represent the first instance in which an architect self-consciously denies the possibility of meaning as *presence* and therefore questions the integrity of atmosphere as both emotional and intellectual: the associated field of *concentus/temperance*. Following Descartes and Malebranche, Perrault rejects synesthetic perception in favor of an associationist psychology that assumes the mechanistic functioning of five independent senses, *partes extra partes*, prone to error, and with their emotional interference confusing our clear intellectual understanding of *res extensa*. This Cartesian concept of perception, sanctioned by later eighteenth-century theories of cognition (like that of Étienne Bonnot de Condillac) and the "scientific" psychology of the nineteenth and twentieth centuries, would have far-reaching consequences for architecture, even to the present day. It would in fact make it difficult for modern humanity to grasp what Merleau-Ponty would call the primacy of embodied and situated perception, affecting issues ranging from science to aesthetics and fundamental to truly life-enhancing design. In Perrault's model of *passive* perception, the senses receive impressions that cause sensations eventually related by the mind to concepts. Meaning can become data, and is grasped through the association of concepts in the mind. If architecture communicates meaning, it does so as if it were a sign offered to autonomous vision, or a language that is primarily denotation. It is liable to perfection like language itself, yet ultimately is a form of prose to be understood only by the intellect.

3
Architecture as Communicative Setting 2: Modern Poetic Atmospheres

It was only after Descartes that philosophers could start to believe that thinking, our self-conscious intellectual understanding (linguistic, logical, mathematical), might be posited as proof of our existence. Conversely, only after Descartes did our emotional experiences become private and internal to the soul/mind. While the Greek "discovery of the mind" disclosed the space of desire that characterizes *philo-sophia*, its reification of the reflective ego never went as far as Descartes's *ego cogito*. A geometrician like Euclid would have emphatically distinguished the precision of the conceptual line or circle in the intellect from its worldly manifestations, while, in contrast, emotions were always acknowledged to be external and sited, inextricable from appearance and cognition. In other words, prior to early modernity the worldly origin of emotions and the limitations of the intellect to master them were taken as the natural order of things.

Whether mental matter was considered innate (Descartes) or wholly external, coming to us from the environment through mechanistic, autonomous senses (John Locke and Condillac), the belief that a person's thoughts and emotions are exclusively within his or her "soul" is one that only slowly became a collective cultural assumption, finally generalized in the Western world during the nineteenth century. As I will explain at the conclusion of this chapter, this sense of interiority, coupled with a *critical recovery* of synesthesia as the primary modality of human perception, became a condition for the discovery of romantic *Stimmung* as a new possibility of attunement for modernity. Yet for the most part, Cartesian dualism became even more entrenched following the spectacular victories of instrumental rationality during and after the Industrial Revolution, exported through European colonization and now very much a part of universal technological civilization. As a result, this belief concerning the subjectivity and interiority of emotions and moods remains current and generally unquestioned to this day.

It is immediately illuminating to compare this belief with Homeric literature, for example, where all sensory experience is qualified with passions and is characterized through distinct verbs as a different relationship with the world, such as: "seeing with pity," "seeing with fear," or "seeing with love." Homer even wondered how Odysseus could keep his feelings private, possibly turning his eyes inside out to cry internally. A few centuries later, Augustine tried to convince Christians that they actually *had* an inner life; such was the foreignness of the concept. A belief in the Christian soul became an obvious precedent for dualistic philosophy, yet for premodern Christianity, well into the Renaissance, the soul was embodied; indeed, eternal life *depended* on the resurrection of the flesh. Only in the fifteenth century did Marsilio Ficino crystallize the notion of an eternal soul truly independent of a corruptible body, a notion that eventually became dogmatic in modern Christianity.

Earlier in the eighteenth century in Europe, the interiority that emerged from philosophical dualism meant that feeling and reason could be separated. Reason was generally deemed superior by the Enlightenment, even held to be the only legitimate form of cognition, while emotion was seen as clouded and getting in the way of reason. Debates on this separation and their consequences became common in the fields of art and architecture. The invention of modern aesthetics and its favorite terms for encapsulating aesthetic experience—the "beautiful," pointing to the measurable, and the "sublime," a characteristic of the immeasurable—were a result of this presumed disjunction. Alexander Gottlieb Baumgarten, the inventor of the "science of aesthetics" (1735),[1] deliberately twisted a term that had originally articulated the possibility of a "sensory understanding" drawn from *all* that appears in synesthetic perception: *aisthésis*. This term originally referred to sensation given to embodied consciousness, comprising feeling, hearing, seeing, scent, and cognitive discernment. Baumgarten, in contrast, used the word *aesthetic* to denote a kind of intellectual *cogitation* that can be both clear and confused, therefore resulting in a *gnoseologia inferioris*, a "lower" sort of understanding than that issuing from clear reason. Rather than describing a comprehensive experience that implied primary cognition, the term came to mean less and less over time until eventually it would not seem out of place in the expression "mere aesthetics."

Baumgarten likely took this concept from Leibniz's explanation of musical affect.[2] In a letter from 1712, Leibniz defines music as "an occult practice of arithmetic in which the mind is unaware that it is counting." The inventor of calculus thought that mathematics structured the universe and accounted for the present "most perfect" outcome of God's creative act. Humans, however, have some confused or insensible perceptions, so that "even if the soul does not have the sensation that it is counting, it nonetheless feels the effect of this insensible calculation," resulting in pleasure from consonances and displeasure from dissonances.[3] Leibniz even grants that dissonances might be pleasing by accident, as they come between consonances, and that our delight in hearing demonstrates there is no pleasure of the senses that may not be reducible to a pleasure of reason, ultimately revealing the perfectly intelligible design of the universe. He concludes that the beauty of music consists of the concord of numbers, even though we may not be aware that we are counting. Likewise, he extrapolates, "The pleasures that sight finds in proportions are of the same nature; and those that cause the other senses will be reducible to something of this kind, though we cannot explain it distinctly."[4]

While one could argue that at a popular level eighteenth-century Europeans still assumed the primacy of undivided perception as the first evidence of truth, the changes brought about by modern scientific epistemology as expressed by Leibniz and Baumgarten were of great consequence for architecture and had a profound impact on how it could be conceived as an attuned, resonant setting for everyday life. Recalling the two word groups that would lead to *Stimmung*: while *harmony* as *mimesis* in the traditional sense became impossible in a mechanistic world governed by modern mathematics, *temperance* and appropriateness to cultural situations became all-important. In the wake of Cartesian cognitive psychology and its dissociation of the senses, eighteenth-century architects struggled to find ways to reconnect the senses through aesthetic and scientific arguments. They often came back to the powerful evidence of music, which became a truly dominant art form. The techniques of temperance to adjust discrepancies arising from the incommensurability of musical intervals in performance were perfected, so that after the seventeenth century the entire octave could be divided into twelve halftones of equal acoustical magnitude (as in the modern piano—in effect an irrational magnitude of twelve times the square root of two). This made it possible for Jean-Philippe Rameau (1683–1764) to refine the system of tonalities and render the theory of music into an efficient theory of composition, one that remains at the basis of tonal music (even unconsciously, particularly for pop), up until the present and all over the world.

* * *

Just as for Leibniz a musician or a scientist had to grasp the mathematics behind a work while the listener simply enjoyed the pleasures afforded by consonance, Claude Perrault believed that knowledge of proportions, though "arbitrary," was fundamental for the architect. Despite questioning many essential premises of previous architectural theories—particularly, as I have noted, the assumed primacy of synesthesia—Perrault never doubted the capacity of classical architecture and its orders to provide appropriate settings for life in his own time, the "golden age" of Louis XIV. In his commentaries to his own translation of Vitruvius's *Ten Books*, he clarifies that the proportions of architecture had their origins not in a cosmic image but in the customs of civil society, in human history, transforming in a way similar to language.[5] Architectural forms and proportions may be arbitrary and not absolute, definitely not based in nature like those of physical science, yet this qualification was not derogatory and did not mean that such a condition might simply condone the vagaries of individual taste. Rather, the issue for architecture was the perpetuation of civil community (in his case, the accomplishments of civilization witnessed under Louis XIV). In architecture, unlike in dress, fashion moves toward stability. In order to "speak properly," architecture had to be cognizant of traditions and history.

As we have seen, the possibilities for an architecture mimetic of a traditional cosmos were vanishing. Rather, a new paradigm emerged—*architecture as analogous to language*—one that recognized, instead, the importance of history in orienting its preferences and formal decisions, and presumed the possibility of speaking both discursively and lyrically, to affect the intellect and our sentiments. Reason and feeling, seen as inner faculties of the dualistic mind, were recognized as distinct yet reconcilable, as we observed in Leibniz, or sometimes as akin through their origin in the empirical world of "experience." This last was particularly true in the wake of Newton, Locke, and Condillac, yet now (and in contrast to earlier times) one could presuppose that the legitimate contents of such "experience" were the results of quantitative experiment (reason), or of sensations perceived by autonomous senses, *partes extra partes* (feeling).

It is pertinent to remember here the enormous influence of Newtonian natural philosophy, particularly after 1735 and until the end of the century. In the Enlightenment world all supernatural phenomena were questioned, and miracles were seldom attributed to divine intervention, yet scientists and philosophers generally recognized the presence of a mathematical God behind Nature, whose creation was made evident in the laws of universal gravitation "discovered" by Newton and corroborated through empirical observations.[6] In this totally transformed manner, the possibility of understanding Nature as the source of truth (reason) and beauty (taste) in human works and architecture was maintained, and a number of writers on architectural theory even argued for their identity; intuition generated taste and rules, both of which governed taste thereafter. Newtonianism promoted a new cultural sensitivity to Nature's wonders and moods, making them exemplary for human works, *all* taking *place* within "divine" (empty) mathematical space and time.[7] It also demonstrated Nature's utter "simplicity" as it revealed its mathematical principles (universal gravitation) to reason, so that mathematics and geometry could be assumed to underscore its paradigmatic beauty and could be extrapolated to architecture, both as a symbolic and metaphysical structure and legitimizing new versions of instrumental theories founded through induction.

***

The Abbé Jean-Baptiste Dubos, writing about art in 1719, made an early attempt to reconnect that which Descartes had separated. For him it is not enough for us to judge a work beautiful (an aesthetic cogitation); it is vital that the work "moves our hearts."[8] He writes that the sublime dimension of poetry and painting touches and pleases, just as that of eloquence persuades.[9] The mission of the artwork is a deep emotional communion without which communication is not possible: it is a question of participation. In other words, art must be both beautiful *and* sublime—in contrast to the disjunction perpetuated later in the century by Burke and Kant, and often taken for granted in later aesthetics. It is important to observe that this notion corresponds to attunement's deep-seated capacity to accomplish *concordia discors*, or discordant harmony, as explained in chapter 2.[10]

In view of these complex early modern assumptions concerning Nature and culture, French eighteenth-century architects conceived several models to create communicative settings, ranging from the scientistic to the linguistic, and thus already anticipated some of our contemporary debates. On one extreme was Amédée-François Frézier, a military engineer by profession who delighted in the intricacies of applied geometry for stonecutting while acknowledging that his speculations were totally useless in practice. Frézier believed that architecture could convey the values of nature, its "positive" beauty, and to this end he applied findings in the science of statics to the proportions of buildings.[11] In his view, such would avoid the pitfalls of historical variation and result in truly absolute beauty—an argument curiously resonant with recent and current attempts to deduce scientific models for the purpose of form generation while disregarding history. Beauty, he thought, should be self-evident to vision; of course, such apprehension of beauty was unrelated to the invisible Pythagorean numbers, but ruled instead by those of mechanics (statics). The imitation of nature always affords pleasure; thus, the universal rules of architecture should be established based on the imitation of natural architecture; they should be simple, like the universal rules of science. So, he argued, masonry structures were better when built using arches and piers rather than columns and lintels, in compliance with the rules of statics. Deploying this same reasoning in regard to the design of columns, Frézier believed there must be only three classical orders (disregarding all issues of ornament), because we build solidly, lightly, or in between. Thus, the orders' proportions are fixed—light for Corinthian (1:9), medium for Ionic (1:8), and sturdy for Doric (1:7)—in line with the rules of Galilean mechanics but also in expressing the related sensation to visual perception.[12] According to Frézier, we *feel* the lightness of the Corinthian column and thus we intuitively know that if it were any more slender, it would *be* dangerous; hence we can set the right proportions. The same argument would apply at the opposite end of the spectrum. All expression would be possible within this range, but Frézier had no interest in qualifying the question of appropriateness further since beauty is assured merely by emulating the mathematics of Nature (in his case drawn from statics). His rhetoric was not unlike that of today's computer-generated biomorphic architecture, and was perhaps as limited.

Abbé Marc-Antoine Laugier, the well-known theoretician of neoclassicism, shared some of Frézier's premises, particularly vis-à-vis the precedence of Nature for beauty and rules; but Laugier arrived at very different conclusions. Interestingly, in his *Essai sur l'architecture* (1753) he opposes his contemporaries' reduction of theory to technical or formal prescriptions and explicitly sets out to recover a philosophy of architecture that would respond to the modern, Newtonian worldview. This philosophy reinstates the metaphysical questions of traditional *theoría*, yet seeks out a "single law" that might derive from inductive observation. As such, he establishes the priority of post-and-lintel architecture: the original form of building closest to "simple" Nature; a unique principle, like our "little rustic hut."[13] The presence of the hut's three elements—columns, beams (architraves), and frontispieces—is a condition of beauty and meaning in building. All else is either necessity (like walls and windows) or abuse (like superfluous ornament). Trees, and not the human body or its articulation, are postulated as the origin of the orders, becoming the very structure of architecture (as opposed to its ornament, as in Renaissance theories). Thus, he concludes, the noble, delicate, and graceful simplicity of the Corinthian order is the most beautiful; it is a particularly appropriate expression for religious buildings when articulated with the lightness of Gothic, in which case it coincides both with French historical taste and natural expression. Yet for Laugier, unlike Frézier, these general principles had to be modulated by the rules of *bienséance* (*commoditas*) in order to attain a form of expression befitting the hierarchy of social institutions that frame human actions.

This question of expression became central to a group of eighteenth-century French writers particularly pertinent to this book's main concern; architectural historians have labeled their work "character theory." These writers clearly recognized that in the absence of a cosmological referent, architects interested in designing communicative settings for society had to consider linguistic analogies to realize their projects. They thought that architecture, like prose and poetry as well as painting and music, should be able to communicate both discursively and/or emotionally, and in ways appropriate to the role buildings play in society. This approach addressed the need for legibility of social hierarchies to preserve the "space of appearance," particularly in larger urban centers such as Paris and London,[14] while drawing on the conviction that character was visible, as, for example, in physiognomy, and that the passionate affect of architecture was based on nature, as had been explained by Dubos.

Thus, character theory placed a special emphasis on *decorum*, "appropriateness" to a human situation. This was already evident, as we have seen, in classical Vitruvian theories, where it complemented (from Greco-Roman antiquity to the Renaissance) the possibility of cosmic *mímesis* for the design of harmonious and well-tempered environments. During the eighteenth century, in the absence of a Pythagorean cosmos, this category addressing cultural values and traditions became the dominant issue of architectural meaning. In this case, all allusion to harmonic proportions no longer referred to determinate "multitudes"—expressed in numbers—but mostly to geometric, continuous magnitudes, like modern music that had shifted from Pythagorean natural numbers to a scale (or octave) divided into twelve equal semitones. This proportion was thus primarily "experienced" directly: present in an emotionally charged Nature and evident in artistic practices such as painting, music, and literature. Associating architectural meaning with character, eighteenth-century authors perceived the ambivalence of the term: *character* is a sign or a letter; when used to characterize an object or a work it is a perceived condition; while the character of a person is itself ambivalent. Individual character is both innate—as when one states, "That man has character"—and acquired, as when used in reference to the role one plays in society or in the theater. As Richard Sennett observed, such theatricality of everyday life was crucial for various aspects of social interaction in the eighteenth century, encompassing personal dress, behavior, and the environment, i.e., the "texture" of cities. Character in architecture was deemed capable of conveying emotions (like poetry) as well as intelligible meanings (like prose). Generally, it was not presumed that the audience would "read" or "decode" buildings, as the problem of meaning would usually be understood starting in the nineteenth century; despite the positions expressed early on by theoreticians like Perrault, meaning as *visible presence* was still largely assumed. Its apprehension involved intelligible and/or emotional experience, yet this was made increasingly difficult by a growing suspicion—fueled by the new science and the writings of many Enlightenment thinkers (ultimately derived from modern Cartesian philosophy and its mechanistic psychology)—of emotions as "hindering" meaning rather than contributing to it.

It is important for my argument to mention, albeit briefly, some of the diverse positions of French writers to embrace this modern paradigm. Earlier character theoreticians perceived history as a positive force and regarded the poetic harmonies in the arts, with their origins in Nature, as experiences to be translated into the realm of architecture. Later in the century, "simple Nature" was privileged as the paradigm of moods that could then be applied to appropriate architectural situations. Classical theoretical assumptions were radically questioned and the classical orders were no longer deemed essential, while history was often construed as a corruption of original conditions.

In his *Livre d'architecture* (1745), Germain Boffrand takes it as an article of faith that somehow the arts and sciences must relate through mathematics:[15] a concept that had been "demonstrated" by Leibniz and absorbed by Baumgarten. Already assuming (and this, it should be emphasized, is an innovation elaborating on insights by Dubos) that "poetry, painting, sculpture, music, and architecture" are sister arts, sharing issues of expression capable of "depicting" the diverse incidents of Nature, even "inciting tender and violent passions,"[16] he was the first to suggest character theory as a strategy to address the "new" problem of decorum in contemporary architecture. He understood character primarily in terms of that expressed by literary genres (as set forth in Horace's *Ars poetica*)—for example, the "epic character" of the *Iliad* or the "lyrical character" of a love poem, which could be conveyed in architecture through the proportions of the classical orders. The importance of proportions was presumed yet only generally specified in his book and discussed as a question of "temperance" or optical correction, one that could even be extrapolated to buildings where the orders were not used.[17] Indeed, Boffrand argues that the five classical orders were akin to different "poësies" expressing different genres (paraphrasing Vitruvius's book 1). Yet he goes on to explain that, for instance, every part of a house must have an appropriate character, such that a stable should not be treated the same as the courtyard leading to the entrance; nor should interiors be handled like exteriors. The issue for Boffrand is to use good judgment ("more important than the ruler and the level"), to ascertain the appropriateness of such characters to the human situations framed by architecture, "which should announce its destination to the spectator," similar to a stage in the classical theater. It is interesting that in the wake of classical theory with its basis in Aristotelian science and cosmology, Boffrand already understood architectural theory not as science, like Perrault and Frézier (in the tradition of *theoría/sophía*), but mostly as a matter of "practical philosophy," or *phrónesis*. He writes, for instance: "In architecture, like in other things, a good sense for judgment is acquired in communication with other ethical people and people of good taste, through the reading of philosophy, through a long experience of careful making, and through the knowledge of ways of life [cultural mores] in the country where one builds."[18]

While classical literature constituted the paradigm in this regard for Boffrand, music became the preferred origin of architectural character for Charles-Étienne Briseux, who published his *Traité du beau essentiel dans les arts* a few years later, in 1752.[19] Although rejecting Perrault's claim concerning the notion of arbitrary beauty in architecture, Briseux also proposed an instrumental theory that could, nevertheless, lead to "positive beauty," in accordance with Nature. Diverging from Boffrand, Briseux agreed with Perrault on the unnecessary nature of optical corrections, thus implicitly accepting Descartes's psychology *partes extra partes*: the autonomy of the five senses and the preeminently visual nature of architecture. He assumed that architectural drawings and buildings must correspond precisely and that their design should be prescribed through rational operations, and yet he ridiculed the a priori nature of Perrault's proportional system, which he held to be the cause of its failure. He thought that inventing proportions a priori was inappropriate; he sought instead to arrive at them through empirical scientific methods, thus proving through "authority, physical explanation, and experience," i.e., experiment, the existence of an essential beauty in architecture.

According to Briseux, the true Natural beauty and character that constitute architectural meaning are expressed through proportions, like those that produce musical harmonies in a diatonic scale. When it came to applying the concept, however, Briseux in his treatise suggests that the set dimensions in the plan of a project merely be taken as a given, determining the base of the building's elevation, to be subdivided according to whole numbers and the desired intervals to produce the appropriate effect. No numbers are specified; the issue is to divide the "monochord," understood as the "fundamental base," literally the base line of the main elevation, into harmonic intervals that are manifested as graphic magnitudes and thus regulate the composition. Within this framework, even the classical orders could become incidental to meaning. Briseux derived his central concept from the writings of his contemporary Jean-Philippe Rameau, a talented composer and author of the first theory of music that could be applied as a theory of composition—unlike traditional theories of music, which, as we have noted, were mostly "contemplative" elucidations of the music of the cosmos based on Pythagoras.[20]

Rameau believed that tonal music derived from nature and even suggested that science, along with all other disciplines based upon mathematics, had its first origins in music—an argument refuted by Jean-Jacques Rousseau, who could already discern that Western tonality was a cultural construct.[21] We all "hear" harmonic tonality, Rameau affirmed, regardless of our knowledge of music theory, and can "resolve" a third into a fifth. Rameau put forward the system of major and minor keys that is now accepted universally. From Rameau, Briseux understood that harmonic proportions in the various keys (C major, C minor, and so on) were capable of diverse emotive expression, *of communicating particular moods*, and he imagined an analogy between proportions and human sensations that could be transferred to buildings, thus contributing to attuned settings for human actions. It bears recalling that this assumption initially emerged in Greek music theory and the characters associated with the diverse *modes* (intervals along the diatonic scale on a monochord), as part of the original concept of harmony discussed in the previous chapter. Aristotle believed music was capable of creating a particular quality of character in the soul, conveying ethos (ἦθος), moral character. In his *Politics* he describes the effect of the different *harmoniai* of music on mood and character formation observed by experts in music education. He explains, for example, how the Myxolydian mode conveys grief and anxiety, the Phrygian creates ecstatic excitement, and the Dorian moderation and firmness, distinct moods appropriate for diverse human situations, ranging from theatrical performances and religious rituals to war.[22] By analogy, Briseux believed that a judicious choice of intervals (divisions) of the primary (base) dimension of a building could lead to an appropriate expression in view of its avowed use.

In order to extrapolate from music to architecture Briseux needed to align the senses of hearing and sight that had been emancipated in the modern psychology of Descartes and by the eighteenth-century *philosophes*. Thus, he adapted a "scientific" argument from Newton's *Opticks* (1704). Newton had established the analogy of light—decomposed into the seven colors of the rainbow—with music's seven tones in a diatonic scale, a metaphor that had an extraordinary impact on poets, painters, and architects of the eighteenth century.[23] Furthermore, it was exemplified by the Jesuit Père Castel's *clavecin oculaire*, an instrument demonstrating correspondences between colors and musical tones built on principles concerning the melody of colors, set out in his writings (which also contained a critique of Newtonian optics), and which the composer Georg Philipp Telemann proclaimed as admirable when he saw it on one of his trips to Paris.[24] For Briseux, this proved that the harmony of music could also be achieved in the visible world, while no longer assuming the entrenched primacy of synesthesia.

Thirty years later, Nicolas Le Camus de Mézières expressed fascination with Newton's *Opticks*, with René Ouvrard's late-seventeenth-century applications of musical harmonic proportions to architecture, and with Père Castel's *clavecin oculaire*. In the opening paragraph of his treatise *Le génie de l'architecture* (1780), he acknowledges his debt to Condillac's mechanistic psychology while seeking to explain the "analogy of architectural proportions with our sensations," a topic, he claims, that had never been treated.[25] Following his introduction, the book opens with sensuous descriptions of important French buildings such as the interior of the dome of Les Invalides, the colonnade of the Louvre, churches such as La Sorbonne and Val-de-Grâce, theaters in Paris and elsewhere, castles like Versailles, and even the "voluptuous and playful new architecture" in some areas of Paris. These examples generally "seduce through their harmony, through the concordance of their parts and manifold decoration," producing appropriate atmospheres to the activities they house. The theater at Versailles, for example, communicates its effect "as if prepared for a ball, promoting feelings (*sentimens*) analogous to games, distractions, and the parties it will accommodate."[26] He also repeats the generally accepted proportions of the classical orders, such as eight diameters of height for a Doric column and nine for an Ionic, but what really matters to him is the character expressed, always in relation to the characters of human bodies, both male and female, their natural grace, their dress and effects.[27]

Le Camus's main stated aim, to design architecture seeking an analogy between its masses, parts, dispositions, and décor and "our sensations," both foregrounds a new crucial awareness concerning the nature of architecture's communicative space as "atmosphere," and surprises us with its claim for novelty, given the story that we have been telling in this book: that a resonance between architectural spaces and experience in focal actions was always at the forefront of classical discourses surrounding harmony and temperance. Yet, given the cultural conditions of late-eighteenth-century France, the question appeared both as new and in need of better articulation. This, in my view, is closely related to the growing identification of the isotropic, homogeneous space of science with lived spatiality (place), whose repercussions on the popular perception of the city and its architecture now began to felt. As I will elaborate in the following chapter, the qualitative perception of *places*, the so-called genius loci, related to focal actions and their emerging language, was a commonplace of European cultures until about this time. The dissolution of such shared experience contributed in a fundamental way to the crisis of meaning in architecture that Le Camus lamented in his treatise. Like other contemporaries, such as Viel de Saint-Maux and Boullée, he declared the importance of philosophical questions for architecture, believing it was imperative to grasp the significance of the discipline amid its challenging present social context.

Le Camus regarded all previous theories as inadequate to the production of a meaningful architecture, one whose character might be appropriate and truly communicated to the inhabitant; *qualities* of space were the issue, and no manner of geometric formal manipulation would be sufficient for the now-homogeneous space of science, the necessary site of each and every building, to recover its emotional content. So, while he perceived the importance of dimensions (proportions) for the characterization of spaces, he rejected his predecessors' attempts at objectifying harmony and consonance through mathematical languages, whether arithmetic or geometric. Instead, acknowledging the modern "interiority of feeling," *he decided to use words in a literary structure* (instead of geometric ratios) to convey the qualities of analogy needed for a resonant "exteriority" in architectural spaces. This would prove to be a remarkable and far-reaching development.

More simply, never before Le Camus had "space," that "in-between" we today identify with atmosphere, become a self-conscious concern in architectural theory to be implemented in the design of communicative settings. This could only have become possible amid a fully constituted modern subjectivity. Yet Le Camus recognized the necessity of attunement (in his words, "the analogy of architecture and our sensations"), and understood that the moods of rooms (space/place) carried the very meaning—the harmonic potential—of architecture, which he deliberately sought. An emerging metaphorical language identifying actions and emotions, and describing rooms' aspects—textures, smells, decoration, and colors, among others—was crucial for the design process, so that appropriate qualities to specific settings would be conveyed to the inhabitant.

As such, Le Camus's book is very different from all previous treatises. Consisting of a qualitative description of architectural "space" *in* a human dwelling, in the rooms that constitute a private house (an *hôtel particulier*), it shuns the use of drawings and engravings. Interiority now comprised the paradigm for understanding qualitative place, communicated through poetic language, a momentous development. Suffice it to recall that architecture's primary concern had always been the public realm, the social space of appearance where humans might recognize an intersubjective order and thus find their place vis-à-vis the cosmos. By contrast, interior rooms are by definition *limited*, as opposed to the generalized "infinite" Cartesian space that was gradually becoming understood as "commonplace."

Le Camus's designation of internal spaces as exemplary, for the first time ever in architectural writing, also bears a significant relationship to changes taking place in the design of stages for the theater. The theater had been a fundamental architectural institution in which the "city" or a public building constituted the unchanging, generalized backdrop for drama. At this juncture, particularly after Denis Diderot's invention of the *drame bourgeois*, interiors started to be used as sets,[28] a practice that would be perpetuated in the nineteenth century and beyond.

These transformations were obviously symptoms of and reactions to the dissolution of the protection that had always been afforded by the "external," limited cosmos, the dome of the sky: a perception common in many cultures that perceive the place of man in the "interior" of nature, and still present in Europe into the late Enlightenment. A remarkable plate from Claude-Nicolas Ledoux's contemporaneous treatise, *La maison du pauvre*, is a wonderful illustration of this condition: a poor man, lacking the material resources to build himself a more sophisticated home, is shown sitting on a stone; Ledoux explains that despite his limitations the man is not really poor, for he dwells under the auspices of divinities and is protected by Divine Nature. Once "infinite" place was identified with lived space, architecture was forced to take a critical position, for its harmonious and temperate *place making* had always been *an issue of limits*; by definition, human "significant" space must be limited (even if it can be understood as hypothetically or theologically infinite).

More will be said about the work of Ledoux and Étienne-Louis Boullée in the following chapters, although Boullée's famous project in honor of Newton is particularly relevant here. As shown in the sectional drawing, the visitor enters the spherical interior through a tunnel and stands at the bottom, in the center. Looking up, the cenotaph "presents" to perception the universe studded with stars, the infinite space/time of Newton's natural philosophy and deism, as a finite interior space. This is the ultimate *coincidentia oppositorum*, the last possible "sacred" space that concludes the possibility of a geometric representation of the Judeo-Christian God, first introduced to Western thinking in the theology of Nicholas of Cusa in the fifteenth century. Boullée, like Le Camus, was skeptical of the potential of earlier discourses in architectural theory to bring about meaningful work, and believed that the articulation of a poetic intentionality through literary language was the best way to express appropriate moods experienced first in Nature, and made present in his projects through the tools of the painter. Harmony is also claimed as crucial. It exists in the analogy between the simple geometries of nature and human experience, yet it cannot be attained by theoretical (mathematical) prescription, only through expressive fictions, engaged through language.

Finally, it is important to point out that the sequence the inhabitant takes through Le Camus's *hôtel* is also crucial as a design consideration for architectural space, not because he is imagined "visiting" the building in the linear time of tourism, as will become common in the nineteenth century, but rather because Le Camus is aware of the fact that for a full "resonance" of the building to occur, spaces must be considered as primordially intertwined with lived time. The characters of rooms are particular to the specific situations to which they are dedicated, like eating, receiving friends, washing, sleeping, or seducing a partner, yet they are complementary, so that further meanings are constituted and growing expectations created, eventually telling a story, a poetic image or metaphor for dwelling. This intertwining of spatiality and temporality is another reaction to the emancipation of time and space as they became autonomous quantitative variables in the physical sciences, and were eventually considered to be real, primary facts of existence. Le Camus thus placed special emphasis on the function of thresholds and the creation of expectations. Theatrical analogies appear everywhere, and, as Louise Pelletier has suggested, architectural meaning appears *as* the space of desire, reconnecting also on this account with the earlier qualification of communicative space I discussed in relation to Vitruvius's *venustas*. This participatory understanding of beauty and meaning, which ultimately challenged the "detachment" of eighteenth-century aesthetic qualities and which André Breton would call "convulsive beauty," capable of making us shiver with pleasure, was to become particularly important for romanticism and surrealism. It is crucial to the concept of *Stimmung*.

* * *

Indeed, it is around this time that this multivalent German word became popular among romantic philosophers, scientists, and poets. Writing between the late eighteenth and mid-nineteenth centuries, this group of European thinkers forcefully reclaimed the ancient understanding of human space as the emotionally charged space of desire. They questioned the dualistic Cartesian understanding of reality and its concept of subjectivity, together with its implied psychology. While their position would remain marginal and polemical in relation to positivism, the applied sciences, and technology, they lay the groundwork for important artistic, philosophical, and even medical endeavors that would have far-reaching consequences. Their use of the term *Gemüt* to characterize human consciousness is illuminating, also anticipating developments in phenomenology, recent neurology, and "third-generation" cognitive science.

It is well established that the first person, a "mind" *in love* with speculative knowledge, emerged in the Western tradition in the realms of philosophy and architectural theory, but prior to Descartes man was never held to be at the basis of reality. Only the Cartesian *ego cogitans*, standing for the self-reflective "I" that thinks, became the origin of being in early modern philosophy ("I think, *therefore* I am"). The romantic self radically questioned this understanding. It prefigures an alternative: a phenomenological "first person," the *me* that wakes up every morning yet is always in flux, revealing a primary human consciousness that cannot be reduced to transparent reason, coemerging with its world and its active engagement, a potential *tuning*. Elaborating on earlier insights from Anthony

Ashley Cooper, Third Earl of Shaftesbury, Jean-Jacques Rousseau, and the *Sturm und Drang* literary movement in the German-speaking countries that flourished around the 1770s, these romantic thinkers started by questioning David Hume's anthropology of impersonality, in which consciousness was construed as a camera obscura: the mind like an empty room receiving all its understanding through impressions acquired from individual, autonomous senses, characterized by their specific organs. In its place, romantic thinkers postulated an imagining, poetic, and ethical self, whose certitude is founded upon an intimate sense.

The evocation of *Stimmung* in this period emerged in response to the enduring quest for an accord between the human being and the universe, at a time when the environment, ultimately characterized by materialism as a mere repository of natural resources available for exploitation and needed for industrialization and economic growth, became perceived as totally *separate* from human consciousness and potentially even hostile. In this context, *Stimmung* became an explicit program for the arts, a means for humanity to seek new forms of attunement. This critical dimension, thereafter required of any poetic project, had a fundamental impact on architecture that I will explore at the end of this chapter and through other examples in this book, expanding its specificity beyond the traditional "performance" of buildings to include other mediations.

In his *Essais* (1795), Friedrich Schelling called for a gnostic turn vis-à-vis the rational world of dominant culture and mechanical time and space. He thought it our prerogative to effect a distance from the times in which we live and contemplate within ourselves eternity in its immutable form, this being the only way to access our most precious certainties, to know "that anything is in the true sense of being, while the rest is only appearance."[29] This intuition appears to us whenever we stop being an object for ourselves, as we are not "in" linear time. Rather, "time, or pure eternity, is in us"—anticipating Edmund Husserl's and later phenomenological and neurobiological revisions of the nature of lived experience, at odds with the mechanical concept of linear time and its nonexistent punctual present.[30] Most significantly, however, the story for Schelling doesn't end here. He adds an important observation that underscores his introspective critical understanding: "Even the most abstract notions retrieve an experience of life and existence … all our knowledge has as a point of departure direct experiences."[31]

Indeed, Schelling's stance is characteristic of romantic philosophy. The questioning of the anthropology of impersonality and the mechanistic theories of perception of the Enlightenment led to a renewed, now self-conscious and critical consideration of the primacy of synesthesia. Throughout European history, synesthetic apperception always bore witness to the idea of world harmony, allowing all the senses to converge into one harmonious feeling. In chapter 5, I will discuss more extensively the term as understood in phenomenology and with reference to enactive cognitive theories. Etymologically, the term means simply "union of the senses," and it is important to mention that this differs from its contemporary common usage as a neuropathology, in which stimulation on one sensory pathway leads to automatic, involuntary experiences in a second sensory pathway. Phenomenological synesthesia is in fact closer to the neologism coined in 1794 by a romantic doctor, Johann Christian Reil, appearing initially in a student's doctoral dissertation. This internal function of consciousness he called *Gemeingefül*, translated into French as *coenesthésie*, defined in opposition to the autonomous external senses and conveying "to consciousness the state of the body by the intermediary of the nerves, distributed throughout the organism,"[32] a coloring or tonality at once biological and affective. Maurice de Guérin (1810–1839) thus emphasized the primary reality of synesthesia in human experience, while rejecting the very possibility of Locke's concept of the mind as a "blank slate." While the interior "feeling" dimension is initially foregrounded, an acknowledgment of the reciprocity between the inner and the outer as a condition of human consciousness immediately follows.[33] For example, Novalis (1772–1801) in *Grains de pollen* (1798) writes: "We dream of trips through the universe, yet the universe is in us."[34] In his philosophical reflections, he always gave priority to the poetic image (disclosed by metaphor), emphasizing it is precisely that which tends to become real. All these thinkers are driven by a struggle for wholeness, abolishing distinctions between the body and the mind, the outside and the inside, physiology and the science of the mind—anticipating the discoveries of contemporary enactive cognitive science. Rainer Maria Rilke (1875–1926) would eventually summarize this feeling in his poem "Ah, not to be cut off" with the verse "The Inner, what is it if not intensified sky?"[35]

This redefined, thoroughly incarnated human consciousness posited *Gemüt* as its central "organ," a feeling mind, with temper and disposition;

a "heart" instead of a brain, yet hardly the biological pump that makes blood circulate (*Herz* in German), but rather the place just over the diaphragm where emotion strikes us. Thus *Gemüt* can be sober, sentimental, cheerful, serene, buoyant, fiery, quick, childlike, even, smooth, sharp, tender, stubborn, sunny, or uneven. Joseph Ennemoser (1849) gives *Gemüt* priority over understanding, *Verstand*. The former is the foundation of certainty, effected by *Stimmung*.[36] According to Friedrich Schlegel, *Gemüt* is "the true vital force of beauty and internal fulfillment." At times he associates it with a feminine dimension of consciousness, at others with the immediate perception of human reality, nuanced at its origin, of sympathy or antipathy, attraction or repulsion, that goes beyond appearance and refers to the totality; it implies physical and moral components in a complex yet simple judgment, impossible to justify through logic alone.[37] Anticipation, presentiment, and affinities are confounded in the unity of divination at the time of an encounter with a work or a person, as can be observed in the common experience of love and friendship. Later phenomenology will refer to this as *prereflective cognition*, fully emotional *understanding*.

For Novalis, *Gemüt* has an *active* function; while passive perception (*partes extra partes*) was assumed to allow a cognitive synthesis that presents an objective exterior reality in geometric space, our innate *Gemüt* already evokes a different apprehension, the geometry of an internal space colored by all the resources of imagination and affectivity. Thus, the first person exercises its right to commandeer material objectivity, a re-creation that consecrates the primacy of the poetic over the real. "We perfectly conceive why, in the last instance, everything becomes poetry. The world, is it not finally, *Gemüt*?"[38] Here the term again resonates with embodied, worldly "consciousness," primarily emotional (prereflective). It has an ontological value where we may find our orientation in the world. According to romantic anthropology, this is one of the essential tasks of human beings, one in which the built environment and architecture should play a crucial role. *Gemüt* thus appears as the very organ of creative inspiration that must be enlisted by the architect, the organ of passionate love and compassion. And it is associated with poetry by Novalis: "Poetry is the representation of *Gemüt*, of the interior world in its totality." *Its medium is words*.

* * *

Allow me to reiterate that *Stimmung* was a distant translation from Latin: *temperamentum (temperatura)* and *consonantia (concordia)*—related to the quest for harmony of classical architecture, in pursuit of psychosomatic health in cities and buildings. Romantic *Stimmung* reflects a similar quest to discover an accord between the human being and the universe, yet with full acknowledgment of the challenges represented by a modern world; its meaning, not surprisingly, is very difficult to transpose to other European languages. It is understood as a search for lost integrity, health, wholeness, and holiness; transforming from *proportion* in the classical and medieval contexts to *atmosphere* or *mood*, it becomes a central concept for artistic works in search of meaning, potentially including architecture, of course. In English *Stimmung* may be also rendered as *tone*, *feeling*, *disposition*, or *frame of mind*. The root in German is *Stimme*, meaning "voice," the "atmospheric" vehicle that carries human language, song, and melody, our original expressive utterance, contiguous to gesture. It implies the primacy of orality over writing, contrary to the recent arguments of poststructuralism and deconstruction. The romantic word designated, according to Charles du Bos (1957), "both the tuning of an instrument and the disposition of soul [mind, as *Gemüt*]."[39] Novalis refers to "an acoustics of the soul," evoking a spiritual dimension that is both interior and exterior, whose constitutive elements are fluid and ultimately defy analysis.

Analytic, discursive language and so-called algorithmic languages aim for denotation and precision. Despite the unintended consequences of technological processes and the opacities that are now perceived as built into the products of our technology, such languages tend to devalorize, exclude to the margins, and ultimately reduce to irrelevance all that cannot be rendered through clear, intelligible logic. At the heart of existence, however, our emotional, prereflective life imposes its feelings on us, like musical modulations inspired by a condition of being that escapes external determinism and conformity.[40] We are traversed by concordant and discordant waves arising from the depths of consciousness, consonances and dissonances with the external world with no more justification than the "mood" of the moment—to which the environment and architecture contribute in a fundamental way. This apparent capriciousness and irrationality expresses in its own way an intelligibility in which the human being finds the essential facets of a life that resembles him or her.

Humors, the way we feel, cannot simply be regulated by a controlling will and clear thinking. We have mentioned how the ancients believed that temperaments expressed the relationship, through the individual, of the external cosmos (a particular planet, for instance) and bodily consciousness: Saturn was responsible for our melancholy, Mars for our aggressiveness. Architecture's role as a mediator in this relationship was well established in traditional classical theory, but was questioned once the built environment became subject to technological instrumentality in early modernity. Romantic *Stimmung*, commandeered as an aesthetic category for artistic production, represents an attempt to recover, in a transformed way that makes sense to the human cultures of the nineteenth to the twenty-first centuries, the same phenomenon: privileging relationships, harmonies, and correspondences. Romantic philosophy recovers the older understanding of the "sensitive soul" in Aristotle's *De anima*, the dimension of consciousness that humans share with animals and that is like "an inner touch," asserting the primacy of feeling (rather than thinking) as evidence of existence.[41] Thus, felt experience, becoming primary, ascertains this deeply rooted Western tradition and justifies the doctrine of *Stimmung*, which gives its form to the individual's *Gemüt*.[42]

Stimmungen correspond to forms of organization of "chaosmic" experience; that is, they designate *forms of intelligibility* that one can perceive clearly through the vicissitudes of a personal life.[43] According to Karl Gustav Carus (1851), the specificity of *Gemüt* is expressed amid the species of four fundamental *Stimmungen*: joy, sadness, love, and hate.[44] It is important to point out that Le Camus de Mézières, introducing the importance of character in architecture, after relating it to the painter Charles Le Brun's theory of the passions in physiognomy, had observed these same four fundamental "sympathies" induced by architectural character: love, hatred, happiness, and sadness.[45] Such affective dispositions denote modes of presence to the world and to the self, resonating in the depths of personal life, ultimately contributing to the harmonious or discordant tone of a person's spiritual destiny, to our "particular meteorology."[46]

The intuition *Stimmung* and *Gemüt* designate is found precisely in the in-*placement* that relates the inner with the outer dimensionalities of human consciousness: the place of the built environment where the magical tuning of architecture can be implemented. It also reveals that visual perception cannot be explained as a passive phenomenon of geometric optics, as already suggested by Goethe in his *Theory of Colors* (1810). Contrary to the positions of Condillac, Locke, and Hume, perception is *active*, and thus "man imposes on landscapes the priority of his intimate climate."[47] As man is "of the world" even before birth, both body and mind contribute to this belonging. Like a glass that may resonate or shatter when subjected to a certain sound frequency, each human being is sensitive to certain influences with which its psychophysical constitution finds affinity or discordance. The network of mostly prereflective relations that negotiate the engagement of self and world is the place of *Stimmung*, always revealing the links between exterior and interior landscapes and "meteorologies." *Gemüt* is the threshold of consciousness to the world and the self,[48] the place of an integrated perception, imagination, and memory. If it is disrupted, harmony must be reestablished in alignment with nature. This became the calling of poetry and architecture.

Novalis spoke of an enigmatic correspondence between mathematics, *Stimmung*, and emotions, as if the *mathemata* could be internalized as a sign of the divine or holy.[49] In this regard, it is intriguing to recall the unprecedented development of the demanding, "contemplative" musical concert and symphony during the nineteenth century, quite at odds with previous social uses of music, representing far more than entertainment for a public in search of personal harmony. While it would be impossible to develop this theme here, we may invoke George Steiner's observation that despite changes of taste in later times, the omnipresence of music in our discordant world civilization is a hopeful sign of our thirst for attunement.[50]

Novalis's insight also suggests the potential reinstatement of "harmonic dimensionality" in architecture, not as an instrumental precept or compositional guideline, but as an "experience," identical to the experience of music. Indeed, resonant with its historical roots, romantic *Stimmung* ultimately aims to attune consciousness, proposing an ideal of harmony—aesthetic, moral, and ontological. This constitutes a sort of peace, difficult to acquire, that could also be a gift of grace; a harmony that might be established beyond all discordance, a perfect accord. It is experienced as spontaneous accord due to a mysterious contact wherein the harmony is not preceded by any intentional or conceptual tuning process on the part of the subject; it has nothing to do with research, conquest, or even the attainment of equilibrium, in the sense of biological homeostasis. *Stimmung* is given and received as a *gift* in all its meanings, and this is the central issue; it is a concordant *discord* since it acknowledges that humans must remain "open toward death."[51]

There is an inescapable ambiguity associated with the term, one that is explicit in its uses by later philosophers, like Martin Heidegger and Giorgio Agamben. I have elaborated on Heidegger's use of the term in chapter 1; for him, moods are ways of being in the world: "attunements which attune us in such a way that we feel as though there is no attunement there at all ... these attunements are the most powerful."[52] In an earlier text, *Being and Time*, he calls *Stimmung* the fundamental existential mode of *Dasein* on the ontological, rather than the ontic plane. Yet on the other hand, since moods come from outside and commandeer us, they are also very noticeable; they make us feel more complete and become participants: through focal actions, our lives matter. Agamben elaborates on and emphasizes the liminality of the term, manifested "neither within interiority nor *in* the world, but at their limit."[53] He offers other insights that will be helpful to retain for the chapters that follow; as prior to conscious knowledge, *Stimmung*, rather than being itself in a place, is the very opening of the world, the very *place* of being. Yet equally, since it discloses *Dasein* as "having been thrown," *Stimmung*'s structure is manifest as *Dasein*'s feeling of *not* being at home.[54] Furthermore, Agamben deduces that *Stimmung* is a privileged place to think through our relation to language, revealing the very articulation between living and language, between *zoon* and *logos*, between nature and culture. It is "the coming into being of the poetic word."[55]

***

For romantic philosophers, knowledge was expected to be rigorous, but it was also to be a lived knowledge of life, prefiguring José Ortega y Gasset's "vitalist" philosophy and Edmund Husserl's search for the most demanding precision while remaining attentive to the primacy of the lived world. Romantic medicine, for example, aimed at holism; it maintained a distance from mechanistic physiology, unconvinced that the Cartesian metaphor was the best model for understanding and healing the human body with all its complexities and dimensions. Thus, romantic philosophy is not merely a fuzzy, reactionary irrationalism but a redefinition of human consciousness and a valorization of reason (of *logos*—the word) as *primarily narrative and historical*.

Indeed, coinciding with the naming of *Stimmung*, romanticism invented the modern novel: the *roman*. Contrary to the demystification of the external world, which reduces nature to mere natural resources, "out there" to be exploited by the applied sciences and technology, reality is felt as *overflowing with meaning* through poetic language; man can merely participate in nature, not be in control. The *novel* became the paradigmatic embodiment of this outlook, a modern (Western) genre that is now a popular form of expression in all modern languages around the globe. The novel became thereafter, and remains still, the privileged receptacle of *phrónesis*, the wisdom conveyed by practical philosophy, whose questions and discursive origins in everyday language are excluded by the official (analytic) philosophy of specialists after Immanuel Kant's *Prolegomena to Any Future Metaphysics*. The poetic form, furthermore, is also the site of "inspired madness," which, as Plato once said, is even superior to temperance (*sophrosyne*), because the latter has a merely human origin, while the former belongs to the divine. Indeed, Dionysus returns through the likes of Friedrich Hölderlin, Friedrich Nietzsche, and the Comte de Lautréamont.[56]

Roberto Calasso argues that while monotheism entered into crisis during the nineteenth century, eventually leading to Nietzsche's famous dictum concerning the death of God, the manifold divinities representing external forces, moods, and emotions, so present in non-Western cultures and pre-Christian Europe, made a reappearance in literature. But these divinities are no longer just of one family; rather, "now they are multitudes, a teeming crowd in an endless metropolis," often with unpronounceable names.[57] The power of their stories is still at work, yet this composite tribe lives *only* in its stories and scattered idols, such as art and, potentially, architecture. It is never a question of inventing "a new mythology"; this would be an arrogant and dangerous impossibility. And yet it is impossible to imagine a "community" whose Zeus is the algorithm.[58] Schlegel writes:

> We don't have a mythology. But I am telling you: we are about to have one ... [it] must be elaborated from the most profound depths of the spirit; it must be the most artistic of all works of art, since it will have to embrace all others, be a new riverbed and recipient for the ancient eternal and original spring of poetry, and be itself the infinite poem that contains hidden within it the germ of all other poems ... the supreme order is still and only the beauty of chaos, and to be precise of a chaos waiting only for the contact of love to open into the world of harmony, like

the world of ancient mythology and ancient poetry. For mythology and poetry are one and the same, indivisible.[59]

Later in the nineteenth century, Nietzsche would state: "Without myth every civilization loses its healthy and creative natural force: only a horizon drawn by myths can hold together a process of civilization in a single unit."[60] These intuitions speak of the work of art outside of its conventional straitjacket (as the official "fine arts"). They suggest already "expanded fields" for painting, sculpture, architecture, and literature, and of course, since the issue of attunement concerns the human environment and it can happen in manifold "media," including "architecture" (as poetic image), beyond buildings, in installations, poems, novels, film, books, or exhibitions. No genuine art will merely "depict" a reified "objective" (or scientific—dispassionate), external world, it will necessarily "construct" it, exactly like fiction and following its path, effecting a distance from the "facts" to reveal the real as such. I will say more about this in a later chapter. Schlegel also divines the possible reconciliation of form and chaos, of nature and artifice, *of formal experimentation and divine epiphanies*; a crucial argument to grasping the potential of architectural meaning in the modern and contemporary world.

Schlegel became fascinated with the redefinition of the work of art as a form of knowledge that matters. "Every artist is a center," he wrote; the work of art represents an opaque "wholeness," conveying this as an ephemeral experience analogous to orgasm: a knowledge of nontransparent Being.[61] He was fascinated with erotic mythological themes, both Western and Eastern, revealing significant human truths. For Schlegel, androgyny was an emblem of intelligibility. The new understanding of truth, connected to narrative structures and the tradition of rhetoric, anticipates Heidegger's "truth as unveiling," an ephemeral manifestation of meanings, which the German philosopher and his followers in the twentieth century would also associate with art's mode of communication. In other words, human truths are not like scientific truths; they are borne from metaphoric language articulating the human condition; they are history and stories. Truth is never given once and for all; it is truly event-like, analogous to our meaningful experiences of art and architecture.

It bears remembering that this is also the moment when history distanced itself from the physico-mathematical sciences in the writings of Wilhelm Dilthey and Friedrich Schleiermacher, to become properly "hermeneutic," i.e., self-conscious interpretation, leading eventually, through phenomenology and existentialism, to the theories of Hans-Georg Gadamer and Paul Ricoeur. Romanticism already understood the failure of "progress" and positive reason, setting the stage for Nietzsche's remarkably perspicacious speculations on the nature of history as both a potential problem and our salvation, in a text on the "uses and disadvantages" of history as relevant then as it is today (1874).[62] He perceived that we must maintain a balance between our historical and ahistorical dimensions. In the absence of a shared cosmology or religion, we should know history for the future, to empower creativity, and particularly to act prudently in view of a common good, but never merely to foster preservation, or arising out of an admiration for past monuments that may stifle action.

***

It is important to emphasize that the crystallization of self-conscious, romantic *Stimmung* took place in view of unpoetic immediate surroundings: the by-product of an alienated objectivity for a fully constituted modern subjectivity. A new relationship to the world was sought, declaring the principle of insufficient reason and the opacity of consciousness in order to preserve the sense of personal life, accepting neither irrationalism nor a despairing nihilism. Not surprisingly, *Stimmung* was first manifested outside of the new and growing cities with their industrial slums: at the top of a mountain, at the seashore, or bathing in the waves of symphonic music. Indeed, the Swedish translation of the term, *stammer*, refers specifically to the melody (or artifact) capable of attuning man in the context of a usually hostile or foreign world.[63]

While quintessentially romantic, an early example of this modern sensibility may be traced in Giordano Bruno's precocious thought (active 1560–1600), searching for *Stimmung* in the absence of bearings brought about by God's infinite universe. Like Galileo, Bruno unified celestial and terrestrial physics; he believed that we inhabit an infinite universe, on a moving earth. Yet because he also believed that nothing is outside the realm of human experience—the mind-body-world continuum as it emerges in consciousness—Bruno believed that the divine is not entirely distinct from the human, and is therefore present in everything, in nature and cultural artifacts. For him, infinity is coupled with the idea of every creature's participation in the divine; in the infinite space of a love-permeated universe, all things are fused. Since the world we experience is not mathematical (in sharp contrast to the harmonic cosmos of Kepler, for example, which, as mentioned in the previous chapter, could be thoroughly described through geometry, but always on the condition of its finitude), Bruno's cosmos is impenetrable to "perspective"; we inhabit its penumbra "between shadow and light" and must use language to aim for ethical actions.[64] The space of lived experience is primarily "poetic," a "coincidence of opposites"; as such, we can't grasp the universe's mystery through reason, but only through artistic and poetic revelations. Humans inhabit a pantheistic landscape inscrutable to mathematics, where *Stimmung*, potentially afforded by the arts and poetry, is the only form of emotional and intellectual understanding.

Writing in 1785, Friedrich Jacobi continued some of these thoughts, foregrounding the tension between our mortality and our insight into eternal duration, leading to *Ungrund*, a sense of a "positive nothingness," that can be seen as a precursor of Nietzsche's affirmative nihilism.[65] This is not a denial of meanings, but a recognition that these can't be found through mathematical reason alone. Indeed, romantic thinkers often realized that the day could often be less illuminating than the night, and that nocturnal journeys might be far more insightful. This awareness already suggested the potential collapse of retinal perspective as a privileged means of pictorial representation, found precociously in the work of painters like Jean-Auguste-Dominique Ingres and definitively asserted by Marcel Duchamp in the twentieth century, while underscoring romantic art's search for perfection in finitude and the incomplete project, the recognition of virtue in the fragment, and the limitations of totalizing schemes.

Already in the eighteenth century, some architects had recognized the enormous difficulties involved in creating attuned communicative settings in a world increasingly characterized by the isotropic space of Cartesian geometry. As I will elaborate further in the next chapter, traditional architecture had "complemented" preexisting genii loci, prefigured by stories and cultural habits. Once such context began to fail, a "critical practice" emerged in the "theoretical" projects of Giovanni Battista Piranesi (particularly explicit in the two stages of *Carceri* etchings, ca. 1745–1750), Étienne-Louis Boullée (the projects collected as large watercolors, and commented on in his manuscript *Essai sur l'art*, ca. 1778–1788), Claude-Nicolas Ledoux (his ideal city of Chaux, with its many novel institutions, drawn and described in his treatise *L'architecture considérée sous le rapport de l'art, des moeurs et de la législation*, published 1804), and Jean-Jacques Lequeu (the collection of projects in his manuscript *Architecture civile*, left by the author to the Bibliothèque Nationale de France upon his death in 1826), among others. I have written elsewhere about the importance of this architectural tradition that continues into the twentieth century in the work of John Hejduk and Daniel Libeskind, for example, and "expands" the field of the discipline while recognizing the difficulties involved in constructing meaningful atmospheres in natural and urban environments stubbornly conceived (and thus perceived) by a dominant technological civilization as merely homogeneous, isotropic space. Such projects are both poetic and critical, and imply that architecture appears *as* etching, painting, or narrative, in models, installations, or in books. Akin to other romantic works, they flaunt their autonomy and "self-referentiality," like Mallarmé's poetry that speaks only "of words," for example, to represent a fully emotional reality that may return meaning to the reader or inhabitant. I will draw on them as examples in the following chapters.

For now, I would like to emphasize that these modes of action are not an "opting out" of some "legitimate practice" (assumed to be the production of buildings) but, rather, a recognition of the difficulties and issues involved in an architecture seeking attunement. To grasp this fully, I must briefly contextualize what this new "autonomy" actually meant for architecture. Prior to the eighteenth century, the "work" of the architect, which embodied his responsibility, was not usually vested in the drawing (or representation) of a future project, as we take for granted today. It is well known that the importance of drawings as externalizations of architectural ideas was first established in the Renaissance, but these artifacts were never reductive or predictive, in the contemporary sense of a working drawing. The work of architecture was "performed" as a translation of intentions expressed in plain language by patrons and experts, mediated by symbolic traces: mostly plans and elevations, and eventually sections (starting in the sixteenth century). The "performance" was its fulfillment; the architect was responsible for this outcome—despite the obvious complexity of the translation and the involvement of many others, of course—and it is clear that it was felt that the work "gained" in richness in translation, from drawing, to physical model, to building. The framing of attuned atmospheres was the hoped-for outcome.

The history of music offers a useful and instructive analogy, incisively described by Lydia Goehr.[66] She has argued that a piece of music by any composer prior to Beethoven (1770–1827) was also only realized in performance: this was the ontological modality of the *work*, not as a score on paper—just as the *work of architecture* was not the drawing. Thus, seventeenth- and eighteenth-century music, accomplished in performance, was preferably conducted or played by the composer himself, and was usually dedicated to a "function"—a party, a dinner, a funeral—intended to convey the appropriate mood and accompany the actions, even sometimes conceived in relation to its imagined architectural setting (a room, a garden, or a barge on the river Thames). Such *works* are not simply equivalent to the scores we can now take from a library to be performed in the neutral space of a concert hall, part of a program often mixed and matched from different contexts and composers. Architecture of the time was similarly distant from our own modern and contemporary buildings erected from ubiquitous computer-generated documents that may land wherever they may in the global village. The music was often "coauthored" by the client, while architects also well understood the crucial role of clients for their works. Famously, in the fifteenth century Filarete claimed in his *Libro architettonico* that the client was the father and the architect the mother of any future building, whose birth was the responsibility of the architect, of course, as well as its care unto death.[67] And during the seventeenth century, Juan Caramuel de Lobkowitz insisted that the "first architect" of every project was the client.

By the mid-eighteenth century, Jean-Laurent Legeay, an architect who favored pictorial practices for architectural expression and who could produce etchings akin to those of Piranesi, also started to teach the architects of his generation and those immediately following that to make architecture one must provide a fully comprehensive picture of the future building, including an aerial perspective and a full set of drawings and specifications.[68] His students perceived this as a great innovation. This concept, so common today, was only institutionalized by the École Polytechnique and the École des Beaux-Arts in the nineteenth century, and subsequently exported and accepted throughout Europe, North America, and eventually the world. The work of architecture thereafter "existed" as "drawings," placeholders of the architect's copyright. These were intended as instruments that might dictate with precision their execution when delegated to others—just as a score by Beethoven or later composers would be filled with modulation marks and metronome readings to avoid "mistakes" of interpretation. Notice, therefore, how this "autonomy" emerging in early modernity resulted in opposing possibilities. The latter participated in a transforming culture of planning and technology, and fueled our still-common delusion: that the Cartesian spaces on which the design takes place—the three planes of the newly invented (ca. 1790s) "descriptive geometry"—are homologous with the lived spaces of man. Such a deluded understanding is opposite (and evidently oblivious) to Piranesi's questioning of Cartesian dispassionate space in his critical *Carceri* etchings. The autonomy of creator and work also contributed to the institutionalization of the passive (i.e., mechanical, eventually photographic) "optical image" as the model of architectural accomplishment, as is evident in the sophisticated renderings of the École des Beaux-Arts from the nineteenth century, and today in our professional journals and Internet publications.

Our present digital tools may still make possible both options, but given how the real is rendered as mathematical information, they are particularly adept at reducing the appearance of physical objects to an optical image and the computer model to an instrument for precise, prescriptive fabrication. What seems inescapable, however, is that as modern architects we must produce autonomous "works," engaging fully the productive imagination. I will elaborate on this condition in the next chapters. Piranesi's etchings already defied the status of the architectural drawing as a mere tool of production and claimed its meaning as *presence*. His works operate metaphorically, enabling a critical and ethical "seeing as," in his designs of spaces impossible to build yet inhabitable at variable scales by the imagination. The aim is to attune by engaging a fictional character, revealing architecture's original vocation as a site of metaphor, granting a *place* for man to dwell. Since that time, theoretical projects have thus become privileged sites for the enactment of *Stimmung*. However, in the absence of a cultural orientation enacting a critique of their "hostile" context, one that is also inevitably political, similar contemporary attempts fail and usually become one more seductive application of digital media in search of novelty.

Of course, it is impossible not to recognize that the more ominous danger lies still in the other possibility, finally offered to architects as prescription in the writings of Jean-Nicolas-Louis Durand (published 1800–1810), and about whom we will say more in the next chapter. The "set of drawings" as a technological instrument would ultimately give rise to the coordinated computer model for robotic fabrication, curtailing the potential enrichment of products brought about by the embodied translation of drawings into buildings—an enrichment that had also taught architects different ways to engage the world. The digital screen easily furthers the delusion that the represented space in the optical image is homologous with the spatiotemporal reality appearing before us in our lives. This is indeed a tragedy that can only impoverish the world and our consciousness as the artifacts it conjures are built into the discordant, postindustrial megalopolis.

***

While the mainstream of building production in nineteenth-century Europe generally became obsessed with fitting its theories into scientistic modes of thinking and adapting modes of production to the expectations of technology and its new materials, the fictional character of the autonomous project in architecture remained resonant with romantic insights. This was manifested for the most part in other artistic media, in literature and at the margins of the "profession." It is not the intention of this book to provide even a brief survey of the numerous and often very significant nineteenth-century examples, nor to explore the manifold ramifications of *Stimmung* in other forms of artistic expression. My central aim being theoretical, I will devote the following chapters to further elucidating the origins of the problem and to explaining the fundamental continuities between romantic philosophies, phenomenology, and the centrality of poetic language for attunement in architecture. Here, I will conclude in setting the stage for later examples by merely tracing a line between romantic concepts of art and beauty, surrealism, and the European twentieth-century avant-garde.

Scholars have recognized an important link between the *surnaturalisme* of Victor Hugo and twentieth-century surrealism in the writings of Gérard de Nerval, whose *Aurélia, Life, and the Dream* (1855) famously opens with the statement: "Our dreams are a second life."[69] De Nerval praises folly, excess, and the delay of fulfillment as imperative to making present the space of desire. This simple insight, at odds with the wish for hedonistic comfort and perfect homeostasis that underscores the technological project, constitutes a prefiguration of the European avant-garde, as conceived by Walter Benjamin and André Breton, among others. In his manifestoes and fictions, Breton would insist that the quest of the work of art is the disclosure of desire *as* wholeness (or itself fulfillment—a "discordant concord") through the creative imagination. Writing in the early twentieth century, Breton stated that the imagination is our true instrument of knowledge, a gift for deciphering the innumerable enigmas that surround us; it is an object of conquest whose task is not to decorate reality (as normally believed by naïve versificators) but to discover, by approaching two distant realities, a new reality that jolts us like a voltaic arc. This is the very definition of a metaphor or a poetic image,[70] crucial in the generation of any significant art and architecture. Breton incites the cultivation of desire toward freedom from conscious inhibitions and manipulations of power. He imagines a supreme point where all things would genuinely be seen to be comparable to all other things, where consequently mind and matter would at last be reconciled and desire would achieve a glorious identification with its object. Erotic space is thus understood as political action, leading to society's liberation from commodification, a concept resonant with Walter Benjamin's "blow," the shock we must receive from the contemporary artwork.

Breton and other surrealist artists understood the fundamental importance of *emerging* language, seeking to reconcile mind and matter through metaphor, analogy, and irony. Like phenomenology, surrealism recognized the primacy of our experience of the lived world: the object as thing-in-the-world rather than as abstract idea. Thus, in order to recover primary meanings through work *for others*, the use of linguistic tropes, often subversive, becomes indispensable. For example, once water has become H_2O, a chemical compound that circulates and is no longer an irreducible primary element with paradoxical powers to quench our thirst, to cleanse and purify, and awaken memories, multiple metaphorical displacements are necessary to recover its primary emotive presence: to restore the evocative experience of a nymphaeum in a contemporary bathing establishment, for instance. As Ivan Illich has suggested, it is not enough to make "artificial lakes" in the middle of postindustrial cities to retrieve the presence of water; its primary poetic presence in nature—as in our surprise in coming upon a freshwater spring—can only be retrieved through a metaphorical operation of consequence for a technologically mediated environment, necessarily a fiction that suspends its primary reference to reality. I will expound on these issues in chapter 6.

Here I will end with a few words about the work of Frederick Kiesler (1890–1965), a twentieth-century architect who was a friend of Marcel Duchamp and whose work has resonances with surrealism. Kiesler was born in Vienna and eventually immigrated to New York. He produced very innovative designs for the theater (questioning the passive role of the spectator), for displays, and for several important exhibitions, as well as an abundance of drawings and projects. His best known built work is the Shrine of the Book in Jerusalem, a building that houses the Dead Sea Scrolls, with a remarkable set of sequential spaces culminating in a dramatic, partially sunken centralized stage for exhibition of the scrolls, under a breast-shaped dome surrounded on the outside by a mirror of water.

Kiesler was extremely critical of the lack of character and atmosphere typical of contemporary functionalism and its industrial buildings. He believed that architecture must defer to ethical imperatives, yet, he stated, form follows vision: it stems from genuine insight. He thought functionalism disregarded lived life; it merely standardized and constrained habits. It enabled a foot to walk but not to dance; an eye to see but not to envision; a hand to grasp but not to create.[71] Arguably his most important project was the Endless House, a lifelong theoretical project with a complex history.[72] Kiesler describes many of his intentions in his book *Inside the Endless House*.[73] "Endless" space is evoked as a metaphor of the poetic image in architecture, curiously resonant with our observations of Giordano Bruno's understanding of the "infinite": "The coming of the Endless House is inevitable in a world coming to an end. It is the last refuge of man for man." He designed his Endless House with perforated egg-shaped shells as walls transformed into ceilings and floors, enclosing uninterrupted, flowing spaces. This stood as a symbol of human dwelling. The form is important as a manifesto against the meaningless orthogonal forms of technological buildings in his time. But it is not a stylistic statement, some sort of early blob or parametric architecture, as it has been recently categorized. The central issues for Kiesler are atmosphere and the qualities of lived space: his dwelling, like a "modern cathedral in a secular age," must respond to dreams as they reveal cosmic order; its light modulations, colors, and dimensionality were to be in dialogue with the inhabitant's psyche, so that the space never became merely "functional" or comfortable. Every quotidian action, like eating a meal or opening a faucet, would call your attention to the present moment, and in so doing would reveal potential meanings. He writes in his journal:

> Every mechanical device must remain an event and constitute the inspiration for a specific ritual. Not even the faucet that brings water into your glass, into the teakettle, through your shower and into the bath—that turn of a handle and then the water flowing forth as from the rock touched by Moses in the desert, that sparkling event, released through the magic invention of man's mind, must always remain the surprise, the unprecedented, an event of pride and comfort.[74]

Kiesler followed through in every aspect of his house: the inclined floors would make one aware of walking, fire would be present in an open pit, bathing would take place in pools throughout his unencumbered space, and light would change according to the moods of the day. Each of the four elements was meant to engage the inhabitant's embodied consciousness. Kiesler even suggested, prefiguring contemporary biomimetism, that "the house, freed from aesthetic tradition, [could become] a living creature."[75] Endless space in the house functions as erotic space, *expressing both lack and fulfillment*: a "correlation" of the present and infinity, bringing the sky down and the earth up: *coincidentia oppositorum*. The architect was very aware of his aim, teasing out the possibility of expanding habits with poetic revelation as his end. He writes: "You wander into habits thoughtlessly because they offer guidance to security. Insecurity, however, is what we search for."[76] It is in the overlap between habits as sediment of culture and new possibilities granted by the built environment, that architecture may imagine truly meaningful innovation in the proposition of attuned atmospheres. Indeed, despite its formal similarities to recent projects by Greg Lynn or Patrik Schumacher, the issues in this project are totally different. Angeliki Sioli has emphasized the fact that Kiesler was also profoundly respectful of the personal habits, personality, and needs of specific clients. His project was never meant to be built "literally" as a one-family home; adaptations were sought in diverse instances. But more likely, given the architect's lifelong involvement with the theater, the Endless House was intended as a participatory "stage" that would have been set up (at 1:1 scale) in New York's Museum of Modern Art, attaining the status of theoretical project. It existed (and exists) in the sense we related to Piranesi above, and becoming, as in the case of Le Camus de Mézières, a paradigm of the architecture of desire, mood, and character, engaging the discipline's inveterate nature as the intersubjective "space of appearance," and its deep historical associations with the theater and the city.

Kiesler fully engaged the technological world with his concept of "correalism," acknowledging the scientific assumptions concerning the infinity of the universe. Yet he grasped the fundamental analogy that allows for *Stimmung* in the coincidence of the inner and the outer and cultivated the primacy of poetic language to express intentionality and appropriateness. Thus he set out to design an architecture of limited, qualitative environments, expressing through boundaries an ineffable endlessness, understanding that moods are ultimately mimetic of nature, and that the emotions conveyed by architecture are a central part of its meaning. His house is a confluence of atmospheres that convey emotion and complement focal actions expressed as narrative programs. This architecture supports a wholesome and healthy life, its habits and actions crystallizing as spaces imbued with qualities (light/shadow, warmth/cold, resonant/silent) and consonant materials to convey appropriate moods. Metaphoricity is at work everywhere, the central metaphor being: the inner *is* the outer, thus we belong, we are at home; the interiority of architecture is the interiority of our place *in* the earth: on the earth, under the sky. In a similar way resonant moods can be created in the city, when envisioning exterior spaces like those addressed by urban design. The paradigm still holds. Despite the obviously prevailing tendencies, it is not that the public space becomes simply privatized; it may still be a "space of appearance," becoming emotive and cognitive through "use," through habits and words. It is perhaps for this reason that literature and cinema have been more apt at conveying such potential qualities in the last two centuries than the scientific surveys and maps of planners.

4
Architecture as an Unveiling of Place

We have seen how the identification and characterization of *Stimmung* in romanticism contributes to an appropriate understanding of atmosphere as the central issue of modern and contemporary architectural *aisthésis*. The task of design emerges as a bringing to presence of qualitative and attuned settings for human action, issuing from the productive imagination of the architect—as opposed to the predominantly mimetic imagination at work in traditional and earlier architecture.[1] It has also become evident how this new possibility, when properly understood, is in accordance with architecture's long-standing concern with conveying significant order (harmony, concordance) in built form, an order both intelligible and emotional, in view of humanity's relationship with the natural world that grants the very possibility of dwelling—addressing the fundamental questions that perennially arise, beyond the dichotomies introduced by eighteenth-century aesthetics between the "sublime" and the "beautiful." Yet this modern valorization of *Stimmung* only came about in view of *unpoetic* immediate surroundings, in confrontation with an external environment whose spatiality was equated with the homogeneous and isotropic space of classical physics: *a world where place was occulted*. Examining some of the same sources already familiar to us, again in a broad historical perspective, this chapter will be dedicated to exploring precisely how this occultation took place.

Contemporary architects still generally assume that the sites they build upon have few, if any, truly intrinsic qualities, beyond those that can be described "objectively" through physical geography, morphology, geometric cartography, and the sciences (for example, geological analysis). This is founded on the belief that the external world is *essentially* an isotropic geometric space, a three-dimensional matrix as first conceived by

Descartes. Since the beginning of the nineteenth century, the assumption has been that architectural space (subsuming all aspects of real place) is easily represented through the geometric systems of descriptive geometry and axonometric projection, which translates seamlessly today into the digital space of the computer screen through standard architectural software. Thus, it seems obvious that architectural meanings would have to be created from scratch, through the ingenious formal manipulations of the architect-artist, assumed to be relevant merely through their novel, shocking, or seductive character. Whenever the physical context is invoked as an argument for design decisions, it is mostly through its visual attributes, imagining the site as a picture or objective site plan that merely provides some formal or functional cues. This is a dangerous misunderstanding. The deep emotional and narrative aspects that articulate places in a particular natural or cultural milieu are usually marginalized by a desire to produce fashionable innovations. These narrative qualities, however, are crucial considerations as we seek the appropriateness of a given project for its intended purpose in a particular culture: framing a "focalized action" (Heidegger) or event that may bring people together and allow for a sense of orientation and belonging.

Modern accounts of architecture often presume that architects have always manipulated "space concepts," that architecture is "the art of space." This position, famously articulated vis-à-vis the history of European architecture by the Italian historian Bruno Zevi,[2] has remained implicit in most modern historical narratives. Yet, perhaps still surprisingly for some readers, in fact "space" was *never* actually conceptualized as an issue in architectural theories prior to the late nineteenth century, never identified as an element that could be brought to intellectual awareness for the control of the architect. The question is complex, and the observations on the philosophy of embodied consciousness that I will be sketching in chapter 5 will contribute to its clarification.[3] We may easily grasp, however, that the "in-between" ourselves and the world's objects, coemerging in the *action* that is perception, i.e., consciousness, is itself not something objectlike (geometrical), but is also not *nothing*.

We can obviously perceive the qualities of *places*, particularly when cities have deep histories and their layers are present to our experience. Yet these are still obvious if we compare the "spaces" of newer urban centers, such as Toronto and Sydney (both with similar colonial pasts), which, indeed, ultimately appear as qualitatively different; despite their Anglo-Saxon character, the two cities have a different light and feel, a different aroma, stemming from such features as the lake or the sea and the "air" of their respective climates. We can also realize that we think different thoughts in different places, necessarily accompanied and enabled by diverse emotions, albeit usually unintended by the generic architecture of modern development; location affects us deeply, as does more generally the geographical environment.

An environment that becomes increasingly devoid of qualities, reduced to a set of coordinates in a global positioning device, for instance, tends to exacerbate our contemporary psychopathologies—our sense of despair in view of the "meaninglessness of existence," contributing to a debilitating nihilism. In other words, while the qualities of space remain directly accessible through our senses and our emotional consciousness, the technological world tends to deny the cognitive value of such perception, and in fact reinforces the opposite assumption: the reality of an isotropic geometric continuum at work in all manner of instruments, telecommunication devices, and productive techniques. Our own culturally generated scientific concept of space, becoming an important part of our intellectual skill set, in turn, impacts our perceptions, so that *place* effectively hides from our experience. Such is the complexity of the problem for the architect. To grasp the full scope of the question for contemporary design, seeking attunement at all levels and in all media, it is important to provide additional historical context.

***

Prior to Greek philosophy and classical literature, the spaces between things were not acknowledged. Writing in the late sixth century BCE, Empedocles still believed that breath, identified with *Eros*, was present everywhere and accounted for the diverse combinations of the four elements in all natural phenomena. Through breath, everything in the universe is capable of touching everything else. Wings and breath (atmospheric air) moved *both* Eros and words, in an inescapable bond.[4] Buildings existed, of course, as they do in all human cultures, but architecture as a discipline had not yet been named.[5] Not until Cicero and Vitruvius, in the first century BCE, would we find the noun in a usage that approximates our own.[6] Buildings were perceived as natural features; the pyramid was a sacred mountain and the Mycenaean *thólos* was a sacred cave, both predominantly natural *places* attuned to significant human actions in the form of rituals.

Indeed, before Anaximander's contributions in the sixth century BCE, geometry did not exist in the sense we understand today. Spatiality was not grasped independently of temporality; temporal intervals (and other material qualities of the environment, such as weight) were often used for spatial measurement. Anaximander introduced the first stable spatial structure into lived experience with his notion of *arché*, identifying the source of all things in a primary, indefinite substance with qualities "other" than those of matter in the world of experience (fire, earth, air, or water). He described this originative substance as *apéiron*, spatially indefinite (implying unlimited extent and duration). Not surprisingly, Anaximander was reported to have introduced the gnomon into Greece from Egypt. For him, this instrument was much more than a technical device; it represented the means to transpose the perceived regularity of the heavenly motions onto the human world, characterizing its potentially stable spatiality. The gnomon thereafter became one of the three artifacts Vitruvius saw architects as responsible for producing, together with buildings and machines, both mimetic of the superlunary cosmos. Perhaps not surprisingly, Anaximander was also known for having created one of the earliest maps of the known world.[7]

In characterizing the nature of the architect's intellectual production during the first century BCE, Vitruvius—admittedly drawing on previous accounts from Greek and Hellenistic sources—stressed the importance of architectural "ideas," immediately specified as kinds of images, externalized as engravings or traces (*graphé*), *ichnographia* (plan, or horizontal drawing), and *orthographia* (elevation, or vertical drawing). In the context of archaic building practices, these were explicitly artificial products, modes of technology akin to writing. But they were not merely similar to pictograms, figurative graphic signs meant to be read as one experiences and interprets nature. Rather, they were associated with a kind of writing that became prevalent in Greek culture around Plato's time: alphabetic phonetic writing that objectified the spoken word, Empedocles' breath, transforming it into a visual artifact for the first time in human history. Anne Carson and David Abram have emphasized the importance of this early technology in the development of the Western mind, severing it from its intimate communion with the natural world.[8] Suffice it to recall how

Plato employed this technology in his famous dialogues while deploring the fact that writing may be an instrument of forgetfulness; he warned that writing could lead us to believe that it portrayed real knowledge, when in fact true understanding could only happen through verbal communication.

Architectural "drawings" (usually engraved in situ), thus became re-presentations, images with the specific connotation of an *eikón*, autonomous realities separate from their referential presence. Such architectural "writing" both posited and occupied "another" space, one kindred to Plato's *chóra*, a word the philosopher deliberately used to stress its cultural dimensions and differentiate it from *tópos*, the primordial *place* of presence. Architectural "writing" was simply not existent in previous cultures. In Greek architecture, space makes the edges of place visible, just as in Greek alphabetic writing vowels made the older Phoenician consonants audible. Space also becomes the physical interval between the work and the new observer/participant, and between the architect and his work of *techné-poiésis-mímesis*, it must be made harmonious and temperate like nature (*physis*, *natura*) itself, as I explained in chapter 2.

There are other important connections between Greek writing and practical geometry. Pythagoras is reported to have obtained great pleasure from tracing letters, "forming each stroke with a geometrical rhythm of angles and curves and straight lines."[9] Unlike hieroglyphs and pictographic writing usually traced with a brush, after the fifth century BCE Greek letters were written with a reed pen on papyrus. This more precise instrument is analogous to the chisels used for epigraphic inscriptions, carving, cutting, and incising in continuous matter—or to the markings on the earth (as with a plow) "setting apart" hallowed spaces, the areas of buildings, from the continuum of nature. The pen was indispensable for tracing the fine lines of the new letters, all ruled by sharp edges and based on geometry. There is an obvious connection between the constructing of letters for epigraphic inscriptions over geometrical guidelines and the making of architectural "drawings": both were inscribed in stone and evoked the perfection of mathematical ideas. These analogies are also evoked in the classical fragments that tell the story of Daedalus, the mythical first architect: while in Crete he designed both a labyrinth to contain the Minotaur and a dancing platform for rituals; ritual dancing typically took place on a sand floor, similar to that of the orchestra of classical theaters, where a dancing chorus would leave traces outlining an ichnography, resembling that of the labyrinth.

The Platonic *chóra* (in *Timaeus*), a neologism that allowed Plato to properly distinguish cultural space from natural place (*tópos*), evolved from this consciousness. He recognized that the appearance and designation of cultural space enabled words to refer *at once* to the singular and the universal. We have already noted that, contrary to modern misinterpretations, the "ideal" in Plato was never truly "outside" human, embodied experience. In prephilosophical usage, the word *chóra* denoted an inhabited region or land, while in Athenian drama, it named the space for politics and participation, the clearing that made culture possible, sometimes brought about by the actions of an *architecktón* and often associated with the performing *chóros,* the choir representing the spectators in the plot.[10] A century after Plato, Euclid used the term *chórion* to denote an area enclosed by the perimeter of a specific geometric figure, associating the pregnant word with geometrically defined limits. As I have suggested previously, contrary to many modern misunderstandings this "Euclidean space" is not merely an equivalent of later Cartesian space; it was not possible to simply assume that it *existed* as physical space. In fact, both Pythagorean and later Neoplatonic mathematicians would insist that the soul produces the mathematical sciences by looking not to its infinite capacity for developing forms but rather introspectively, by considering the properties of the geometric figures that appear "within the compass of the Limit."[11]

Soon after Plato, Aristotle gave renewed priority to the world of synesthetic (primarily tactile) experience, thus denying the existence of Anaximander's originating substance. With this denial, he would also question the possibility of space as an existing empty substance.[12] Aristotle's "great chain of Being" remained normative for philosophers until the end of the Middle Ages and beyond; what existed, primarily, was qualitative *place*, experienced synesthetically and articulated in a vertical cosmography from the solid earth under our feet to the crystalline, starry heavens. This bottom-up directionality became a foundational constituent of all architectural symbolization. Furthermore, Greek *physis* and Latin *natura* imply in their etymologies the idea of organism, of growth and harmonious development. To know was to perceive and decipher certain constitutive correspondences of reality; by implication the subject and the object of knowledge formed a single being. Man existed within this ontological domain; it would have been inconceivable to pretend to escape it, to reduce external reality to an epistemological field across objectified space.

It was only during the Renaissance that Western architecture manifested greater confidence concerning the potential geometric (Euclidean) structure of *existing* sublunary space. This came about due to a renewed interest among humanists in Euclid's texts, one that was also central to the invention of *perspectiva artificialis*. This development is perhaps most explicit in the theoretical formulations of Andrea Palladio (1570), whose work I discussed briefly in chapter 2. Influenced by mathematicians like Sylvio Belli and Daniele Barbaro, he sought the harmonic experience of buildings by relating the proportions of sequences of rooms.

It is important to emphasize here the scope of this historical achievement, which we understandably take for granted in view of our own presuppositions. Despite subsequent misreadings, Plato's articulation of reality was not a simple duality of Immutable Being (the ideal realm of heavenly motions) and Becoming (the concrete realm of mortal life). His first, unshakable observation was that the two realms were distinct and autonomous: there is nothing purely ideal in our mortal realm, which is always undergoing change. Yet both aspects ultimately appear for human consciousness *in place*: in *chóra*, the "receptacle," a third and ineluctable element of reality, the (architectural) space for the human dance (*chorós*) of culture. As Aristotle would write a few years later, the physical realm is not compatible with mathematics, yet both he and Plato believed that these two realms were related in some way. Aristotle's interpretation of "forms," as things that the eye could see, helped carry the transcendental speculations of *Timaeus* into the natural sciences and through Stoicism, into mainstream Western architectural theory. Aristotle wondered about the organization of the world we experience and observed perfection in living creatures. He often used *eídos* (idea) and *morphé* (form) interchangeably, as inseparable from matter.[13] In his *Parts of Animals*, he acknowledges the disgust one experiences when the human body is dissected, but insists that blood, flesh, and bones are not what anatomy is about. The anatomist does not focus on the immediately sensible stuff of the body, but instead seeks Nature's purposive design (*theoría*).[14] Significantly, Vitruvius identifies the *theoría* of the physician with that of the architect in the first book of his treatise on architecture, thus suggesting that this purposiveness is what the harmonious and temperate visible body of architecture ultimately signifies.[15] Indeed, taking through Stoicism Aristotle's reinterpretation of "forms" as something that the eye could directly see, the circle in architecture could become potentially interchangeable with the *thólos*, for example, the circular temple in which the Greeks celebrated a feminine deity, or with any other circular structure.

Aristotle further struggled to understand the "intermediate" reality of geometry also when discussing optical phenomena in his *Physics*. He observes that the geometer works with naturally occurring lines "but not as they occur in nature," while optics deals with mathematical lines "but as they occur in nature rather than as purely mathematical entities." Since nature (*physis*) ambiguously refers to both form and matter, it must be understood from two points of view.[16] This is the sort of arithmetic and geometry that serves the mimetic intention of traditional architecture, including Palladio's, bounding a human situation and thus establishing places for communication that recognize nature as the goal for the sake of which the rest exists.[17] In Stoic philosophy, mathematical truth was initially and generally related to empirical truth. Stoic doctrine claimed that the only things that truly exist are material bodies, meaning that even the soul and the divine must be corporeal, potentially excluding any mediating space. It is very likely that Vitruvius borrowed some of his central ideas from Posidonius and Geminus, the two Stoic philosophers best known for their interest in the mathematical heritage of the Greeks.

Thus, as we have observed, for Vitruvius architecture's primary concern with atmosphere is tacit. *Limited* and qualitative space is implicit: a communicative space for political and religious action in the city—mostly centered in the public institutions of the *agora/forum*, the *acropolis*, and the theater. Yet architecture is explicitly characterized by the commensurate *dispositio* of forms, by harmony and consonance, mimetic of the Pythagorean cosmos. Evoking the precision and permanence of the divine mathematical superlunary realm in the mortal, ever-changing world, architecture resonates with the space of dreams; this was an image Plato used in *Timaeus* to facilitate the "difficult" comprehension of *chóra*'s actual existence. Following Anne Carson and Bruno Snell, elsewhere I have characterized this archetypal Western architectural space as *fundamentally* erotic, characterized as meaningful by Vitruvius's use of the Latin term *venustas*—the seductive quality of Venus—to designate architectural value. Vitruvius's word choice connotes connection and separation, an essentially "bittersweet" condition of *discordant concordance*.[18] Erotic space is not given a priori, it is not an objectified geometric or topological reality. It encompasses at once the physical space of architecture at the inception of the Western tradition, the space opened up by the discovery of contemplative philosophy (and *scientia*), and the linguistic space of metaphor in literature and poetry.

* * *

Ancient Greek and Roman architects inscribed (*graphéien*) geometric figures (resonant with a superlunary order) into *tópos* (place). In so doing, they contributed to the disclosure of qualities *already* present and recognized in the experience of places. To varying degrees, the place recognized and named as the site was a central part of the architecture's meaning, of its appropriate presence or "atmosphere," conducive to culturally attuned rituals. As such, the topographic site of a Greek temple, for example, was articulated by local myths and cultural mores, becoming eloquent and emotionally charged as soon as it was delimited and the *témenos* or holy precinct was made visible. Regardless of similarities of style and morphology, this is what made "Temples of Apollo" in Attica, Peloponnese, Anatolia, or Sicily into distinct communicative settings for particular, local communities, rather than examples of some "international style." The qualities of place were always enacted through myths: oral, ever-transforming stories that were deeply shared by the people and intertwined with the landscape. The Acropolis in Athens for example, while obviously possessing striking topographical features, became a hallowed *place* as a result of the struggle between Poseidon and Athena for the tutelage of the city; we know that a *xoanna* with the effigy of the goddess fell from heaven and landed on the hill, and the site was marked by the trident of Poseidon, indicating a saltwater well, while Athena's spear hit a rock from which sprouted an eternal olive tree. The inscription of the geometric limits of the temples transforms the place into a cultural space, into a realm appropriate for the rituals associated with Athena.

Christianity generally continued this practice, acknowledging the pregiven, linguistically articulated qualities of places more or less until the late Renaissance, even in cases when as a result of colonization and conversion it had to refound its own architecture over more ancient sacred sites that belonged to other religious practices, or even, negatively, argued for the desecration of "pagan" sites. This linguistic priority is particularly evident in foundations associated with miraculous events or the martyrdom of saints. For example, on September 24, 1445, a young man by the name of Hermann Leicht, working as a shepherd for a Franciscan monastery near Bamberg in Bavaria, saw a crying child roaming the fields that belonged to the nearby Cistercian monastery at Langheim. Moved by a deep compassion, he approached to care for the child but as he reached out, it suddenly disappeared. Leicht remained attentive, and the child soon reappeared on the same spot, first with two candles burning by its side and a third time, in June 1446, accompanied by thirteen other children. At that point, the child told Leicht that they were "the fourteen helpers and wish to erect a chapel here, where we can rest. If you will be our servant, we will be yours!"[19] Leicht then witnessed the divine light, in the form of two candles descending from heaven to mark the *place* where miraculous healings allegedly began almost immediately, ascribed to the intercession of the "fourteen saints."

This holy group thereafter became known (after the Virgin Mary and Saint Joseph) for their efficacy in conveying messages to God and granting favors to those in danger and affliction.[20] An altar was consecrated as early as 1448 and pilgrimages have taken place almost continuously to the present day. The modern baroque church of Vierzehnheiligen, designed by Balthasar Neumann and built between 1743 and 1772, is dedicated to the same narrative program, celebrating the fourteen saints in a remarkable altar. However, the altar is not, as one might expect, at the center of the crossing of the two arms of a traditional Latin cross plan—the *axis mundi* marked by God's initial, luminous signal identifying the site— but effectively "decentered" and under one of several shallow vaults that interweave to form the ceiling and reveal the architect's virtuosic manipulation of geometry. The church already expresses a different sensitivity to space: the "in-between" appears eloquently, the atmosphere is tensed and expressive of desire, as if the natural site were no longer enough; the place is transmuted into space *as* light, the very medium for God's magnetic compassion. His miraculous manifestation is now made present through the geometric mechanisms of design, a willful innovation of the architect's imagination that nevertheless acknowledges its debt to the narrated *place* to work its magical attunement.

Yet, most significantly, Christianity must also be credited with fostering the possibility of ubiquitous architectural (sacred) space. This became possible for the first time in the synthesis of Platonic cosmology (through Stoic interpretations) and the Jewish Old Testament produced by Philo of Alexandria (also called Philo Judaeus, ca. 20 BCE—ca. 50 CE) and finally crystallized in the tradition of Christian church building, becoming most clear in the early modern period. Identifying as a singular creator the Platonic Demiurge that manufactured the universe (in *Timaeus*) according to Pythagorean harmonies, and the Jewish God, who gave Moses exceptionally detailed prescriptions concerning materials, measurements, and even colors for the building of the portable tabernacle (meaning "residence" or "dwelling place" in Hebrew) in Exodus (25–27 and 35–40), Philo inaugurated the possibility of a significant architecture *independent of its site*, necessary for the chosen people in their pilgrimage through the desert—yet mimetic of a musical, harmonic *cosmos* and ruled by the sacred (ritual) prescriptions of God in the story told by Moses. Philo's exegesis, a fascinating architecture in words that stands out in contrast to the general Jewish disinterest in human artifacts, had practically no impact on rabbinical traditions in Judaism. The Jewish God was always ambivalent about any need for a physical residence on earth (together with the well-known prohibition of graven images). Yet, compounding Philo's synthesis with a belief in the Incarnation of Christ, which instead was later interpreted as a call for the building of physical temples on earth, Christians took Philo's insight to heart. Thus, after Emperor Constantine's "official" conversion of the Roman Empire to Christianity, the new religion would eventually deploy traditional Roman building forms such as the basilica and the centralized temple, to house its cultic practices: creating appropriate atmospheres that mostly appeared through the rituals of the *ecclesia*, in the retelling of the biblical stories and the performance of sacraments.

Arguably until the end of the Renaissance, architecture's significant, mostly sacred, theatrical, and political spaces fulfilled the role assigned by Plato to *chóra*, remaining distinct from *tópos*, Aristotle's natural place. In these communicative settings made available by architecture, individuals could attain self-understanding through ritual, dialogue, and intersubjectivity; human culture could flourish, cultivating the coupling of being and becoming, of words and objects, of objects as "ideas"—or words objectified "as if written"—and objects in their ephemeral presence, both simultaneously present. Sublunary *tópos*, on the other hand, provided a qualitative site to all things that "appeared," invariably in the midst of a living, more-than-human natural world. In Aristotelian physics, movement was not a "state"; becoming, a property of life, implied movement and change. Indeed, objects changed their being when they moved; an ontological difference existed between rest and movement. Within this common understanding of reality, *chóra* could still operate as both a separation and a link, a space of contemplation that was a mode of participation. The ideal was elsewhere, and yet present, in a vertical structure, here and now. Many Renaissance architects remark in their treatises that the physical point or line that we can trace with our drawing instruments *is not* the ideal point or line in our minds. For John Dee, for example, the operations of Euclidean geometry take place "betwene thinges supernaturall and natural"; they are "thinges immaterial and neverthelesse, by material things able somewhat to be signified."[21]

During early modernity the ambiguity and complexity of *chóra*, understood as Plato's "third term" articulating the holistic understanding of human reality in embodied consciousness, became practically incomprehensible. Modern science could easily understand only Being and becoming, reducing any relational structure mediating between the *res cogitans* and the *res extensa* (through the new mechanistic psychology of perception outlined in chapter 3) to the objectified, indefinite, homogeneous, quality-free, and isotropic space of Cartesian geometry. This was nothing but a bastardized consequence of Platonic theories that the ancient Greek philosopher would not have recognized. I have also suggested that a key figure in this transformation was Galileo Galilei, whose imaginary experiments on motion led to the laws of inertia that were eventually taken up by Newton.[22] The concept of inertia implies that motion and rest could be conceived as "states," incapable of affecting being. Alexandre Koyré has explained that this hypothesis could only be "proven" by Galileo by imagining motion as taking place in empty geometric space, one literally "out of this world." While only approximating the results of real physical experiments, such motion was believed to take place *in geometric space*, not through qualitative *topoi*. This is motion as conceived by classical (Newtonian) physics, eventually making possible technology and modern transportation, i.e., our "mobile society" and its so-called "no-places"; it is movement as commonly understood today nearly anywhere in our global village. Indeed,

Galileo conceived a physics that differed greatly from Aristotle's. In Galileo's world the ontological difference between the superlunary heavens and the sublunary world was obliterated. The universe became a homogeneous geometric void in which bodies, both celestial and terrestrial, were objectified and described in accordance with the same mathematical laws.

Descartes, for his part, still shared Aristotle's belief that nature "abhors a vacuum"; he thought that sublunary space and matter were cosubstantial, yet, contrary to Aristotle, he assumed they were only truly knowable through mathematics. In contemporaneous baroque architecture, such as the example of the Vierzehnheiligen basilica described above, the presence of a geometrically constructed space filled with light, mimetic of the operations of the divine mind, became a central feature of the emotionally charged sacred atmosphere, respectful and resonant with meanings articulated by the stories that revealed the "spirit of the place" and the corresponding rituals and litanies housed by the church. Descartes, on the other hand, posited geometric perspective as an epistemological model connecting the two terms of his dualistic reality, the pineal gland (the point of *res cogitans*, the subject) and the object (*res extensa*), deployed through a similar geometric space (also associated with divine ideas). He was not interested in qualities or emotions, which he thought were merely a source of error and confusion produced by the body. Descartes was obsessed with constructing vision on the basis of a conceptual model rather than through perception, effectively ignoring all optical and physiological issues. Disembodied vision was understood as the transparent organ of mathematical thought. Thus, Descartes must be held coresponsible, with Galileo, for the thinning and objectification of space. Empty space (and time) became the concealed presupposition of the Newtonian system of the world and its law of universal gravitation, held as the final solution to the puzzle of the universe during the eighteenth century. While Newton still identified absolute space and time with God, these associations were gradually evacuated, and modern Europeans started to assume that they actually lived their everyday lives not in *places* (*topoi*), but in a homogeneous, isotropic, geometric space. This assumption thus became a new cultural "common sense" that, like any other motor and intellectual skill, significantly affected perceptions, leading to the occultation of *place* for modern Europeans. Subsequently, during and after the nineteenth century, it became a generally assumed condition throughout the world.

***

Given the entrenched codependence of architecture and *place—chóra—*in antiquity and the Renaissance, it is not difficult to understand how this progressive occultation would have radical repercussions for the discipline. The substitution of *tópos* by geometric space eventually lent credence to the possibility that architectural meaning might fully result from an architect's formal manipulations, as well as to the fallacious notion that creative genius could be a viable substitute for the richness of culture. The failures stemming from this assumption led, conversely, to a more or less generalized skepticism concerning architecture's capacity to disclose culturally relevant meaning (as emotional and cognitive presence) in the built world, its products being mostly regarded as hardly indispensable "aesthetic" commodities. This has also resulted in a sense of crisis in the attitudes of architects engaged in critical practices, such as those discussed in chapter 3, and has even led some critics to issue pronouncements on the inevitable demise of architecture in its traditional sense.

The assumption of Cartesian space as the place of architecture is first evident in the theoretical writings of Claude Perrault, earlier introduced in chapter 2. Perrault understood architectural representation as thoroughly systematized, a set of "sections" along orthogonal (Cartesian) planes, analytical by definition, like those of an anatomical dissection. His rejection of optical correction as a central technique for the architect to "adjust" his ideas to the perceptual realities of a project and the qualities of *place*, for the first time ever in the history of architecture, together with his unabashed reduction of theory to a demystified system of prescriptions for the classical orders, demonstrate how he had internalized the central Cartesian concepts. He eliminated from his discourse both theory as philosophy and the irreducible nature of technical knowledge: craft wisdom. His "applied theory" intentionally bypassed the crucial moment of translation that had always enriched architecture as it was built, a translation acknowledging the fact that architecture's meaning was manifested through, and was made manifest to, embodied consciousness. I have explained that for Perrault meaning was never merely "present" to synesthetic perception. His Cartesian psychology would no longer allow this premise; he believed instead that meaning was constructed in the mind through associations of "data" provided by autonomous senses. In his view, therefore, the precise drawings of an architect should be literally transcribed into building—no adjustments necessary—thus avoiding the pitfalls of potentially bad craftsmanship. The precision of architecture, its intended perfect order, would be plainly evident to its inhabitants, who would automatically render perspectival distortions in true measure. Since we were all now assumed to dwell in Cartesian space, Perrault believed that we perceived the world via geometric perspective, enabling us to grasp the precise dimensionality of architecture through our privileged and autonomous sense of vision.

During the eighteenth century, this assumption became clearly articulated by Johann Heinrich Lambert. Greatly admired by Kant, Lambert assumed that God had given humans perspectival vision precisely to be able to "know" scientifically. We effectively see in perspective, and therefore there is a direct homology between a "plan" and a "perspective drawing," his metaphor for the very nature of legitimate inductive knowledge.[23] Lambert thought we were called, in all our epistemological endeavors, to "deduce" the orthogonal projection (Cartesian, objective truth) from the perspective (subjective vision).

Giovanni Battista Piranesi (1720–1778) was perhaps the first modern architect to realize the limitations imposed upon the discipline by the identification of lived *topoi* with geometric space. Piranesi's *Carceri* etchings provide a remarkable demonstration of this awareness, perhaps the earliest historical evidence of "experimental research through design"—an elusive and important topic that is discussed in architectural education today, but that unfortunately often results in nothing more than self-referential, if somewhat intriguing, formal novelties. Piranesi's etchings follow a dynamic transformation from a "first stage," in which internal spaces are constructed according to the rules of perspective in Cartesian space (specifically through the two-point perspective method of the Galli Bibienas—*perspectiva per angolo*),[24] into an exploded "second stage," questioning the increasingly more established cultural assumptions as articulated by Lambert. This second stage produces emotionally charged spaces, congruous with their program as "prisons": an architecture that would in fact be impossible to "build" as if it were coherent with orthogonal plans and elevations. This project represents a totally self-conscious and deliberate attempt to retrieve the depth of real vision as it appears in synesthetic, embodied experience, and which is anything but identical with the timeless "third dimension" in Cartesian perspective. In this it represents a precocious anticipation of the subsequent accomplishments in the construction of significant pictorial depth familiar to us in the work of painters like Paul Cézanne, followed by early-twentieth-century European avant-garde. Piranesi understood his etchings as true architecture, not dependent on any further translation or execution; it is well known that he deliberately rejected building commissions.

His *Carceri* project already embraces strategies that Octavio Paz attributes to later poetic works in the Western tradition, being by necessity critical (of its present culture) in order to be truly poetic. The *Carceri* invite existential orientation by confronting darkness, the very darkness that humans ultimately cannot escape, at a time when Western culture had opted for the exclusive light of reason. In contrast to Perrault and other contemporaries for whom beauty had become a problem of aesthetic composition, Piranesi grasped the original sense of Vitruvius's *venustas*: the quality of seduction driven by ethical wisdom (*phrónesis*), this being *the issue* of architectural meaning. His spaces seduce in order to manifest the divine *in* the world, beyond theological dogmatism, perhaps inspired by Giambattista Vico's expectation of the presence of divine providence in human poetic creation. Piranesi's awareness of perceptual depth as the "first" and fundamental dimension of meaningful architectural experience, rather than merely being one of "three dimensions," is crucial. It is a precocious insight, one fundamental to the artistic avant-garde in the twentieth century and addressed by Maurice Merleau-Ponty in his writings on modern painting.[25] This awareness was a necessary precondition for the emergence of romantic *Stimmung* and of atmospheres in later architecture, whose communicative potential might retrieve its rootedness in cultures and go beyond the impact of merely novel effects.

A fascinating alternative response to this fundamental dilemma that emerged in architecture in eighteenth-century Europe is to be found in Étienne-Louis Boullée's theoretical projects. Like Piranesi, Boullée considered these imaginary projects to be the most relevant expression of his abilities, over and beyond his many buildings. In his short manuscript on "the art of architecture," written ca. 1790,[26] Boullée expressed his concern over the cultural value of architecture, which he thought now faced great difficulties when it tried to express poetic truths and act as a truly relevant setting for society. Declaring his anguish in view of this uncertainty, he sought to establish firmer principles for a truly poetic rather than a merely rational architecture; such principles would go beyond classical theories, which he recognized as dealing mostly with instrumental issues. Boullée accompanied his reflections with a series of theoretical projects represented through carefully rendered watercolors, where he tested architecture's capacity to express moods consistent with those of nature. Boullée was convinced that architecture had *both* a capacity to express harmony and emotions much like music, emulating those expressed by nature, *and* the possibility of making present Nature's intelligible order, which he thought had been definitively explained by Newton's natural philosophy and its law of universal gravitation. Thus he criticized and rejected the classical orders as largely inappropriate to these aims, putting forward instead a "Platonically" inspired theory of elemental bodies as the formal—natural—principles of architecture.

Similar to Piranesi's *Carceri*, Boullée's projects exist only on paper and are autonomous. They are poetic "works" of architecture by virtue of their critical dimension, but in this case—and in contrast to Piranesi's work—they seem to accept the veracity of space as three-dimensional, along with its potential for emotional expression in painting. Boullée had learned from his teacher Jean-Laurent Legeay that a "work" effectively existed on paper, whether conceived as a predictive tool or as an autonomous critical statement. His stated aim was to explore how architecture (imagined as built) could "present" nature's atmospheres with their associated emotions and thus demonstrate architecture's superiority over the other visual arts that merely represent them.[27] Boullée characterized his work as *architecture parlante*. Only an architecture that "speaks" can be truly poetic, emphasizing the participatory and primarily oral nature of human communication. This is not architecture as "sign"; rather, akin to a poem, this architecture is intrinsically emotional and not merely semantic: it cannot be paraphrased. Boullée pursued an architecture that communicates by conveying the characters of an expressive nature, taking cues from the seasons, from the optimism of spring or the melancholy of winter, for example, conveying wonder and emotion through sensations appropriate to a given program. The atmospheres made present by such works would thus be in harmony with appropriate moods.

It is important to add a few words about how geometric space could still, for Boullée, be both expressive of transcendental order *and* emotional, both "beautiful" and "sublime," rather than one *or* the other.

Boullée dedicated his best-known project to Newton, the man whom he thought had solved the riddle of the universe. He wished to "surround Newton with his own discovery," an empty spherical space studded with stars (simulated through perforations in the dome). Here we find the best example of nature being "implemented": the visitor is surrounded by empty geometric space, the essence of the cosmos as "demonstrated" by the British scientist. This emptiness, however, is the *Pleroma*, Newton's God, identified with "absolute space and time" in his *Mathematical Principles of Natural Philosophy*: the one and only "hypothesis" that makes the law of universal gravitation operable and is therefore the foundation of all incontrovertible truths;[28] this work renders it immediately present to the senses in all its majesty. Thus the "infinite," the utter externality of the human condition, the more-than-human world, is ultimately "limited," in the sense that it offers protection and harmony, allowing us to come to terms with our finitude as we are moved and recognize ourselves as part of the same order. This is a poetic/religious experience consonant with the theological drive of early modern science, as explained even by Voltaire,[29] still engaging with the very limits of the European tradition of *armonia/concentus* we have described in earlier chapters.

* * *

While, as I have shown, romantic thinkers and artists identified *Stimmung* as a central aesthetic issue through its initial recovery of synesthesia, mainstream philosophy and science during the nineteenth century became obsessed with the nature of space as being either subjective *or* objective. Immanuel Kant, whose doctrine of the transcendental ideality of space dominated idealistic philosophy during the first half of the nineteenth century, was deeply absorbed with this question throughout his life. He famously concluded in his "Dissertation" (1770) that "space is not something objective or real, neither substance nor accident, nor relation, but subjective and ideal, arising by fixed law from the nature of the mind," constituting "the foundation of truth in external sensibility."[30] He regarded both space and time as the two principles of sensuous cognition that are "single and nevertheless pure intuitions," and that have their seat "in the subject only, as the formal capacity."[31] Such a priori intuitions would not be possible "unless infinite space as well as infinite time be given."[32]

On the other hand, continuing Newton's work and rendering it in the language of differential calculus, Pierre-Simon de Laplace posited the indisputable existence of objective geometric space as a precondition for his celestial mechanics (and all classical physics). He offered a "complete solution of the great mechanical problem presented by the solar system," and notoriously claimed that God was no longer necessary to explain seeming irregularities, since eventually the whole cosmos would appear as a system of regularities.[33] Thus he crystallized the late modern assumptions that would be taken for granted by industrial and postindustrial world civilization: that natural geometric space enabled instrumental control and production, by which the contents of the external world could become material "natural resources" exploited for humanity's benefit.

This polarization, with its inevitable contradictions, marked nineteenth-century theories of space pursued in many disciplines, such as pure geometry, physics, physiology, and psychology. In art history and philosophical aesthetics the theorizing of space occurred relatively late, mostly in the German context. The best-known figure in this regard is Alois Riegl (1858–1905), who, in attempting to articulate architecture's differences with other "fine arts" such as painting and sculpture, defined it as a useful art whose aim is to create "limited spaces that allow man the possibility of free movement."[34] In his historical studies, he characterized ancient classical architecture as being more interested in the "limitations of space" than in the "creation" of space, as "one filled with atmosphere."[35] Like Heinrich Wölfflin (1864–1945), Riegl understood that architecture conveyed meanings to more than simply a visual perception; both scholars recognized that the human body, its structure and other sensory perceptions, played a fundamental role through empathy in such aesthetic appreciation. Yet space remained characterized as an objective three-dimensionality, a distinction fundamental in his discussions of differences among the arts, and the Cartesian duality was not questioned. Even when first acknowledged in architectural writings, like in the book of art nouveau architect August Endell, space was characterized as the negative of solid shape, in opposition to structure: "What is to most effect is not the shape [of the facades, the columns, the ornaments] but its inversion, the space, the emptiness that spreads out rhythmically between the walls, is delimited by them, and that vibrancy is more important than the walls."[36]

Perhaps the most significant figure in this part of our story, particularly since he seems to come closest to contemporaneous and later phenomenological intuitions, is August Schmarsow (1853–1936).[37] In lectures and theoretical writings from 1893 to 1919, he established the importance of the notion of space for architecture. This was a totally unprecedented position at odds not only with all traditional treatises (where, as I have argued, *place* is tacit and there is no mention of space), but with the established understanding of architecture in his own time as "the art of building" or, at best, a "bedecked tectonic structure," or ornamented shed. He pressed his point against both Wölfflin and Gottfried Semper, arguing that what all historical architecture had in common, from the hut to sophisticated contemporary buildings, was that all were "spatial structures" (*Raumgebilde*). Any human attempt to produce an "enclosed portion of space" revealed an intention of order and "a disposition to a form of intuition which we call space."[38] Lecturing in 1893, he elaborated on the relationship between human beings and space through his own understanding of the psychology and physiology of the human body. While his psychology remained *partes extra partes*, he argued for visual experience, together with the structure of the body, muscular, and tactile sensations, as the origin of our "understanding" of three-dimensionality, "whose axes of direction intersect in us."[39] This is the basic "capital" of architectural creation, spatial sensation, and imagination. Thus, he concludes, architecture is the "creatress of space"; its task is to externalize the same intuitions that the "science of space" (and physics) have described with mathematical rigor.

In later lectures and writings, Schmarsow discussed the nature of the "three distinct [orthogonal] dimensions" of space in relation to the structure of the body, arguing in favor of height as a primary human dimension, since it represents a fundamental distinction between our bipedal organization and that of other animals. The third dimension, depth, was for him a consequence of *movement*, real or imagined, yet it alone brings our experience of space into full awareness. Schmarsow's fundamental argument with Riegl is precisely around this notion: that human beings experience space not only visually but above all through movement.[40] While only much later would Merleau-Ponty question the understanding of spatial perception as homologous with Cartesian three-dimensionality, positing the *primacy* of depth in experience and a full understanding of embodied perception *as* action, Schmarsow's last essay (1919)[41] stresses not only the importance of movement with regard to the third dimension but also an understanding of life as "embodied," departing from earlier mechanistic physiology and psychology and approaching the phenomenology of Edmund Husserl.

* * *

Only a few years after Boullée's design for the "Cenotaph to Newton," his most notable student, Jean-Nicolas-Louis Durand (1760–1834), would declare his preference for similar buildings free from classical ornament, minimal and rigorously geometric, yet the product of diametrically different convictions. Durand believed that the meaning of architecture depended upon nothing more than an efficient, mechanical understanding of structure and a cost-effective use of materials, expressed automatically through the buildings' forms. Basing his theory on the assumptions of eighteenth-century aesthetics and the generalized cultural expectations of positivism, he believed that the only legitimate meanings would necessarily appear as a semantic pair (like a mathematical equation), establishing an unambiguous relationship between a sign and its significance. It is easy to grasp how this assumption contributed to diminishing the possibilities of architectural meaning, equating it with the reading of signs: the communication of "information." This is in sharp contrast with Boullée's *architecture parlante*, which had explicitly engaged the temporal and musical dimensions of experience in its evocation of atmospheres.

Indeed, Durand already seemed blind to Boullée's anguish over architectural meaning for a technologically oriented culture. He questioned his immediate predecessor's concern with character and his interest in expression. For him architecture was essentially shelter, a social need, and that is precisely the origin of its significance.[42] Architecture represented the objective Cartesian space through which it operated, automatically marked by the practical uses to which it was devoted. A building signified its use—like scientific prose—and any emotion or feeling thus became immaterial. Furthermore, his understanding of the subject as a passive observer inhabiting architecture went further than Perrault's. Durand noted explicitly that the observer invariably perceived in perspective, and this led him to reject the idea that "harmonic" proportions in design might be of any consequence whatsoever (even for "aesthetic" composition)—since dimensions always shifted following our point of view. He favored instead strictly instrumental, orthogonal design mechanisms, believing the space of architecture to be the objective space of descriptive geometry (*géométrie descriptive*), Gaspard Monge's translation of

Cartesian geometry and its isotropic space into an instrument of design and industrial production in the late eighteenth century.

Monge's new application taught the systematically precise drawing of three-dimensional objects, reduced to mechanical constructions operating through "objective" geometric space.[43] Descriptive geometry became a crucial discipline for the Industrial Revolution, instilled in all future architects and engineers at the École Polytechnique between the late eighteenth and early nineteenth centuries and subsequently stipulated as an entry requirement for architectural students at the École des Beaux-Arts (after 1823). Despite its familiarity to us—it is the space of the computer screen in conventional architectural software—this geometry's novelty in the early nineteenth century cannot be overstated. We should recall that the very concept of space as three-dimensional was also new in the philosophy of Kant and Hegel, and the systematic rendering of machine pieces (or building projections) in this manner was unprecedented. Thereafter it became possible to control and dictate the production of any complex building or machine from a drafting table, without needing to worry about the messiness of "translation" that had always been assumed between drawing and execution. This is the central delusion, one still operational today in digital fabrication. The images produced by this method are no more than instrumental "signs," and reality is consequently construed through the optics of the subjective observer.

Indeed, a set of very serious contradictions emerges from the new imperative of reductive design appropriate to a Cartesian, dualistic consciousness. Regardless of the ultimate intention, architectural space in effect appears as a production of the personal imagination, rather than a disclosure of *place*. Architects associated objectivity with orthogonal projections, their preferred mode of production resonant with the expectations of the new scientific culture; they now found perspective subjective, yet an essential tool for the presentation of ideas to the public (or a client), capable of provoking desired emotional responses. As Durand's compositional methods were adapted by the École des Beaux-Arts, perspectival renderings were increasingly used to demonstrate architecture's connection to the fine arts, emphasizing purely visual and compositional attributes as the values of so-called artistic buildings—architecture as picture, as a consumable spectacle, of even greater value if signed by some well-known figure. This most common assumption is still very much with us. It would thereafter be more or less at odds with the "real" value attributed to the built environment in a technological society, as defined through *firmitas* (solidity, durability) and *commoditas* (practical fitness for use). This had already been anticipated by Perrault, for whom *venustas*—beauty reduced to aesthetics in the sense of Baumgarten—could become subsidiary:[44] a position emphatically espoused by Durand. Nineteenth-century perspective and its related artistic products aimed exclusively at optical accuracy (eventually becoming "photographic"). It is thus truly "subjective" and, despite obvious superficial similarities due to its Euclidean origin, paradoxically at odds with the seventeenth- and eighteenth-century notion of perspective as a central "hinge" of representation, deemed analogous to orthogonal plans and elevations, as for Andrea Pozzo (ca. 1695) or Johann Heinrich Lambert (ca. 1760): the hinge that had previously been capable of associating architecture with transcendental—religious, political, and scientific—truths, but no longer.

This occultation of *place* in mainstream Western architecture coincides with Durand's articulation of *functionalism* as a central intention of design. He described the principles of his theory and the main goals of his architectural pedagogy in the textbook for his lessons at the École Polytechnique. Initially published in 1802–1805 and subsequently republished and reprinted in numerous editions, this text had a profound impact on architectural education the world over.[45] It is worth repeating his main line of reasoning: architecture, borne of necessity, provides shelter and is thus fundamental to human life. Its objective is therefore that of public and private utility; no other external justification is necessary. Due to architecture's elevated cost, convenience and economy are its central priorities and should guide all formal decisions once structural necessity is assured. In other words, the primary determinant of architectural form and its dimensions is mechanics (statics), followed by economy and convenience. All else (ornament, for instance) is merely arbitrary and not really necessary. Architecture's affinity is therefore with engineering and *not* with the fine arts; it is "problem solving," for which absolute rules are essential.

It follows that the main issue in architectural design is to solve efficiently and economically the basic problem of space planning; the "form" of a resulting building simply follows its "function." Architects should therefore *not* be concerned with meaning, and if aesthetic questions are raised by clients or society at large, these could only be admissible as issues of subjective composition or style (formal syntax). *Durand's functionalism represents a clear attempt to bypass not only musical harmony* (like Perrault) *but also poetic language as a paradigm for architecture.* His position has persisted (largely implicitly) in architectural practice and education for over two centuries.

Functionalism articulated an explicit position against eighteenth-century character theory and its desire to deploy metaphorical language as a model for form generation in the realization of a communicative architecture—itself a response to the demise of a "cosmic" referent for architectural form in traditional theory. As I have suggested, character theories drew upon linguistic analogies in a full range of registers, from the expression of emotion—as in poetry (or music), where words "rebel against words" (Paz)—to more denotative meanings, such as the representation of status and hierarchy, such that architecture can help constitute a social world. However, starting with Durand, implementing increasingly sophisticated, instrumental tools of representation and production, architects have aimed at bypassing the word when it comes to designing architecture, whereby their projects (effectively promises to Others) are "wordless," made only through forms and volumes, more or less innovative and usually nonresponsive to cultural and natural contexts. The assumption became that objects generate their own meaning, one justified by the self-evident permanence of architecture in comparison to the ephemerality of human lives. *The architect was actually encouraged to abdicate his customary responsibility to help achieve expressive, well-tuned settings for human activity.*

This stance was fueled by a growing hedonism, already present in Durand's theory and his misrepresentation of meaning as pleasure, which he claimed was corroborated by the architecture of previous eras, failing to recognize anything other than psychotropic tendencies in human evolution. Thus, *comfort* would become an exclusive objective: the avoidance of all painful conditions, an attitude already pointing toward a utopian dissolution of the human condition and obliterating the bittersweet space of desire that characterizes human existence, the historical raison d'être of architecture. Today, parametric strategies in design and other extrapolations of "scientific" theories and tools into form generation are built upon similar presuppositions. The obsession with algorithmically generated form thrives on a distrust of the capacity of words to recount the experiential qualities of a site and to propose meaningful, attuned environments for human cultures, a distrust justified by the inherent opacity that always operates in the gap between the words we speak and the things we make.

**

So what can we conclude in regard to the "existence" of space and its distinctions from and relations with natural place? Is space *something* (objective—as in classical physics) or *nothing* (subjective—as in Kant's philosophy and, later, Jean Piaget's psychology)? This is of course an immense topic, argued brilliantly by philosophers like Jeff Malpas and Edward Casey within the phenomenological tradition.[46] While a substantial philosophical elaboration is beyond the scope of this book, our architectural stories provide interesting insights that we will now summarize. Following Merleau-Ponty's *Phenomenology of Perception*, we may start by observing that there is always a dialectic at work between conceptual (reflective) and perceptual (prereflective and emotional) dimensions of consciousness. While perception primarily yields a bodily spatiality whose meanings are in the natural and the cultural world, our concepts, in turn, ultimately have an impact on how the world appears to us. This condition explains the occultation of place in late modern technological culture, and reveals that its "recovery" by the architect for intersubjective perception is not a simple matter.

On the other hand, what is also evident is that any conceptual space can never be *in itself* generative of architectural meanings, of attuned atmospheres for human life. It can produce objects that we might find novel and even astonishing, but that would ultimately fail to move us or to orient us (both emotionally and intellectually), as might be expected from authentic *Stimmung*. Ancient monuments in non-Western and pre-Greek European and Mediterranean cultures were fundamentally mimetic of meanings embedded in perceptual, prereflective, and emotional places. As I suggested earlier in this chapter, the first intuition of spatial stability in the lived world is likely Anaximander's *arché*, followed by Plato's *chóra*, but the Aristotelian critique of empty space always prevailed until the first successes of early modern science. In medieval Gothic architecture and painting, for example, space conceived as simultaneity (as in the modern drawing of a plan) was totally absent. Architecture was a choreography of rituals, a temporal spatiality. Despite its primarily metaphysical connotations through its associations with the divine light, Renaissance perspective contributed significantly to the stabilization of space as a concept through the "image," particularly in painting. Paolo Uccello and Andrea Mantegna famously deployed Euclidean geometry to paint architecture into their works. Conversely, facades could also be conceived and experienced as images, a true innovation during this period, signaling an initial link between perceptual and geometrical space.[47] In pre-nineteenth-century European cultures, however, there were always limits placed on this association. Even after Galileo and Newton, the Aristotelian critique held sway; the "subject" of architecture was not yet a disembodied (passive) optical apparatus. A case in point is the debate about the importance of sensations and their dependence upon temporal experience to convey appropriate character in eighteenth-century gardens and buildings.

The preponderance of geometric space over *place* could only occur during the nineteenth century, due mainly to the final crystallization of Cartesian dualism into a divided reality: on the one hand the "subject" as citizen, passive observer, and *flâneur*, with innate political rights, and on the other hand a material and objectively measurable external reality, assumed to be totally disconnected from the subject to the extent of becoming inanimate "natural resources." I have already detailed some of the ambiguities present in late-nineteenth-century theories of space in aesthetics. In science, Laplace is hardly the end of the debate. Albert Einstein (1879–1955), as is well known, ultimately questioned the stability of classical space in physics, arguing against Newton's absolute geometric space, while much earlier, Henri Poincaré (1854–1912), the eminent scientist and mathematician, understood that intuition was the life of mathematics and even asserted that the assumed geometry of physical space was conventional. According to Poincaré, this was particularly evident in the attempt to make sense of problems in thermodynamics. However, he thought that we were so accustomed to Euclidean geometry that we would prefer to change the physical laws to save Euclidean geometry rather than shift to a non-Euclidean physical geometry. In fact, he set forth a theory of differential geometry capable of better describing dynamic qualitative phenomena, a tool that is now crucial in neurobiological models seeking to explain cognition with a full acknowledgment of phenomenological observations about embodied consciousness in the world. Such is apparent, for example, in the enactive approaches of Thompson and Varela that I will discuss in the following chapter.

Nineteenth-century architecture witnessed an unprecedented polarization of positions on architectural space, yet all underscored by the fundamental assumptions made clear in Durand's writings. Thus, Eugène-Emmanuel Viollet-le-Duc believed in the primacy of a conceptual space, one kindred to engineering and structural analysis, driving tectonic architectural form, while Charles Garnier, the designer of the famous Paris Opera House, could argue polemically that architecture operated in perceptual, scenographic space, usually characterized as the places for reciprocal "observation," epitomized by Walter Benjamin's urbanite, the *flâneur*. Regardless, a full understanding of the issues involved in architecture's communicative settings, always entailing the disclosure of natural and/or cultural *place*, was rarely present; even when invoking artistic intentions, architects remained caught up in the assumptions of eighteenth-century aesthetics, concentrating on issues of composition—"beauty," for a dispassionate observer—rather than meaning or *Stimmung*, in its full embodied, cognitive, *and* emotional sense, as grasped by romantic philosophy.

It is important to remember that the nineteenth century saw the invention not only of unprecedented "optical" methods of perspective (such as three-point and spherical perspective) but also of isometry and axonometry.[48] These became the accepted means of representation for architects, planners, and engineers, eventually presupposed as obvious (like the "objective" space that characterized the art of architecture) and rendered invisible (like in our own computer software), producing works that as authorial creations existed "on paper" (or, later, as digital models). The significance of this change cannot be overemphasized. Axonometric drawing externalizes conceptual (geometric, Cartesian) space into a matrix presumed to be the very space of architecture; it is generated as a "synthetic" descriptive geometry, representing all "real" dimensions *and* angles of a future building, regardless of orientation, in a preexisting, objective space. Axonometric drawings are additive or constructive, that is to say, tectonic, and usually generated from the plan, a central condition of functional architecture. This graphic tool allows for both instrumental production (engineering, i.e., the production of working drawings, eventually BIM models) and formal ("aesthetic") manipulations of all sorts, from the simple tectonics of the international style to the impossibly complex expressions of "parametricism." Yet, given the very nature of the tools of representation, such "aesthetic" judgments are almost entirely visual, generally excluding other sensory and embodied dimensions of spatial experience. Given that the transcription from design to production is also expected to be as seamless as possible (to the extremes of contemporary "fabrication"), this typically modern mode of conceiving and producing the built environment contributes fundamentally to the homogenization of urban space that I described in my introductory chapter. Indeed, due mainly to the imperatives of technology and production, the conceptual space favored by science and engineering became identified with architecture's "modern tectonic space," as famously expressed by Le Corbusier in the journal *L'Esprit nouveau* and exemplified through the well-known axonometric representations of historical buildings in the books of Auguste Choisy (1841–1904).

* * *

In the early twentieth century, European artists came to recognize the limitations of optical or perspectival space in painting. This awareness had already started to emerge within the practices of impressionism and pointillism, despite their avowedly "scientific" interests in representing the "retinal image." As Juhani Pallasmaa has repeatedly observed, it is clear that a great deal of significant architecture of the last two hundred years has been inspired by the realizations of painters and filmmakers. This awareness is clearly in line with the project of phenomenology, dedicated to the recovery of the primacy of fully tactile and sensuous, embodied perception over conceptual constructions. The story of how art "recovered" a sense of *place* through constructed space is one that has been told from different angles. Merleau-Ponty, for example, explains how Cézanne's paintings of the landscape, most notably his many versions of *Mont Sainte-Victoire*, demonstrate the artist's obsessive search for a meaningful depth in painting, one that simply could not be rendered in the manner of classical (perspectival) painting.[49] Duchamp is well known for his declaration of the end of "retinal painting" during the second decade of the twentieth century, anticipating his remarkable later work, where he explores human depth as fundamentally erotic through manifold manifestations, ranging from his *Large Glass* to his *Étant données*. This story has resonances in architecture as well. I have described elsewhere how Le Corbusier, learning about these issues through his painting, managed to recognize axonometric representation on a canvas as a new possibility of embodied depth beyond perspective, transcending its earlier applications as reductive architectural space.[50] In his late works, Le Corbusier privileged depth (and the temporality of lived presence), understanding it as not simply homologous to height and breadth, or deployed as an optical sequence, but truly the dimension of architectural *places* conveying appropriate qualities to the embodied inhabitant. Today, the issue of atmosphere is often appreciated by architects through other visual arts and multimedia installations.

This is all very encouraging. Yet the fact that the appreciation of "atmospheres" usually arises from artistic "effects" makes extrapolations problematic, often not rigorous, potentially glossing over crucial ethical and political issues, particularly in the absence of a critical (historical) understanding of the cultural context in which the architect operates and the specific conceptual skills (the assumed truth of objective space, for example) that radically affect the contemporary perceptions of inhabitants. Indeed, it must already seem obvious that for *Stimmung* to operate effectively it should be understood outside the presuppositions of eighteenth-century aesthetics, *with full consideration of the importance of language and synesthesia as its central components*, since it concerns cognition as a whole and not merely our "emotional brain centers." *Stimmung*, we may recall from Agamben, is at the hinge between living (*zoon*) and language (*logos*).

***

Before engaging in a more comprehensive examination of both *synesthesia* and *emerging language* in the following chapters, I would like to conclude the present one by briefly examining a work by John Hejduk (1929–2000) in which poetic language enables the architect to disclose the meanings of his site as *place*, and to project its possibilities into the future by means of literary configuration. Hejduk was one of the great architects of our time, yet he is not known best for his (very few) buildings but, rather, for his books and numerous theoretical projects. He was educated in a totally modern context, belonging, in his own words, to a "third generation of modern architects"[51] after the heroic figures of Le Corbusier, Mies van der Rohe, and Frank Lloyd Wright. The assumption of an "objective" space of precise architectural representation and axonometric projections was a given in the first stages of his career. Following up on the discoveries of Cézanne, Juan Gris, Piet Mondrian, and other modern artists, Hejduk soon came to realize the limitations of conceptual space, the enigmatic depths that became manifest by simply shifting a square plan forty-five degrees, or employing frontal axonometric projections. While always believing, with Alain Robbe-Grillet (writing about Franz Kafka), that a "hallucinatory effect derives from [the] extraordinary clarity [of objects, gestures, words] and not from mystery or mist [for] nothing is more fantastic ultimately than precision,"[52] he came to understand the limitations of a progressive (instrumental) and optimistic modernity. In his more mature work, he acknowledged the central importance of storytelling and poetic language in architectural design.

Hejduk's work is complex; like much excellent poetry, it draws on multiple and deep life experiences to speak not about itself (or the author) but about the world, often defying paraphrase. Here I wish to offer only a few observations on his project *Victims*, a proposal for a barren site in Berlin that used to house the headquarters and torture chambers of the Nazi SS and the Gestapo—a site marked and cursed by the stories of all the atrocities that took place during the Third Reich.[53] Today the site, known as the Topography of Terror museum, houses a functional documentation center and features a few remnants of existing structures (most of which were destroyed during and after the war), as well as a fragment of the Berlin Wall bounding its north side. The present structure was built after a complicated sequence of competitions that included the infamous failure of Peter Zumthor's winning project, halted and demolished in 2004, officially due to cost overruns. Compared with the existing museum, which objectifies the site in its past horror, Hejduk's design was not concerned with preserving and documenting physical remnants; it has no didactic aspirations and does not set forth an objectified memory for selective consumption. The conventional Topography of Terror museum reveals documents to a passive visitor, who, dumbfounded by the atrocities orchestrated by the Nazi state apparatus, usually exits hurriedly in search of a stiff drink, thus perpetuating the paradox of either resentful memory or guiltful forgetting. Hejduk's project, by contrast, aimed at involving the inhabitants and visitors in a process of remembering that is also a process of healing, through settings for participatory focal actions that bridge normally opposed dimensions of experience: linking the quotidian

Architecture as an Unveiling of Place 137

with the extraordinary, the past with the future in a thick present, angelic play with demonic action, the city and the garden with the concentration camp. The site, a marginal and devastated plot of land after the war, long perceived as a no-place, is obviously loaded with negative meanings. The challenge for Hejduk was to acknowledge them by charging Berliners with the role of caretakers of memories that also included other "victims" of torture and technological warfare elsewhere in the world, acknowledging both the particularities of the situation and the wider universal issues of human violence to others, and its potential catharsis.

The project consists of sixty-seven structures presented to the city and its citizens that might be built over two thirty-year periods, wholly or selectively, or—he writes—might even not be built at all, while the site gradually becomes transfigured into an enclosed garden of evergreen saplings on a tight grid.[54] Each structure is *named* and characterized through drawings and words. A set of precise plans, elevations, and sections (whenever necessary), systematically descriptive through the three orthogonal directions, are intertwined with a story or stories, usually the description of a potential inhabitant (some biographical traits or anecdotes), and/or his or her activities. The structures on the site are connected consistently one to the next, touching each other at a single point. The drawings are clearly referential: a means to the end of an imagined building, yet in conjunction with their texts. These narratives are written in the "objective" manner of Robbe-Grillet; avoiding subjective emotional qualifications, they generate poetic images and above all the experience of attunement between environment and task, action and habit; in doing so, they recall rituals from the past, usually engaging the ineffable. Hopeful atmospheres appear in between drawings and narrative: on the one hand the precise images that are never merely "novel" but generated from recognizable Euclidean figures coming from our architectural, urban, and landscape traditions; and on the other, the words that characterize actions or habits. Such atmospheres charged with meanings concern action and the habitual; they cannot be perceived from the detached position of a museum visitor.

Hejduk reminds us that in the end, there are only a handful of basic interventions: a double hedge (to grow up to fourteen feet high) marking the perimeter of the site; a trolley track running between the hedges; telephone poles running along the tracks whose lines serve the park alone (there are no calls beyond the hedges); a bus stop, drawbridge, and gatehouse marking the only access to the site and flanked by two clock towers (whose blades ironically conceal the present hour, signaling the exclusion of real presence from any mathematical time); and, inside, a grid locating the placement of the evergreen saplings that grow in cycles of thirty years. This is an "incremental place ... a growing vision"[55] whose architectural character and atmospheres are defined through the stories of the inhabitants of the city. Thus, through poetic language, the occulted *places* of a modern metropolis, even when cursed by war and tyranny, may be returned to a meaningful architectural production.

5
Stimmung, Phenomenology, and Enactive Cognitive Theory: From Habit to Language

We have accounted for the historical roots of *Stimmung* and its association with basic issues of architectural meaning (*armonía/concentus*), as well as for the inception of the concept itself as a central concern for artistic expression in view of the adverse cultural conditions of the late eighteenth and early nineteenth centuries. For architectural practice in the twenty-first century to fully grasp the possibilities of *Stimmung* and its implementation, creating atmospheres responsive to human action and to *place* in the fullest sense (as both natural and cultural context), a proper understanding of consciousness and perception beyond Cartesian misunderstandings is indispensable.

It is a fact that the practices responsible for the design of the environment in our technological world, generally understood as no more than clever "problem solving," have been largely uncritical of the assumptions of Cartesianism, including its underlying cognitive models and concept of space. The critique of Cartesianism and its consequences in all disciplines is a vast topic that has been and continues to be the subject of much debate. I shall sketch out some important aspects of this critique in the work of modern and contemporary philosophers, and this will lead us to a discussion of the most relevant concepts for our argument in phenomenology, cognitive science, and neurobiology. My intention will always be to draw out their potential impact on the design and practice of architecture.

As I explained at the close of chapter 2, the Cartesian understanding of mind and perception first appeared in architectural theory toward the end of the seventeenth century, in the writings of Claude Perrault.[1] Contrary to Aristotle, for whom mind and the living body were always united—since "soul" is the capacity of the organism to *act* in manifold ways from vegetative nourishment, sentience, motion, and volition, to intellectual conceptualization[2]—Descartes must be held responsible for imagining and promoting the *separation* of consciousness and life, transforming the former into an inner experience accessible to the intellect, the *ego cogitans*. In his "Second Meditation," he goes so far as to doubt the very existence of the body's sentience; indeed, he even claims it is possible to doubt the existence of one's own body. The power of the imagination belongs to his thinking, and therefore "it *seems*" to him that he sees or touches.[3] This, Descartes concludes, cannot be false (regardless of the origins of the sensation in fact or delusion); but sensing, understood in this particular way, is simply "thinking."

Following in Descartes's footsteps, Perrault similarly believed that architecture communicates its meanings to a disembodied soul, thoroughly bypassing the body with its complex feelings and emotions. He assumed perception to be passive, and meaning to be merely the result of the association of concepts and images in the brain. Implicit in his theory is Descartes's presumption that human consciousness was enabled by the pineal gland at the back of the head, conceived as a geometric and monocular point of contact between the measurable, intelligible world—*res extensa*—and the disembodied, rational soul—*res cogitans*. This consciousness was capable of perspectival visual perception, manifested as a picture composed with precise lines, like a copper plate engraving; it ensured the human capacity to grasp the immutable geometric and mathematical truth of the external world, bridging the divide between the two heterogeneous elements of reality. As I have explained, this is why Perrault could question, for the first time ever in the history of architectural theory, the bodily experience of "harmony" applicable to all the senses in *action*, embedded in kinesthesia. This phenomenon had always been presumed since classical antiquity and constituted the primary quality to be observed in architectural design. For Perrault, sight and hearing were autonomous and segregated receptors, and therefore the inveterate experience of "musical" harmony expressed in architectural settings appeared to be a fallacy. Consequently, the quality of desire (*venustas*) to be conveyed by the architectural object in order to generate harmonious (good, meaningful) *place* was substituted by abstract aesthetic composition producing a dispassionate beauty through the capable manipulation of exclusively visual, instrumental proportions.

Given what we now know about perception and consciousness, the immense staying power of Cartesian dualism in European and world technological civilization is puzzling. Many of its assumptions remain unquestioned by virtue of the extraordinary successes of the instrumental sciences, which build upon dualism and ignore its inherent contradictions. The *ego cogito*, or "soul," which Descartes still believed had contact with God, was eventually identified with a "brain" by behaviorism and early-twentieth-century neuroscientists and cognitive theorists; the material brain came to be understood as the exclusive seat of consciousness and conceptualized as an information processor. Despite the obvious differences between Descartes's ultimately metaphysical interests and twentieth-century science, the Cartesian dualistic model remained intact. The issue of the "absent body" is complex, having been wonderfully elucidated by Drew Leder:[4] "It is *the body's own tendency toward self-concealment* that allows for the possibility of its neglect or deprecation. Our organic basis can be easily forgotten. … Intentionality can be attributed to a disembodied mind given the self-effacement of the ecstatic body," particularly in healthy-functioning individuals, so that "freeing oneself from the body takes on a positive valuation." Mainstream, technologically driven planning and architectural practice has remained caught in this framework of understanding up until the present. Buildings evidently acquire meanings by virtue of their existence, and these are identified with "information," salient when it is communicated by novel and unusual forms so that little else seems to matter, leading to a significant disregard for more primary sensory meanings offered to a fully embodied consciousness by their materiality. Ignoring the living body's fundamental condition as earthbound and *placed*, avant-garde architects obsessed with complexity for its own sake have even celebrated architecture's "liberation" from gravity.[5]

While Cartesian epistemology eventually prevailed in European culture, the issue of feeling or *sentiment* as a crucial dimension of art could not be easily dismissed. Not long after Descartes, French writers on art, like the celebrated Abbé Jean-Baptiste Dubos, started to argue that artistic judgment pertained to feelings, perceived by a "sixth sense."[6] Yet during the eighteenth century, aesthetic feelings (taste) could easily become reasonable rules; convertibility was often argued, facilitated by Descartes's epistemology, and supposedly generated inductively, in emulation of rational Nature. French philosopher Marie-François-Pierre Maine de Biran (1766–1824), however, began to recognize the limitations of Descartes's epistemology, and therefore tried to grasp the source of the personal "I" in a "feeling of existence," meaning the *bodily experience of exercising effort in movement*.[7] This heralded the start of romantic philosophy, as described in chapter 3, itself a precursor of the late-nineteenth-century American pragmatism of William James and John Dewey, and of the early- and mid-twentieth-century phenomenology of Edmund Husserl and Maurice Merleau-Ponty. This realization thus lay at the root of later developments in American philosophy, among them the contemporary work of Mark Johnson, contemporary American and European existential phenomenologists, as well as the recent revolution in the cognitive sciences that has reconciled this discipline with the previously mentioned philosophical positions, particularly in the works of Evan Thompson and Alva Noë.

Despite the various differences among all these positions, they are united by a fundamental questioning of Cartesian dualism and a comprehension of the deep continuities between mind, life, and world. It is important to stress as well that these developments underscore the fact that phenomenology is not "antiscientific," as it has been regrettably misunderstood. Merleau-Ponty himself explains: "The entire universe of science is constructed upon the lived world, and if we wish to think science rigorously, to appreciate precisely its sense and scope, we must first awaken that experience of the world of which science is the second-order expression."[8]

Indeed, the latest approaches in cognitive science have jettisoned any reliance on analytic philosophy and computer brain models, and instead begun acknowledging the relations between cognitive processes and the real world. "Embodied dynamicism," the most recent stance in cognitive science that arose in the 1990s, has called into question the conception of cognition as a disembodied and abstract mental representation, adopting a critical attitude toward the extrapolation of all manner of computer models and its processes to explain the mind.[9] The mind and the world are simply *not* separate and independent of each other; nor is the mind merely a neural network in the head. Rather, the mind is an embodied dynamic system *in* the world. For Francisco Varela, Evan Thompson, and Eleanor Rauch, who coined the term neurophenomenology in *The*

Embodied Mind (1991), cognition is the exercise of skillful know-how in embodied and situated action, and cannot be reduced to prespecified problem solving. In other words, the perceiver (subject), the perception (invariably affective *and* cognitive), and the thing perceived (object) could never be said to *exist* independently; they are always codependent and coemergent.[10] In the same book, they introduced the concept of cognition as "enaction," linking biological autopoiesis (the notion that living beings are autonomous agents that actively generate and maintain themselves) with the emergence of cognitive domains. In this view, the nervous system of any living being does not process information like a computer; rather, it creates meaning, *i.e., the perception of purpose in life*, the articulation of which becomes more sophisticated with the acquisition of language in higher animals, culminating in humanity's symbolic communication.[11] Indeed, in the human world the relationship of purposeful action to biological imperatives, such as primary homeostasis, is always opaque, since human actions are part of complex symbolic economies.[12]

The "lifeworld" in this model is not a prespecified outward realm represented externally by the brain, but a relational domain enacted by a being's particular mode of coupling with the environment, beyond distinctions between nature and culture, and one in which cities and architecture play a prominent role. Let me emphasize the obvious: architecture is part of the lifeworld, not of "objective nature." For humans, the lifeworld is linguistic and symbolic, a setting of "perceived situation-work," beyond the "perception-action" of most animals and life in general.[13] According to this view, embodied experience is not a secondary issue (as it was after Descartes) but becomes central to the understanding of the mind itself; as such, it requires careful examination in the manner of phenomenology, an approach explicitly adopted by Thompson (2007), relying upon the findings of Edmund Husserl and Maurice Merleau-Ponty. A more extensive discussion of mind is not our aim here, although it is important to point out that Merleau-Ponty's understanding of the "I" as a *bodily subjectivity* radically negates Cartesian dualism.[14] If, as he states, "I am my body," this is never to be understood in a materialist sense. The body is unlike any other physical object, but is instead like a work of art, "an expressive being" of my subjectivity. Being-in-the-world is thus beyond any subject-object dichotomy; it is neither first-personal (subjective) nor third-personal (objective), an existential structure that remains prior to all abstractions.

Enactive understanding and embodied perception are crucial to our grasp of *Stimmung* (or atmosphere) and its potential implications for contemporary environmental and architectural design. In his 1907 lectures, Edmund Husserl recognized that every visual or tactile perception was accompanied and intrinsically linked to the sensing of one's body movements: in watching a train go by, for example, the train is experienced in conjunction with my sensing of head and eye movements. Husserl believed that kinesthesis was therefore a constitutive condition of ordinary perception, and this became a central point of departure for Merleau-Ponty's *Phenomenology of Perception*. In this seminal text, Merleau-Ponty rejects the explanations of associationism and behavioral psychology, along with the idea of perception as the mere sum of stimuli conveyed by independent senses, simply communicating data to a brain where a synthesis of some kind might take place. Perception is not the later stage of sensation, with the sensory receptors as the starting point of any analysis. Rather, both perception and emotion are dependent aspects of intentional action: our engaged bodily, sensorimotor knowing of the world. Merleau-Ponty argued for the primacy of embodied perception at the roots of being and understanding, grounding other modalities of intellectual articulation, following Husserl's explanation of the limitations of hypothetical thought. For example, we first know through our sensorimotor awareness that the earth does not move. This is a primary certainty for our bodies, one indispensable to ultimately constructing an endless number of scientific or mythical explanations of the universe that may be more or less credible as we "prove" them through instrumental means. But the first phenomenological truth is a precondition for all others.

The ideas developed by Husserl and Merleau-Ponty continue to be revisited today. Alva Noë (2009) has lucidly explained the enactive understanding of perception and cognition, emphasizing particularly that in order to understand consciousness in humans and animals we must look not inward, but rather to the ways in which an animal continues to live in and respond to its world.[15] Consciousness is always of something, it is always of things other than itself, and any inward turn of our gaze, as Schelling had already understood, must inevitably find itself back in the one and only "outer" world.[16] Consciousness is not merely contained in the brain, bounded by the skull. This absence of limits has to do with complexity, the distributed nature of mental processes, and the involvement of the body in consciousness. Neurologist Frank Wilson puts it thus: "We will never know how the brain works … it is even more complicated than we thought it was when we realized that it had both sequential and simultaneous operations (which we gratefully assigned to … a 'dominant' and 'nondominant' hemisphere). But the brain can also work with 'intermaths,' massively complex sets of minute data that are themselves in constant flux." Wilson argues that the concept of brain functional centers is tantamount to simplistic scientific reductionism. "The brain is changed by its active involvement; in that sense, it remembers." Moreover, "[t]he brain does not live inside the head, even though that is its formal habitat. It reaches out to the body and the body reaches out to the world. We can say that the brain 'ends' at the spinal chord, and that the spinal chord 'ends' at the peripheral nerves," but "brain is hand and hand is brain, and their interdependence includes everything else right down to the quarks."[17]

Alva Noë's work allows us to understand how the traditional view of perception operative in all premodern architectural theories (one that was "musical" and primarily synesthetic, and that espoused harmony as a central architectural value), is vindicated by the recent understanding of the senses as "modalities" that transgress their functional boundaries and defy any exclusive association with the physical organs to which they have been conventionally attached (like "eyes" to "vision").[18] Among many other cognitive phenomena, this understanding explains the now demonstrated capacity of human consciousness to experience "visual perceptions" through touch, as is possible for blind individuals with the aid of a device that transforms a digital image into electrical impulses on the skin.[19]

According to Shaun Gallagher, developmental studies also demonstrate that perception is intermodal from the start. This is not an intellectual trait acquired after much practice, but an innate feature of our embodied existence.[20] Perception is less the result of an internal processing of sensory information and more the result of an interaction between body and environment. As an innate system designed for motor control, the *body schema* (Gallagher's term for the prereflective, nonobjectified "living body") is better understood as a set of pragmatic (action-oriented) capabilities embodied in the developing nervous system. In the human infant, it accounts for the capacity to recognize and imitate other humans, the mimetic and empathic faculties crucial for later self-understanding.[21] Only after the age of four do children come to realize that others are capable of having beliefs different from their own, potentially gaining access to a "stable" intersubjective space upon which philosophical and historical concepts such as we described in chapter 4 can be established. Prior to this, our understanding of others has already been established by embodied practices that are emotional, sensorimotor, perceptual, and nonconceptual; these continue to be our primary means of understanding others' minds, and constitute the foundation of later possibilities of interpretation.[22] Human perception grasps the intentions of others as "experienced realities," not as objects in a detached or intellectual sense. This insight underscores the importance of the environment's "animate" presence: literally, its physiognomy.

If, as Husserl and Merleau-Ponty first suggested, perception is something we do, not something that happens to us (like other autonomous internal physiological processes such as digestion), it is obvious that our intellectual and motor skills are fundamental to cognition.[23] By the same token, *the external world, the city and architecture, truly matter*. All living organisms are not only reactive but also proactive in both perception and action; their environments are particular, not "objective."[24] There is circularity in all organisms' relationship to their environments; our behavior is both affected by the environment and affects it. We could therefore not merely abandon our intersubjective, emotionally charged spaces of communication, the necessarily bittersweet space of human desire, for the visual space behind our computer screens, as some might naively think, without also abandoning a fundamental dimension of our human consciousness. Neither do we relate to our symbolic environment as if it were a text in need of interpretation or "information" conveyed to a brain; interpretation comes after we have the world in hand.

Thus, architecture affects us, along the full range of awareness, from prereflective habits to reflective wonder. We are "already" in a shared social context; our subjectivity is intersubjective; we are "in the "game," just as we might participate in a sports match, depending on motor intentionality and skills for our perceptions. As Merleau-Ponty illustrates through his well-known example: the consciousness of the soccer player "is nothing other than the dialectic of milieu and action. Each maneuver undertaken by the player modifies the character of the field and establishes in it new lines of force in which the action in turn unfolds and is accomplished, again altering the phenomenal field."[25] Human consciousness, understood as action in this playing field, is by definition a skillful attunement to the environment. For humans, the playing field—the architecture of the city—is symbolic, framing focal actions and habits, enabling some and curtailing others, setting limits and thus making possible human freedom; *it does not appear primarily as an object, but becomes "present as the practical end" of the inhabitant's intentions.*

Thompson clearly explains how reflective self-awareness is not the only kind of self-awareness.[26] This is a crucial point for understanding the nature of architectural meaning, and has been a challenge for philosophers in the existential and phenomenological traditions, one that was acknowledged as such by Merleau-Ponty. It became a hotly contested issue for poststructuralists (after Derrida), who used this argument to deny art its capacity for "meaning as presence." Experience also comprises a prereflective self-awareness *that is not unconscious*. Merleau-Ponty always believed it was possible to have legitimate access to this prereflective state through "radical reflection," but he did not have access to the neurobiological evidence that now vindicates this possibility. Indeed, it has now become evident, as I will explain later, that the *present* temporality inhabited by the conscious, living body is not merely a nonexistent point between past and future, but a looped network of immediate and mediate memories and projections. Thus, significantly, present experience includes the prereflective bodily self-consciousness profoundly affected by the environment (architecture), which may be passive (involuntary) and intransitive (not object-directed).

Thompson adds that there is every reason to think that this sort of prereflective self-awareness animates skillful coping.[27] Indeed, in the *Phenomenology of Perception* Merleau-Ponty describes a double engagement of our embodied conscience with the world. At a primary level, our body *knows*: this is a body inhabited by motility and desire, the motion of life itself, a body whose foundational knowledge becomes stabilized through habits. As I will explain below, habits (or *habitus*) entail far greater personal agency than conditioned reflexes as understood by behaviorism, and yet they *are* habits and thus challenge any overintellectualized conception of the agent rooted in propositional mental acts.[28] There is no "will" as a cause of action (like in waving hello to a friend across the street). We can of course plan or imagine a particular goal state, but in action there is no intermediary "will."[29]

This prereflective body is fundamentally our sexual body, closest to our animal reality, and also to our sense of the sacred, for there is an intimate intertwining between this sense and our fruition through sexuality or meditation. Our body recognizes its location in our surroundings without "paying attention," through "motor intentionality." This is the body capable of unspeakable athletic feats when threatened, as well as the body that knows another person or a place long before exchanging a word with the stranger or reading a travel guide. It is also the body in action that is housed by architecture (not necessarily a subject that contemplates it as an aesthetic object) and that may be extended through prosthesis and digital media. Upon this primary understanding, diverse and often diverging cultural body images, and both poetic and reductive articulations of space and time, can be constructed.

No one will deny the importance of measurement; time and space can indeed be conceived in mathematical terms, and this has proven immensely useful. Rather, phenomenology shows that in human perception the mystery of simultaneity is always at work: both the ideal essence of the snow, its whiteness, and the particular shade of color are given at once, regardless of ambient light. Neither is possible without the other. This is the enigmatic nature of human perception, the foundation of meaning and linguistic understanding. It translates into what we perceive as most authentic in human artifacts, the presence of Being, which is also a potential absence or vacuity: an opening to the most abysmal (*das Ab-gründigste*).

When we address the issue of architectural meaning, thinking about either the creation or the reception of architecture, this primary reality made present to perception must not be forgotten. Architecture is not what appears in a glossy magazine: buildings rendered as two-dimensional or three-dimensional pictures on the computer screen, or comprehensive sets of precise working drawings. The most significant architecture is not necessarily photogenic. In fact, often the opposite is true. Its meanings are conveyed through sound and eloquent silence, the tactility and poetic resonance of materials, smell and the sense of humidity, among infinite other factors that appear through the motility of embodied perception and are given *across* the senses. Furthermore, because good architecture fundamentally offers a possibility of attunement, atmospheres appropriate to focal actions that allow for dwelling in the world, it is very problematic to reduce its effect (and critical import) to the aesthetic experience of an object, as is often customary. Strictly speaking, architecture first conveys its meanings as a situation or event; it partakes of the ephemeral quality of music, for example, as it addresses the living body, and only secondly does it become an object for tourist visits or expert critical judgments.

* * *

Granting the radical primacy of embodied perception leads us to question all mechanistic or causal models of human understanding that have been prevalent since the seventeenth century, especially the commonly accepted notion of visual perception as a picture. Merleau-Ponty was particularly critical of Descartes's *Dioptrics*, emphasizing that sight is not simply a representation in the brain: "It is by means of the perceived world and its proper structures that one can explain the spatial values assigned to a point of the visual field in each particular case."[30] The next step for Merleau-Ponty was to demonstrate how sight is integrated with the other senses in order for us to "make sense" of our experience of the world. This is what he set out to do in *Phenomenology of Perception:* "The senses translate each other without any need of an interpreter, they are mutually comprehensible without the intervention of any idea." Stressing the primordial temporality of experience, he stated: "The lived perspective, that which we actually perceive, is not a geometric or photographic one."[31]

Contemporary philosophers and cognitive scientists like Evan Thompson and Alva Noë have further explained how vision is all-important, yet our experience is not picturelike.[32] This is a complex and fascinating issue that we can only summarize here. The optical image is fragile at best, a condition well understood in the call for optical correction in traditional architectural theories I discussed in previous chapters. Merleau-Ponty and Noë use the well-known experiments with inverting glasses to prove the precariousness of the retinal image. After one wears goggles that invert the field of vision and thus create significant initial discomfort, orientation and normality are recovered in a relatively short time. Furthermore, the act of covering one's eyes in a movie so as not to see danger or a bloody scene expresses "the greatest degree of our belief that what is for us *absolutely*, that a world that we have succeeded in seeing without danger *is* without danger … our vision goes to the things themselves." Perhaps this experience teaches us better than any other what the perceptual presence of the world is: "beneath affirmation and negation, beneath judgment ... it is our experience, prior to every opinion, of inhabiting the world with our body."[33] Noë further explains how seeing is not a process that starts from a retinal picture, for in fact there are no retinal *pictures*. The image at the back of the eye is incredibly imprecise and hardly a rendition in "high definition" of the world around us. Thus, seeing itself is not pictorial; its "high-definition" quality is a result of our primary motor and sensory skills.[34] One may recognize the building in the picture or the drawing—it "shows up"—but it is also obviously *not* present in the same way that the building might be in real embodied experience. The building is present *as absent*.

This is of course a major issue when it comes to questions of architectural representation in design, dependent as it often is on the assumption of the identity between represented visual form and the experienced reality in buildings. Thompson carefully analyzes and rejects the presuppositions of perceptual experience as pictorial, especially in the photographic sense presumed by many theorists.[35] He concludes that in fact *we visualize an object or a scene by mentally enacting or entertaining a possible perceptual experience of that scene*; language plays a crucial role in this, something architects seldom consider and that will be a central issue for discussion in the following chapter.

Georges Perec offers us a sharp meditation on optical perception. He describes how our field of vision, considered "objectively," reveals a limited space, something vaguely circular, which ends very quickly to left and right, and doesn't extend very far up or down.[36] If we squint, we can manage to see the end of our nose; if we raise or lower our eyes, we can see there is an up and down. If we turn our head in one direction, then another, we don't even manage to see completely everything there is around us. We have to twist our bodies around to see properly what was behind us. And yet we take for granted the stability of the environing world, of both objects and space; our *present perception* includes all that is available to us, the back of the chairs we don't actually see and even the corridor just beyond the door.[37] We never hesitate to negotiate an unfamiliar room or a building, or to use technical extensions of our bodies, like keyboards, musical instruments, and cars. Our gaze travels through space and we recognize depth, a fundamental quality of our stable world.

Depth is a primary dimension, unlike all others, irreducible to breadth and height. Depth is not the prosaic interval between nearby and distant objects that one observes from above, or the concealment of layered things that a perspective drawing represents. "The riddle of depth," writes Merleau-Ponty, lies in the connection between these two views: "the fact that it is precisely because things disappear behind each other that I see them in place, [and] the fact that it is precisely because each is in its place that they are rivals for my gaze."[38] Depth is therefore not a "third dimension." If it were any dimension at all, writes Merleau-Ponty, it would be the first. "But a dimension which contains all others is not a dimension," at least not in the conventional Cartesian sense of measurement.[39] Depth is, furthermore, the dimension of human love and longing, hardly analogous to "perspective," an enigma made manifest by every human culture in its architecture and other significant artifacts.

Our spatiality is constructed with an up and a down, a left and a right, an in front and a behind, a near and a far. When nothing arrests our gaze, it carries a very long way. But if our gaze meets with nothing, it sees nothing. Space is itself also the obstacle, whether consisting of bricks or a "vanishing point." Properly understood, human space *is* limits, most clearly when it makes an angle, when it stops. There is nothing ghostly about space; it has edges. Human space is in fact all that is needed for the parallel lines of the straight road to meet *well short* of infinity; it is *not* Cartesian space.

* * *

Understanding fully the true nature of time consciousness for a living body is crucial in this discussion, for ultimately temporality and spatiality are intertwined in our primary experience of place. Reducing visual perception to a picture can be seen as the equivalent of eliminating time from the experience itself, producing a "lie," as Guarino Guarini already argued in the seventeenth century as he rejected the use of perspectival illusionistic frescoes in churches. This realization offers immediate challenges for architectural representation and a proper understanding of atmosphere.

In the phenomenological tradition, the point of departure for discussions on time consciousness is Edmund Husserl's observation that it would be impossible to experience "temporal objects," like a piece of music, if our consciousness of the present moment were the experience of a *punctum*, of an instantaneous "now" that is in fact never "here."[40] At a different level, there are temporal "syntheses of identity" at work in the experience of "permanent objects" (such as buildings) that are given to us as partial aspects, like when we walk or engage in a focal action in place. William James had also suggested that "the practically cognized present is no knife's edge," but rather operates like a block, a temporal expanse with a "bow and a stern."[41] Husserl's central contribution was to disclose the structure of the intentional processes that constitute the experience of a "thick" present moment. According to him, time consciousness has a threefold structure, including primal impression, protention (looking forward) and retention (looking back); these work together and cannot operate on their own; their unified operation underlies our experience of the present moment as having "temporal width." Husserl further distinguishes between retention as "primary memory" and recollection, or "secondary memory"; between protention, or "primary anticipation," and expectation, or "secondary anticipation." While primary protention and retention are "present," the secondary types of temporality are *re-presentational*; they are, properly speaking, memory (ultimately history, orienting reflective action) and foresight: our capacity to promise, which may become an architectural project. Husserl describes the "living present" as "standing-streaming." It "stands" because it does not move in or through time; as a structure of awareness it does not change or vary. Yet it also "streams" in that, as the continuous operation of primal impression-retention-protention, it underlies *all* appearances of flow, including that of consciousness itself as flow.[42]

According to Thompson, Husserl's description of the absolute flow or "standing-streaming" of the living present corresponds precisely to prereflective self-awareness (which is, as we have noted, anything but "unconscious"), an argument now corroborated by neuroscientists interested in the temporal dynamics of consciousness.[43] In the lived experience of architecture, while one is working or engaged in focal actions, place is first *given* in this mode. The contents of the present moment arise and perish at different rates, depending on the nature of things; some have more permanence, while others are inherently ephemeral. Buildings themselves are relatively permanent objects, stabilizing cultural memories; they can be judged through rational and even scientific criteria. The proper, primary temporality of architectural atmospheres, however, is not of this order. Rather, it is effectively kindred to music, addressing the primary prereflective and engaged bodily consciousness, framing *actions*, like ritual or work, articulated in a narrative program. We can also now better grasp why the concern with architectural meaning in the architectural treatises of the Western tradition was so emphatically connected to music, starting with Vitruvius's *eurhythmy* and including key concepts analyzed in previous chapters, such as harmony and temperance, and why romantic *Stimmung*, as in Novalis's "acoustics of the soul," retains this musicality.

It is crucial to emphasize how this differs from the living temporality at work in regard to objects, which is the one more easily apprehended by modern aesthetics, starting in the eighteenth century, when architecture became more firmly associated with the "fine arts." Buildings became "objects" to be experienced "out of time" as dispassionate, beautiful "compositions," or, at best, in the linear time of voyeuristic criticism or tourism, as keenly reported by visitors to ancient ruins during the 1700s; experience became aesthetic "judgment," connecting to emotions as mental associations, effectively bypassing the kinesthetic bodily senses and explaining its effects through Cartesian psychology. This understanding of architectural meaning came to fruition in the *parcours* deployed at the École des Beaux-Arts in the early nineteenth century to judge the value of projects and adjudicate prices, a precedent for the well-known devices used by modernist architects in the early twentieth century, and still often implemented in contemporary building design. Today, the concept of scientific time is at the root of the popular "fly-through," computer-generated presentations of building projects, and of the misplaced claims of the "dynamic" and "flowing" experiments in parametric design that freeze a frame from an algorithmically generated "changing" form, similar to Eadweard Muybridge's famous stop-motion photography of the nineteenth century. This is merely a "representation" of time that doesn't acknowledge the true nature of the lived present as described above. These cinematic representations and "flowing" buildings may therefore provide surprising experiences and "neat" effects, but amount to nothing more; they are not "cognitive" in the way that the emotional experiences in a narrative program, ritual, or piece of music, are interwoven with an "emplotted" whole.

In view of this we can speculate that architectural meaning, offered to our *presence*, unfolds in two different temporalities: one pertaining to the building as object, obviously imbued with relative permanence, and the other to the temporality of the event, more elusive yet primary. Form embodied in the materials that make up buildings is of immense importance in architecture, something that matters at the level of representation as it becomes *memory* and contributes a poetic image. I have written about this elsewhere and will summarize in the next chapter.[44] In regard to the configuration of atmospheres for focal actions, however, form matters in a different, arguably more fundamental way; it creates a stage whose properties, available to the inhabitants, both limit and make possible their actions and habits. While these communicative functions of architecture have traditionally been integrated, the reflection offered here becomes particularly relevant in our times of "divided representation,"[45] where symbolic representations of "world" are simply unattainable for a fragmented, cosmopolitan society.

Elaborating on Husserl's understanding of lived temporality, enactive cognitive science has identified the importance of emotions in relation to protention, which is manifested as desire, always unfulfilled in the living present, motivated by emotions in the environment. Thompson explains that human consciousness is *self-constituting* between retention, which falling into the past becomes *determined*, and protention, which appears open, the realm of freedom, pulled by the affective valence of the world.[46] Thus consciousness (mind *in* life) "makes its road while walking," to borrow a line from a famous Spanish poem by Antonio Machado. These words are used by Humberto Maturana and Francisco Varela to relate enactive cognition to problems of human evolution, beyond distinctions between culture and nature, and the well-trodden polarities of determinism and chance.[47] A lived world without affective valence—and this especially concerns the urban environment and architecture for twenty-first-century humanity—would significantly curtail a sense of purpose in human action.

This scientific analysis substantiates earlier philosophical insights by Maine de Biran and other romantic thinkers, most notably Husserl and Jan Patočka, relating emotion to intentionality: an impulse moving outward, as an arrow directed at a target, the way primary motor intentionality was described by Merleau-Ponty; "active" embodied perception. I must emphasize that this is already a form of knowing: the foundation of all knowledge, in fact, and not merely a secondary phenomenon. Thompson argues that there is a gradation of affection from the "affectively ineffective" to the "affectively salient," with various intermediate gradations.[48] This is a helpful articulation of the complex range of architectural experience for both prereflective and reflective consciousness. Trying to grasp how experience comes to be formed as one is affected precognitively, Husserl distinguishes between "passivity" and "receptivity." *Passivity* designates how one is involuntarily affected while engaged in some activity, for example the focal actions and rituals framed by architecture; while *receptivity* means responding to an involuntary affection by "noticing" the alluring "something" and even paying attention, such as the formal and material qualities of a building. The key point here is that ultimately, in both of these cases, *"affection" as the allure or pull of architecture does not refer to a causal stimulus-response relation, but to an intentional "relation of motivation" that must account for cultural grounds and habits.*

***

Neurobiology now recognizes the continuity of consciousness (sentience) in life, ranging from single-celled organisms to human self-consciousness. Despite obvious differences among different classes of biological entities, this realization is crucial: consciousness is not something "other" than life, like a "soul" added to our biology and which animals lack (as in Descartes's thought), but is actually inherent in life. The question is vast and certainly not our topic here. However, what I must stress is that in the case of humans, culture is no mere external addition or support to cognition; it is woven into the very fabric of each human mind from the outset. Symbolic culture, in particular the human linguistic, architectural, and urban environment, shapes the cognitive potentiality of the human mind. Stripped of culture, we would simply not have the cognitive capacities that make us human. It has been argued that socially isolated humans do not develop language or any form of symbolic thought and have no true symbols of any kind; such a human brain has no greater symbolizing power than that of an ape.[49] For this reason, among others, architecture cannot be simply mimetic of animal shelters, however clever, functional, or rational they may appear to us. Since the environment and the mind, human or animal, are deeply entangled, and specific bodily morphologies and environments shape their respective minds, there is a radical limitation to our "objectification" of the animal worlds, in the direction of biomimetism, for instance.[50] Neuroscientific evidence now indicates that experience-related brain activity, in particular environmental contexts, plays a major role in the development of the individual brain. Human architecture cannot be assumed to be simply driven by material or hedonistic factors, associated with psychotropic processes, and our human biological homeostasis (equilibrium) necessarily involves cultural issues, like our culturally framed sexuality and our awareness and openness to death.

Individual subjectivity is *from the outset* intersubjectivity, as a result of the communally handed down norms, conventions, symbolic artifacts, and cultural traditions in which an individual is already embedded.[51] While emerging from the world of perception, linguistic symbols create a break with sensorimotor representations.[52] This is the world of architectural communication, the real "context" of architectural endeavors, one that cannot be understood as being neatly divided into culture and nature, and presuming its objectivity for analysis through aesthetic rules or by means of mathematical languages. Human mentality arises from developmental processes of enculturation, beyond the dichotomy of "nature versus nurture."[53] The enculturation of the mind culminating in language acquisition is first made possible by empathy, a particular form of intentionality; a projection of the *feeling* kinesthetic body, ultimately allowing for recognition of myself through the other, feeling *as* the other. Empathy, we may recall, first appeared as a concept in nineteenth-century aesthetics, not surprisingly in conjunction with the identification of space as a question in art.[54] Merleau-Ponty, among others, has shown how empathy in the human child makes possible a prelinguistic understanding of moods and emotions, which, revealing the possibility of the other's perception of myself in reciprocity to mine, opens up "stable space" out of bodily, kinesthetic spatiality. This is a fundamental characteristic of human cognition at the root of linguistic communication—*the natural languages we speak*, which are the vehicle for the transmission of most cultural knowledge. In other words, since the subject is the outcome of a habitually structured interaction between the body and the environment, the reflective subject then emerges from the prereflective realm, a function of spoken language.[55] This *emerging language* of the first person that we are in our life stories is the language of emotions, perceptions, and feelings, a language articulated in myths and eventually formalized by literature and, as I will argue in the next chapter, crucial for architects in the act of design.

It will be useful to reiterate here the primary question we have been pursuing in slightly different words: how it may be possible for architecture and urban design, whose central vocation is form generation in the material world, to create attuned environments, *significant* settings for human life beyond the prevalent fixations with stylistic novelty (the pornographic impulse—desire as commodity) or pragmatic, technology-driven sustainability (the moralistic impulse—ethos as commodity) that often appear as dead ends, ultimately contributing to our general malaise. To grasp effective alternatives it has been crucial to establish that human *understanding* is first embodied and enactive,[56] evident in our competent behavior as evidenced in a multitude of quotidian situations. As Gallagher puts it, the body is already acting "before you know it."[57] One's body anticipates one's conscious experience; my hand shapes itself in the best possible way to grasp an object. This is not merely a deterministic behavior, however; free will is real but it involves deliberative consciousness, a feedback or looping that corresponds and is made possible by the thick dimensionality of the living present.[58] Thus, the Aristotelian insight that the human soul is the expression of the human body finds significant verification in contemporary scientific studies of human experience. "Before you know it, your body makes you human and sets you in a course in which your human nature is expressed in intentional action and in interaction with others."[59]

The fact that computers can solve mathematical problems doesn't justify imagining them as a model for human reasoning; we are neither metal and plastic nor digital.[60] Propositional thought is not the paradigm of mental life. Even a philosopher's analytical understanding is first and foremost embodied; his activity is not unlike a boxer's, a practical and skilled engagement, a "doing" in the world rather than merely a cogitating on it, even if what philosophers do is cogitate.[61] Thus, modern philosophers in the hermeneutic tradition, for example Ernesto Grassi and Hans-Georg Gadamer, have criticized analytic philosophies that pretend to dissociate propositional, syllogistic thinking from action. Grassi and Gadamer valorize instead the Aristotelian concept of *practical philosophy*, engaged and constructed from the bottom up, woven out of the polysemic, indicative, narrative living language of cultures. It bears noting that if authentic thinking is a mindful and embodied know-how, it has a bearing on well-grounded foresight, crucial for architectural and urban projects. It is at odds with instrumental know-how, one exclusively framed by logic and reduced to algorithmic languages, and the sole value of which is to efficiently enact some prior concept, robbing know-how of its potential wisdom and ethical sense.

Merleau-Ponty explains how I am my body, and how this body of mine is not for me like an external object. I move my hand to move a book; the act is intentional, but it is not the result of a prior intellectual intention causing an action. The knowledge involved in combing my hair, or that of a master organist arriving to play on an instrument that she has never seen before (with more keyboards or stops than the one she is used to at home) is not intellectual or reflective knowledge. Starting with proprioception and culminating in habit and skillful action, it is an embodied form of "knowing without knowing," challenging Cartesian duality and consisting in a capacity to act, tangled with what it knows.[62] This sensorimotor knowledge stabilizes primarily as *habits*. Habits eventually result in stable gestalts: mostly acquired flexible skills and competences, established yet always open to change.[63] All human actions share in the habitual. Habit is a trace left by actions. Present actions are shaped by habits, because previous actions have given rise to habits. Such actions are never deterministic but always situated in *place* and motivated by purpose and meaning.[64] Habits are not like mechanical reflexes; habits and agency imply plasticity for humans. Alva Noë states, "Habits are basic and foundational aspects of our mental lives. Without habit there is no calculation, no speech, no thought, no recognition, no game playing. Only a creature with habits like ours could have a mind like ours."[65] They are a form of practical understanding or know-how that manifests itself as competent and purposive action and attaches to the world by way of the meaning it discerns therein. The importance of the environment in general and of architecture in particular is obvious in this regard, as are the stakes involved in significant formal "innovation." Noë suggests that, paraphrasing Goethe, we think of the city as "frozen habit." Habits are neither intellectual knowledge nor involuntary action, but knowledge that is forthcoming through the body's motricity and effort.[66]

The body doesn't impose instincts upon humans, but it does develop action into stable dispositional tendencies.[67] In other words, the nature of human beings is their culture; patterns of behavior settle into that nature, which is a cultural world. Our environments are both physical (air, water, trees) and manmade (computers, airplanes, words). We don't just adapt to environments but adapt *them* through material culture. Even biological evolutionary traits, like our adult tolerance to lactose, are now believed to be the result of cultural preferences for milk and milk products. Furthermore, it would be a mistake to think that any form of animal intelligence (or instinct) can operate independently of a respective environment.[68] Shaun Gallagher is perhaps more emphatic in recovering for phenomenology an old intuition from "Aristotelian neurobiology": the soul is the form (*morphe*) of the body, literally its shape, with its inherent orientation (its upright posture, for example) upon which depend all its abilities, including cognition. Thus, the instantiation of the human soul in any other shape, animal, or computer, is simply impossible.[69] And the world for such embodied consciousness is not constructed as a mental image; rather, we "tune into it." Our animal-embodied nervous system "must be a self-tuning device,"[70] operating in a prereflective mode, which has to be aligned with our reflective understanding. This is how language and architecture must play a role.

The example cited earlier in this chapter of the soccer game in which we (as the players) are immersed, is not only a demonstration of the relationship between perception and action, but also an illustration of how human agents relate in the social world.[71] We don't first think objectively about the game, its "form" or "space" (or society); we are tuned into it in such a way that our very perception and action embodies its structure and logic. Nick Crossley concludes that both man and society have two poles, subjective and objective, yet always constituting a united whole. The player doesn't exist independently of the game and vice versa.[72] This means that neither absolute freedom nor simple determinism are useful concepts for characterizing the human condition. According to Merleau-Ponty, meaningful freedom presupposes choice and this, in turn, necessitates a prior engagement and belongingness to the world.[73] Such "situated" freedom is crucial to grasp the possibilities of significant architectural innovation. Radical novelty is almost impossible, or would appear to be without lasting value. We are free to change, but to be "new" whatever we propose must be "old"; it must refer to existing habits. Meaningful freedom presupposes choice, which in turn necessitates a prior engagement and belongingness to the world. Good architecture might thus offer such "situated" freedom. *The comprehensibility of architecture depends on acknowledging habits and framing them in new settings with appropriate atmospheres that may reveal limits and remain open to the ineffable.*

If culture is primarily habitual and this manifests itself as environment—if it is our "equipment," to use Heidegger's term—we can better grasp the reasons why Amsterdam and Venice are so different from Toronto. This is also why some architects and urban designers have come to appreciate the richness embedded in so-called slums or informal settlements that often reveal a better quality of life than that issuing from the more hygienic and efficient housing proposals of planners aimed at substituting them. The issue, however, is not merely one of material means and services, as if an informal settlement could simply "develop" to become a good city. As I will establish in the following pages, much more is at stake for the spiritual well-being of humanity. And yet, if historical cities are richer in moods and emotive atmospheres than modern cities, this has less to do with decisions of traffic engineers and planners than with the sedimented habits of cultures over longer or shorter historical periods.

There is no way that one individual, architect, or planner can subsume culture. This is a crucial aspect of our contemporary architectural crisis, one that has been brilliantly explained by Dalibor Vesely.[74] There are real limitations to the concept of the architect as "creator," imagining that his or her formal talent and skills may compensate for the flatness of our technological world. When habits sediment into environments that convey negative or hostile emotions, however, what is the architect to do? It is my belief that despite such limitations and with a clear understanding of the stakes, the architect must act in search of culturally specific poetic images, perhaps taking clues from expressive moments in contemporary art and literature, accepting the "experimental" nature of the search and perhaps even emulating the necessary "blow" which, Benjamin has argued, the artist must inflict on a complacent society. And yet again, this cannot amount to a mere search for novelty. A consideration of viable tools of representation for an architect in the creation of fitting moods and atmospheres is central to this concern.

* * *

The subject that inhabits and builds cities is the outcome of a habitually structured interaction between the body and the environment. The reflective subject emerges from the prereflective realm; *it is a function of speech, of natural language.*[75] Emergent speech breaks the silence of the perceptual world and spreads further layers of significance over it; it brings the subject into relationship with itself. Speech cannot be planned without speaking; it is originally a prereflective act that brings the subject and object of speech, the speaking subject, into being: an embodied activity, a corporeal technique that Alva Noë suggests may be closer to the grooming of chimpanzees than to the indicative character of semantics in reasoned discourse.[76] Languages are in fact gestural habits, the debris or sediments of the past communicative acts of a community, stored within the bodily schemas of the contemporary population.[77] Language embodies the shared practical sense of a society; it gives durable form to habits of perception, conception, and reflection that have formed within the group.[78] Yet speech is the medium of reflective thought.[79] Natural language is thus the appropriate way to negotiate enactive knowledge toward further action; as such, it is indispensable in driving the architectural project.

Speech and orality are primary.[80] This is language understood in a sense very different from that of conventional poststructuralist linguistics, a topic that will be developed in chapter 6. It is not an arbitrary or "constructed" system of signs but, rather, the emerging breath (air) that breaks the silence of the perceptual world and is capable of first giving shape to an atmosphere, disseminating another layer of significance over the world of perception. It is language as Vitruvius evokes it, as primary expression at the dawn of culture, emerging at the origins of architecture in that momentous occasion when humans, brought together by the need to keep a fire going, first assembled and *spoke*, contemplated the heavens, imitated nature, and then built their first dwellings.[81] Emerging language brings a subject into relationship with its self through an articulated story, which is a life lived; it allows for the recognition of the ethical self that (after about the age of four) recognizes itself as invariable and distinct every morning, despite the constant mutations in an individual's lived experience. It enables the "me" that is constructed in the web of narrative discourse and imaginative representation and that is distinct from the "I" that embodies and repeats its history in the form of habits.[82] This is the language that enables one to negotiate enactive knowledge toward further action, the language of ethical promises, such as architecture.

Heidegger has also explained that this emerging language "speaks through us,"[83] emphasizing that speech cannot be planned without speaking; it is originally a prereflective act that brings the subject and object of speech, the speaking subject, into being. As Merleau-Ponty explains:

the body materializes language by means of movement that is already expressive. (Even in primates there is evidence of expressive movement.) Speech language is an embodied activity, a bodily technique. Thus, in continuity with gesture, "speech is the body of reflective thought, its flesh."[84] Languages are the debris or sediments of the past communicative acts of a community, stored within the corporeal schemas of the contemporary population—they are gestural habits that can therefore be grasped through reflection and placed in the service of poetic and ethical making.

Linguistic habits are practical. Words are not primarily concepts, as understood by conventional linguistics, but tools for interaction; we learn language by learning to do things with words.[85] Heidegger has suggested that the word is originally a poetic utterance, and only later flaunts its capacity to emulate mathematics, arguing "truths as correspondence" through syllogisms.[86] In *Rhetoric as Philosophy*, Ernesto Grassi, one of Heidegger's eminent students, emphasizes the crucial role of emerging language, constituted from the bottom up in cultures.[87] Tracing an alternative trajectory to "scientific philosophy," starting from Aristotle's "practical philosophy" and his understanding of truth as *phrónesis* (prudence or wisdom), through Cicero, Renaissance humanist writers (including Leon Battista Alberti), Giambattista Vico, and twentieth-century phenomenological hermeneutics, he demonstrates how it is only through this sort of emerging language (and its storytelling) that one can truly grasp human truths to formulate strategies for ethical action and embrace effective communication in aesthetics. Any creative act that, like much modernist architecture, tries to avoid natural language and its archetypal expressive function would be doomed to failure; avoiding natural language is tantamount to avoiding thought; early functionalism and contemporary design through algorithms cannot be appropriate substitutes.

***

We have established that speech derives from gestural communication, both being largely forms of emotional expression.[88] The deep continuity between language and emotion must be emphasized. Given the central role played by emotion in attuned architecture, this continuity will be important for our discussion on language in chapter 6. And emotions like love, hate, or anger are not "inner realities" or psychic facts, they are types of behavior, styles of conduct, *visible from the outside*. They exist on the face and on gestures, not behind them. One "reads" anger directly, immediately—it is unmediated by intellectual thought.[89] The gesture of the other moves me or fails to do so because we share collective habits of emotion; they are culturally grounded. Emotions, we should recall, are ways of being-in-the world, bodily transformations, which operate at a prereflective level.

Giambattista Vico was among the first to suggest that our initial human speech acts were poetic utterances, the language of *mythos*, a "mute" poetics in continuity with the gestures of rituals, rather than the language of prose. While language is affective, perhaps primarily a manner of "singing the world," expressing the emotional attitudes of members of society toward the world and a "style" of living by a culture, it obviously allows us to grasp the world by condensing and mapping it; it is our primary tool of cognition.[90] To learn a language is to enter the symbolic milieu of a group; new creative significations perpetually burst forth and then sediment; living languages are never stable codes established once and for all.[91] Speech and thought are inseparably intertwined sides of the same coin. *Language is the body of thought and thus its means of real existence.*

It is therefore not unreasonable to claim that a thoughtful and emotional architecture must be grounded in metaphoric language; bypassing it in the process of design and replacing it with visual styles or parameters is always problematic, particularly in view of the all-too-evident limitations inherent in the representational tools of architecture since early modernity. As I have suggested, the most common outcomes of this condition are cities organized as traffic networks, populated by buildings that are no more than technological shelters, ideological signs, or solipsistic sculptural forms. Indeed, if Giorgio Agamben is correct, the aim of architecture—attuned atmospheres, or *Stimmung*—lies precisely at the point of articulation between embodiment (in the form of habits) and language (which brings them to awareness and reveals their full affective and cognitive value), between *zoon* and *logon*. The challenge in the following chapter will be to explore more widely the nature of *emerging* language and how forms of linguistic expression may intersect with the better-known tools of architectural and urban design.

6
The Linguistic Dimension of Architecture: Attunement and the Poetic Word

In the preceding pages, I hope to have established the primary connections at work between natural language and *Stimmung* in embodied consciousness. At this point, I would like to explore further the phenomenology of language, unpacking its potential for architectural design. Our entry point will be a clarification of the divergences and connections between the "language of architecture" proper and the language through which the architect may represent his or her intentions in the design of attuned environments. Both aspects are complex, and much confusion arises from both a misunderstanding of the nature of language itself (obviously still a highly debated issue among linguists, philosophers, philologists, media theorists, and cognitive scientists) and the expectations commonly associated with the products of our technological civilization. The result has been a reluctance to consider the possibilities of poetic language in the design process, while privileging functional, typological, stylistic, or parametric strategies. Natural language is marginalized to operate at best as the language of rational consensus in architect-client negotiations, or serving as the "specifications" in traditional hands-on construction or the language of industry standards in more recent technological fabrication.

Furthermore, even in cases where modern and contemporary architects have pursued interests in narrative and associated architecture with language, fundamental assumptions have usually been drawn from Saussurian semiotics and Derridian poststructuralism. Strikingly, these assumptions also underscore the otherwise positive recent trend in cultural studies to consider art and architecture as "media" communicating in multiple registers, yet often limited and misleading in their characterization of architectural "messages" as mostly ideological. Such top-down constructivist theories of language will be shown to be at odds with the concept of emerging language in phenomenology and hermeneutics. Regarding languages as ultimately arbitrary codes more or less independent of lived experience and built upon a misconception concerning the nature of lived temporality (as explained in the last chapter), constructivist theories prioritize writing over orality as the primary modality of meaning. Transferred to the realm of architecture, such theories fail to do justice to the human experience of communicative settings for action in the lived present.

I. The Voices (*Stimme*) of Architecture

In *The Bow and the Lyre*, his remarkable study on the nature of poetry, Octavio Paz explains why it is no accident that critics speak of "plastic" or "musical languages" and extend the notion of the poetic beyond the crafting of poems. As soon as brute sounds or colors are perceived by human consciousness (remember—perception is action) and touched by human hands, their nature changes and they enter a linguistic horizon, becoming the materials for works. As Paz summarizes: "And all works end as meaning; whatever man touches is tinged with intentionality."[1] The human world is a world of meaning, one that "tolerates ambiguity, contradiction, madness, or confusion, but not lack of meaning."[2] Frank Wilson writes succinctly: "Language is not just words, semantics, syntax. It is also melody, and sometimes it is a dance. Sometimes, as in the deaf, it is a silent dance of the hands. It is a voice, a face, and the words between the lines. It is a small carved object, a submarine, a chair, underarm odor, a hairdo, a chant, a puff of smoke from the Vatican chimney."[3] For Paz, there is a fullness of meaning in the vertical thrust of a Gothic church, in the "tense balance of a Greek temple, the roundness of the Buddhist stupa or the erotic vegetation that covers the walls of the sanctuaries of Orissa. All is language."[4]

While there are profound differences among the "languages" of the arts and spoken language, in all cases we find "expressive systems endowed with significative and communicative force."[5] Paz observes how architectural or sculptural systems relate to their respective spoken languages, whereby it is much easier, for example, to translate Aztec poems into their architectural or sculptural analogues than into Spanish or French, or surrealist paintings into surrealist poems rather than into cubist paintings. The reason for this is to be found in the very nature of *poetic* language, which is the manner in which such works convey their significance. Paz reminds us that today we valorize the prose of univocal meaning, implying reflection and analysis, which nevertheless involves an unattainable ideal, because the word refuses to be mere concept, bare meaning: "In prose the word tends to be identified with one of its possible meanings, at the expense of the others." In fact, Paz suggests, "this is an analytical operation and is not performed without violence, since the word possesses a number of latent meanings, it is a certain potentiality of senses and directions."[6]

It is therefore important to repeat that, contrary to common assumptions, *poetic language is original language*; my use of the qualifier *original* here encompasses the sense of language as a "natural" and "emergent" phenomenon. Merleau-Ponty devoted an important segment of his body of work to explaining how human natural language can be understood as part of the flesh of the world. He explains: "All perception, and all action which presupposes it ... every human use of the body, is already *primordial expression*. This means that perception is not derivative ... but the primary operation which first constitutes signs as signs."[7] Like movement, gesture is a prereflective performance, but the expressive movement on which language depends is also different from others organized primarily by bodily motor intentionality, actions aimed at achieving a particular end.[8] A gesture that signifies the picking up of a glass depends to some extent on the fact that the gesture serves an entirely different purpose than the actual grasping—a cognitive and possibly communicative function that requires the generation and expression of meaning. The relevant feedback from an interlocutor will not be proprioceptive but, rather, cognitive and linguistic.[9] Thus the body materializes language by means of movement that is already expressive. Insofar as it involves an "open and indefinite power of giving significance," language transforms and transcends the natural powers of the body without leaving the body behind.[10] Expressive movement doesn't convey something internal and already formed, like a thought, a belief, or an idea. It *is*, instead, like language and gesture, "the subject's taking up a position in the world of his meanings."[11] The relationship between language and embodiment is self-organizing and self-reciprocating only if there is another person. The body generates a gestural expression; it is, however, the other person who moves, motivates, and mediates this process.[12]

We can therefore understand why what one culture produces has a meaning for another culture, even if it is not the original meaning, both synchronically and diachronically. "If it is characteristic of the human gesture to signify beyond its simple factual existence and to inaugurate meaning, it follows that every gesture is *comparable* to others."[13] Arising from a single syntax, each gesture is both beginning and continuation, never opaque or enclosed like a circumscribed event. Moreover, the human gesture is not only a possibility simultaneous with all other expressive efforts, it also assumes a structure within them in the built world, including architecture; and especially in the case of architecture, its trace remains and its heritage is transmitted. As such, it is the essence of the architectural gesture, once made, to modify the situation of the universal enterprise in which we are all engaged. "Once the work is finished, it constructs new signs from signs, putting new significations at our disposal, and expands culture the way a new organ might expand our bodily capacities."[14]

Given its origins in embodied consciousness, "Language leads us to the things themselves to the precise extent that it *is* signification before *having* a signification.[15] In an essay entitled "Indirect Language and the Voices of Silence," Merleau-Ponty writes that language more closely resembles a type of being than a means to an end; it does not presuppose its table of correspondence, but unveils its secrets itself. Precisely in its self-referentiality it is a "monstration": comparable to a universe. Since our language is *not* the translation or cipher of an original text, *complete* expression is nonsensical. All language is indirect and allusive—it is, if you will, deeply akin to silence.[16] Even in everyday speech, every language is subject at each moment to the twin but contrary demands of expressivity and uniformity.[17] This is why language is "completely accidental and completely rational."[18] There is no such thing as "definitive expression"; for something to be said, it must not be said absolutely.

To speak is not to put a word to every thought; if it were, nothing would ever be said.[19] "Language signifies when instead of copying thought it lets itself be taken apart and put together again by thought"; it "bears the meaning of thought as a footprint signifies the movement and effort of a body."[20] In this essay, Merleau-Ponty also elaborates on the distinctions between the empirical "already established" language (our common prose) and its creative, literary use.[21] He argues that empirical language, famously described by Mallarmé as "worn coin," can only result from creative language and its capacity to render *l'absent de tous les bouquets*, which is silence for empirical language. *This is of course the central paradox: poetic or literary language demands great work, and yet to merit its status (as opposed to mere contrivance or innovation) it must also be akin to humanity's original utterance.* It goes without saying that language is oblique and autonomous, and that its ability to signify a thought or a thing directly *is only a secondary power* derived from the inner life of language.[22] Like a weaver, the writer works on the wrong side of his material. He has only to do with language, and thus he suddenly finds himself surrounded by meaning. In other words, language is neither primary nor secondary to meaning; it is not meaning's servant, and yet it does not govern meaning.[23]

Merleau-Ponty explicitly examines how the algorithm and the analytic prose it inspires comprise "a revolt against language in its existing state."[24] This observation is crucial for my critical arguments in this book directed at the modus operandi favored by architects in the last two centuries. Refusing the confusions of everyday language, the algorithm is "an attempt to construct language according to the standard of truth, to redefine it to match the divine mind ... to tear speech out of history."[25] Drawing further implications from this insight, Merleau-Ponty in "The Phenomenology of Language" explains how the universality we desire from communication is only accessible through the specific given languages we learn to speak—and not from some ideal Esperanto, a transparent articulation of fact.[26] This observation is obviously valid for all expressive systems, including architecture, dooming its efforts to generate meaningful forms from the reduction of "variables" in the world of experience to algorithms.

What is necessary, instead, is an understanding that organized signs have their immanent meaning, which does not arise from the "I think" but from the "I am able to," a function of enactive consciousness.[27] The "action at a distance by language," bringing significations together as we speak without ever exhausting them, is a case of corporeal intentionality: embedded in the prereflective dimensions of consciousness, even as we utter discursive thoughts.[28] Thus the spoken word (uttered or heard) is pregnant with a meaning that can be grasped in the very texture of the linguistic gesture—a hesitation, a shift in intonation, can change everything—and yet is never contained in that gesture. Every expression appears as a trace, it has a degree of opacity, while, in contrast, ideas are given to a person in transparency. It is interesting to observe that when a word is written, the trace seems to vanish; the impression is created that the word *is* the transparent idea, and that something is lost (even if the sign may later be reactivated by a reader's act of interpretation).

It should be emphasized that in architectural settings (atmospheres) articulated by frozen gestures (buildings) and not words or discourse, the primary receptor is the prereflective consciousness of the inhabitant *in action*, with indications of discursive meanings encoded in formal iconography and narratives that constitute the program. Signification arouses speech as the world arouses one's body. The gesture is a "significative intention" or determinate gap—even if it later fructifies in "thoughts."[29] A fundamental fact of expression is "a surpassing of the signifying by the signified which it is the very virtue of the signifying to make possible."[30]

As a primary modality of language, speech "is that moment in which the significative intention (still silent and wholly in act) proves itself capable of incorporating itself into my culture and the culture of others—of shaping me and others by transforming the meaning of cultural instruments. It becomes 'available' in turn because in retrospect it gives us the illusion that it was contained already in the available significations, whereas by a sort of ruse it espoused them only in order to infuse them with new life."[31] Merleau-Ponty emphasizes that, for this very reason, phenomenology can be said to envelop philosophy, since the object's relationship to subjects in idealistic philosophy is radically questioned.[32] This is particularly the case for speech and expression in general: its phenomenology *is* its philosophy. Phenomenology is all or nothing. That order of instructive spontaneity—the body's "I am able to," the "intentional transgression" that gives us others, the "speech" that gives us the notion of an ideal or absolute signification—cannot be subsequently placed under the jurisdiction of a pancosmic consciousness without becoming meaningless again.[33] Conveyed most succinctly in defiance of the semiotic model, the central phenomenon of language is *the common act of the signifying and the signified*.[34]

***

In a primarily physiognomic lived world, with the characteristics of its *presence* to consciousness as described in previous chapters, and in view of this brief introduction to the phenomenology of language, the meaning of architecture—a building, garden, or ephemeral artifact that frames human actions—is best understood as a form of gestural speech. While obviously possible, the analogy of architecture with objectified writing, emphasizing its capacity to last through time, is subsidiary, and can be misleading when believed to fully subsume meaning. It is interesting to recall the insightful association that Vitruvius makes between the origins of human speech and architecture in the celebrated passage in book 2.[35] The emergence of speech among primitive humans that can both wonder at the poetic beauty of the starry heavens and keep a fire under control is coemergent with human dwelling, the beginnings of architecture. Walter Ong, Ernesto Grassi, and David Abram have eloquently demonstrated the primacy of orality in human cultures.[36] The issue is obviously not to advocate orality as a permanent state of culture; literacy revealed possibilities to the word and to human existence unimaginable without writing, yet orality was able to produce works like the *Odyssey*, beyond the reach of the literate members of society. Nor is orality ever eradicable: reading a text oralizes it; real, effective understanding depends on a reader's *dialogue* with an absent author; and both orality and literacy have proven indispensable to the evolution of consciousness.[37] With its intensely animistic or participatory frame of mind, orality is the form of awareness that has shaped human communication for more than 95 percent of humanity's presence in the biosphere. Even within the European tradition, reading was always enacted as vocalized utterance; reading aloud was the norm well into the eighteenth century. While the technologies of alphabetic writing and architectural representation that originally developed in early classical Greek culture eventually transformed human consciousness and its relationship to the outside world, the oral primacy of our linguistic capacities is important for our discussion.

Architecture speaks in many registers. If speech involves sounds, then it follows that architecture can speak literally, for example in the manner in which Vitruvius imagines the classical theater served as a resonant vessel for the harmonious articulated sounds and music of drama.[38] This is the acoustic character of atmospheres, understood since the very beginning of the Western tradition. But as I have emphasized, Vitruvius mainly addresses harmony as it applies to the experience of architecture as a whole, and relates it to the problem of proportions. I have alluded to the multiple misconceptions that result when we identify the problem as merely one of formal composition of buildings and their elements. The real issue is, rather, how the theater as fabric is resonant with the event that it is designed to house; the building thus "speaks" harmoniously, creating the appropriate moods that are conducive to the cathartic experience intended by the dramatic actions and by the melodic and rhythmic dimension of the drama with the ultimate aim of orientation and psychosomatic health—an epiphany of beauty that is also an incentive to a just and ethical life. It is not a question of literal acoustics but of emotions, understood through the basic (embodied) metaphoric dispositions of human consciousness.[39]

Phenomenology has argued that things "speak" to us, that perception is by definition meaningful—the world is expressive, and this is because we have human speech; this is *our* nature, distinct from other animal forms of communication and yet part of the animate earth and its multiple creatures. Indeed, our speech being our "nature" also belongs to wider Nature. Divinities in polytheistic traditions are embodied in natural forces and objects, and men used to "talk" to them. The environing world is expressive, and our ancestors could easily listen to it and "understand" it by engaging all interwoven sensory modalities—including, of course, sight—in a manner that resembles "reading." Hieroglyphic, pictographic, and ideographic writing systems established a distance from primary orality, but still maintained a link to the expressiveness of the world at large; functioning as "windows" to the external world. This relationship became more distant after the invention of alphabetic writing, with its capacity to objectify and freeze the voice of speech. Using a pertinent metaphor, Abram calls phonetic letters "mirrors" as opposed to "windows," reflecting back on human consciousness, and eventually making possible the monotheistic religions "of the Book."[40]

It is in terms of human language, its ambivalence and consubstantiality with our flesh, that we "understand" all communicative acts. Similarly, architecture speaks to us; an office building may make me tense, or I may relax in a sensuous environment. Abram has suggested that for primarily oral cultures prior to the hegemony of monotheistic religions, prayer was tantamount to speaking "to" things (rather than about things). Reciprocally, after Nietzsche and in the wake of monotheisms, we may perhaps imagine how any architecture that speaks to us may be an invitation to commune with the spiritual. Such architecture, beyond conventional distinctions between sacred and profane space, may reveal an "ongoing transcendence wherein each sensible thing is steadily bodying forth its own active creativity. … Like the spell quietly cast on a garden by a blossoming tree."[41] I will expand on these thoughts in chapter 8.

It is often said that architects make drawings (or models), not buildings. In a previous chapter I qualified this potentially misleading assumption—sometimes mistakenly believed to operate throughout the history of our discipline—and I will return to questions of representation in the next chapter. However, it's helpful to recall here that Vitruvius indeed first spoke of "architectural ideas" as *ichnographia*, *orthographia*, and *sciographia*, the inscriptions we readily identify with "plan," "elevation," and "profile drawing," which may have been mostly engraved in situ, yet are a reference to a tradition of *writing* (*graphein*) that, while initially pictographic, was already associated with the new forms of alphabetic writing in the Greco-Roman cultural world. The term *idea* (or *form*) in Plato's philosophy, at the origins of Vitruvius's formulation, is visually based, and it unwittingly signals a rejection of the old world of oral culture, epitomized by the archaic poets. Plato himself linked the technology of writing with death and with the destruction of memory, a paradox in view of the fact that the deadness of the text, its removal from the living lifeworld, makes it accessible to a potentially infinite number of living readers. The word in Greek and Latin alphabetic writing externalizes the voice and makes it objective, while the Platonic *chóra* is both the space of architectural representation and the matrix that makes possible the connection through the word (as *gráphein*) between the designated ideal and the specificity of lived objects. It epitomizes for Plato the very potential for meaning to emerge in the space of human culture (the ideal chair *in* the very particular chair in front of us), the reason why the things of the world "speak" to us and nothing is meaningless. Thus the *architectural idea* functions like the written word in a script, and, despite its indicative propensities, we can recognize that the "images" originate in our linguistic consciousness, in the primacy of speech as man's natural mediation: the speech of everyday language, distinct from that "special case" which is indicative language; the particular, unambiguous sort of language of analogy (rather than metaphor) that today we take for granted as language *tout court*.

On this basis, it is possible to argue in favor of the possibilities of the poetic as an attribute of architecture. The physical elements of architecture, its form and materials, textures and colors, have both the capacity for communication, creating attuned atmospheres framing and enhancing habits and meaningful action, and for the revelation of "something else." In Paz's words, such materials in a poetic work, regardless of its nature, refuse mere utility to become "bridges to another shore, doors that open on another world of meanings inexpressible by means of ordinary language."[42] That is, the poetic work conveys sense and transmits it, and yet it is something that is beyond language. "But [in a poem] that thing beyond language can only be reached through language":[43] it is the poetic image that is brought into being by what seems to be a paradoxical and contradictory operation at the heart of all artistic creation; *its ultimate cognitive function becomes the ineffable*: an openness to mystery which is the eloquence of silence, the fullness of emptiness. For Gaston Bachelard, the poetic image never duplicates present reality, nor is it merely an echo of the past; rather, it "reverberates" in the reader's consciousness and leads her to create anew.[44] Paraphrasing Merleau-Ponty: precisely because it comes to dwell in the world in which it makes us at home though we do not hold the key to it, the work of art and architecture teaches us to see and makes us think as no analytic work can.[45]

What seems hazardous or ambiguous and irreducible to a single theme in great works of art and architecture is not a weakness to be overcome. Ambiguity is inherent in language, and the "price we must pay to have a conquering language which, instead of limiting itself to pronouncing what we already know, introduces us to new experiences" that can never be only ours, so that language "destroys our prejudices."[46] We would never see any new landscapes or urban environments if our eyes did not give us the means of catching, questioning, and shaping patterns of space and color hitherto unseen. "We would not accomplish anything if our body did not enable us to leap over all the neural and muscular paths of locomotion in order to reach our projected goal."[47] It is in the same brief, imperious fashion, often without transitions or preparations, that the architect offers us a new world. Just as our body guides us among things only on the condition that we stop analyzing them in order to use them, so, too, architectural forms and places can offer new possibilities only on the condition that we make common cause with them, that we stop examining their origins in order to follow where they are going, that we allow the means of expression in a building to envelop us in that haze of signification that derived from its particular arrangement, and, finally, that we let the whole work veer toward a second-order tacit value where it may speak through a mute radiance.[48]

The essential meaning in both literature and architecture is initially perceptible as a *coherent deformation* imposed on the visible and the habitual.[49] Prior to any semantic signification, our experience is transformed when gripped by a transforming atmosphere, *atmós*, either in the textual spaces of a poem or novel or the *emplacement* of a building, even by the way a figure, volume, or space acquires a new shape with the addition of an extra line.[50] Today's architecture, even though it is possible only through its past, denies history deliberately to be free of it, responding to Paz's definition of modernity as "a tradition against itself." Today's architecture can only forget the past; it is "condemned" to perpetual experimentalism—more about this below. The ransom it pays for its novelty is that, in making what came before it appear to be unsuccessful, it foreshadows another architecture that tomorrow will make the present appear failed as well. Thus, architecture often presents itself as an abortive effort to say something that still remains to be said.[51] The architect unwillingly or unwittingly accommodates and destroys cultural mores, often all at the same time, an act that only awakens half-dead significations. Each new work of architecture occurs in the world inaugurated by the first dwelling: the public space of communication around the fire or the first mimetic hut. But it does not contain the past in a manifest state; it is a memory for us only if we also know the history of architecture.

***

I explained in chapter 2 how Vitruvius described the importance of the mathematical and linguistic disciplines (the liberal arts) as contributing to the communicative potential of the architect's work. He could take for granted the congruent and complementary functions of mathematical analogy (proportion—*dispositio* with all its subcategories, namely *symmetría* and *eurhythmia*) and rhetorical tropes (metaphor, crucial for the weaving of stories—the basis of décor) as being simply different modalities of natural language, which he understood as essentially poetic. Indeed, *dispositio* itself, emblematic of the ultimate aim of architectural order, was a term he likely imported from rhetoric that originally applied to the composition and arrangement of sentences in discourse. Both the mathematical analogies and their linguistic counterparts were crucial in the creation of communicative settings appropriate to specific cultural programs. They enabled the production of order on the earthly plane through architectural ideas believed to be mimetic of the cosmos by virtue of their geometric and mathematical properties, materialized as structures clad with appropriate ornament. While allowing for a healthy (just and beautiful) life, this also made possible the creation of a poetic image—the "stereoscopic effect" of a metaphor stating "this" (sublunary *urbs* and architecture) is "that" (harmonic supralunary cosmos). This coincidence of opposites allowed for similarity to be apprehended in spite of and through difference.

The condition of continuity between natural language and mathematics was generally preserved in the architectural discourses and practices of European cultures until the end of the baroque period. Only after the Enlightenment did geometry and mathematics definitively lose their culturally sanctioned symbolic capacities to become formal sciences, capable of algebraization and intrumentalization—eventually giving rise to non-Euclidean geometries.[52] Elsewhere I have shown that Durand's writing constitutes the first instance in architectural theory where geometry became plainly and simply an instrument for efficiency devoid of its traditional symbolic qualities.[53] His mathematization of design processes is still with us in all our contemporary fashions and infatuations with the computer. I have explained how city planners prevailed over architects and urban designers, adopting the values of engineers in the service of political power and economic expediency; reason, utility, and efficiency became the determining factors of the physical environment. If needed, they were assumed to communicate clear semantic messages (usually ideological, concerning religious or national identity in the nineteenth century) unencumbered by emotional intentionality.

Thus the relationship between algorithmic "languages" and natural language was forever altered. Algorithmic languages became the triumphant language of science, technology, and instrumentality; they "made things happen" and radically changed the physical world, while the poetic was pushed aside as an illegitimate aspiration to knowledge. Rather than mutually contributing to meaning, these two mediations of reality pulled in opposite directions, best expressed in Merleau-Ponty's famous formulation quoted above: algorithmic language (a language reduced to grammar) is in frank opposition to natural language. We have already examined the romantic reaction to this condition. Out of this juncture, architecture inherited its fundamental and prevailing dilemma: on the one hand, the incapacity of geometries to generate intersubjective meaning, while the tools for attaining formal complexity and novelty become ever more powerful through the computer; on the other, the imperative of aesthetic experimental innovation in search of appropriate forms for an ever-evolving world culture, whose normative dynamics is to be a "tradition against itself."

The latter imperative, seemingly at irreconcilable odds with the values transpiring from this book, bears further clarification. Confronted by the inability of traditional (classical) forms and processes to engage new materials and express modern values after the French and industrial revolutions, the modern architect has had no option but to "experiment," engaging creative processes to develop novel forms. Generally ignoring the origins of poetic expression in natural language as we have sketched above, trying as well to respond to the new cultural expectations for direct and unambiguous expression, architecture affirmed its autonomy through its associations with the pragmatic values of engineering or through syntactic (stylistic) formal composition. It thus has suffered during the last two centuries from either the banality of functionalism (an architecture that attests to its own process) or from the limitations of potential solipsism and near nonsense, the syndrome of "architecture made for architects." This has prolonged the crisis—even, some would claim, the agony of the discipline. Yet both the need for continuing formal exploration in a fluid and changing world *and* the fundamental existential questions to which architecture traditionally answered—the profound necessity for humans to inhabit a resonant world they may call home, even when separated by global technological civilization from an innate sense of place—remain as pressing as always. Like other artistic disciplines engaged in poetic making—a making that attempts not imposition but disclosure, architecture must propose the revelation of something that is "already there" and is therefore familiar to a culture while also being new. As Franz Schubert reportedly claimed, "to compose a good song you choose a melody that everyone recognizes but that no one has heard before."

Mallarmé is unquestionably the poet who most lucidly reflected on the paradoxes inherent in the realization of poetic work in modernity. His poetry is primarily "about" words, taking full account of the irreversible transformations between the traditional and nineteenth-century worlds. His insights partially stem from the same romantic sources in Eastern thinking that we evoked in chapter 3. He writes: "Having discovered Nothingness, I have found the Beautiful."[54] Marcel Proust refers to this awareness as the black marble on which Mallarmé's images of things are reflected. Thus, according to Roberto Calasso, his poetry, which does not state things but, rather, resonances of things, is nevertheless not self-referential. We do not only think in words, as if these were arbitrary semantic signs, self-identical across languages and in every utterance; rather, words are "like archipelagos scattered in the ocean which is the mind," and the mind is embodied and *in* the world. Yet, for contemporary instrumental culture, "to recognize this sea in the mind seems to be something forbidden."[55]

Inaugurating for modernity the insights into the primacy of poetic language we have already discussed through Paz, Mallarmé provocatively argued that "prose doesn't exist; that everything is verse, that human consciousness is a 'rhythmical knot.'"[56] Besides supporting our rhythmic consciousness and activities, consciousness (in its broad post-Cartesian sense, embodied and in place, as defined in chapter 5) puts us in contact with the divine. And this has nothing whatsoever to do with either an acceptance of religious dogma or a quest for novelty in art (or architecture) that flaunts its self-referentiality. However, what seems clear is that a correspondence between style and society, emerging from the bottom up, is no longer possible: "Above all what has gone is the unquestionable notion that in a society with neither stability nor unity one cannot create a stable art, a definitive art." Hence "the restlessness of minds," "the unexplained need for individuality of which contemporary literary [and architectural] manifestations are the direct reflection."[57] Style can (finally) escape from society, opening up a "land of rhythmical knots." At the same time, Mallarmé rejects the cavalier posturing of the avant-garde against history: "I cannot see, and this remains my firm opinion, that anything that was beautiful in the past is cancelled out by this."[58]

Writing in the mid-twentieth century, Canadian literary critic Northrop Frye also insisted on the inevitable self-referentiality of modern poetry. Yet he also explained that "the unity of the poem is a unity of mood … poetic images express or articulate the mood. The mood is the poem, not something else behind it ... what it says is always different from what it means."[59] Referential meaning is recovered at the deepest and most significant level, beyond the ordinary meaning of "words," precisely because what one "says" (both words and emotions) is what one means. *Moods are "semantic."* The dilemma opened up by self-referentiality as characterized by Frye is indeed artificial once one considers the insights of phenomenology and contemporary cognitive science. Emotion in poetry (and architecture) is "linked with the object." As Mikel Dufrenne writes, poetic sadness is "felt as a quality in the world." "To feel is to experience a feeling as a property of the object, not as a state of my being."[60] Much more recently, Alva Noë has argued that the feelings conveyed by moods have an ontological status different from the relationship at a distance characterized by *concept*; they facilitate *participation* in things.[61]

Merleau-Ponty echoes this understanding when he asserts: "It is certainly correct to condemn formalism ... [yet] formalism's error is not that it overestimates form but that it esteems it for so little that it abstracts it from meaning. ... The true opposite of formalism is a good theory of speech that distinguishes speech from any technique or device. Speech is not a means in the service of an external end. It contains its own ebbing, its own rule of usage and vision of the world, the way a gesture reveals the whole truth about a man."[62] It is in this sense that architecture must be a form of speech, arguably the explicit aim of Boullée's *architecture parlante*, which largely fell on the deaf ears of his modern and contemporary successors.

***

Indeed, architects and designers today usually bypass spoken and poetic words, considered imprecise and subjective, incapable of unambiguously guiding the hand of the creator from conception to realization. In our technological world it is easy to imagine that the only legitimate kind of language is one that speaks unambiguously, where sign and signified correspond like a mathematical equation, in a fixed one-to-one relationship. The languages we use in everyday speech don't have this character, and humans in a technological civilization tend to ascribe to this condition many problems associated with misunderstandings and subjective opinions. Curiously, the main characteristic of technological, instrumental "languages," easily reduced to digitized information, coincides with the nature of Adamic language, a language to which humans (in the

Judeo-Christian tradition) were supposed to have had access before their fall from grace and their expulsion from Paradise. God created the universe by naming, particularly as rendered in the Christian New Testament, and humans today believe that the instrumental relationship between the algorithm and the fabricated object is the only possible model for language. This dominant view overlooks the kenotic potential also inherent in Christianity (and present in other world religious traditions) in which God is seen to create by "emptying" Himself, for example, in the case of Christ, by becoming mortal. A secularized kenotic view of creation, one open to situations and conditions and responsible to Others, has been adopted by Gianni Vattimo as the most viable attitude to avoid arrogant imposition of values and political violence in a postmodern world.[63]

The initial conceptions of architecture as grammatical style date from the early nineteenth century,[64] a position taken up by art history and uncritically embraced by modernism as well, in its attempts to liberate itself from the determinism of "function," and still fervently espoused by Peter Eisenman and his many direct or unwitting disciples the world over. Eisenman has often flaunted the "self-referentiality" of architecture as its greatest potential, conceptualizing architecture as a formal object, deliberately ignoring its relationships to the life it houses and frames. It is not surprising that younger architects interested in digital form generation have found this position fertile. Yet, despite the apparent successes of such instrumentalizing of "language" through digital implementations in architecture, it is easy to argue that most resulting architecture has little or no resonance with places and cultural values.

As I have explained, however, nothing in human experience is meaningless—and that complicates and clouds the issue for architects in the quest for appropriate tactics and ethics in design. Digital novelties issuing from complex geometries and flows are rather short-lived thrills, ultimately becoming as trite as intentionally utilitarian buildings. John Keats insightfully observed that "Poetry should be great and unobtrusive, a thing which enters into one's soul, and does not startle or amaze it with itself, but with its subject."[65] It could be argued that in architecture the subject is not a building, but the meaningful event made present: life itself. This immediately points to the limitations of any position that regards architecture's aim as that of "aesthetic" object.

The concept of architecture as autonomous grammar or aesthetic object is intimately related to the nature and limitations of the tools of representation used in producing modern buildings, starting with Durand's "mechanism of composition," and made increasingly efficient through digital media. It is also congruent with the belief in the "image" as reductive and substitutive: the top-down concept guiding the production of technical images that is at odds with the bottom-up reality of spoken languages. It is no exaggeration to say that the very possibility of communicating anything that matters to us as humans, depends on our able crafting of those everyday languages we speak as well as our capacity to integrate them into our creative making.

II. The Voice of the Architect

We established above that emerging language is always polysemic, though it is often intended as indicative as we seek to avoid confusion in speaking to others and in sharing, through words, our perceptions of reality. Reality always overflows language; in fact, this is the reason why true poetry is eminently translatable, though it must always be rewritten in the host idiom; it speaks primarily about the world, not about a "subjective author" and purported internal feelings. Language is often used indicatively in architecture, not only as extrapolated into the discipline's obsessions with functions and parameters, but also literally, in the drafting of contracts and specifications. I wish to argue, however, that the language that is truly central for the design of culturally grounded *Stimmungen*, the language that may eventually give rise to an architecture with greater claims to universal sense—or at least suitable for cultural accommodation in pluralistic societies, so crucial for our global village— is poetic or literary language, the language whose elemental unit is the metaphoric sentence. Indeed, of all the forms of language it is metaphoric language—the language of both practical philosophy (in the Aristotelian sense) and literature—that best allows the nature of reality to appear. It is by embracing strategies that make use of metaphoric language that the architect may start designing more culturally relevant *places* that operate like Giambattista Vico's "imaginative universals."[66]

Paul Ricoeur's *The Rule of Metaphor* (1977) remains to this day an authoritative source on its subject. Ricoeur acknowledges Aristotle's insight in identifying the seemingly paradoxical role of metaphor as central in his *Rhetoric* and his *Poetics*, essential *both* (1) to speak persuasively (in his *Rhetoric*) of "probable" truths in the realm of "practical philosophy," appropriate in the world of human actions and distinct from the realm of *epistéme*, with its "scientific" propositions dependent upon identity (a special case of analogy); and (2) to "redescribe" reality (in his *Poetics*) through affective, ultimately cathartic poetic fictions. To this, Ricoeur adds his phenomenological and hermeneutic grasp of language to identify metaphor's centrality for human understanding. Recognizing the initial metaphoric impulse in emerging language leads to a radical questioning of the conventional oppositions between "prose" and "poetry," "proper and figurative [uses of language], ordinary and strange, order and transgression. It suggests that the idea of order itself proceeds from the metaphoric constitution of the semantic fields, which themselves give rise to genus and species."[67]

For Ricoeur, metaphor's "most intimate abode" is neither the name, nor the sentence, nor even discourse, but the copula of the verb *to be*. Of course, metaphor is implied in all of the above. The mobility of nouns, *transference*, is the origin of Aristotle's concept: a kind of change with respect to location that acknowledges the polysemy of words versus their indivisible meaning. The sentence, which for Ricoeur is in fact the kernel of discursive meaning (giving priority to semantics over semiotics), is a whole that cannot be reduced to the sum of its parts—for only in conversation do we have an idea of a meaning for a word. *To make metaphors* is a particular verb for Aristotle,[68] a sign of "genius" or ingenuity, implying an intuitive *active* perception of similarity in the dissimilar: the very structure of knowing. Its ultimate aim is the eventual weaving of sentences into works, which is discourse, the subject of hermeneutic understanding. Ricoeur explains: "Sign [the word] differs from sign, discourse refers to the world. Difference is semiotic, reference is semantic: What is intended by discourse, the reference, is irreducible to what semiotics calls the signified. But these are not simply distinct oppositions: the sign owes its very meaning as sign to its usage in discourse."[69]

Yet beyond these complexities, the metaphorical copula *is* at once signifies both "is not" and "is like"; it is therefore not simply a simile or analogy, though it may encompass both. Metaphor is more than the "master" figure of speech; it is the central form of linguistic expression for enactive consciousness once it finds itself facing external reality. It is an articulation of truth in the manner of the Greek *alétheia*, Heidegger's "revealing-concealing" that must take the place of "truth as correspondence" as normative for human understanding.[70] The "genius-stroke" of metaphor marking the work of both the poet and the philosopher (the architect as maker and thinker) is that it characterizes perception as the apprehension of similarities in things remote from each other. It potentially generates an affective voltaic arc through a coincidence of opposites; it has, as Aristotle put it, an eye for resemblance.[71]

Metaphor emerges from embodied consciousness oriented in the world, affording possibilities for communication among humans both in ordinary situations and in the extraordinary occasions when artistic artifacts speak "out of time and place." At the same time, it is capable of semantic innovation by extending the possibilities of perception, opening up its cognitive availabilities in the present moment. This circularity of metaphor has been described in various ways. Ricoeur employs it to demonstrate the untenability of Saussure's linguistic model with its dichotomies of signifier and signified: "initial polysemy equals language, the living metaphor equals speech, a metaphor in common use represents the return of speech to language, and subsequent polysemy equals language."[72] In an important 1980 book, George Lakoff and Mark Johnson (a student of Ricoeur) demonstrate how metaphor is far more than a rhetorical flourish; it is pervasive "not just in language but in thought and action. Our ordinary conceptual system, in terms of which we both think and act, is fundamentally metaphorical in nature."[73] Their study thoroughly establishes metaphor's rootedness in embodied orientation and prereflective action, its "experiential" nature. There is continuity between kinesthetic preconceptual experiences and meaningfulness.

At the other side of the spectrum, metaphor is cognitive and poetic, comprising our mediated access to reality through language. This function of metaphor is beautifully evoked in the frontispiece of Emmanuele Tesauro's *Il cannocchiale aristotelico* (Turin, 1654), arguably the most important book on rhetoric for the baroque period. *Poiésis*, personified as a woman, looks through an "Aristotelian telescope" (the emblem of metaphor) pointed directly at the sun, obviously blinding yet also representing the Platonic and Christian light capable of revealing truth. The "impossible" act reveals the sunspots in the engraving—the blemishes of the life-giving divine luminary, a "scientific model," while *Pictura* points to a conical anamorphosis and reveals that "All is One." The light of the Sun, the truth of reality, is something we can never contemplate directly; truth is always mediated, yet accessible through metaphor. Even scientific models have the same status, the only difference from other metaphors being their liability to instrumentalization, their capacity to become technologies. Indeed, Ricoeur writes succinctly, "Metaphor is to poetic language what the model is to scientific language."[74] I will elaborate on this in the following chapter.

As cognitive *and* embodied, metaphor plays an important role in our grasping of the "language of architecture" (on the side of reception), of its manifold voices, as discussed in the previous section. The kinetic body is the source of metaphors that, in turn, through their own specificity in artifacts, organize habits and life (consciousness, i.e., thought). I have argued that since human cognition is inseparable from bodily experience in the physical world, cities and architecture frame and afford possibilities for knowing, operating at both a cognitive and affective level.

As a creative and poetic device, moreover, linguistic metaphor is vital for the generation of appropriate atmospheres, claiming a central role in the "language of the architect." This is the topic that I wish to examine here, and it is also best discussed by way of Ricoeur. Following in the hermeneutic tradition, Ricoeur is concerned with the relationship between language and embodiment, but his particular interest is in how poetic metaphor aspires to the condition of the human body, the effect of flesh.[75] This focus enables him to account for artistic specificity: for the fact that metaphor allows for semantic innovation in poetics (in architecture) while being untranslatable to normal (conceptual) language through paraphrase.

Indeed, a most significant implication of Ricoeur's work for the architect and designer stems from his argument that there is a fundamental dimension of lived human experience intrinsic to "figured" discourse.[76] *Figura*, "plastic shape," was eventually used by Quintilian to describe the classical "figures of speech." *Figure* in Latin was applied only to bodies, expressing contours and features. In its different ways of signifying and conveying, discourse is akin to the differences in forms and features to be found in real bodies; it was on the basis of this analogy that the metaphor "the figures of discourse" was coined.[77] Furthermore, Ricoeur observes that a figure becomes "physical" to the extent that it infringes on grammatical rules.[78] When Philippe Soupault writes "Paris is Georgette," in his *Last Nights of Paris* (1928), the city under his narrative feet is immediately characterized by the particular mood of desire.[79] Language here leaves behind its literal horizon, compelling the reader to infer a productively metaphorical meaning; it "reveals" a truth that refers us back to experience and can be useful in design considerations. Language is liberated "from its first-order referential level" to become "stuff" for the poet/architect, precisely like other materials for the hand of the craftsman.[80] Indeed, it is not difficult to discern that this is the key to the "material imagination" that Gaston Bachelard famously admired in great poetic works;[81] conversely, the very possibility of acknowledging the predominance of materiality for meaning in architecture hinges upon the primacy of metaphor for signification and its appropriate uses by an architect.

Earlier in this chapter I cited the example of classical architecture in Vitruvius's treatise, in which geometry functions metaphorically. Given its clear cosmological referents, and Vitruvius's own statements about signifier and signified at the outset of book 1,[82] historians have tended to interpret the issue of meaning through semiotics (imagining this model as a historical constant, extrapolated from modernity). In fact, Vitruvius is merely articulating the appearance of meaning in embodied perception, exactly as we described it in the previous chapter, and then claiming the importance of discourse (the full scope of theory) to generate such meanings; he is not reducing architecture to a sign. A circular temple, such as the *thólos* in Epidauros, Greece, for example, already exhibits the character of "heuristic fiction,"[83] whose value is proportional to its "denial" of the more-than-human natural world; the *thólos is* and *is not* the figure of the horizon and the cosmic limit. Ricoeur characterizes metaphors as having "split reference"; similarity is apprehended in spite of and through difference. Hence, the language or material that has become separate from denotation is never static; it is tense and alive and thereby creates "images."

Octavio Paz shares Ricoeur's understanding of metaphor when he writes:

Nothing precludes our regarding plastic and musical works as poems, if they are able to meet the two stated conditions: on the one hand, to return their materials to that which they are—sparkling or opaque matter … on the other hand, to be transformed into images and thus to become a peculiar form of communication. Without ceasing to be language—sense and transmission of sense—the poem is something that is beyond language. But that thing that is beyond language [the poetic image] can only be reached through language."[84]

In a similar vein, Gaston Bachelard argues that the image is not a residue of impression, but an aura surrounding speech: "The poetic image places us at the origin of speaking being."[85] The poem gives birth to the image. The poetic image reverberates into the depths of existence; it is a source of psychic activity. What was a new being in language becomes an increment to consciousness, or, better, "a growth of being."

There is a profound affinity between the metaphor's ability to make visible and its capacity to render a description active or alive. It is important to note the similarity of this primary cognitive operation with the enactive theory of perception's understanding of how we actually "see images," being not simply passive pictures formed in the mind's eye but the reenactment of embodied action in the world (chapter 5). "In the realm of perception, the productive imagination produces concepts; in the realm of language, it produces emergent semantic innovation."[86] Words in a sentence give way to the reference of discourse to the world; there are always prereflective cognitive dimensions that in some ways transcend language. The "seeing as" involved in the metaphor harnesses the nonverbal and the verbal at the core of the image-making function of language.[87] Most importantly for our arguments, Ricoeur also holds that metaphor acts on the body in the form of *feeling*, a dimension that for him is both cognitive and affective.[88] Feeling is cognitive because it is referential, and it is referential because it fosters a *mood* capable of attuning the inhabitant (or reader) to the world of the work. In addition, this referential quality is what allows for identification and "participation" with the text/work as an autonomous product (different from a verbal utterance, outside the place and time of its production), through the dynamics of distanciation and appropriation that make up the "circle" of understanding as described by hermeneutics. In this way the work projects its "aesthetic force."[89]

All of this leads to an important conclusion, deeply challenging for the architect so used to working with visual images: Ricoeur's own assertion that *the human imagination is primarily linguistic*.[90] Earlier phenomenological accounts of the imagination still reiterate Aristotle's assumptions and apprehend the imagination (*phantasía*) as ultimately derivative of visual perception: as a picture, regardless of its specific role. This is of course the "common sense" of optics and psychology that we questioned in chapter 5. Phenomenology ultimately rejected this passive understanding of visual perception (Merleau-Ponty), and this critique has now been corroborated, as I have shown, by cognitive science. Supported by considerations on the role of emerging language (hermeneutics), some of which I have summarized above, the privileging of description in phenomenology was revised: it moved from description to interpretation. In other words, while the body (the morphology of our particular embodied consciousness) and our world (our oriented engagement in it) shape the mind and set limits to perception, our motor and reflective knowledge also determine what "appears"; for example, when we visit a gallery and a well-informed guide conveys to us relevant knowledge about the artwork in front of us, we effectively perceive it differently.

Ricoeur's preference for a linguistic model of imagination over a visual one embraces the poetic role of imagining, its creative potential. Imagining is folded into the function of metaphor: the ability to say one thing in terms of another, or several things at the same time, creating something *new*. This creative copula is always complemented by "seeing-as," which "contains a ground, a foundation … resemblance."[91] Thanks to the character of "seeing-as" as "half thought and half experience, it joins the light of sense with the fullness of the image. In this way the non-verbal and the verbal are firmly united at the core of the image-ing function of language."[92]

While the above is a philosophical characterization of the human imagination regardless of its changing historical and cultural conditions, it is particularly germane for modern *creation* seeking relevance and appropriateness in the wake of modernity's epistemological transformations from ancien régime to romantic paradigm. This is a central question for architecture I have evoked in previous chapters, and one made even more critical by the boundless creative options now granted by digital media. Fundamentally, the linguistic (hermeneutic) imagination permits the search for an appropriate relationship between *tradition* and *innovation*, crucial for the proper social functioning of architecture. The two terms are no longer understood as polar opposites but as mutually determined.[93] For a linguistic imagination, "[i]nnovation remains a form of behavior governed by rules," writes Ricoeur;[94] it is bound to tradition's paradigms at many levels, from habits to ideas. Ultimately the range of solutions may be vast, deployed between the two poles of servile application and calculated deviation within a particular discourse. Classical and premodern architecture, for example, gravitate toward the first pole, while modern architecture tends toward the second.

Like Ricoeur and Heidegger, Gaston Bachelard believed that representational meaning does not exist prior to words. In his theory of the poetic imagination, images are not primarily visual, auditory, or tactile but "spoken." While fundamentally in agreement with all that we have established, Bachelard contributes greatly to our celebration of the poetic imagination's role for architecture by insisting on the correspondence between the materiality of things and the materiality of (emerging) words.[95] Seeking to understand the essential nature of poetry through its relationship to primordial matter (the dynamic transformations of fire, earth, water, and air that may account for all phenomenal substances), his poetic materialism amounts to a devaluation of the imagination of visual forms, prioritizing depth over surfaces. The material imagination of poetics is "this amazing need for *penetration* that, going beyond the imagination of forms, thinks matter, dreams in it, lives in it or, in other words, materializes the imaginary."[96] For Bachelard materiality is not a property added to images or a characteristic of objects, it is the imagining act itself that operates through language.[97]

Put in these terms, it is easy to grasp the importance of poetic language for an architecture that, for its meanings, should valorize the extraordinary primacy of material. The inherent dynamism of metaphor ($\mu\varepsilon\tau\alpha\varphi\circ\rho\acute{\alpha}$) corresponds to the inherent dynamism of matter, responding to the primary kinesthetic dimension of human perception. According to Bachelard, this is evident in the best poetry, always remaining incomplete in its perfection, much like the *Slaves* of Michelangelo, thus suggestive of further creation and translation, or similar to the feminine water touched and tasted by Novalis in his dream,[98] pure dynamism without ever becoming fixed figures. Such material dynamism is suggestive also of the demiurgic nature of poetry shared by the poet and the world: a cocreation in words whose ultimate authorship must remain uncertain. If given the conditions of modern architectural practice as we have described them, the architect can no longer be a craftsman and is thus estranged from such primary ways of knowing matter from the inside, the best option available is to let design be guided by the poetic word, the only one capable of material dreaming.

The linguistic imagination is central to understanding as interpretation, and it is also *active*, like perception. Not surprisingly, Elaine Scarry has noted that literary texts activating the linguistic imagination have a greater capacity to recall the vivid nature of perception, its very "solidity," than conventional pictures.[99] By projecting new worlds—the very task of architecture—the linguistic imagination provides humanity with projects for action. As Richard Kearney explains, quoting Ricoeur: "the traditional opposition between *theoría* and *praxis* dissolves to the extent that 'imagination has a projective function that pertains to the very dynamism of action.'"[100]

Ricoeur's argument echoes Mallarmé's insights, whose profound relevance for modernity I suggested previously, in stating that while poetic reference suspends literal reference and thereby appears to make language refer only to itself, it in fact reveals a deeper and more radical power of reference to those ontological aspects of our being that cannot be spoken directly.[101] Thus, a true poetic work is not a shadow or reduction of reality (like a Platonic *eikón*, for example) but the opposite: a "depiction" of reality that enlarges our existential horizon by augmenting it with meanings intrinsic to its own universe of discourse.[102] This is indeed the nature of significant architecture.

Ricoeur places the referential power of narrative works under that of poetic works in general. Historical narratives, crucial for a project's ethical dimension and cultural appropriateness, borrow from this imaginative power of redescription, since, insofar as they constitute a "reference through traces," the past can only be reconstructed by the imagination.[103] I have discussed elsewhere the importance of hermeneutics for architectural discourse, as the proper form of historical understanding; crucial for the architect to define a position in view of a particular task and the common good.[104]

It is in fictional narratives, however, that the productive power of the human imagination to configure and refigure human time and space is most dramatically evident.[105] *Metaphor is the ideal vehicle for bringing moods to presence.* I will close this chapter by arguing that the architectural project itself, a cohesive proposal, can be understood as a multilayered story that involves aspects of poetic narrative that Ricoeur identified in his major work on the topic, *Time and Narrative*.[106] While I maintain a distance from some conclusions in Ricoeur's own interpretation of the connections between literary texts and architecture (understood mostly as buildings or aesthetic objects) in his essay "Architecture and Narrative," he uses the three analytical categories from *Time and Narrative* that are most convenient for our discussion:

(1) *Prefiguration*, which for Ricoeur draws from the narrative nature of life itself, the stories we tell (and which we effectively *are*)—that constitute our identities, and are the precondition for literary work. In the case of architecture, I take this to refer to the contextual preconditions of the project that may be best understood through poetic language, such as the character of a natural site or a city (*place*, as I argued in chapter 4), the stories of the living and future inhabitants, and the historic, artistic (i.e., paintings or other narrative works), and literary works (such as modern and contemporary novels) that recount and express the topology of places and the cultural habits that must be accommodated (often much better than statistics, sociological studies, or cartographic maps).

(2) *Configuration*, which is for Ricoeur the literary text itself, giving shape and human significance to time. For architecture, this is the physical design that organizes space and proposes attuned atmospheres for significant events and eventually reveals poetic images; generated from figural language guiding other tools of representation that should be congruent with narrativity (from sketches to "immersive environments"), with the aim of producing a proposal that ethically limits and frames habits and human events.

(3) *Refiguration*, which in the case of the literary text involves the reader's interpretation, the "fusion" of her horizon of expectation with the author's proposal. In architecture it concerns the inhabitant, "refiguring" the "configured" spaces through life itself, which must be accounted for by the architect as a consideration of *program*, not a simple list of parts but a literary narrative of proposed human actions and events for which architecture must provide suitable moods, and through which it will ultimately grant its significance. While in the end this last aspect is "open" and unpredictable, since it is the inhabitant that "refigures" the architecture and obtains its meaning, the architectural project demands active consideration of this issue from the outset of the proposal. The potential variability of use through

time for any building is perhaps the main condition that has given credence to the belief that what matters in architecture is simply the material durability of a structure and its objective aesthetic qualities. I hope to have shown the limitations of that understanding in our previous discussions of the historical continuities between dwelling and building—often ephemeral, always intertwining temporality and spatiality, and so *not* fundamentally about durability. My observation concerning the importance of a narrative program that may also incorporate in its fictional structure issues of refiguration is particularly pertinent when the issue is *how* the architect can enact architectural intentionality in the attainment of meaning, that is, in relation to the generative questions that are central for the project.

This three-part structure suggests a notion of architecture as a literary work with a discernible plot, rather than a "formal syntax" (Eisenman), a collage or montage of "fundamental elements" (Koolhaas), or simply a collection of diagrams, tables, specifications, legal documents, physical models, and sets of drawings of various nature and codified information for fabrication. The project is fundamentally an ethical promise, communicated through emotion and reason. In engaging hermeneutic and poetic language, we can imagine how architecture may offer better alternatives, beyond obsessions with fashion and form, to reconcile the architect's personal imagination with an understanding of local cultures and pressing political and social concerns: the crucial dilemma we have inherited with our modern condition.

***

It can be said that while literature represents a "leap" beyond ordinary language, architecture is likewise a "leap" in regard to everyday uses of space.[107] But we must be careful with this characterization. The issue is not merely one of special or "ornamented" buildings as opposed to ordinary utilitarian ones. Rather, as I think we can now better understand, it concerns a distinct relationship to human action, culturally transmitted as habits and stories. Just as in literature there is the paradox created by the primacy of poetic language as speech that only subsequently becomes ordinary, a similar situation arises in architecture. Arguably, poetic dwelling is present at the origins of "primitive" humanity, for any story about life (our ability to speak) unfolds in a space of life, already a significant "space of appearance" (to employ the famous formulation of Hannah Arendt). While the self-awareness of this "cultural place" as distinct from natural *tópos* was signaled by Plato's *chóra*, it is impossible to imagine a space of human communication that is not *already* "a line of fracture and suture between nature and culture."[108]

We are all beings of action: perception itself is active and our primary wisdom is psychomotor, the knowledge of embodied consciousness that is about 80 percent prereflective. We are thus capable of intervening in the course of events, inscribing action in things.[109] As we have seen, actions become habits with their particular plasticity, unlike reflexes. Yet they are endowed with stability, often becoming rules and entering into symbolic orders; they are rendered as the stories that are our lives. Thus, when attempting to describe the essence of the poetic work, Aristotle associated it with a plot creating imitation: *the mimesis of action*, signaling both the continuity *and* the break between the "ordinary" account of our lives—famously defined by Ricoeur as "stories in search of a narrator"[110]—and the poetic work.

Significant action is also the subject of architecture, for which it endeavors to provide or "configure" appropriate atmospheres, "spaces of appearance." Emulating rhetorical practices based on Aristotle's *Poetics* and passed on to Cicero—and clearly evident in Vitruvius—this project of "configuration" became a self-conscious activity, guided (as I have explained) by *epistéme, phrónesis*, and *techné* ("theory"). This is the distinct contribution of Greco-Roman culture to the discipline. Architecture (like dramatic literature) composes and constructs the very thing it imitates; it orders life through "lived-in" plots (read "projects"). It innovates, but never in an anarchic fashion; we may recall that until early modernity the concern for innovation was not an explicit issue for architectural writers—only becoming dominant after the end of the eighteenth century, precisely as political and social orders were uprooted and architecture's customary links to language and rhetoric were severed. For Aristotle the structure of the plot in a dramatic work constitutes *mímesis*, so that "*poiésis* is *mímesis* and *mímesis* is *poiésis*." It is crucial to stress that this original concept of "imitation" has nothing to do with copying. If mimesis involves an initial reference to reality, this reference signifies nothing other than the very rule of nature over all production: *its "biological" expression of meaning, sense, or purpose.*

Actions and habits usually mark the physical environment and become *traces*. This is of course the physical (cultural) context that architects often consider, either to restore it, reuse it, or make tabula rasa out of it. The traces preserve histories of previous lives and should be considered carefully; they contain a richness that usually enhances design. And yet, I would argue, it is also important not to confuse such traces with the full horizon of prefiguration alluded to above, which is the living culture sedimented in habits and stories. Responsiveness to site in any case means that the traces of stories in buildings and cities are not simply vestiges of the past preserved for visiting tourists; rather, they become living testimonies, incorporated into the life of the present and enabling a future. This would be the first, essential step toward a meaningful "regionalism."

If, as I have stated repeatedly, perception is action and motility is at the root of consciousness, architecture must resonate with our actions to grant the gift of dwelling. Thus, rather than be content with expressing technological processes, personal style, or arbitrary formal innovation, the architect must take very seriously the notion that architecture should "imitate our actions at their best," which traditionally were rituals and today are what Heidegger has termed "focal actions." Architecture takes place amid the duality that characterizes this imitation. It is not merely a literal trace or container of actions, like a nest, which could be construed as the frank, wise, and sustainable "imitation" of the bird's life. While accounting for this basic condition that humans share with other animals, it must also reflect fabulous invention and ennobling elevation.[111] Unlike the relationship between the nest and the bird's actions, architecture deals with plastic human habits within a symbolic (linguistic) horizon. This duality constitutes the referential function of metaphor in poetry. "Abstracted from this referential function, metaphor plays itself out in substitution and dissipates itself in ornamentation or language games,"[112] the fate of much architecture of the last two hundred years conceived on the basis of biological and mechanical analogies.

Rem Koolhaas's curatorial project at the 2014 Venice Biennale merits some further comment in this context. His concern with establishing a distance from the dominant formalist practices of star architects, preoccupied with solipsistic grammars and personal "styles," is encouraging. In *Fundamentals*, the "elements" of architecture such as doors, windows, ceilings, and escalators are rendered as "words" and are considered through their historical constitution, so that, for example, the window of the seventeenth century appears in continuity with the modern window. This understanding suggests the layered richness of the element, usually ignored by architects. In his practice, Koolhaas must be recognized for his efforts to find specific solutions to modern programs, rather than imposing a style. However, while his semantic interest is valuable, it is also limited. Fundamental elements must be used propositionally (as sentences) to mean anything at all. In the Inuit language spoken in Quebec, the word for *door*, for example, is exactly the same as that for *vagina*: a sameness that opens up a dimension of metaphoricity for architects working in the North, enabling a potentially fruitful connection with its specific culture, physical context, and tendencies beyond the "concrete" materiality of the object.[113] Privileging language over the concretized building element that seems to have a life "outside of history" is crucial for architecture's "configuration" of space, bringing about a synthesis of heterogeneous elements and enacting its capacity to provide attuned atmospheres for human action.

Additionally, given all that has been said, the architectural project as poetic discourse implies a more extensive composition than a predication (a sentence). A text implies categories of production and labor, involving *dispositio* (the term from ancient rhetoric that Vitruvius also preferred), "composition" or "arrangement," whereby the work is irreducible to a simple sum of elements or sentences. It generates its own formal rules, akin to those set out for old literary genres, and yet particular to the contemporary habits and actions at stake today, a code revealed a posteriori that ends in a particular work (with its own traits or "style") and that is not the basis for a universal style, being irreducible to theoretical categories. Paz remarks: "Technique and creation, tool and poem are different realities. The technique is repetition that improves or deteriorates; it is heritage and change: the gun replaces the bow. The *Aeneid* does not replace the *Odyssey*. Each poem is a unique object, created by a 'technique' that dies at the very moment of creation."[114] A speaking architecture, one endowed with a voice (*Stimme*), may bring forth its "aesthetic intent," enacting the semantic innovation of a productive poetic imagination, ethically framing habits to reveal their cognitive value and resulting in a poetic image.

The architectural project as a poetic hypothesis "is the suggestion or proposal, in imaginative, fictive mode, of a world."[115] The framing of the

The Linguistic Dimension of Architecture

habitual *otherwise* suspends reference to the ordinary and becomes the condition of access to a virtual mode of reference. Similarly to poetry, architecture proposes *other* possibilities of existence, yet possibilities that would be most deeply our own.[116] Under the rubric of mood, an extra-linguistic factor is introduced, which is the index of a manner of being: a "state of the soul," a way of finding or sensing oneself in the midst of reality. In Heidegger's language: a way of finding oneself among things. We should note one last time that "bracketing" or distancing from natural reality is the condition that enables architecture to develop a world, and one attuned to the mood that the architect has deemed appropriate. The creation of a concrete (poetic) object suspends the inhabitant's reliance upon signs, while at the same time opening up access to reality in the mode of fiction and feeling.

Echoing Antonio Damasio's discoveries in neurobiology, Nelson Goodman has pointed out that "[i]n aesthetic experience the emotions function cognitively."[117] Ricoeur would nevertheless insist that only a feeling transformed into *mythos* (a story) can reveal and discover the world.[118] I shall end with one more turn to Aristotle, helpful in clarifying this important and always seemingly paradoxical issue, particularly when we think about architecture. I will do this by contrasting two forms of poetry: tragic and lyric. Tragic poetry is the imitation of human actions (mimesis) through *mythos* (the plot-making activity); as I have suggested, it is most interesting in this context for its resonances with "program" (or "prefiguration" and "refiguration" in architecture). In lyric poetry, on the other hand, *mythos* is substituted by *moods*.[119] I would argue that in lyric poetry the metaphoric "action" reveals an "arch-plot," a plot that comprises the seeking out of, and failure to reach, the basic human motion/emotion: *desire*. Under this rubric, lyric poetry and literature are therefore more appropriate than their tragic counterparts for the aims of the "configuration" of architectural atmospheres.[120] This lyric *mythos* (the mood) is joined by a lyric mimesis, in the sense that the mood created becomes a sort of "model" for "seeing as" and "feeling as." Analogous to a lyric poem, the effect of architecture is to orient humans, through their actions, to reality—through a heuristic fiction.

7

Representation and the Linguistic Imagination

I have been arguing for the importance of poetic narrative as a—generally overlooked—tool of architectural representation. While for a hermeneutic approach to architectural theory, historical narratives (like those in this book) are the fundamental source of orientation for philosophical questions and ethical decisions, literary narratives can contribute greatly to the design of programs for future living woven from significant actions, and to the configuration of properly attuned atmospheres. Fundamental to this argument has been the observation that the imagination is *primarily* linguistic, since emerging poetic language is inherently innovative and open; its very nature is polysemic and metaphoric. Much work is needed to develop methodological frameworks that facilitate the implementation of this insight in design, taking full account of the issues from the perspective of phenomenology and hermeneutics.[1] The seemingly unshakable expectations of technological production are hard to question, yet it should become evident from these pages that the stakes for humanity are high, going far beyond mere issues of physical survival and economic development.

Though modern and contemporary architects have sometimes spoken of narratives and fiction in relation to their projects, it is not always obvious how such interests are reflected in their work. Often the concern with literature becomes vague inspiration (as might a concern with music or cinema), or a structural mechanism for organizing form. Dialogue among partners in an office or with clients has been theorized and even embraced in practice in recent years, often under the influence of the Frankfurt School, observing the importance of oral exchanges that may lead to design decisions. Such exchanges might be seen as a form of narrative, yet their underlying assumptions are usually the possibility of rational consensus and accommodation.[2] These are excellent aims in themselves, but they usually fall short of attunement: the conciliation of the creative capacity and ethical responsibility of the architect, as author, with the cultural and physical values needed to ground a project and produce emotive and meaningful atmospheres for human events.

On the other hand, given the linguistic nature of human cultures, even when language is not used self-consciously in design, meanings emerge that are specific and appropriate to given cultures and situations. Resonance among artistic practices in a particular time and place is common and has often benefited architecture in profound ways. Architects that have taken seriously such reverberations—like Le Corbusier, Luis Barragán, Frederick Kiesler, and Alvar Aalto, to name a few—have produced poetic atmospheres appropriate to culturally grounded situations. Nevertheless, the critical problems generated for life by the instrumental mentalities of planning and formalism to which I earlier alluded are prevalent in cities all over the world. While political and economic forces undeniably play a major role in this situation, it is certainly fueled by the current intentionality and modus operandi of architecture and building design practices in our technological global village.

In past eras, the spoken word was deemed central for making design decisions. It facilitated the client's involvement as a fundamental part of the process, as in the exchanges between an abbot and the master mason in the Middle Ages, or with patrons during the Renaissance—Filarete famously called the client the "father" of the project, while the architect he characterized as the "mother." Their oral intercourse was literally the seed of the project, fructifying into drawings, models, and buildings. The spoken word was also crucial to building operations; oral transmission was fundamental between the master or architect and the masons, leading to remarkable accomplishments, like the building of Milan's cathedral (without a final "picture" of the building) in a complex and highly compromised urban site, or Michelangelo's buildings, often in the absence of "proper" architectural drawings. Today, however, we would find it inconceivable to build without precise working drawings and legal documents, and the skeptical reader will rightly wonder about the contributing role of poetic words in the realization of a complicated building or urban design in view of our contemporary technological expectations.

Architects over the last few decades have been consumed with the promises of the computer and digital design software. There is a curiously uncritical optimism concerning these tools, based on the belief that they have brought about a radical transformation in design. The perspectival visualization of projects on a screen, the coordination of design decisions through programs such as Autodesk Revit, the recent trends in computational design where measurable data and parameters are transformed into uncanny shapes and architectural forms, and the production of numerous glossy renderings disseminated daily through the Internet all convey the feeling that an immense change has taken place. In a fundamental sense, however, this is largely a delusion. Elsewhere, I have explained at length how the fundamentally reductive and instrumental aims of such software were already present in Jean-Nicolas-Louis Durand's early-nineteenth-century "mechanism of architectural composition."[3] The so-called "digital revolution" can only be grasped through a careful historical analysis and should in fact *not* be reduced to an issue of hand drafting versus computing. The cultural and epistemological transformations that took hold in Europe during the early nineteenth century and prompted architecture's scientific reduction greatly explain why, as architects entered the age of computation, the tools chosen have been those that work in a totalizing abstraction: software such as Autodesk's AutoCAD and Revit. Here I don't wish to revisit these issues nor examine the larger particularities of digital design. My aim is simply to try to draw out some suggestions about ways the reflections in this book may have an impact on or profit from present conditions.

While dedicated architectural software affords the architect the means to produce seductively appealing renderings and facilitates formal innovation, there remains an uncritical assumption, inherited from the nineteenth century, concerning the univocal relationship between the drawings (or, at present, the digital model) and the building to come. This is the very premise of software like Revit that offers the user tools "to define forms and geometry as real building components for a smoother transition to design development and documentation."[4] The architectural design operation is therefore conceived as the production of the "picture" (a digital model) of a future building, with its components related syntactically at multiple levels (technical, formal, and so on), inherently resulting in technical and/or aesthetic, more or less self-referential objects. Since the software also optimizes the processes of construction, the dream (or nightmare) of seamless fabrication—an unquestioned expectation and absolute value of the technological world first expressed by the likes of Durand and Jean Rondelet two hundred years ago—comes closer to realization. We can imagine building as one manufactures cars, starting with a stylish, marketable, and enticing picture, increasingly internalizing the external world into generalized parameters to produce buildings from the top down, as absolute manifestations of a creative will to power.[5] This strategy innately curtails architecture's referential potentiality as a necessarily emotional, kinesthetic, and multisensorial form of communication, an atmosphere responsive to the natural world and specific cultural values; all issues that involve experience and language, and are irreducible to binary information.

Vilém Flusser has proposed a useful distinction between traditional images, such as painting and drawing, and technical images, in which he includes *both* analog and digital photography and imaging. Traditional images, he argues, are "first-degree abstractions," in direct relationship with the concrete world. Technical images, on the other hand, are "third-degree abstractions," since they are abstracted from "texts" that are themselves abstracted from the concrete world.[6] Rather than referring to phenomena, like traditional images, technical images refer to "concepts."

Flusser's studies have been very valuable in their questioning of the naive polarization of "analog" versus "digital," one that is often taken for granted and explains very little about technical images and our present dilemmas. While the distinctions drawn by Flusser in view of the images' genetic constitution and their relationship to the visual world are helpful, there are more fruitful ways of understanding the problem. Placed within the framework of the present study, the technical image is actually made possible by the same disconnect between a reified nineteenth-century subject and his "objective" world that enabled both non-Euclidean geometries and modern "autonomous" poetry (like Mallarmé's). In the world of architecture, it sees its inception in the teachings of Durand. The "virtual image," in the sense often evoked today, fabricated out of "information"—1s and 0s—and translated into pixels, is already the underlying concept behind Jean-Victor Poncelet's projective geometry (1821), nurturing the possibility of creating a world out of the individual mind—a geometry generated by mathematical functions—bypassing experience, both visual and linguistic.[7] Flusser's distinctions are useful for characterizing the nature of modern and contemporary architectural representation, but instead of conceiving of the break between the traditional and the technical image (exemplified for him by painting and photography respectively) in terms of the self-referentiality of the technical media (like chemicals or pixels), I would like to argue that *the problem resides in the nature of their disconnect from language*—not from a "visual" world, but from a world articulated by natural, inherently metaphoric language. This break is precisely what makes the label "digital culture," often used by Antoine Picon to designate the current situation, a lamentable contradiction in terms.

Here it is important to briefly recall a point established in chapter 5. The visual world is not simply given as "pictures" in the mind's eye. Visual perception, what we regard as our "high-definition" images, is constructed from a vast array of sensorimotor knowledge, both reflective and prereflective. Translating Husserl's initial insights into the specific fields of contemporary artistic practices, Merleau-Ponty proposed an elaborate critique of perspective as "natural" vision in a number of essays.[8] He established that "it is certain that classical perspective is not a law of perceptual behavior. It derives from the cultural order, as one of the ways man has invented for projecting before himself the perceived world, and is not a copy of this world."[9] In spontaneous, kinesthetic vision, things vie for a person's attention. Once anchored in one of them, through a focal action, the person feels the solicitation of the others, which make them coexist with the first.[10] In spontaneous vision, the inhabitant experiences "a world of teeming, exclusive things which could be embraced only by means of a temporal cycle in which each gain is simultaneously a loss."[11]

As I have already pointed out, Alva Noë and Evan Thompson have elaborated this position.[12] Thompson explains that the content of our experience is not picturelike in a number of ways; for example, given the kinesthetic nature of human vision (whereby the eyes and the head are always in motion), which picks up things in a scene and throws them into view, the focus is never uniform from center to periphery. There is no precise match between what we experience in perception and whatever internal representations are in our brains (an observation that always troubled Kepler), so that "we visually experience the world to be rich in detail not because we must represent all this detail inside our heads at any given moment, but because we have constant access to the presence and detail of the world, and we know how to make use of this access."[13] Most importantly, "whatever impression we supposedly have of there being pictorial representations in our head when we perceive is not a first-person impression of experience but a third-person [ultimately Cartesian] theoretical belief."[14]

The scene of spontaneous vision is of course the space of life and architectural atmospheres, and one that is at odds with a picture generated through Cartesian space (as in our computers), where "backgrounds resign themselves to being only backgrounds" and things no longer vie for the person's attention: "nothing looks into one's vision and adopts the figure of being present."[15] So we can dispense with the notion of architecture as an image in the creative mind of the architect, suddenly externalized on the proverbial restaurant paper napkin. Whatever is externalized was not already "there," and depends greatly upon the local conditions: available paper, pens, or crayons, the texture and topography of the table offering support, and the like. Classical (perspectival) painting, no less than contemporary painting, is a creation dependent on cultural ("linguistic") intentions.[16] In contemporary painting and literature, the artist or writer endeavors to restore "the encounter between the one who has to exist with what does exist."[17] If it is this very encounter in the world of action that the mediating devices in architecture must signify, it is clear that architectural drawings and models cannot accomplish their task by merely *resembling* the things of the world.

While in the far longer-lasting, premodern traditions of architecture representation functioned as a simile, taking for granted the imperative of *translation* between the "model" (or set of drawings, regardless of their specific nature) and built architecture,[18] in the modern context the model functions more appropriately when it recognizes its affinity to metaphor, embracing its "split reference," and thus potentially conveying appropriate affective and cognitive meanings. Indeed, Ricoeur writes that with respect to their relation to reality, metaphor is to poetry what the model is to scientific language.[19] This is illuminating when we think of the functions of digital models in design. In science, a model is a heuristic fiction that seeks to break down an inadequate interpretation of the physical world. Owen Barfield has remarked on the grave dangers of identifying models with reality, a veritable idolatry that has dire consequences for scientific practices, as in the identification of the brain with "man" by some outdated neurophysiologists.[20] Extrapolated to language, the model corresponds to an extended metaphor: a tale, story, or allegory, even suggesting the possibility of "narrative models" in view of our findings in the previous chapter. The cognitive function of metaphor overlaps with the model. According to Alva Noë, a proper model is not reductive yet is always referential, a tool for "seeing as."

In his most recent book *Varieties of Presence*, Noë elaborates on the enactive theory of perception and its understanding of visual images. He introduces the concept of the picture as model. All pictures, he argues, are actually models; they function not unlike the way a relationship between arbitrary objects on the table in front of a person may represent monuments in that person's city by which he or she explains to a visitor how to navigate and arrive at a given destination.[21] Models enable specific understanding in view of circumstances and interests; in architecture they don't represent the absent building, for example, but they are their "representatives." Anything can be a model, as the saltshaker can be a model of the Eiffel Tower under certain circumstances, but nothing is a model "in itself."[22] The issue is always relational, like metaphor. On the other hand, whether something is a fitting substitute, relative to certain purposes, can depend on its intrinsic properties.[23]

This insight applies to all graphic modes of architectural representation; they must therefore always be considered carefully in view of a signifying intention. Since visualizing is actually not pictorial but "the activity of mentally representing an object or a scene by way of mentally *enacting* or entertaining a possible perceptual experience of that object or scene," action (narrative) must be intertwined with the models that lead to architectural form generation. Thus we again conclude that, despite our assumptions, representations are not neutral—*not even* the supposedly objective "picture" of the future building in Revit. Unless this condition is understood and incorporated into the processes of building production, the result will always be disappointing: the material "dumbness" of the built environment resulting from reductive fabrication. Given the resonances between model and metaphor, we may also add that there is a difference between a model that explains a more or less partial aspect of a phenomenon and one that achieves the status of a work of art capable of augmenting lived experience—in parallel to the very difference between simile and metaphor, whose copula always involves an ontological wager.

To further elucidate the possibilities of the model in current architectural representation I would like to return briefly to the eighteenth-century work of Giovanni Battista Piranesi, whose significant accomplishments I have already mentioned in previous chapters. By challenging the "reality" of Cartesian (three-dimensional) space as the site for the poetic imagination of the architect, Piranesi's *Carceri* etchings, particularly their dynamic transformation from a three-dimensional "first stage" into an exploded "second stage," inaugurates a tradition of modeling in architecture that is of great significance in our age of digital media. They are both "models" and "works of art." Piranesi's works are places inhabitable by the imagination, leading to a poetic revelation: the depth of experience that is other than a banal rendering of depth in optical perspective and that we have identified as a necessary precondition for *Stimmung*. By implicitly questioning their possible translation into three dimensions—it is "impossible" to build them as if they were coherent, with orthogonal plans and elevations at scale—Piranesi's "second stage" models function metaphorically, offering the possibility of "seeing as" that open up a world of fiction. They are inherently noninstrumental. Indeed, these models challenge the assumption that the appearance of the world can be accounted for by an "optical image" self-constituted in the back of the eye's camera obscura and magically transferred to the brain to constitute our consciousness. Piranesi's works reveal, instead, the significant human "image" as a construction, a metaphor, a fiction, in the sense we outlined in the previous chapter: an image "made" by each of us as we literally construct our perceptions by "acting" in the world, embedded in language as a fully embodied consciousness. Conversely, were we to build these spaces as atmospheres for human action, a further imaginary translation involving poetic language would be indispensable.

* * *

Two modern architects, Claude-Nicolas Ledoux and John Hejduk, are significant for having explored literary language and its relationship to architectural drawing as a means of architectural representation in their theoretical projects, reconciling the imperative of a creator's productive imagination with a careful consideration of cultural mores to achieve a poetic and ethical architecture of attuned situations. Their oeuvres are vast, and it would be impossible to explore them extensively in this chapter, but a few words will here suffice as examples for our present argument.

Ledoux was a well-known and controversial practicing architect, closely associated with the aristocracy of the French ancien régime. He was the architect of the Salines d'Arc-et-Senans (1775–1780), a salt mine and processing facility near Besançon, and of the Barrières (tollhouses) and wall around Paris (1785–1789), an unpopular project built on commission from the Fermiers Généraux for the purpose of levying taxes on merchandise entering the city; this project nearly cost Ledoux his head at the guillotine. Despite his contentious practice, he was aware of the need to rethink the role of urban architecture beyond monarchic regimes, based on a new sense of social responsibility and respect for nature that would result in greater human happiness. He dedicated many years to writing his massive book *L'architecture considerée sous le rapport de l'art, des moeurs et de la législation* (1804; 1847),[24] a remarkable and original text, where theory becomes poetic narrative and the story describes the project for the city of Chaux, the model (in the sense outlined above) of an ideal city, conceived by him as "crowning" his realized project for the Salines. The projects for the institutions in this city are housed in simple geometric volumes and their combinations, in accordance with a Newtonian and deistic concept of Nature—forms he deemed more appropriate than the older (and decadent) classical syntax—and novel programs that strive to establish a new harmonious urbanity for a postrevolutionary society. Bringing together insights from Le Camus and Boullée, the seemingly objective reality of the architectural structures that are proposed as drawings is complemented by descriptions of life experience. New institutions are created and designed, and the character of architecture—both its intellectual and moral meanings and its emotional impact—is articulated through literary language.

The title of Ledoux's book is itself noteworthy. He is in search of an architecture whose meanings may be drawn from art, particularly from painting and its ability to render eloquent and harmonic atmospheres (a concept present in earlier character theory), and from mores or customs, that is to say, from the values embodied in the citizens' everyday life and initially manifested as habitual actions. Thus architecture, shaping habits, could set forth an urban environment that was truly desirable, just, and ethical, operating in analogy to legislation. It could seek to frame human actions in view of a good life in accordance with nature, a concept most likely inspired by Jean-Jacques Rousseau.[25]

While written in prose, Ledoux's text is highly poetic, often taking a grandiloquent tone. It describes the experiences of a traveler visiting the city, yet the story often disappears amid the characterizations of the human situations framed by the new architecture and the urban order. Despite some formal similarities with later utopian social organizations, Chaux is not a "panopticon"—an instrument of political power, control of nature, and surveillance. Rather, the issue for Ledoux was to consider new possibilities for the space of appearance: a public space that might be effective after the fall of the old regime, framing *both* the rights and responsibilities for a new human subjectivity. The latter, for Ledoux, involved in particular a recognition and respect for the natural environment. This is the grounds for a natural sense of morality—a deistic divinity present in the natural order is invoked frequently, and Ledoux asks rhetorically why He has designed nature with such perfection, yet supplied so few rules for the human architect to do a proper job. This is not nature reduced to resources (Heidegger's "standing reserve"): the oval shape of the overall plan of Chaux celebrates the geometry of the heavens as the earth moves around the sun; nature itself, instead of walls, provides the limits of the city.

Ledoux's language is descriptive of situations, but never of the forms of the buildings that give them place. The envisioned architecture appears in the juxtapositions of text and image. The architectural drawings show precise plans, elevations, and sections (which nevertheless are not always constructively coherent), creating the sense of monumental solidity and objectivity, expressing with the limited choice of simple geometries the moving and poetic character of the institutions and their "proportionality." In counterpoint, the texts describe ephemeral situations that impact human action, mold behavior, and frame habits, revealing self-evident values that constitute customs and thus contribute to a happier life. That life foregrounds a sense of presence and feeling as sensuous experience, a "thick" present in the sense we outlined in chapter 5. Furthermore, as I suggested, the tone of Ledoux's language itself is deeply poetic: expressive through its rhythms and turns of phrase, and not only through the semantic meanings of the words.

A few prominent examples of institutions may be mentioned in closing. The well-known house for the caretakers of the city's water source (the river Loue) is highly innovative, articulated through simple volumes whose geometry originates in nature, like the circles made by a stone dropped into a pond. The intention is to convey the purpose of the building while recognizing the precedence of Nature, framing the life-giving water, so crucial for the common good, as it comes gushing through from the depths of the earth. The perspective emphasizes through its atmosphere the appropriateness of the form and its connection with the qualities of the source's natural setting. The situation portrayed in the text, however, is about family life and its values, about playing billiards in the room on the top floor.

Several projects for new institutions celebrate such values as peace, memory, and virtue. In this context, Oikéma, a brothel for the city, stands out and resists easy interpretation for appearing to encourage vice rather than virtue.[26] Ledoux plays with the "character" of his architecture by appropriately "hiding" its reference in the plan (where it takes the form of an erect phallus), as opposed to the evident eloquence of symbols in his other institutions. In this instance the story told is about the sensuously titillating experience of visiting the brothel, its vibrant diverse atmospheres eloquently portrayed, along with its importance, since sexuality is at the root of human actions and desire is the basis of all meaning. Imagining the outcome of different scenarios through literary imagination, Ledoux demonstrates how a visitor would realize the futility of a sexual encounter devoid of a spiritual dimension, thus apprehending the value of reciprocal and respectful romantic love as a foundation of society. As such, we can only grasp the project as a theoretical proposition, necessarily "told" as a story, revealing what may in fact be most essential for the social fabric of the new city.

His project for the cemetery of Chaux is also remarkable. The building is approached on the ground; all that appears is a pristine half-sphere suggesting its completion underground. Ledoux describes the terrifying experience of entering the underworld and confronting the emptiness that is death; as you glance into the central sphere pierced by a single source of light, you are frozen with fear and terror. This is resonant with the emotions associated with our finitude and with the sadness of parting from a loved one. And yet, the spherical shape also reveals, in the paradoxical drawing of the "elevation," a vision of the universe—of "outer space"—filled with planets and stars, the light and order of divine providence: not a religious paradise but an understanding of purpose for a human life well lived, as Ledoux himself writes, celebrated among the atoms of light. This extraordinary juxtaposition of a vision of the light-filled cosmos with the frightening emptiness of the cemetery reveals the importance of metaphor and the poetic word itself as tools of representation and kernels of architectural meanings—obviously demanding further poetic translation if the model were ever to materialize as a physical building *in* the world.

* * *

John Hejduk is perhaps the twentieth-century architect who has most thoroughly explored the relationship between architectural drawing and literary language. For his deep insights into the nature of architectural representation, his work also belongs to the critical tradition initiated by Piranesi, encompassing works that are poetic precisely by virtue of their distance from the world of practice, manifesting the characteristics of modern poetry as described by Paz and as expected by romantic philosophers. For this reason, his drawings are not representational in the conventional sense and operate more like metaphors or models, in the way described above. He himself spoke of his books as his "works of architecture."

It would be impossible to do justice to the richness and heterogeneity of Hejduk's work here. His most fruitful projects addressing the overlaps between literary language and drawing are his "Masques," which themselves display a great diversity and almost defy characterization.[27] I have already introduced his Victims project. For the purposes of this discussion, I will only speak briefly about some aspects of his Lancaster/Hanover Masque, given a final form in a book published in 1992. Like some of the other Masques, the Lancaster/Hanover Masque proposes new ways of dwelling in society, new urban organizations framed by an appropriate architecture. Taking the "program" as a fundamental aspect of the project, one that is rendered into literary language, Hejduk's work also inherits the concerns first introduced into architecture by Ledoux to contribute to a new "social contract" in the sense we outlined above. In Hejduk's project, the central area of the "farm community" is designated by an open quadrangular space, marked as "Void" by the architect—a "space of appearance" framed by four "houses" on two opposing sides, the Court and Prison House, and the Church and Death House, and two facing walls with thirteen suspended chairs on them, interweaving the biological and political life (*zoon* and *bios*) that make up human settlement. Hejduk thus recovers the understanding of such space of communication as the very essence of the *polis/civitas*: itself the ground and sufficient precondition of any further architecture as had been suggested by Vitruvius.[28] He characterizes the drawings for this "kernel" of the city as an "x-ray … apparitions … that may seem somewhat ethereal [yet are] in fact absolutely precise: that is, everything drawn is sufficient, no more—no less."[29]

These remarks come from a short passage entitled "On the Drawings," where Hejduk (exceptionally) introduces his work and discloses some of the intentions, underscoring his use of literary text and drawings. He points out that the texts of the Masque are meant to explain the community's "functions," the ritual and theatrical dimension of life, while the "drawing is like a sentence in a text, in which the word is a detail … a detail that helps to incorporate a thought."[30] While Hejduk is referring here to the specific drawing of his Court House project, he believes his drawings for all sixty-eight structures of the Masque, in many cases enigmatic composites of plan, elevation, and section superposed in a single image (never merely conventional, instrumental graphics), "reveal the whole structure … the whole story. It's life that is there."[31] It is important to emphasize how Hejduk depicts the "emergence" of poetic language and drawing as interwoven moments; the drawing is "propositional" (like a sentence, the unit of discourse, in the terms of Ricoeur discussed in chapter 6); it "encompasses the whole of a dematerialized thought."

Like many of the others in Hejduk's oeuvre, this Masque is organized in terms of "objects" and "subjects," presented as columns on a page, numbered and arranged face to face. The "objects" are architectural structures with names and drawing(s), often described in diverse, appropriate terms: from technical specifications, to literary or artistic references (for instance, Edward Hopper's paintings for the atmosphere of the hotel rooms), to modes of operation (the small Ferris wheel completing a revolution every twenty-hour hours that is "The Time-Keeper's Place"). To each of these corresponds a "subject," an inhabitant with a life story expressed in poetic yet precise language. These are engaged in activities and sometimes in interactions with other "subjects," often revelatory of human purpose and the spiritual dimensions of the quotidian—for example, the citizens who paradoxically become observers participating in the public space, easing themselves into the chairs on the wooden walls to contemplate how "the old cloth of the spinning wheel is placed in the Voided Centre and through age and the normal elements becomes dust."[32] For Hejduk, architectural meanings are only made manifest through a lived life (action, for which the architect is also accountable). This life is lived in a physical, formal context framed by the designer, one that may afford the proper attunement between "objects" and "subjects."

* * *

Digital design software, substituting for conventional architectural drafting, has unquestionably played a part in the continuing impoverishment of the built environment in our exploding universal megalopolis. Implicit in the software is an instrumental imperative that devalorizes the crafts that had formerly been involved in the translation of drawings and models to buildings. Its facility to manipulate form has generally resulted in blindness to the experiential meaning of materials at the expense of formal innovation. Dedicated architectural software has enabled extreme standardization and gratuitous novelty: formal repetition, giving rise to identical buildings with homogeneous components, and one-of-a-kind sculptural pieces, often assembled from complex heterogeneous components, yet both unresponsive to their location (cultural and physical) and the preexisting qualities of *place*. Indeed, these powerful tools that have captivated building practices the world over participate in a societal tendency to engage less and less with the physical world around us, trusting GPS for orientation, Facebook for our "social" interactions, or Google to supply all the information we need to know about a place. The result is a world designed for a technological way of life that curtails our sensorimotor skills, a flattened world that as a constitutive part of our consciousness enhances our sense of nihilism.

As I started to suggest above, however, despite this dominant trend, fueled by society's unquestioning belief in the reduction of reality to numerical data ("information"—assumed to be the "intelligence" or even the potential "human consciousness" of the machine), the historical roots of our problem run much deeper, and cannot be attributed solely to digital media. The digital tools are not the "cause" of our pathological environments. The task that stands before us, if we wish to design a more meaningful and healthy environment, is to engage the tools critically, mindful of the observations that have been raised in these pages. This task must necessarily be for others to pursue, but some observations may be drawn. Indeed, besides a need to maintain a place for different modes of graphic expression that involve the body in continuity with gestures and skills like hand-drawing, physical modeling, and working with materials, all of which actually qualify our understanding of reality and thus should not be regarded as merely reducible to computer graphics, in view of our argument it seems particularly crucial to seek ways to harness the linguistic imagination to the digital tools themselves.

Is it possible to "return" to the world of experience through mediations that reduce the wholeness of such experience to a binary code of 1s and 0s? Obviously, given what we have discovered about the opposition between natural and algorithmic languages, the problem is not simple. While the tendency of digital technologies is reductive and substitutive, it is evident that the media engaged by artists can augment experience by revealing new encounters with reality, much like Cézanne, for example, accomplished through his numerous paintings of Mont Sainte-Victoire that obsessively questioned the equating of visual perception with optical perspective. In a recent book on dance, digital technologies, and phenomenology, Susan Kozel insightfully describes her experiences as performer in the installation entitled *Telematic Dreaming* by Paul Sermon. Lying on a bed, her image was projected live onto another bed located in a separate room where any visitor could interact with her virtual body. Viewing a projection of her own body on the other bed, she describes how she could at times feel great intimacy while at one point she became distressed, as she felt violated by a particularly cruel guest. Kozel concludes that the "virtual," when properly understood, has ultimately little to do with disembodiment and computer screens. Drawing particularly from Merleau-Ponty's late philosophy and his concept of flesh, she points out how this notion is consistent with his understanding of the prereflective as a region prior to the duality of object and subject. Merleau-Ponty writes: the flesh "is not matter, not mind, is not substance. To designate it we should need the old term 'element,' in the sense it was used to speak of water, air, earth and fire. ... [It is] the formative medium of the object and the subject ... [being] incomparably agile ... [it is] capable of weaving relations between bodies that this time will not only enlarge but will pass definitively beyond the circle of the visible."[33]

Understanding virtual experience as an iteration of the flesh of the world, Kozel demonstrates how participatory and responsive events, in her case dance performances that include digital telepresence, challenge the dualistic concepts prevalent in Cartesian space, revealing significant depths and fostering intersubjective communication.[34] If, as V. S. Ramachandran famously wrote in regard to the phantom limb phenomenon, "*Your own body* is a phantom, one that your brain has temporarily constructed purely for convenience," explaining why "[i]f your hidden hand and a rubber hand in front of it are stroked simultaneously while you concentrate on the rubber hand, you will feel the sensation on the rubber hand," there may be grounds for the belief that *moods* can be simulated.[35] In other words, it is possible to experience one's sensations in another object. We may recall that for enactive theory, moods and feelings are not "internal," they are *in the world*, a result of the very conditions of embodied consciousness. More recently, BeAnotherLab in Barcelona, an interdisciplinary art collective dedicated to investigating embodied and telepresence experiments, has been running "The Machine to be Another," where participants, usually in pairs, wearing immersive head-mounted displays, experience their movements while seeing the body of the other. The performances offer fascinating first-person perspectives on gender and racial difference.[36]

Translating this understanding of virtual reality into tools for graphic representation that may result in nonreductive and narrative-driven models for architecture, however, is certainly not easy. Rather than maintaining the usual "third-person" relationship with his architectural models, the designer, in order to ascertain the moods of atmospheres for human action in a virtual world, would have to occupy a "first-person" position. The "interface" for the design of not-yet-existing environments is usually a screen of some sort, which, as I suggested, is at odds with spontaneous visual perception. Video game software designers have better explored the first-person position behind the screen. But in some circles there is excitement about the possibilities of bypassing the screen through immersive environments such as those described above. While provoking human consciousness to recognize itself as another is not difficult in such immersive environments, particularly when movement is limited or carefully choreographed between two people, simulating spontaneous vision in a purely visual designed environment is another issue. The first-person interaction with the virtual world must be like in the lifeworld, kinesthetic and synesthetic, sensing the body moving through the room, drawn to get a better grasp of what's going on, and so forth. This is possible in performances and art installations that depend upon interactions with a physical environment, but is hard to imagine in a visual model of a nonexistent building. The ultimate simulation of spontaneous perception in time and space—of *depth*—is probably impossible, since embodied perception is always an enacted solicitation rather than a passive optical experience, the backing away from large things in order to better grasp others close by, the feeling of being attracted by some colors (always shifting in ambient light—color is another aspect of quotidian embodied perception that is very difficult to simulate in digital environments) while recoiling from others. After pondering this issue some years ago (while still taking the computer screen as a necessary interface), Hubert Dreyfus concluded that "it looks likely that in the virtual world the mood of the background space cannot come to resemble the mood of a similar space in the real world and so give guidance to the architect."[37]

Recent modeling software has even attempted to question its presumed Cartesian ordering systems to allow for a more embodied engagement with the process—as, for example, is the case with 3ds Max and other three-dimensional animation and rendering programs where the camera can simulate our vision so the designer/inhabitant can move around the designed building. This is of course an intriguing development, albeit one that to a great extent still represents a fallacy, since our vision is not merely homologous to photographic perspective. Even more sophisticated recent software (although extremely difficult to use properly) allows one to work in non-Cartesian space and draw without having to deploy precise measurements, facilitating drawing as a thinking process. Such is the case with Maya, software initially designed to create artifacts based primarily on narrative structures, as with interactive 3D applications, video games, animated film, and visual effects,[38] recently engaged by some architects. At McGill University, we ran a research project on the use of digital media in design using software designed for the entertainment industry (Crytek's CryEngine and Unity3D), intended to create atmospheres in which a narrative could be constructed.[39] Models for such applications might be narrative video games now on the market that center on telling stories and creating different experiences for the game players that "act" in the environment, similar to open-ended versions of cinema. Some of these games tease out connections between actions, stories, and narratives, often to be discerned by the game player, and frequently in collaboration with other players.

What always makes this issue truly complicated is the discrepancy between the way the software is intended to operate and the way architects may use it, as well as the fact that software tends to be more and more complex, such that to adapt or subvert it in view of the designer's aims requires a very deep knowledge of the program's "digital architecture." In the end, the issue for the architect is to skillfully master the design tools available in view of an expressive intention that recognizes the primacy of the world of experience, the meanings already given in the natural and cultural worlds and articulated in poetic language. This is still a tall order for present digital media.

8
Architecture and *Spiritus* in the Twenty-First Century

I have sought in these pages to provide the historical context of the concept of *Stimmung*—atmosphere—in architectural theory, traced its proper foundations in phenomenology and cognitive science, and drawn a line to the linguistic imagination. I have suggested this may be a strategy for a meaningful architecture in the twenty-first century, one that, while "authored," may truly take into account the values and habits of the diverse cultures on our compressed planet. Much remains to be researched and tested to find appropriate tools of representation to achieve this aim, finding methodological strategies to implement the literary imagination in design while engaging other contemporary tools of imaging and production. In this last chapter I wish to elaborate upon some of the central questions that have been raised throughout this book, summarizing our findings and reaching some additional conclusions.

Even after we correct our understanding of *aisthésis* to grasp, as I have explained elsewhere, following Hans-Georg Gadamer, "the relevance of the beautiful" for the prospering of human cultures, architecture stands apart from all other arts.[1] As numerous excellent studies have demonstrated, our discipline shares many attributes with art forms that include temporality as an aspect of their configurations, such as literature and cinematography.[2] The moving image emulates human motion, and cinematography's techniques of montage, framing, and collage can be profoundly instructive in the creation of moods. With painting and sculpture, also evidently media of emotions, architecture shares its lasting presence as object, one that has the capacity to move us regardless of our relationship to the rituals and habits of the culture for which it was produced. Something similar is obvious, however, in major literary or musical monuments from past epochs; in all cases, works gifted to us in the present moment demand interpretation from embodied consciousness. Like a Mozart symphony or Michelangelo's *Pietà*, these works transcend the particularities that root them to their respective times and places, to communicate universally, especially at the level of emotions and passions.

Trying to better articulate the nature of the poetic image in architecture, I have cited Octavio Paz, who believes that given the primarily linguistic dimension of reality, we can indeed consider plastic arts and musical works as poems on two conditions: first, that they "return their materials to that which they are—sparkling or opaque matter," evoking the primary poetics of material studied by Gaston Bachelard and setting aside their instrumental utility; and, second, that they "be transformed into images ... to become a peculiar form of communication." This is none other than the poetic image: that which a metaphor "says" and yet cannot be paraphrased (so it's nothing like a picture), which even for a written poem is paradoxically something that is beyond language.[3] It is important to point out, however, that when Paz speaks of the universality of the poetic image across the arts, he is writing about experience in the presence of the painting, the monument, the poem or the symphony, all as aesthetic objects. In architecture this characterization does not suffice, for "use" and "materials" can never merely become inconsequential to meaning—though as I will argue, they may resolve into the perception of higher purpose and emptiness. To claim, as John Hejduk did and as I recalled in the previous chapter, that architecture may "be" its representation is therefore always a "critical" operation, justifiable by the cultural conditions of modernity since Piranesi's time, but bracketing the conditions of bodily *emplacement* necessary in architectural and urban atmospheres. *Presence* in architecture operates through different temporalities, the phenomenological "thick present" of prereflective experience, in and through our actions (everyday life), and as (reflective) representation, through memory and imagination. It operates as a poetic image that, like Giambattista Vico's "imaginative universals," may have the capacity to communicate universally and transcend its present time.

Indeed, I have emphasized in this book that architecture's primary subject matter is life as lived, accessible as a narrated story whose elements are human habits. Its purpose is to give resonance to situations as events, accounting for their familiarity while disclosing poetic options in the manner of linguistic, semantic innovation. Other arts can be distorted to appear merely decorative, be kept in museums, or stored in basements, but architecture, to be truly what it is, must concern itself with psychosomatic health, with the spiritual (literally "atmospheric") dimensions of life. In order to address life as lived, a life always and already possessed of sensorimotor skills afforded by the body and structured by cultures, architecture must create appropriate transformative atmospheres accommodating habit as well as bringing about productive (poetic and ethical) change. This architectural power emulates that of the classical gods in the physical realm, present in the very meanings and uses of the Greek word *atmós*.

In ancient Greek, *atmós* doubled as both "vapor" and "steam," and was sometimes associated with breath; it could be poisonous, like that of the Furies in Aeschylus's *Eumenides* (line 138), or beneficial, as in the divine vapors emanating from the ground in Delphi that inspired the Oracle (Pausanias, *Description of Greece*, 10.5.7).[4] Tracing the roots of the term back to Sanskrit we find *atman*, meaning "inner self" (or soul—in a nondualistic sense), the "first principle" or true self of the individual prior to identification with phenomena. In Hinduism, in order to be liberated, the individual must realize that one's true self (*atman*) is identical with the transcendent self. According to Plutarch, the *atmós* of moving water or foggy air is capable of carrying fleeting images—like the imagination of the inner self (or soul);[5] it can bear words like human breath. From Latin we inherit *spiritus* (breath), in words such as *spirit* and *spiritual*. In architecture, prereflective transformative atmospheres can indeed give place to reflective poetic images, completing its cognitive and communicative function, affective and intellectual. This is, in essence, its spiritual function.

***

Are we asking too much from architecture in our secular world, consumed at worst with selfish financial gain and marketing, and at best with the goals of providing affordable housing (or comfortable accommodation) for large populations in Africa and Asia? Is it possible for cultural survival to be content with a soulless environment good enough to house the needy or the affluent, to expect nothing more than the production of merely functional, physically sustainable, and at times fashionable buildings? What about humanity's spiritual needs? Traditional Catholic churches in Quebec are now empty and being converted to gyms and condominiums, while in downtown Los Angeles old cinemas are being transformed into spaces for new cults. The polarization of traditional religions through ideological distortions is evident in our war-torn world, while the power of new cults is undeniable, even when their site is a television studio. Traveling through Jamaica, one notices the poverty of the housing stock, and yet every five hundred meters there is a well-appointed building for a different cult, testimony to an important human need. How is architecture to respond authentically to these questions? By building a "traditional" temple in the suburbs of Toronto?[6] Pretending that the old religions remain unaffected by contemporary questions and their own internal corruption? Designing sterile "interdenominational" buildings?

Romanticism dreamt about bringing back the gods but found the way of cults and rituals already barred, either because there was no longer a group of devotees to carry out the ritual gestures after the French Revolution, or because the gestures involved in traditional religions themselves were insufficient. The cult of the gods and the religious feeling migrated into the realm of the arts and their reception: *aisthésis*.[7] Literature's capacity to communicate a poetic image is closely associated with spiritual experience, which may explain the unprecedented popularity of the novel (and related narrative forms such as film) in all cultures during the last two centuries.

Indeed, the embodiment of the gods as events, moods, or atmospheres in literature may thus function as a point of departure for our own projects of lived space. Literary invocations of atmospheres appear in diverse genres. In novels and in drama, for example, spatial atmospheres are evident whenever the moods, feelings, or motivations of protagonists are shown to be affected by the environment. In an essay on the work of Gernot Böhme, Kate Rigby points out that the philosopher's literary examples are most commonly taken from lyrical verse.[8] This is far from a simple personal preference. In its use of metaphor, metonymy, rhythm and rhyme, alliteration and assonance, poetic writing, even in narrative fiction, is a particularly effective medium not only for the communication of atmosphere, but also for its production: namely, in the bodily and affective responses of readers. This is similar to the position put forward by literary critic Hans Ulrich Gumbrecht in his recent book *Atmosphere, Mood, Stimmung*, foregrounding the expression of atmosphere and mood through the music and prosody of language itself, as language communicates through aural presence and not exclusively though representation.[9] Roberto Calasso suggests a further reciprocity between poetic language and the visual idea evident at the origins of our philosophical tradition in ancient Greece: Socrates described himself proudly as *nympholeptos* ("captured by the nymphs"); the knowledge that comes from the nymphs, mediators between mortals and divinities, is both terrible and precious. The nymphs are poetic language, the flowing voices of water, the substance of literature; they are "the quivering, sparkling, vibrating, *mental matter* that forms an image, an *eídolon*."[10]

In the aftermath of Nietzsche's lucid questioning of monotheism in *The Gay Science* (1882–1887), any discussion about spirituality in modern culture possesses little legitimacy within the province of old, discredited dogmas and fanatic sects. Mallarmé perceptively realized that he must kill the God (of monotheisms) to access the underlying divine ground; this defined his poetic task: "Having discovered Nothingness, I have found the Beautiful."[11] I suggest that we productively consider that the old, sharp divisions so cleverly set out by Mircea Eliade and easily extrapolated into our architectural heritage between the sacred (literally that which is "set apart") and the profane are no longer operative, so that the spiritual might be expected to appear in the realm of everyday life, with architecture as one of its important mediators.

* * *

Nineteenth-century Europe ushered in the possibility of positive reason, a very different type of rationality from that of classical and medieval European periods, and even different from the reason of the eighteenth-century Enlightenment. Distinct from the Divine Nature of the eighteenth century, still implicit in Newton's natural philosophy and present in the pages of Ledoux's literary and graphic project for the city of Chaux, for example,[12] nineteenth-century nature became generally identified with mere "natural resources," a characterization of external reality now taken for granted the world over despite real or alleged cultural differences. Nature became the repository of animals, plants, and inanimate matter deemed separate from our consciousness: merely existing to be exploited, however rationally (or, in our present time, sustainably). Contrary to the animate materials of traditional architecture, inert matter after the nineteenth century was believed to be no more than a composite of chemical substances, quantified through their atomic weight in the periodic table of the elements. Neither fire, water, air, nor earth were real elements any longer; their qualitative manifestations could be explained away by molecules and their chemical reactions. Life itself was reduced to carbon and atoms of gases. Once Laplace came to explain through mathematics the workings of a universe larger than Newton's—one that accounted for the less obviously predictable motion of comets, for example—and could tell Napoleon that he didn't need God as a "hypothesis," the very concept of the cosmos (order) appeared as a hypothesis, to be demonstrated through increasingly sophisticated instrumentation. The privileging of positive scientific reason led inevitably to the conundrum of subjective science, as eventually expressed by Werner Heisenberg's indeterminacy theory, particularly evident in the theorizing of the phenomenon of light.[13]

Continuity between *mythos* and *logos*, between literary narratives (religious, social, political), with their focus on metaphor and polysemy, and logical discourse, with its emphasis on indicative language, had always been the rule for Western humanity's articulation of the truth of reality. But positive reason excluded all speculation and metaphorical language, seeking its foundation and legitimacy in the pure logic of mathematics. This was precisely Immanuel Kant's plea in his *Prolegomena to Every Future Metaphysics* (1783). No future philosophy would be valid unless it strictly adhered to the rules of mathematical reason. Aristotelian *phrónesis*, "prudence" or "wisdom," expressed in the language of everyday life, was no longer granted authority; rhetoric, its technique, was evicted from higher education and instead became associated with deceit. Romanticism put forward the alternatives we have been contemplating in previous chapters: the novel as the new art form and affective truth over logic. Meditating upon the limitations of reason in the age of science in more recent times, Hans-Georg Gadamer has explained how the great novels took the place of traditional philosophy in articulating the fundamental questions of humanity, while during the nineteenth and twentieth centuries professional philosophy generally became mired in its own formal systems.[14]

I have been arguing that in its quest to provide communicative settings for cultures, traditional European architecture mirrored precisely the continuity between logic and narrative language, with harmonic proportions dictating formal disposition and narrative language guiding ornamental considerations, producing attuned atmospheres through mimesis and ultimately cohesive urban environments. The settings created out of this tradition accommodated the political orders associated with ancient democracy, theocracies, monarchies, and empires. This continuity in architecture was ruptured in the nineteenth century, as reflected in the theories and teachings of Jean-Nicolas-Louis Durand, coinciding with the advent of a new politics—one that has radically impacted our global village, despite present cultural differences and our recovered awareness of the limits of scientific reason. The French Revolution was not just one civil war among others; it marked an end to millennia of political systems premised on the notion of a sovereign's capacity for transcendent judgment. After Louis XVI finally lost his head, all human beings could be considered equal; no modern ruler was thereafter deemed divine, despite the futile pretensions of all manner of dictators.

Every individual today is born with a set of universal rights still generally encapsulated by *égalité, fraternité, liberté*. These are the rights of a new, truly autonomous subject, modeled on Descartes's dualistic premises, endowed with almost absolute free will and who must be totally responsible for his or her actions. Despite the undeniable benefits of the new dispensation for most human beings, there was also a tremendous cost to our humanity. Such a subject would find it increasingly difficult to participate in rituals, the most important focal actions traditionally framed by architecture, since ritual by definition involves a belief in external agencies having true and effective responsibility for outcomes. The new subject's will-to-power aimed to be fully in control, never hesitating to exploit through increasingly more efficient instrumental methodologies a reality deemed to be totally *other* than him- or herself. This gave rise to great physical perils, such as the ecological crisis that is now taking a toll on our habitats, but also a more insidious crisis of participation for modern humans: a potential alienation from the worlds of nature and culture resulting in a sense of purposelessness, which paradoxically also explains the ideological polarization of religions and the endless emergence of new cults. This condition has also resulted in great difficulties for architecture in its customary role of framing significant actions. Architecture should, to the extent of its capabilities, resist contributing to the vicious cycle of instrumentalism and commoditization; it must do more than merely produce comfortable and consumable environments with a planned expiration date.

According to Giorgio Agamben, once we all become sovereign (like the kings of yore), we all become sacred, *homo sacer*, reduced to our biology.[15] What becomes questioned is the very difference between the common man and the sovereign; the common man—who according to Aristotle was given both *zoon* (the biology shared with all animals) and *bios*, dependent on *logos* or speech—is fundamentally transformed. *It is the very effectiveness of natural language to attain political order, i.e., human equilibrium and well-being, that is being questioned.* To govern human beings reduced to their biology, equal "in law" and free to act, "democratic" regimes had to put in place rules, regulations, and an apparatus of control, discipline, and surveillance (as clearly articulated by Foucault) necessary to ensure order, and which we now even willingly accept. Not surprisingly, their legislative and policing institutions often become corrupt. Even the most "open" governments become police states, and we find the extreme manifestations of the cherished values of the French Revolution in economic corporatism (liberty), communism (equality), national socialism (fraternity), producing in their polarization the worst authoritarian nightmares of our last two centuries.

Durand, of whom much has already been said, set forth the first architectural theory for humanity reduced to bare life (*zoon*), one where architecture would serve its purpose as a comfortable biological shelter constructed in the most efficient manner possible. Durand argued convincingly that the importance of architecture was precisely that it allowed humans, thrown into a hostile natural environment, to avoid pain and maximize pleasure, this being in his opinion the only self-evident universal human aim, putting an end to all other speculations about beauty, meaning, or expression. Despite the discussions about the role of pleasure and pain in human sensation and action that had already emerged during the Enlightenment, no previous architectural theory had dared contract its values to their simple opposition. All forms of subsequent functionalism, biomimicry, and biomimetism, from the sublime wish to build houses with the delicacy and fitness of bird's nests, to the ridiculous contemporary obsession with creating "intelligent" buildings, find their origin in this position. It is important to consider why this view was embraced by modern disciplines and increasingly by societies the world over after 1800, its argument for hedonism (the individual's pursuit of pleasure) appearing as "common sense" to most modern humans.

Daniel L. Smail has explained that from the perspective of evolutionary neurobiology, considering not only recent humanity's history but also our "deep history" (including the Paleolithic and Neolithic eras), it is possible to argue that the progress of civilization is "an illusion of psychotropy."[16] While he realizes that this may be an overgeneralization, like the grand narratives of sacred historians that may see the unfolding of history as God's plan, he believes there are sufficient grounds for the hypothesis. What passes for progress "is often nothing more than new developments in the art of changing body chemistry."[17] While it is impossible to summarize Smail's argument here, his position is important to consider in view of our search for attunement through architecture. It may be cynical or reductive to see humanity's historical accomplishments in this light, but what is certain is that once a dualistic understanding of reality (the Cartesian mind/body split) was generally taken for granted in the early nineteenth century, the disappearance of the painful, mortal body was celebrated, and psychotropic tendencies accentuated.

In fact, given the current homogenization of global society and the universality of basic human physiology, Smail speculates that it is likely all humans "will be tempted by the same package of sensory inputs and body stimulations, and that the capitalistic marketplace, evolving as it does towards optimal solutions, will eventually hit on the perfect package of psychotropic products and mechanisms."[18] While perhaps ultimately impossible to accomplish due to its unsustainable demand for energy, this thrust points to the "end of history" prophesied by Francis Fukuyama: a radical "animalizing" of human beings, and hardly a state of attunement. The real difficulty, as Smail concludes, is that we grow increasingly numb to the mechanisms that stimulate our moods and feelings every day. We usually get bored by what only a decade ago might have been an exciting environment, creating a neurochemical insensitivity that reinforces our alienation.

Indeed, it follows that for a mentality driven by hedonism, architecture would be best if it functioned like a high-tech drug: providing maximum comfort and just enough titillation to avoid boredom between the cradle and the grave, promoting the forgetfulness of death while science forever seeks its elimination. Michel Houellebecq, in a brilliant piece of literary science fiction entitled *The Possibility of an Island*, considers the possible outcomes of our present culture of hedonism as he projects it into the future (approximately twenty-five generations from the present, to be more precise). Poignantly describing through Daniel, his central character, the pain associated with aging and the loss of sexual vitality in our youth-obsessed society, he narrates Daniel's association with a sect that seeks the total elimination of physical and emotional suffering while devoting its energy to making cloning of humans a reality: humans at their peak of vitality that will eventually feed like plants, through a process similar to photosynthesis. Daniel eventually provides his DNA to the sect, which we then learn is the reason for his ultimate survival through successive cloning—down to generation twenty-five.

The oracle of the sect teaches that jealousy, desire, and the appetite for procreation originate in the suffering of being. It is this suffering that "makes us seek the other, as a palliative"; we must go beyond this stage, leaving behind our social world to reach the state "where the simple fact of being [biological life] constitutes in itself a permanent occasion of joy." All forms of sexuality, in a few generations reduced to "intermediation" through computer screens, constitute "nothing more than a game, freely undertaken and not constitutive of being." In other words, only the "freedom of indifference" would bring about serenity.[19]

Houellebecq's advanced humans have no need for architecture: no need for settings for embodied communication, for emotionally charged spaces of desire. They reside in plain houses that are no more than shelters with computer screens, linked by efficient telecommunication networks. They exchange information via written words and precise codes, but only through their terminals, and everyone is encouraged to write an autobiography for his or her successors. They live out their allotted number of years for pure telematic enjoyment, to be replaced by one more incarnation. They spend their lives trying to eliminate whatever remains of desire, preparing for final salvation (the coming of the "Future Ones"), studying the "tragic" lives of their predecessors toward this greater goal. Outside of their compounds, surviving hordes of "neohumans" roam a planet decimated by wars and ecological disasters, and yet still evoke for the insiders the mysteries associated with passion.

Indeed, despite all the rational efforts of the advanced humans and the impeccable logic of the project, contradictions emerge and eventually the experiment fails: at least for the main character. Daniel 25 (his twenty-fifth clone) escapes his comfortable environment looking for a woman he had met online, herself driven out into the world by a belief in the survival of love and its importance for happiness. We learn from an oracle that she has been "poisoned" by a delirious poem written by

Daniel 1 in which he had affirmed eternal love to a young promiscuous Spanish woman who had abandoned him (just before committing suicide out of despair, having realized he was simply too old for her). She had also read Plato's *Symposium* (his dialogue on love); this was deemed by the sect to be one of the most pernicious texts ever written, for its intoxication of Western mankind and finally of mankind as a whole. Plato's text, according to the oracle, "had inspired in [humanity] disgust at its condition as rational animal," engendering a dream that it had failed to shed entirely, even after two millennia. Its persistence was such that it was even taken up by Christianity so that St. Paul could write: "Two will become one flesh; this mystery is great, I proclaim it, in relation to Christ and the church."[20]

After walking for several days out in the inhospitable world, unable to find the woman he is seeking, Daniel 25 dehydrates and finally and truly dies, not before exclaiming, "I was. I was no longer. Life was real."[21]

* * *

Thus we may rightly ask, what is real life? And what is this specifically human life for which architecture must provide attuned atmospheres? Is it merely the material, pleasure-seeking process described in these scenarios and often assumed by our contemporary cultures? Chilean biologists Francisco Varela and Humberto Maturana famously coined the term *autopoiesis* to characterize metabolic, autonomous life (cells and bacteria, as distinct from other chemical compounds and even parasitic viruses), always seeking homeostasis, perceiving (and pursuing) food as "meaning." This is precisely the biological life we share with other living organisms, already sentient and thus possessing an elemental "mind": Aristotle's *zoon*.

Given our observations, it is not surprising that Patrik Schumacher co-opted the term *autopoiesis* to evoke self-organization in parametric design approaches,[22] also extrapolated to the now popular desire to create "intelligent," efficient buildings that cater to our comfort and pleasure by emulating the systems of a "computerized mind." Significantly, however, neurophenomenology's own understanding of architecture is rather as a *heteropoietic* system, capable of harmoniously complementing the metabolic processes of human consciousness, to provide for prereflective purposeful action and a reflective understanding of our place in the natural and cultural world. *Architectural "limits" would thus be articulated not as a self-generating part of a system (as in a cell contained by its membrane) but through language, that fundamental characteristic of human life, in view of intersubjective expression.* I must insist here on one of our primary previous discoveries: language also has its roots in the prereflective realm of gesture and the body as a primary expressive system. It is not a more or less arbitrary, constructed code. Language is "emergent"; it "speaks through us" and captures meaning in its mesh; words point toward meanings but never fully coincide with them.[23]

Given architecture's heteropoietic character, one can better grasp that its unique gift is to offer experiences of sense and purpose not in the mere fulfillment of pleasure, but in the *delay* (Marcel Duchamp's famous word to characterize the experience of meaning in his own works) that reveals the space of human existence as a space of desire. Such desire is actually bittersweet as characterized by Sappho, never concluding in biological homeostasis; it is irreducible to the search for ever-increasing comfort or fulfillment. The so-called meaning of existence appears profoundly grounded in our biology, as a true *human* alternative where desire is never-ending, yet one that may always be sensed as purposeful in our actions, particularly when framed by attuned works of architecture. Contrary to Antonio Damasio, who has argued that the arts are further "causes" of homeostasis for a reflective mind, I might characterize them as symbolic mediations through which humans deal with the paradoxically open-ended quality of our own biological homeostasis, as we experience it in view of our awareness of death.[24]

In other writings I have explained that the space of desire is no a posteriori construct but rather the given spatiality of human (sexual) embodied consciousness; it is also the spatiality of human linguistic consciousness. Plato called it *chóra*, whereby the word for the specific wood-and-leather chair in front of me, with its cracks and imperfections, coincides with *chair*, its ideal, one that exists always *in* the world; the space therefore where the particular and ephemeral meets the ideal and eternal. Regardless of its distinctions from *tópos*, the natural places we may share with other animal species, this enigmatic, coemerging site of enactive consciousness is often hidden today behind pseudo-scientific assumptions. Beyond stylistic preferences, fashion, generative geometries, and formal predilections, architecture's calling is to represent such space to humanity: one attuned to our worldly actions and habits yet emotionally resonant, open to uncertainty and external forces, one where *Stimmung* may become manifest as "the scattering of a quake of being as an event in *Dasein*."[25]

Another important aspect of architecture's gift of *place* is to reveal in itself *the true temporality* of this space of human experience, a constitutive dimension of what we may call our access to *spirituality*. This is the experience of a present moment that, while it can be conceptualized by science (and our clocks) as a quasi-nonexistent point between past and future, is experienced as thick and endowed with dimensions—in a sense, eternal. This has always been the time "out of time" that is the gift of rituals, festivals, and art, evoked by Hans-Georg Gadamer,[26] or the time of "silence," celebrated by Louis Kahn and Juhani Pallasmaa for architecture. This present "with dimensions" corresponds to Merleau-Ponty's *écart*, the delay between prereflective experience and reflective thought in all its modalities that is paradoxically present in experience and substantiated by neuroscience. Indeed, as I have noted, the formal structure of time-consciousness, or phenomenal temporality (as first described by Husserl, and paraphrased in chapter 5), has an analogue in the dynamic structure of neural processes.[27] This uniquely human temporality is generally concealed by scientific and hedonistic interpretations of meaning, whereby we may simply assume that the present "does not exist" and continue cultivating our destructive obsessions with the future. Giving place to such *presence* in the events it frames has been architecture's well-documented accomplishment throughout history, as it has been poetry's, allowing humans to perceive meaningfulness in the coincidence of opposites: being and nonbeing, life and death, reconciled beyond theological dogma.

***

Despite prevailing assumptions concerning the dualistic structure of reality that are constantly reinforced by instrumental technologies, by much contemporary science and old religious beliefs, as well as carried through metaphorical systems that characterize our minds as disembodied, I hope to have sufficiently demonstrated that there is no disembodied mind (or soul). "We" are not simply our brains; our full nervous system is embodied and *in* the world. Consciousness is in continuity with our biology, truly "mind in life." Likewise, the properties of the mind (like moods and feelings) are not primarily internal; they are shaped by the physiology of the brain, of course, but more importantly by the living body and its actions in the world. Gilbert Ryle would go even further in denying the existence of a substantive "inner world,"[28] claiming that there is nothing to see inside a human skull. Introspection is only retrospection (about past experiences—whether recent or long term). This is confirmed by George Lakoff and Mark Johnson, who in this regard follow in the footsteps of Merleau-Ponty and David Abram; since the embodied mind is part of, and dependent on, the living body for its existence, in order to properly speak of the spiritual experiences accessible to cultures around the world and crucial for psychosomatic health, it is necessary to realize that this experience is embodied.[29]

Lakoff and Johnson remind us that a major function of the embodied mind is empathic.[30] Our capacity for imaginative, mimetic projection is a vital cognitive faculty, the origin of our social selves. In contrast to Sartre, who postulated the ultimate alienation of the "Other," seemingly unknowable to us, Merleau-Ponty's phenomenology demonstrates that we only know ourselves through such projection; we know ourselves *through* the other, in embodied communication, situated through architecture and urban space (and for which Skype on the computer screen is always a poor substitute). Experientially, this is a form of "transcendence." Lakoff and Johnson add that imaginative empathic projection comprises a significant portion of what has been called spiritual experience, as cultivated in meditative practices. I have insisted in these pages that the environment is part of our consciousness; it is not an "other," or a collection of objects, but is indeed part of our being. Through empathic projection, we understand that we are part of the environment.

In many religious traditions, a connection with the natural world is regarded as an encounter with the divine present in all things. In theology this is known as panentheism, affirming simultaneously both the transcendence and the immanence of God: God does not exist as a separate being "out there"; it is more than everything, yet everything is in God; God is "right here" even if it is also more than "right here."[31] This condition describes the possibility of an authentic spirituality for modernity in the wake of dualism. For this reason, Hölderlin goes beyond and behind the gods to arrive at the pure divine or "immediate": *enargeîs*.[32] The sacred is the awesome itself—an alignment of *cháos* and *nómos*—precisely what Heidegger admired in Hölderlin's poetry. For the poet, chaos is the sacred, reminding us of the relationship Plato elicits in *Timaeus* between *cháos* and *chóra*—cultural space. Chaos is the gap where light appears and which itself flaunts all location in measurable time and space.[33]

Granting the possibility of a panentheistic spirituality for nondualistic embodied consciousness in the contemporary world, it is easy to recognize that appropriate environments are crucial in the realization of this goal. If perception is something "we do," and self-conscious life appears as a result of our bodily sensorimotor articulation in the world, then the environment is the "equipment" of consciousness (in the Heideggerian sense), and architecture is an event. Architecture must be resonant, "empathic" for us to attain a spiritual wholeness; postindustrial environments are seldom receptive to empathy, but they could be, as is amply demonstrated in literature and cinema, and they must be part of everyday life: no longer "set apart" like old ritual spaces. Architecture is not an encounter with an unusual, uncanny, or even supernatural dimension that is deployed somewhere beyond everyday life experience. Rather, if it is magical, it discloses a dimension, *Stimmung*—an attunement of being that is always operative beneath conventional consciousness, in that carnal realm of exchange with our animal bodies, our true embodied minds. Thus, great architecture and moving urban spaces do not simply sweep you away, they gather you up into the body of the present moment so thoroughly that explanations can fall away; revealing the ordinary in all its plain and simple outrageousness and allowing it to shine.[34]

Indeed, it is interesting to observe that for the Greeks *theós* has no vocative case; a god can't be "called." *Theós* has a predicative function; it designates something that happens, an *event*; it thus relates to architecture, to atmospheres and moods. Euripides in *Helen* writes: "O gods: recognizing the beloved is god."[35] According to Karl Kerenyi, it was indeed common parlance in ancient Greece to characterize an event as *theós*.[36] *Theós* could easily become Zeus. Aratus (third century BCE) writes: "From Zeus let our beginning be, from he whom men never leave unnamed. Full of Zeus are the oaths and the places where men meet, full of Zeus the sea and the seaports. Every one of us and in every way is in need of Zeus. Indeed, we are his offspring."[37] Virgil then follows with his famous statement: "Iovis omnia plena"; God (Jove) is everywhere … it is the light.[38] In 1797, Siegfried Schmidt translated this feeling through the sensibility of romanticism: "All is life, if God animates us, invisible, felt. / They are light touches, but of sacred power."[39] Thus *atheós* generally meant "to be abandoned by the gods"—or, we might say, "devoid of architecture." This is the result of environments that alienate rather than resonate with our empathic potential.

Cognitive scientists in the wake of phenomenology have explained how conceptualization can only happen through the body, and since the body is the mind engaged in its environment, the qualities of this external reality matter immensely for cognition.[40] Language is the mediation that allows us to articulate issues concerning this relationship: metaphoric language that accounts for emotions and feelings, and that may unearth dimensions of consciousness that are concealed from analytic thought. In this book, we have been reconsidering the relationship between what architects do as they design and the language we speak, and how this affects the process in various ways, consistent with the discovery of the identities between natural and poetic language. These are manifested primarily in the form of narrative programs that may foreground the significant habits and actions to be shaped by form, actively engaging the ethical issues of the project and bringing to bear historical understanding. This is a true fusion of horizons coming from the personal concerns of clients and the grounds of culture. Primarily metaphoric language can also bring about lyrical narratives that imagine the emotional quality of spaces, their articulation as resonant vessels for cultural programs and shared values leading to empathic spaces of dwelling. This experience must be passionate—the body and architecture make it possible. Lakoff and Johnson write: "The mechanism by which spirituality becomes passionate is metaphor. ... Through metaphor, the vividness, intensity and meaningfulness of ordinary experience become the basis for passionate spirituality."[41]

* * *

Since, according to Ricoeur, the ontological function of metaphorical discourse is to reveal the "Real as Act,"[42] we may easily imagine that architecture likewise has this capacity. It is well known that in the past architecture found one of its most important expressions in religious and political institutions, those that gave meaning to collective and personal lives by framing rituals. For contemporary panentheism, the connections between the enactive theory of perception and ancient Buddhist psychology are most illuminating.[43] In the second century of the Christian era, the Buddhist philosopher Nargajuna put forward a carefully argued and comprehensive case for the theory of codependence, explaining the appearance and meaning of reality.[44] He asserted that even though the subject of an action may easily assume his positive existence apart from the world, or, even more easily, the persistence and absolute existence of objects after his demise, upon closer examination this makes little sense. We can neither talk about a seer of a sight who is not seeing its sight, nor of a sight that is not being seen by its seer. Nor is it possible to assume that the action itself has a positive, independent existence. Finally, after testing all possible logical arguments, he concludes: "nothing is found that is not dependently arisen. For that reason, nothing is found that is not *empty*" (my emphasis).[45] In other words, if subjects and their objects, things and their attributes, and causes and their effects exist independently as we habitually take them to be, then they must not depend on any condition or relation. Yet nothing in our experience can be found that satisfies this criterion, and therefore there is nothing that can be found that has an ultimate or autonomous existence; everything is "empty" and originates codependently.[46]

Where does this leave us with regard to our all-too-real everyday experience? Nargajuna explained that there are two truths, the truth of worldly convention and the ultimate, supreme truth. Relative truth is the phenomenal truth as it appears; in Tibetan this is called *kundzop*, meaning "dressed up, outfitted, or costumed." It is *sunyata*, or absolute truth (emptiness, groundlessness), but costumed in the colors of the phenomenal world, everyday experience. This distinction is not metaphysical in the Western sense; it doesn't imply for *kundzop* relativism or subjectivity, but simply acknowledges the codependent origin of reality, where mind, its objects, and their relations appear as devoid of any independent or abiding existence—subsuming, of course, our personal mortality and even the scientifically ascertained entropy of the universe.

Within this framework, the ethical first person is real but "empty," characterizing our responsibility, allowing us to let go from both strife and pernicious attachments and making it easier to avoid pain and violence. We might recall through phenomenology that there is no "will" as a cause of action (like in waving hello to a friend across the street). We can of course plan or imagine a particular goal state, but in action there is no intermediary "will."[47] The "alternative" between "freedom of will" and determinism is false. The elusive "I" or "ego cogito" (discussed as a fallacy by many early-twentieth-century philosophers and crystallizing in deconstruction) reflects the fact that our attempts at self-examination exclude of necessity our one current activity—the process of inspection—but the ethical self is nevertheless real. Yet because it is not about a punctual will preceding an action, the creation of "dispositions" though habits (in architecture) and education are of central importance. Claude-Nicolas Ledoux understood this precisely when he claimed the power of legislation and cultivation of mores for architecture, expressed through his literary narratives.[48]

There is, moreover, always a connection between *sunyata* and compassion in experience. In Buddhism, "sense" therefore ultimately arises not from the self, its object, or the relationship between the two, but from emptiness itself, the feeling that is primordial consciousness; inherent also in Aristotle's animal soul. In the wake of Nietzsche, the modern and contemporary world resonates strongly with the Buddhist concept of being without ground. "Emptiness" is the void encountered by Mallarmé on his way to finding the divine through his poetry. This, it must be emphasized, is in fact the opposite of despairing nihilism that may deny the meaning of life.

Ecologically responsible building and sustainable cities do not in themselves connect us to a meaningful life; simply adopting such approaches will not protect us from slipping into a cynical instrumentalism. We might see evidence of this in the way standardized systems for sustainable design can easily reduce complex ecological and energy-driven relationships to oversimplified (and commoditized) technical checklists, subject to manipulation for profit. If we are to curtail a nefarious nihilism, our understanding must extend beyond the merely positive aspect of ecology to the more polyvalent and subtle environmental relationships at stake. True psychosomatic health depends on attuned environments.[49] The issue is cultural sustainability, our ever-sought ambition to peacefully coexist with others on a shared living planet. Thus, architecture should aspire to create atmospheres conducive to moods appropriate for skillful focal practices where "emptiness" may be understood to underscore fulfillment, arising as action disclosed in its fully *present* temporality. Recall here the previously noted etymological genealogy linking atmosphere, *atmós*, and the Sanskrit *atman*: nondualistic being. This is, in Heidegger's language, the attunement of *Dasein*, perhaps the possibility of *Gelassenheit*: the understanding of reality that emerges "beyond" both our instrumental relation to objects as *ready-to-hand* equipment (through work—in the temporality of action) and our intellectual attention as *presence-at-hand* (for example, analytic or aesthetic cognition). Such atmospheres, never merely about sensuous pleasure or consumable novelty, could function as the contemporary alternative to the sacred, paradigmatic architectural space of world cultural traditions. If so, we can hope they might foster the weakening of the strongly held values that are always at the root of human discord and violence.

Notes

Introduction

1. See Antonio Damasio, *Descartes' Error* (Toronto: Penguin, 2005).

2. Cited by Evan Thompson, *Mind in Life: Biology, Phenomenology, and the Sciences of Mind* (Cambridge, MA: Harvard University Press, 2010), 362–363.

3. See Daniel Heller-Roazen, *The Inner Touch: Archaeology of a Sensation* (New York: Zone Books, 2007), 21–41.

4. Vitruvius (Marcus Vitruvius Pollio), *Ten Books on Architecture*, ed. Ingrid D. Rowland and Thomas Noble Howe (Cambridge: Cambridge University Press, 2002), book 1, 26–32.

5. For a more philosophical study of this issue, see my own *Built upon Love: Architectural Longing after Ethics and Aesthetics* (Cambridge, MA: MIT Press, 2006).

6. See Martin Heidegger, "Building, Dwelling, Thinking," in *Poetry, Language, Thought*, trans. Albert Hofstadter (New York: Harper and Row, 1971).

7. Richard Sennett, *The Fall of Public Man* (Cambridge: Cambridge University Press, 1977).

8. See, for example, *Architecture and the Crisis of Modern Science* (Cambridge, MA: MIT Press, 1983).

9. Hubert Dreyfus and Sean D. Kelly, *All Things Shining: Reading the Western Classics to Find Meaning in a Secular Age* (New York: Free Press, 2011), 190–223.

10. Jean Baudrillard, *The Ecstasy of Communication*, ed. Sylvère Lotringer, trans. Bernard Schutze and Caroline Schutze (New York: Semiotext(e), 1988), represents the point of departure for later discussions on virtual space. Despite the fact that Baudrillard was only addressing television culture in the late 1980s, he was already describing the ways our grip on reality was waning as we identified with our avatars in a global network of communications; simulations would be the new reality, our body almost useless as we interfaced with screens (now through a click of the mouse or a tap of a finger), and the notion of public space (and its distinctions from the "private") would be rendered obsolete, reduced to an "ephemeral connecting space." Already in 1909, E. M. Forster's short novel *The*

Machine Stops, first published in *The Oxford and Cambridge Review*, brilliantly staged the consequences of a world ruled by telecommunications (http://www.ele .uri.edu/faculty/vetter/Other-stuff/The-Machine-Stops.pdf). Michel Houellebecq's *The Possibility of an Island* (New York: Vintage, 2007) takes up this nightmare, one on which I will comment in the concluding chapter. See also Louise Pelletier, *Downfall: The Architecture of Excess* (Montreal: RightAngle International, 2014), another novel in which architects argue the pros and cons of Baudrillard's position, wittily summarized, and its repercussions for parametric design (140–143).

11. Semir Zeki, *Splendors and Miseries of the Brain: Love, Creativity, and the Quest for Human Happiness* (Malden, MA: Wiley-Blackwell, 2009).

12. See Sarah Robinson, *Nesting: Body, Dwelling, Mind* (Richmond, CA: William Stout, 2011).

13. Vitruvius, *Ten Books*, book 2, 34.

Chapter 1

1. Pierre Patte, *Mémoires sur les objets les plus importans de l'architecture* (Paris, 1769), 1–70.

2. Ivan Illich, *H$_2$O and the Waters of Forgetfulness* (Berkeley, CA: Heyday Books, 1985).

3. Ibid., 63, n. 37.

4. See Richard Coyne, *The Tuning of Place* (Cambridge, MA: MIT Press, 2010).

5. Daniel Heller-Roazen, *The Inner Touch: Archaeology of a Sensation* (New York: Zone Books, 2007), 253–290.

6. Mark Wigley, "The Architecture of Atmosphere," *Daidalos* 68 (1998): 18.

7. Gernot Böhme, "Atmosphere as an Aesthetic Concept," *Daidalos* 68 (1998): 112ff. See also *Architektur und Atmosphäre* (Munich: Wilhelm Fink, 2006) and *Atmosphäre: Essays zur neuen Ästhetik* (Frankfurt am Main: Suhrkamp, 1995).

8. Cited in Kate Rigby, "Gernot Böhme's Ecological Aesthetics of Atmosphere," in Axel Goodbody and Kate Rigby, eds., *Ecocritical Theory: New European Approaches* (Charlottesville: University of Virginia Press, 2011), 143.

9. Ibid.

10. Gernot Böhme, "Atmosphere as the Fundamental Concept of a New Aesthetics," *Thesis Eleven* 36 (1993): 113–126.

11. David Abram, *The Spell of the Senses* (New York: Vintage, 1997), 225ff.

12. Ibid., 226.

13. Ibid., 227.

14. Ibid., 226.

15. I will be arguing this more fully in chapter 5. See Alva Noë, *Varieties of Presence* (Cambridge, MA: Harvard University Press, 2012), 30–33.

16. Jean-Nicolas-Louis Durand, *Précis des leçons d'architecture* (Paris, 1819), 1:34.

17. Étienne-Louis Boullée, *Architecture: Essai sur l'art*, ed. J. M. Pérouse de Montclos (Paris: Hermann, 1968).

18. Wigley, "The Architecture of Atmosphere," 19, 26.

19. Ibid., 25.

20. See Bart Lootsma, "En Route to a New Tectonics," *Daidalos* 68 (1998): 34–47.

21. Cited in ibid., 37.

22. J. G. Ballard, "The Thousand Dreams of Stellavista," in *Vermelion Sands* (London: Vintage, 2001), 183–208.

23. Adolf Loos, "Das Prinzip der Bekleidung," in *Ins Leere Gesprochen* (Vienna: Georg Prachner, 1981), 139–145.

24. Ibid.

25. Peter Zumthor, *Atmospheres* (Basel: Birkhäuser, 2006), 11.

26. Ibid., 11–13.

27. Ibid., 15–17.

28. Ibid., 19.

29. Michael Asgaard Andersen and Henrik Oxvig, eds., *Paradoxes of Appearing: Essays on Art, Architecture and Philosophy* (Baden, Switzerland: Lars Müller, 2009), 7ff.

30. Christian Borch, ed., *Architectural Atmospheres: On the Experience and Politics of Architecture* (Basel: Birkhäuser, 2014).

31. David Leatherbarrow, "Atmospheric Conditions," in Henriette Steiner and Maximilian Sternberg, eds., *Phenomenologies of the City: Studies in the History and the Philosophy of Architecture* (Burlington, VT: Ashgate, 2015), 85–100.

32. David Abram, *Becoming Animal* (New York: Vintage, 2011), 153–154.

33. Ibid., 154.

34. Alberto Pérez-Gómez, *Architecture and the Crisis of Modern Science* (Cambridge, MA: MIT Press, 1983), 17–47.

35. See Alva Noë, *Out of Our Heads: Why You Are Not Your Brain, and Other Lessons from the Biology of Consciousness* (New York: Hill and Wang, 2009), 97–128; and Nick Crossley, *The Social Body: Habit, Identity, and Desire* (London: Sage, 2001). This topic is expounded in chapter 5.

36. Most recently, in an interview he criticized Rem Koolhaas's stewardship of the 2014 Venice Biennale (June 12, 2014), http://newsletter.dezeen.com/t/r-l-xhiitg-juiriijydi-ih/.

37. Peter Eisenman in Cesar Pelli, ed., *Yale Seminars on Architecture 2* (New Haven: Yale University Press, 1982), 49.

38. Hubert Dreyfus, "Why the Mood *in* a Room and the Mood *of* a Room Should Be Important to Architects," in *From the Things Themselves: Architecture and Phenomenology* (Kyoto: Kyoto University Press, 2012), 23–37.

39. See Alberto Pérez-Gómez and Angeliki Sioli, "Drawing *with/in* and Drawing *Out*: A Redefinition of Architectural Drawing ...," in Azucena Cruz-Pierre and Donald Landes, eds., *Exploring the Work of Edward S. Casey* (London: Bloomsbury, 2013), 153–162.

40. Dreyfus, "Why the Mood *in* a Room," 34.

41. I provide a summary of their positions in chapter 5.

42. Dreyfus, "Why the Mood *in* a Room," 26.

43. Cited in ibid.

44. Crossley, *The Social Body*, 22–37.

45. Ibid., 42.

46. Ibid., 45.

47. Ibid., 85–86.

48. Martin Heidegger, *The Fundamental Concepts of Metaphysics: World, Finitude, Solitude*, trans. William McNeill and Nicholas Walker (Bloomington: Indiana University Press, 1995), 66–67.

49. Ibid., 67–68.

50. Crossley, *The Social Body*, 86.

51. Dreyfus, "Why the Mood *in* a Room," 35.

52. Maurice Merleau-Ponty, *Phenomenology of Perception*, trans. Donald A. Landes (New York: Routledge, 2012), 156–160.

53. Crossley, *The Social Body*, 87.

54. Jean-Luc Marion, *Le phénomène érotique* (Paris: Grasset, 2006).

55. Cited in Crossley, *The Social Body*, 88.

56. Ibid.

57. Ibid.

Chapter 2

1. I have proposed such a reading drawing from Gadamer in other writings. See, for example, *Built upon Love* (Cambridge, MA: MIT Press, 2006), 44–47.

2. Leo Spitzer, *Classical and Christian Ideas of World Harmony: Prolegomena to an Interpretation of the Word "Stimmung"* (Baltimore: Johns Hopkins University Press, 1963), 6.

3. Ibid., 7.

4. For a full account, see ibid., 79–83.

5. Sophrosyne was a Greek goddess, the spirit of temperance and moderation, representing a healthy mind. Cicero writes that "temperans, quem Graeci σώφρονα appellant, eamque virtutem σωφροσύνην vocant quam soleo equidem tum temperantiam, tum moderationem appellare, nonnumquam etiam modestiam; et distemperantia [Greek δυσκρασία]." Ibid., 81–82.

Notes to Chapter 2

6. See Lian Chikako Chang, "Articulation and the Origins of Proportion in Archaic and Classical Greece" (Ph.D. dissertation, McGill University, 2009). Chang's dissertation convincingly argues that architectural proportion and its associated terms, rather than being simply a formal mathematical conceit, have their origins in the valorization of *articulation* by a living Greek culture, having to do of course with the joining of parts to make an object, but primarily, as well, with how persons, things, and the world could be beautiful, healthy, and just. Ideas of articulation thus bound together the ordering of bodies, of the cosmos, and of crafts, including architecture.

7. *Oxford English Dictionary*, s.v. "harmony."

8. Spitzer, *Classical and Christian Ideas of World Harmony*, 85ff.

9. Ibid., 9.

10. Indeed, the issue of "tuning" cannot be reduced to "comfort," usually through technological gadgets, as is sometimes the case in contemporary criticism. See Richard Coyne, *The Tuning of Place* (Cambridge, MA: MIT Press, 2010).

11. Spitzer, *Classical and Christian Ideas of World Harmony*, 16.

12. Ibid., 17.

13. Vitruvius, *Ten Books on Architecture*, ed. Ingrid D. Rowland and Thomas Noble Howe (Cambridge: Cambridge University Press, 2002), 35.

14. Spitzer, *Classical and Christian Ideas of World Harmony*, 119–120.

15. See Daniel Heller-Roazen, *The Fifth Hammer: Pythagoras and the Disharmony of the World* (New York: Zone Books, 2011), 21.

16. Spitzer, *Classical and Christian Ideas of World Harmony*, 13, citing Plato, *Timaeus*, 47d.

17. Ibid., 64.

18. Ibid., 71–73.

19. The fundamental communicative task of architecture (often misunderstood through semiotic interpretations) is evoked at the very outset of book 1, in the third paragraph. See Vitruvius, *Ten Books*, 22.

20. See http://en.wikipedia.org/wiki/Geminus, accessed September 7, 2014.

21. Vitruvius, *Ten Books*, book 1, ch. 2, 24–26.

22. Alberto Pérez-Gómez and Louise Pelletier, *Architectural Representation and the Perspective Hinge* (Cambridge, MA: MIT Press, 1997), 87–104.

23. Vitruvius, *Ten Books*, book 1, ch. 3, 26.

24. Spitzer, *Classical and Christian Ideas of World Harmony*, 108.

25. Ibid., 16. See Marsilio Ficino, *The Book of Life* (*De vita coelitus comparanda*), trans. Charles Boer (Dallas: Spring Editions, 1986).

26. Spitzer, *Classical and Christian Ideas of World Harmony*, 126.

27. Ibid., 16.

28. Ibid., 19–20.

29. Ibid., 21.

30. Ibid., 23.
31. Ibid., 26.
32. Ibid., 27.
33. Ibid., 30.
34. Heller-Roazen, *The Fifth Hammer*, 49–53, 65–68.
35. Spitzer, *Classical and Christian Ideas of World Harmony*, 35.
36. Heller-Roazen, *The Fifth Hammer*, 17.
37. Ibid., 41.
38. Hugh of St. Victor, *The Didascalicon of Hugh of St. Victor: A Medieval Guide to the Arts*, trans. Jerome Taylor (New York: Columbia University Press, 1966).
39. Most notably by Otto von Simson in the classic work *The Gothic Cathedral* (New York: Harper and Row, 1964).
40. See Rudolph Conrad, *Artistic Change at St-Denis: Abbot Suger's Program and the Early Twelfth-Century Controversy over Art* (Princeton: Princeton University Press, 1991).
41. *Abbot Suger on the Abbey Church of St. Denis and Its Art Treasures*, 2nd ed., trans. and ed. Erwin Panofsky, ed. Gerda Panofsky-Soergel (Princeton: Princeton University Press, 1979).
42. See Jason Crow, "The Hierurgy of Stone in Suger's Restoration of Saint-Denis" (Ph.D. dissertation, McGill University, 2013), 11.
43. Ibid., 125.
44. Suger, *De consecratione*, in *Abbot Suger on the Abbey Church of St. Denis*, 115.
45. Ibid.
46. See Elie Konigson, *L'espace théâtral médiéval* (Paris: Centre National de la Recherche Scientifique, 1975).
47. Leon Battista Alberti, *Ten Books on Architecture*, trans. James Leoni (1755), ed. Joseph Rykwert (1955; repr., London: Tiranti, 1965), 113.
48. Ibid., 194–195.
49. Ibid., 112–113.
50. By 1591 we find in Fray Luis de Leon's "Noche Serena," *concierto* as the primary quality of a serene starry night, involving proportion, harmony, concord, peace, and temperance, ultimately conveying *sosiego*, a beautiful Spanish word that alludes to bodily and mental rest after the subsiding of a painful or stressful experience. Spitzer, *Classical and Christian Ideas of World Harmony*, 112–113.
51. Francesco Colonna, *Hypnerotomachia Poliphili*, ed. Giovanni Pozzi and Lucia A. Ciapponi (Padua: Editrice Atenore, 1980), 34–49. See also Alberto Pérez-Gómez, "The *Hypnerotomachia Poliphili* by Francesco Colonna," in Vaughan Hart, ed., *Paper Palaces* (New Haven: Yale University Press 1998).
52. Marsilio Ficino, *Commentary on Plato's Symposium on Love*, trans. Sears Jayne (Dallas: Spring Publications, 1985), 91.

Notes to Chapter 2

53. See Marsilio Ficino, *The Book of Life*, trans. Charles Boer (Dallas: Spring Publications, 1968).

54. Spitzer, *Classical and Christian Ideas of World Harmony*, 127.

55. Giovanni Pico della Mirandola, *Oration on the Dignity of Man* (1486) (Chicago: Regnery, 1956).

56. Spitzer, *Classical and Christian Ideas of World Harmony*, 43.

57. Ibid., 55, 44.

58. Luca Pacioli, *Divina proportione. Opera a tutti gli ignegni perspicaci e curosi necessaria que ciascun studioso di Philosophia Prospettiva Pictura Scultura architectura Musica e altre Mathematice suavissima sottile e admirabile doctrina consequira e delectarassi co varie questione de secretissima scientia* (Venice, 1509); Spanish translation by Aldo Mieli, *La divina proporción* (Buenos Aires: Losada, 1959), 151–159.

59. See Alberto Pérez-Gómez, "The Glass Architecture of Fra Luca Pacioli," in A. Pérez-Gómez and S. Parcell, eds., *Chora: Intervals in the Philosophy of Architecture*, vol. 4 (Montreal: McGill-Queen's University Press, 2004), 260–269.

60. Ibid., 270–281.

61. Spitzer, *Classical and Christian Ideas of World Harmony*, 130–131, citing Z. K. Pyne (London, 1922).

62. *Dieci libri dell'architettura di M. Vitruvio*, trans. Daniele Barbaro (Venice, 1556).

63. Particularly in Rowe's famous essay "The Mathematics of the Ideal Villa," in *The Mathematics of the Ideal Villa and Other Essays* (Cambridge, MA: MIT Press, 1976), 2–27.

64. Andrea Palladio, *The Four Books of Architecture*, trans. Robert Tavernor and Richard Schofield (Cambridge, MA: MIT Press, 2002), 203–205.

65. Ibid., 213.

66. Ibid., 58–59.

67. Robert W. Wienpahl, "Zarlino, the Senario, and Tonality," *Journal of the American Musicological Society* 12, no. 1 (1959): 27.

68. Vincenzo Galilei, *Discorso de Vincentio Galilei nobile fiorentino intorno all'opere di messer Gioseffo Zarlino da Chioggia* (Florence, 1589).

69. Heller-Roazen, *The Fifth Hammer*, 68.

70. Hans Blumenberg, *The Genesis of the Copernican World* (Cambridge, MA: MIT Press, 1987), 135–230.

71. Amos Funkenstein, *Theology and the Scientific Imagination from the Middle Ages to the Seventeenth Century* (Princeton: Princeton University Press, 1986), 3.

72. Kepler referred to Pythagoras as his "guide, master, and precursor" and paid him homage throughout his life. See Heller-Roazen, *The Fifth Hammer*, 113–114.

73. Cited in ibid., 118.

74. Cited by D. P. Walker, "Kepler's Celestial Music," *Journal of the Warburg and Courtauld Institutes* 30 (1967): 228–250.

75. Heller-Roazen, *The Fifth Hammer*, 75–79.

76. Ibid., 79.

77. Athanasius Kircher, *Musurgia universalis* (Rome, 1650); see Michael Spitzer, *Metaphor and Musical Thought* (Chicago: University of Chicago Press, 2004), 151.

78. Kircher, *Musurgia universalis*, cited by Spitzer, *Metaphor and Musical Thought*, 156–158.

79. See Joachim Burmeister, *Musica poetica* (Rostock, 1606).

80. Marin Mersenne, *Traité de l'harmonie universelle* (Paris, 1627) and *Harmonie universelle: Contenant la théorie et la pratique de la musique* (Paris, 1636).

81. Mersenne, cited by M. Spitzer, *Metaphor and Musical Thought*, 154–157.

82. Johannes Kepler, *The Harmony of the World*, trans. E. J. Aiton, A. M. Duncan, and J. V. Field (Philadelphia: University of Pennsylvania Press, 1997), 290.

83. Dante Alighieri, *The Divine Comedy*, trans. John Ciardi (Toronto: New American Library, 2003), *Paradiso*, canto 10, lines 139–149.

84. Pérez-Gómez and Pelletier, *Architectural Representation and the Perspective Hinge*, 55–58, 199–205.

85. Guarino Guarini, *Architettura civile* (Milan: Il Polifilo, 1968), 10–11.

86. Bianca Tavasi La Greca, "La posizione del Guarini in rapporto alla cultura filosofica del tempo," appendix to ibid., 439–459.

87. Guarini, *Coelestis mathematicae* (Milan, 1683).

88. The belief in geometry as a universal science, a *combinatoria* or science of permutations, which, in analogy with divine creativity, becomes a mirror of perceptual reality, was common in the seventeenth century. This possibility was a common assumption among scientists and philosophers such as Gottfried Wilhelm Leibniz, Baruch Spinoza, and Claude-François Milliet Deschales, among many others.

89. Guarini, *Architettura civile*, 12.

90. Janine Debanné, "Guarino Guarini's SS. Sindone Chapel: Between Reliquary and Cenotaph" (M.Arch. thesis, McGill University, 1995), 69–80.

91. Ibid., 81–95.

92. Ibid., 134.

93. Guarini's contemporary, Juan Caramuel de Lobkowitz, was probably the first architect to have explicitly considered in his treatise historical genealogies (with its origins in the Temple of Solomon in Jerusalem) as a source of legitimacy and orientation for present practices.

94. Debanné, "Guarino Guarini's SS. Sindone Chapel," 46ff.

95. Spitzer, *Classical and Christian Ideas of World Harmony*, 120–121.

96. This is a couplet sung at the end of both acts: "Dann ist die Erd'ein Himmelreich, uns Sterbliche den Göttern gleich."

97. Isaac Newton, *The Mathematical Principles of Natural Philosophy*, trans. R. Motte (London, 1803), 2 vols., 1:6ff, 2:311ff.

98. See Alberto Pérez-Gómez, "Charles-Étienne Briseux: The Musical Body and the Limits of Instrumentality in Architecture," in George Dodds and Robert Tavernor, eds., *Body and Building: Essays on the Changing Relation of Body and Architecture* (Cambridge, MA: MIT Press, 2002), 164–189.

99. Novalis, *Christenheit oder Europa* (1798), cited in Spitzer, *Classical and Christian Ideas of World Harmony*, 76.

100. Many excellent works have been published in the last few decades dealing with this shift. Besides others quoted in this chapter, we should add: Thomas Christensen, *Rameau and Musical Thought in the Enlightenment* (Cambridge: Cambridge University Press, 1993); Richard Leppert, *The Sight of Sound: Music, Representation, and the History of the Body* (Berkeley: University of California Press, 1993); and Cynthia Verba, *Music and the French Enlightenment: Reconstruction of a Dialogue, 1750–1764* (Oxford: Oxford University Press, 1993).

101. Spitzer, *Classical and Christian Ideas of World Harmony*, 76.

102. I have discussed Perrault's theories in the introduction to his *Ordonnance for the Five Kinds of Columns after the Method of the Ancients*, trans. Indra Kagis McEwen (Santa Monica, CA: Getty Center for the History of Art and the Humanities, 1993), and in Pérez-Gómez, *Architecture and the Crisis of Modern Science* (Cambridge, MA: MIT Press, 1983), 18–39.

103. Perrault was the author of two important texts on architecture: *Les dix livres d'architecture de Vitruve*, the first modern French edition of Vitruvius (1673, 1684), with a remarkable scholarly apparatus, so modern in its outlook that it is still in print, and the *Ordonnance des cinq espèces des colonnes* (1683), the first modern instrumental theory of the classical orders.

104. See Pérez-Gómez, *Architecture and the Crisis of Modern Science*, 31–47. For Blondel's association of musical ratios and architecture, see George Hersey, *Architecture and Geometry in the Age of the Baroque* (Chicago: University of Chicago Press, 2000), 37–41.

105. Claude Perrault, *Essais de physique ou recueil de plusiers traitez touchant les choses naturelles* (Paris, 1680), tome II, 382–383.

106. Claude Perrault, *Ordonnance*, preface, 48–49.

107. Ibid., 50–54.

108. This is the explicitly stated intention behind his writing of the *Ordonnance*, first published in 1683. In his preface, where most of the important arguments are made, he shows awareness of the polemical nature of his propositions. He insists he has not invented new proportions, but merely altered them so that "they are truly balanced in all parts of every order in such a way as to establish a straightforward and convenient method," and has reduced all obscure numbers "to commensurable dimensions which I call probable." He argues that he has arrived at his proportions through a simple mathematical method, averaging to find the "juste milieu" for every detail of every order of column, the largest and smallest dimensions stipulated either in the main classical treatises, or in the great buildings of antiquity.

Chapter 3

1. The term was introduced by Alexander Gottlieb Baumgarten in *Meditationes philosophicae de nonnullis ad poema pertinentibus* (1735), section 117, and further developed in a major treatise on the topic published in 1750.
2. Suggested by Daniel Heller-Roazen, *The Fifth Hammer: Pythagoras and the Disharmony of the World* (New York: Zone Books, 2011), 83–88.
3. Letter to Christian Goldbach, cited in ibid., 83–84.
4. Gottfried Wilhelm Leibniz, *Philosophical Essays*, trans. Roger Ariew and Daniel Garber (Indianapolis: Hackett, 1989), 212.
5. Claude Perrault, *Les dix livres d'architecture de Vitruve* (Paris, 1684).
6. Newton's theory of universal gravitation is presented in his *Mathematical Principles of Natural Philosophy* (1687), where he declares "hypotheses non fingo": mathematical laws are revealed (not assumed a priori, as in the case of his seventeenth-century predecessors), arguably through empirical observation, becoming the ultimate symbol of God's presence in Nature. Nevertheless, in his theory he postulates the existence of absolute quantitative time and space and identifies these with God, becoming a fundamental (if often invisible) premise of his physics: "God endures forever and is everywhere present; and by existing always and everywhere He constitutes duration and space … in him are all things contained and moved, yet neither affects the other." This primary existing being, whose emanative effect is measurable space and time, was consequently responsible for the order, regularity, and harmony of the structure of things. Newtonianism excludes atheism, a point made by Voltaire in his *Eléments de la philosophie de Newton* (Paris, 1738). Cited from Isaac Newton, *The Mathematical Principles of Natural Philosophy* (London, 1803), 2 vols., 1:6ff, 2:311ff.
7. Voltaire jokingly compares Descartes's and Newton's concepts of space by associating them with Paris and London, both mathematical and intelligible, yet full of substance in the former case and empty in the latter. He explains that Newton's laws of gravitation (attraction) express the quantitative essence of the cosmos that had previously been represented to the senses by the Cartesians. The order of the world is composed of matter and movement in an empty and homogeneous space, which Newton associates with God's presence.
8. Abbé Jean-Baptiste Dubos, *Réflexions critiques sur la poésie et la peinture* (Paris, 1719), 1:24.
9. Ibid., 2:1.
10. See chapter 2.
11. Amédée-François Frézier, *Dissertation sur les ordres d'architecture* (Strasbourg, 1738), 4–18. Also published as part of his *La théorie et la pratique de la coupe des pierres et des bois, pour la construction de voutes et autre parties des bâtiments civils & militaires, ou traité de stéréotomie à l'usage de l'architecture* (Paris, 1737–1739). See also Alberto Pérez-Gómez, *Architecture and the Crisis of Modern Science* (Cambridge, MA: MIT Press, 1983), 53–55, 233–235.
12. Frézier, *Dissertation sur les ordres d'architecture*, 16.

13. Marc-Antoine Laugier, *Essai sur l'art* (Paris, 1753), 9.

14. See, for example, Richard Sennett, *The Fall of Public Man* (Cambridge: Cambridge University Press, 1977), for a description of the exaggerated theatricality of eighteenth-century public life. Hannah Arendt characterizes this moment as the inception of "social space" as a place of public interaction, slowly replacing the public space of the *polis*, *urbs*, and *ecclesia*. See Arendt, *The Human Condition* (Chicago: University of Chicago Press, 1958).

15. Germain Boffrand, *Livre d'architecture, contenant les principes généraux de cet art* (Paris, 1745), 16.

16. Ibid.

17. Ibid., 25.

18. Ibid., 29.

19. I have written more extensively on this in "Charles-Étienne Briseux: The Musical Body and the Limits of Instrumentality in Architecture," in George Dodds and Robert Tavernor, eds., *Body and Building: Essays on the Changing Relation of Body and Architecture* (Cambridge, MA: MIT Press, 2002), 164–189.

20. Rameau's theory, first published in 1722 in his *Traité de l'harmonie reduite à ses principes naturels*, changed somewhat throughout the century and was reiterated in various writings with increasing epistemological and metaphysical ambition. By midcentury his position had become contentious and a subject of dispute among *philosophes* of the *Encyclopédie* such as D'Alembert and Diderot.

21. Jean-Philippe Rameau, "Conclusions sur l'origine des sciences," in *Journal encyclopédique* 5 (1762), 91–101; and Jean-Jacques Rousseau, *Dictionnaire de musique* (Paris, 1969), 236–237.

22. Aristotle, *Politics*, trans. T. A. Sinclair (London: Penguin, 1992), VIII, 1340a40–1340b13.

23. See Marjorie Nicolson, *Newton Demands the Muse* (Princeton: Princeton University Press, 1966).

24. Louis Bertrand Castel, *L'optique des couleurs* (Paris, 1740).

25. Nicolas Le Camus de Mézières, *Le génie de l'architecture, ou l'analogie de cet art avec nos sensations* (1780; Geneva: Minkoff, 1972), 1.

26. Ibid., 17–21.

27. Ibid., 23–40.

28. For a thorough study of the work of Le Camus and in particular its relationships with eighteenth-century theater, see Louise Pelletier, *Architecture in Words: Theater, Language, and the Sensuous Space of Architecture* (London: Routledge, 2006).

29. Friedrich Wilhelm Joseph Schelling, *Lettre sur le dogmatisme et le criticisme*, trans. S. Jankelevitch (Paris: Aubier, 1950), 109.

30. Evan Thompson, *Mind in Life: Biology, Phenomenology, and the Sciences of the Mind* (Cambridge, MA: Harvard University Press, 2007), 312–359. More about this in chapter 5.

31. Schelling, *Lettre*, 111.

32. Cited by George Gusdorf, *L'homme romantique* (Paris: Payot, 1984), 36–37.

33. Ibid., 34–35.

34. Novalis (Baron Georg Philipp Friedrich von Hardenberg), "Grains de Pollen," in *Petis écrits*, trans. L. Bianquis (Paris: Aubier, 1947), 35.

35. See http://gladdestthing.com/poems/ah-not-to-be-cut-off, consulted September 8, 2014.

36. Joseph Ennemoser, *Der Geist der Menschen in der Natur oder die Psychologie in UebereStimmung mit der Naturkunde* (Stuttgart and Tübingen, 1849), 613.

37. Schlegel (1800), cited in Gusdorf, *L'homme romantique*, 93.

38. Novalis, *L'encyclopédie*, collected fragments by E. Wasmuth, trans. into French by M. de Gandillac (Paris: Minuit, 1966), 308.

39. Charles du Bos, "Fragments sur Novalis," *Cahiers du sud* (May-June 1957): 183.

40. Gusdorf, *L'homme romantique*, 96–97.

41. For a remarkably comprehensive history of this problem in Western philosophy, see Daniel Heller-Roazen, *The Inner Touch: Archaeology of a Sensation* (New York: Zone Books, 2007).

42. Gusdorf, *L'homme romantique*, 97.

43. Karl Friedrich Burdach (1842) defined them as "durable constitutions that impose their mark, corresponding to personal expressions, providing a tone to the development of external life, while also determining the degree of receptivity for impressions coming from the outside, and the vivacity of the reaction." Cited in Gusdorf, *L'homme romantique*, 97.

44. Cited in Gusdorf, *L'homme romantique*, 97.

45. Le Camus de Mézières, *Le génie de l'architecture*, 4.

46. Gusdorf, *L'homme romantique*, 97–98, citing Henri Frédéric Amiel, *Fragments d'un journal intime* (1853).

47. Ibid., 99.

48. Ibid., 105.

49. Georges Gusdorf, *Fondaments du savoir romantique* (Paris: Payot, 1982), 468–469, citing Novalis, *Fragments mathématiques*.

50. George Steiner, *Real Presences* (Cambridge: Cambridge University Press, 1985).

51. While Montesquieu, Voltaire, Condorcet, Locke, Hume, and Kant were not interested in death, the personal experience of the death of others (which can be profoundly personal) becomes a central concern for romantic writers. See Gusdorf, *L'homme romantique*, 188ff.

52. Martin Heidegger, *The Fundamental Concepts of Metaphysics: World, Finitude, Solitude,* trans. William McNeill and Nicholas Walker (Bloomington: Indiana University Press, 1995), 66–67.

53. Jenny Doussan, *Time, Language, and Visuality in Agamben's Philosophy* (London: Palgrave Macmillan, 2013), 22–23.

54. Ibid., citing Giorgio Agamben, *Language and Death: The Place of Negativity*, trans. K. Pinkus (Minneapolis: University of Minnesota Press, 2006).

55. Ibid., 23.

56. Cited by Roberto Calasso, *Literature and the Gods* (New York: Vintage, 2001), 58–59.

57. Calasso, *Literature and the Gods*, 21.

58. Ibid., 46–47.

59. Cited in ibid., 59.

60. Ibid., 58.

61. Cited in Gusdorf, *L'homme romantique*, 62–64.

62. Friedrich Nietzsche, "On the Uses and Disadvantages of History for Man," in *Untimely Meditations* (*Unzeitgemässe Betrachtungen*, 1874), trans. R. J. Hollingdale (Cambridge: Cambridge University Press, 1983).

63. Leo Spitzer, *Classical and Christian Ideas of World Harmony: Prolegomena to an Interpretation of the Word "Stimmung"* (Baltimore: Johns Hopkins University Press, 1963), 140–142 and footnotes.

64. I provide an analysis of Bruno's philosophy with this emphasis in *Built upon Love: Architectural Longing after Ethics and Aesthetics* (Cambridge, MA: MIT Press, 2006), 54–56.

65. Friedrich Jacobi, *Lettres à Moses Mendelssohn sur la doctrine de Spinoza* (1785), cited in Gusdorf, *L'homme romantique*, 44.

66. Lydia Goehr, *The Imaginary Museum of Musical Works* (Oxford: Clarendon Press, 2002).

67. Filarete's manuscript was never published during his lifetime. Today there is an Italian edition, *Trattato di architettura*, 2 vols., ed. Anna Maria Finoli and Liliana Grassi, with introduction and notes by Liliana Grassi (Milan: Il Polifilo, 1972), and an English translation by John Spencer, *Filarete's Treatise on Architecture*, 2 vols. (New Haven: Yale University Press, 1965), 1:15–16 (fol. 7v–8r).

68. See Alberto Pérez-Gómez and Louise Pelletier, *Architectural Representation and the Perspective Hinge* (Cambridge, MA: MIT Press, 1997), 216–227.

69. Gérard de Nerval, *Selected Writings*, trans. G. Warner (St. Albans, UK: Panther, 1973), 119.

70. I discuss the importance of the poetic image in architecture, following the definitions of Octavio Paz, in *Built upon Love*, 67–110.

71. Frederick Kiesler, "Pseudo-Functionalism in Modern Architecture," in *Frederick Kiesler 1890–1965*, ed. Yehuda Safran (London: Architectural Association, 1989), 57; cited in Angeliki Sioli, "Is the Endless a House?," in A. Pérez-Gómez and S. Parcell, eds., *Chora: Intervals in the Philosophy of Architecture*, vol. 7 (Montreal: McGill-Queen's University Press, forthcoming).

72. See Sioli, "Is the Endless a House?"

73. Frederick Kiesler, *Inside the Endless House: Art, People, and Architecture; A Journal* (New York: Simon and Schuster, 1966).

74. Ibid., 568.

75. Sioli, "Is the Endless a House?"

76. Kiesler, *Inside the Endless House*, 395.

Chapter 4

1. I employ these descriptors of the imagination as explained by Richard Kearney in *The Wake of Imagination* (Minneapolis: University of Minnesota Press, 1988).

2. Bruno Zevi, *Architecture as Space* (New York: Horizon Press, 1974).

3. See, for example, Evan Thompson, *Mind in Life: Biology, Phenomenology, and the Sciences of the Mind* (Cambridge, MA: Harvard University Press, 2007); and Alva Noë, *Action in Perception* (Cambridge, MA: MIT Press, 2004), and *Out of Our Heads: Why You Are Not Your Brain, and Other Lessons from the Biology of Consciousness* (New York: Hill and Wang, 2009).

4. Anne Carson, *Eros the Bittersweet: An Essay* (Princeton: Princeton University Press, 1986), 49.

5. It is important to emphasize here the "invention" of architecture as a culturally specific discipline, with a *theory* (comprising the three forms of knowledge identified by Aristotle, as explained in chapter 2), and, after the seventeenth century, with a *history* (in the sense of self-conscious, human-generated, progressive change). Any discussion of architecture and particularly of the beginnings of "modern architecture" in non-Western cultures must pay close attention to this fact.

6. See Stephen Parcell, *Four Historical Definitions of Architecture* (Montreal: McGill-Queen's University Press, 2012).

7. For an account of Anaximander's theory and its sources, see G. S. Kirk, J. E. Raven, and M. Schofield, *The Presocratic Philosophers* (Cambridge: Cambridge University Press, 1983), 100–110. Also interesting, though somewhat speculative, is Robert Hahn, *Anaximander and the Architects: The Contribution of Egyptian and Greek Architectural Technologies to the Origins of Greek Philosophy* (Albany: SUNY Press, 2001).

8. Carson, *Eros the Bittersweet*; and David Abram, *The Spell of the Sensuous* (New York: Vintage, 1997), chs. 4 and 5.

9. *Grammatici Graeci*, ed. A. Hilgrad, 3 vols. (Leipzig, 1901), 1.3.183, cited in Carson, *Eros the Bittersweet*, 56.

10. See Lisa Landrum, "Chora before Plato: Architecture, Drama, Receptivity," in A. Pérez-Gómez and S. Parcell, eds., *Chora: Intervals in the Philosophy of Architecture*, vol. 7 (Montreal: McGill-Queen's University Press, forthcoming).

11. Proclus, *A Commentary on the First Book of Euclid's Elements*, trans. Glenn R. Morrow (Princeton: Princeton University Press, 1970), 30–31.

Notes to Chapter 4   249

12. Carson, *Eros the Bittersweet*, 111.

13. Aristotle, *Physics*, 193a, trans. Robin Waterfield (Oxford: Oxford University Press, 1999), 34–35.

14. Aristotle, *Parts of Animals*, 645a, cited in Shigehisa Kuriyama, *The Expressiveness of the Body and the Divergence of Greek and Chinese Medicine* (New York: Zone Books, 1999), 127.

15. Vitruvius, *Ten Books on Architecture*, ed. Ingrid D. Rowland and Thomas Noble Howe (Cambridge: Cambridge University Press, 2002), book 1, 21–24.

16. Aristotle, *Physics*, 194a10–26, 37.

17. Ibid.

18. Alberto Pérez-Gómez, *Built upon Love: Architectural Longing after Ethics and Aesthetics* (Cambridge, MA: MIT Press, 2006), ch. 2.

19. Http://en.wikipedia.org/wiki/Basilica_of_the_Fourteen_Holy_Helpers, consulted January 28, 2014.

20. The fourteen saints are: Saint Blase, invoked against diseases of the throat; Saint George, invoked against herpetic diseases; Saint Acathius, invoked against headaches; Saint Christopher, invoked in storms, tempests, plagues, and for avoidance of accidents in traveling; Saint Pantaleon, invoked against consumption; Saint Barbara, invoked against lightning and sudden death; Saint Denis of Paris, invoked for persons possessed of devils; Saint Giles, invoked against panic, epilepsy, madness, and nocturnal terrors; Saint Margaret, invoked against pains in the loins and for expectant mothers; Saint Erasmus, invoked against diseases of the stomach; Saint Cyriacus, invoked against diseases of the eye and diabolical possession; Saint Vitus, invoked against chorea, lethargy, and the bite of venomous or mad beasts; Saint Eustace, invoked for preservation from fire whether eternal or temporal; and Saint Katherine, invoked by students, Christian philosophers, orators, and barristers. Ibid.

21. John Dee, *The Mathematical Praeface to the Elements of Euclid* (London: John Day, 1570).

22. See Georges Gusdorf, *La révolution galiléenne* (Paris: Payot, 1969), 1:85–102; and Alexandre Koyré, *Metaphysics and Measurement* (London: Chapman and Hall, 1968), chs. 1–4.

23. Johann Heinrich Lambert, *La perspective affranchie de l'embaras du plan géométral* (Zurich, 1759). See Alberto Pérez-Gómez and Louise Pelletier, *Architectural Representation and the Perspective Hinge* (Cambridge, MA: MIT Press, 1997), 180–198.

24. Galli-Bibiena was the last name of a family of several generations of architects involved in theater and stage design, authors of several compilations and books. See Ferdinando Galli da Bibiena, *Architettura civile* (Parma, 1711).

25. See, for example, Maurice Merleau-Ponty, "Cézanne's Doubt" and "Eye and Mind," in Galen A. Johnson, ed., *The Merleau-Ponty Aesthetics Reader* (Evanston: Northwestern University Press, 1993), 59–75, 121–149.

26. Étienne-Louis Boullée, *Architecture: Essai sur l'art* (Paris: Hermann, 1968), ms. at the Bibliothèque Nationale de France, available online at http://gallica.bnf.fr/ark:/12148/btv1b9061529g.r=Papiers+de+%C3%89tienne -Louis+BOULL%C3%89E%2C+architecte.langEN.swf.

27. A claim to reproduce nature by harnessing its processes rather than merely copying it was one that had been made in the past by alchemists, asserting the superiority of their aims to those of artists, who were merely concerned with reproducing superficial forms. See William Newman, *Promethean Ambitions: Alchemy and the Quest to Perfect Nature* (Chicago: University of Chicago Press, 2004).

28. Isaac Newton, *The Principia: Mathematical Principles of Natural Philosophy*, trans. I. Bernard Cohen and Anne Whitman (Berkeley: University of California Press, 1999), 408–415.

29. Voltaire, *Élémens de la philosophie de Neuton* (Paris, 1738).

30. Immanuel Kant, "De mundi sensibilis atque intelligibilis forma et principiis" [Dissertation on the Form and Principles of the Sensible and Intelligible World], in *Sämtliche Werke* (Berlin: Prussian Academy of Sciences, 1902), 2:65–67.

31. Immanuel Kant, *Critique of Pure Reason*, trans. J. M. D. Meiklejohn (London: Dent, 1979), 45.

32. Kant, "De mundi sensibilis," 67.

33. Pierre-Simon de Laplace, *Exposition du système du monde* (Paris, 1813), 443.

34. Alois Riegl, *Spätrömische Kunstindustrie* (Vienna, 1901), 25.

35. Ibid., 26.

36. August Endell, "Die Schönheit der grossen Stadt," in *Vom Sehen: Texte, 1896–1925; Über Architektur und "Die Schönheit der grossen Stadt"* (Basel: Birkhäuser, 1995), 199ff.

37. See Eleftherios Ikonomou, "The Transformation of Space in the Architectural Thinking of the Late 19th and Early 20th Century" (Ph.D. dissertation, University of Cambridge, 1984); and Harry Francis Mallgrave, ed., *Empathy, Form, and Space: Problems in German Aesthetics, 1873–1893* (Santa Monica, CA: Getty Center for the History of Arts and the Humanities, 1994).

38. August Schmarsow, *Das Wesen der Architektonischen Schöpfung* (Leipzig, 1894), 10; cited in Ikonomou, "The Transformation of Space."

39. Ibid., 11.

40. August Schmarsow, *Grundbegriffe der Kunstwissenschaft am Ubergang vom Altertüm zum Mittelalter* (Leipzig, 1906), 16.

41. Cited in Ikonomou, "The Transformation of Space," 246–247.

42. Jean-Nicolas-Louis Durand, *Précis des leçons d'architecture données à l'École Royale Polytechnique* (Paris, 1819), 1:18–21.

43. For further specifications, see Pérez-Gómez and Pelletier, *Architectural Representation and the Perspective Hinge*, 304–307.

44. This is most explicit in his comments to the section of the first book of Vitruvius, where the Roman architect sets out his famous trilogy of values. See *Les*

dix livres d'architecture de Vitruve, trans. and ed. Claude Perrault (Paris, 1684), book 1, ch. 3.

45. Durand, *Précis,* 6–8, 16.

46. See, for example, Edward Casey, *The Fate of Place: A Philosophical History* (Berkeley: University of California Press, 1997); and Jeff Malpas, *Place and Experience: A Philosophical Topography* (Cambridge: Cambridge University Press, 1999).

47. The relationship between perspective and architecture in the Renaissance is complex and multifaceted. See Pérez-Gómez and Pelletier, *Architectural Representation and the Perspective Hinge.*

48. Ibid., 307–316.

49. Merleau-Ponty, "Cézanne's Doubt."

50. Pérez-Gómez and Pelletier, *Architectural Representation and the Perspective Hinge,* 340–370.

51. John Hejduk, *Mask of Medusa* (New York: Rizzoli, 1985), 26.

52. Alain Robbe-Grillet, *For a New Novel* (Evanston: Northwestern University Press, 1989), 165. The quote is reproduced in Hejduk, *Mask of Medusa,* 39. Hejduk had a framed version of the quote in his office at the Cooper Union School of Architecture in New York.

53. John Hejduk, *Victims* (London: Architectural Association, 1986).

54. Ibid., introduction, n.p.

55. Ibid.

Chapter 5

1. Claude Perrault, *Ordonnance for the Five Kinds of Columns after the Method of the Ancients,* trans. Indra Kagis McEwen, intro. Alberto Pérez-Gómez (Santa Monica, CA: Getty Center for the History of Art and the Humanities, 1993); and Claude Perrault, *Les dix livres d'architecture de Vitruve* (Paris, 1684).

2. Aristotle tried to explain his concept with a fascinating analogy: "if the eye was a living creature, sight would be its soul," *De anima,* II, I, 412b19. Cited in Evan Thompson, *Mind in Life: Biology, Phenomenology, and the Sciences of Mind* (Cambridge, MA: Harvard University Press, 2007), 226.

3. René Descartes, *Meditations of First Philosophy,* trans. J. Cottingham (Cambridge: Cambridge University Press, 1986), 19.

4. Drew Leder, *The Absent Body* (Chicago: University of Chicago Press, 1990), 69.

5. Greg Lynn, Michel Maltzan, and Alessandro Poli, *Other Space Odysseys,* exh. cat. (Baden: Lars Müller/CCA, 2010).

6. Jean-Baptiste Dubos, *Réflexions critiques sur la poésie et la peinture,* 2 vols. (Paris, 1719).

7. Thompson, *Mind in Life*, 228.

8. Maurice Merleau-Ponty, *Phenomenology of Perception*, trans. Donald A. Landes (New York: Routledge, 2012), xxii.

9. Thompson, *Mind in Life*, 10.

10. This insight is present in the Buddhist teachings of Nagarjuna from the second century, titled *Stanzas of the Middle Way*, cited in Francisco Varela, Evan Thompson, and Eleanor Rosch, *The Embodied Mind* (Cambridge, MA: MIT Press, 1991), 220–221.

11. See Hans Jonas, *The Phenomenon of Life: Toward a Philosophical Biology* (Evanston: Northwestern University Press, 2001).

12. Nick Crossley, *The Social Body: Habit, Identity, and Desire* (London: Sage, 2001), 70.

13. Ibid., 76–77.

14. Ibid., 245–247. See also Evan Thompson, *Waking, Dreaming, Being: Self and Consciousness in Neuroscience, Meditation, and Philosophy* (New York: Columbia University Press, 2015), for a recent study of the nature of "self" that takes into consideration Hindu and Tibetan Buddhist insights and tests them through neurophenomenology.

15. Alva Noë, *Out of Our Heads: Why You Are Not Your Brain and Other Lessons from the Biology of Consciousness* (New York: Hill and Wang, 2009).

16. Crossley, *The Social Body*, 46, citing G. Ryle.

17. Frank Wilson, *The Hand* (New York: Vintage, 1999), 302–307.

18. See Alva Noë, *Action in Perception* (Cambridge, MA: MIT Press, 2004), 1–17.

19. Ibid., 106–113.

20. Shaun Gallagher, *How the Body Shapes the Mind* (Oxford: Clarendon Press, 2006), 170.

21. Thompson, *Mind in Life*, 226.

22. Ibid., 123–124.

23. Noë, *Out of Our Heads*, 7.

24. Crossley, *The Social Body*, 70–73. See also Louise Barrett, *Beyond the Brain: How Body and Environment Shape Animal and Human Minds* (Princeton: Princeton University Press, 2011).

25. Merleau-Ponty, *Phenomenology of Perception*, cited in Thompson, *Mind in Life*, 80.

26. In addition, he elaborates on how self-consciousness (in various modalities) is present in dreams and even in dreamless deep sleep, an ancient position found in Hindu and Buddhist thought that can now be ascertained through neuroscience. See Thompson, *Waking, Dreaming, Being*, 1–20, 356–366.

27. Thompson, *Mind in Life*, 315–316.

28. Crossley, *The Social Body*, 54–56.

29. Ibid., 57.

30. Cited in Martin Jay, "Sartre, Merleau-Ponty, and the Search for a New Ontology of Sight," in David M. Levin, ed., *Modernity and the Hegemony of Vision* (Berkeley: University of California Press, 1993), 164.

31. Maurice Merleau-Ponty, *Phenomenology of Perception*, trans. Colin Smith (London: Routledge and Kegan Paul, 1962), 235.

32. Thompson, *Mind in Life*, 278–279; Alva Noë, *Varieties of Presence* (Cambridge, MA: Harvard University Press, 2012), 82ff; and Noë, *Out of Our Heads*, 35ff.

33. Maurice Merleau-Ponty, *The Visible and the Invisible*, trans. Alphonso Lingis (Evanston: Northwestern University Press, 1968), 28.

34. "Despite the poor quality of the visual apparatus, we have the subjective experience of great richness and 'presence' of the visual world. But this richness and presence are actually an illusion." Thompson, *Mind in Life*, 276–277, citing John Kevin O'Regan (1992).

35. Thompson, *Mind in Life*, 278–279.

36. Georges Perec, *Species of Spaces and Other Pieces*, trans. J. Sturrock (London: Penguin, 1999), 188.

37. The issue of "availabilty" to characterize "presence" is a central topic in Alva Noë's *Varieties of Presence*.

38. Cited in Edward S. Casey, "'The Element of Voluminousness': Depth and Place Reexamined," in M. C. Dillon, ed., *Merleau-Ponty Vivant* (Albany: SUNY Press, 1991), 20–21.

39. Ibid.

40. Husserl discusses this problem in multiple writings, starting with the "Lectures on the Consciousness of Internal Time from the Year 1905," in *On the Phenomenology of the Consciousness of Internal Time (1893–1917)*, trans. J. B. Brough (Dordrecht: Kluwer Academic Publishers, 1991). The discussion and commentary on the topic are abundant and often highly technical. Thompson, *Mind in Life*, 317–328, offers a very lucid summary of Husserl's analysis.

41. Cited in Thompson, *Mind in Life*, 318.

42. Ibid., 326.

43. Ibid., 328–329ff.

44. See also Alberto Pérez-Gómez, *Built upon Love: Architectural Longing after Ethics and Aesthetics* (Cambridge, MA: MIT Press, 2006), 69–73ff.

45. This is a term coined by Dalibor Vesely to designate the profound dilemmas facing modern and contemporary practice. See Dalibor Vesely, *Architecture in the Age of Divided Representation* (Cambridge, MA: MIT Press, 2004).

46. Thompson, *Mind in Life*, 361–362.

47. The first four verses of the poem read: "Caminante son tus huellas / el camino y nada más. / Caminante, no hay camino, / se hace camino al andar." Antonio Machado, "Proverbios y Cantares XXIX," in *Selected Poems of Antonio Machado*,

trans. Betty Jean Craige (Baton Rouge: Louisiana State University Press, 1979). This is a bilingual edition.

48. Thompson, *Mind in Life*, 377.

49. Ibid., 403, citing Merlin Donald, *Origins of the Human Mind: Three Stages in the Evolution of Culture and Cognition* (Cambridge, MA: Harvard University Press, 1991).

50. See Barrett, *Beyond the Brain*.

51. Thompson, *Mind in Life*, 403. See also Crossley, *The Social Body*, a remarkably lucid treatment of the issue of intersubjectivity through Merleau-Ponty, and its consequences for the understanding of the social body.

52. Ibid., 409–410.

53. Ibid., 403.

54. This is known as the theory of *Einfühlung*, which was put forward by Robert Vischer and Theodore Lipps and subsequently influenced Alois Riegl and Wilhelm Worringer.

55. Crossley, *The Social Body*, 79.

56. Noë, *Varieties of Presence*, devotes particular attention to unpacking this issue. He insists that for "enactive direct realism [in recent cognitive theory] there is no perceptual experience of an object that is not dependent on the exercise, by the perceiver, of a special kind of knowledge. Perceptual awareness of objects ... is an achievement of the sensorimotor understanding" (65).

57. Gallagher, *How the Body Shapes the Mind*, 237.

58. Ibid., 241.

59. Ibid., 247–248.

60. Crossley, *The Social Body*, 50. See also the two important books by Hubert Dreyfus on the limitations of artificial intelligence, still relevant today: *What Computers Can't Do* (Cambridge, MA: MIT Press, 1972, rev. ed. 1979) and *What Computers Still Can't Do* (Cambridge, MA: MIT Press, 1992).

61. Crossley, *The Social Body*, 51.

62. Ibid.

63. Ibid., 73.

64. Ibid., 121.

65. Noë, *Varieties of Presence*, 125.

66. Crossley, *The Social Body*, 127.

67. Ibid., 129.

68. See Barrett, *Beyond the Brain*. Barrett emphasizes the importance of specific worlds for animal behavior, which are given to particular species' sensorimotor mechanisms in close reciprocity with their body morphology. (We humans don't really share the same world as a lion or an ant, even though they may overlap.) Thus the shape of the body and the environment are crucial, and can bring about very complex behavior with very small brains, and in both animals and humans

"it becomes very hard to decide where 'perception' ends and 'cognition' begins" (56). All animals need to behave adaptively in their respective worlds, and it may be that the larger the brain, "the greater complexity of the tracking device that accompanies sensorimotor mechanisms, means that animals require a much larger number of innate predispositions than do simpler animals in order to ensure that their environment derived knowledge does not go off on some useless tangent. It is not a simple tradeoff—more flexibility equals less instinct—but a complex interaction between the two" (86–87).

69. Gallagher, *How the Body Shapes the Mind*, 147.

70. Barrett, *Beyond the Brain*, 110.

71. Ibid., 77.

72. Ibid., 78–79.

73. Ibid., 133–134.

74. Vesely, *Architecture in the Age of Divided Representation*.

75. Ibid., 79.

76. Noë, *Out of Our Heads*, 107.

77. Ibid.

78. Ibid., 133.

79. Crossley, *The Social Body*, 80.

80. See Walter Ong, *Orality and Literacy: The Technologizing of the Word* (London: Methuen, 1972).

81. Vitruvius, *Ten Books on Architecture*, ed. Ingrid D. Rowland and Thomas Noble Howe (Cambridge: Cambridge University Press, 2002), 34.

82. Crossley, *The Social Body*, 148.

83. Martin Heidegger, "The Thinker as Poet'" and "Language," in *Poetry, Language, Thought*, trans. Albert Hofstadter (New York: Harper and Row, 1971).

84. Crossley, *The Social Body*, 80. Interestingly, studying the hand-thought-language nexus from a neurological perspective, Frank Wilson has also ascertained a deep-seated relationship between the anatomical change of the hand in *Homo erectus* and the evolutionary origins of language. He remarks that while you could stop humans from learning to write or drive a car, you can't stop them from learning to speak. If human language is a heritable trait but not one that is continuous with other animal communicative behavior, where did it come from? It is not easy to understand the functional origins of human language. We may explain through the evolution of the voice mechanism the utterance of words, but not the production of meaning, without acknowledging its continuity with the expressive and functional role of the hand. Wilson, *The Hand*, 54–57.

85. Ibid., 81.

86. Heidegger, "Language," 185ff.

87. Ernesto Grassi, *Rhetoric as Philosophy* (Carbondale: Southern Illinois University Press, 2001).

88. Crossley, *The Social Body*, 84, citing Merleau-Ponty.
89. Ibid., 85.
90. Crossley, *The Social Body*, 81, citing Merleau-Ponty.
91. Daniel Heller-Roazen, *Echolalias: On the Forgetting of Language* (New York: Zone Books, 2005), 9–12.

Chapter 6

1. Octavio Paz, *The Bow and the Lyre* (Austin: University of Texas Press, 1991), 9.
2. Ibid.
3. Frank Wilson, *The Hand* (New York: Vintage, 1998), 307.
4. Paz, *The Bow and the Lyre*, 9.
5. Ibid., 10.
6. Ibid.
7. Maurice Merleau-Ponty, *The Prose of the World*, trans. John O'Neill (Evanston: Northwestern University Press, 1991), 78.
8. Shaun Gallagher, *How the Body Shapes the Mind* (Oxford: Clarendon Press, 2005), 126.
9. Ibid.
10. Maurice Merleau-Ponty, *Phenomenology of Perception*, trans. Colin Smith (London: Routledge and Kegan Paul, 1962), 194.
11. Ibid., 193.
12. Gallagher, *How the Body Shapes the Mind*, 128.
13. Merleau-Ponty, *The Prose of the World*, 79.
14. Ibid., 80.
15. Ibid., 14.
16. Maurice Merleau-Ponty, *Signs*, trans. Richard C. McCleary (Evanston: Northwestern University Press, 1964), 43.
17. Merleau-Ponty, *The Prose of the World*, 35.
18. Ibid., 36.
19. Merleau-Ponty, *Signs*, 44.
20. Ibid.
21. Ibid.
22. Ibid.
23. Ibid., 45.
24. Ibid., 5.
25. Ibid.
26. Ibid., 87.

27. Ibid., 88.
28. Ibid., 89.
29. Ibid.
30. Ibid., 90.
31. Ibid., 92.
32. Ibid., 93.
33. Ibid., 94.
34. Ibid., 95.

35. Vitruvius, *Ten Books on Architecture*, ed. Ingrid D. Rowland and Thomas Noble Howe (Cambridge: Cambridge University Press, 2002), 34.

36. Walter Ong, *Orality and Literacy: The Technologizing of the Word* (New York: Methuen, 1985); David Abram, *Becoming Animal: An Earthly Cosmology* (New York: Vintage, 2010), 264–274; and Ernesto Grassi, *The Primordial Metaphor* (Binghamton, NY: Medieval and Renaissance Texts and Studies, 1994), 14–28.

37. Ong, *Orality and Literacy*, 171–172.

38. Vitruvius, *Ten Books*, 65–70.

39. See George Lakoff and Mark Johnson, *Metaphors We Live By* (Chicago: University of Chicago Press, 1980).

40. Abram, *Becoming Animal*, 177.

41. Ibid., 170.

42. Paz, *The Bow and the Lyre*, 12.

43. Ibid.

44. Gaston Bachelard, *On Poetic Imagination and Reverie*, trans. and intro. Colette Gaudin (Putnam, CT: Spring Publications, 2014), 39.

45. Merleau-Ponty, *The Prose of the World*, 90.

46. Ibid.

47. Ibid.

48. Ibid.

49. Ibid., 91.

50. Ibid.

51. Ibid., 99.

52. The important consequences of this transformation for early modern architecture are the subject of my first book, *Architecture and the Crisis of Modern Science* (Cambridge, MA: MIT Press, 1983), inspired by Edmund Husserl's insights in *Phenomenology and the Crisis of Philosophy*, trans. Quentin Lauer (New York: Harper and Row, 1965).

53. *Architecture and the Crisis of Modern Science*, 298–314.

54. Roberto Calasso, *Literature and the Gods* (New York: Vintage, 2001), 112.

55. Ibid.

56. Ibid.

57. Ibid., 130.

58. Ibid.

59. Paul Ricoeur, *The Rule of Metaphor*, trans. Robert Czerny et al. (London: Routledge and Kegan Paul, 1977), 226.

60. Ibid., 228.

61. Alva Noë, *Varieties of Presence* (Cambridge, MA: Harvard University Press, 2012), 153–155.

62. Merleau-Ponty, *The Prose of the World*, 89.

63. See, for example, Gianni Vattimo, *Beyond Interpretation: The Meaning of Hermeneutics for Philosophy* (Stanford: Stanford University Press, 1997), 42–57.

64. It is well known that "style" becomes a central issue for nineteenth-century architects. I have traced the origin of the concept in relation to "syntax" in the theoretical writings of Charles François Viel. See Alberto Pérez-Gómez, *Built upon Love* (Cambridge, MA: MIT Press, 2008), 174–176.

65. John Keats, "Letter," February 3, 1818, cited in John O'Donohue, *Beauty: The Invisible Embrace* (New York: Harper, 2004), 80.

66. For a remarkable study on the importance of metaphor in relation to the humanistic tradition, from Aristotle to Vico, see Grassi, *The Primordial Metaphor*.

67. Ricoeur, *The Rule of Metaphor*, 23.

68. Aristotle, *Poetics*, 1459a3–8, and *Rhetoric*, 1412a10.

69. Ricoeur, *The Rule of Metaphor*, 216–217.

70. Ibid., 257ff. In his late philosophy Martin Heidegger uses this Greek concept to characterize philosophical truth arrived at through "meditative" rather than "calculative thinking." See *Poetry, Language, Thought*, trans. Albert Hofstadter (New York: Harper and Row, 1971); and *Discourse on Thinking*, trans. John M. Anderson and E. Hans Freund (New York: Harper and Row, 1966), 45–47.

71. Aristotle, *Poetics*, 1458a8, and *Rhetoric*, 1412a10–15; Ricoeur, *The Rule of Metaphor*, 27.

72. Ricoeur, *The Rule of Metaphor*, 121.

73. Lakoff and Johnson, *Metaphors We Live By*, 3.

74. Ricoeur, *The Rule of Metaphor*, 284.

75. Ibid., cited in Michael Spitzer, *Metaphor and Musical Thought* (Chicago: University of Chicago Press, 2004), 79.

76. Ricoeur, *The Rule of Metaphor*, 143.

77. Ibid.

78. Spitzer, *Metaphor and Musical Thought*, 95.

79. Philippe Soupault, *Last Nights of Paris* (1928), trans. William Carlos Williams (Cambridge, MA: Exact Change, 1992).

80. Ricoeur, *The Rule of Metaphor*, 209.

81. I am referring here to the cycle of works relating the Aristotelian elements to literature and poetry, such as *La psychanalyse du feu* (1938), *L'eau et les rêves* (1942), *L'air et les songes* (1943), *La terre et le rêveries du repos* (1946), and *La terre et le rêveries de la volonté* (1948).

82. Vitruvius, *Ten Books*, 22. The passage reads: "In all things, but specially in architecture, there are two inherent categories: the signified and the signifier. The signified is the proposed subject of discussion … carried out according to established principles of knowledge."

83. Ricoeur, *The Rule of Metaphor*, 239.

84. Paz, *The Bow and the Lyre*, 12.

85. Cited in Ricoeur, *The Rule of Metaphor*, 214–215.

86. Spitzer, *Metaphor and Musical Thought*, 98, citing Ricoeur.

87. Ricoeur, *The Rule of Metaphor*, 213.

88. Spitzer, *Metaphor and Musical Thought*, 99, citing Ricoeur.

89. Ibid., 100.

90. Ricoeur developed his theory of the hermeneutic imagination throughout his life, changing emphasis from his earlier books that shared the descriptive conventions of eidetic phenomenology. Summarizing his remarkable thought is out of the question here. For the purposes of my arguments, I will be referring to Richard Kearney's summary of his later positions, "Paul Ricoeur and the Hermeneutic Imagination," in T. Peter Kemp and David Rasmussen, eds., *The Narrative Path: The Later Works of Paul Ricoeur* (Cambridge, MA: MIT Press, 1989), 1–31, and to Ricoeur's essay "The Function of Fiction in Shaping Reality," *Man and World* 12 (1979): 123–141.

91. Kearney, "Paul Ricoeur and the Hermeneutic Imagination," 15.

92. Ricoeur, *The Rule of Metaphor*, 199–200.

93. Kearney, "Paul Ricoeur and the Hermeneutic Imagination," 19.

94. Ibid.

95. Bachelard, *On Poetic Imagination and Reverie*, 40.

96. Gaston Bachelard, *L'air et les songes: Essai sur l'imagination du mouvement* (Paris: José Corti, 1943), 14.

97. Bachelard, *On Poetic Imagination and Reverie*, 43.

98. That is, the water that enticed him to communion and then became countless women lapping against the breast of the bather. Gaston Bachelard, *L'eau et les rêves: Essai sur l'imagination de la matière* (Paris: José Corti, 1942), 174–177.

99. Elaine Scarry, *Dreaming by the Book* (Princeton: Princeton University Press, 2001), 3–11.

100. Kearney, "Paul Ricoeur and the Hermeneutic Imagination," 6.

101. Ibid., 16.

102. Ibid., 17.

103. Ibid., quoting Paul Ricoeur, *Time and Narrative*, trans. Kathleen McLaughlin and David Pellauer, 3 vols. (Chicago: University of Chicago Press, 1988), 1:81.

104. Pérez-Gómez, *Built upon Love*, 203–211.

105. Kearney, "Paul Ricoeur and the Hermeneutic Imagination," 17.

106. Ricoeur, *Time and Narrative*.

107. Paul Ricoeur, "Architecture and Narrative," *19th Triennale di Milano: Identità—differenze*, exh. cat. (1996), 65.

108. Ibid., 66.

109. Ibid., 65.

110. Paul Ricoeur, "Life: A Story in Search of a Narrator," in M. C. Doeser and J. N. Kraay, eds., *Facts and Values* (Dordrecht: Martinus Nijhoff, 1986), 121–132.

111. Ricoeur, *The Rule of Metaphor*, 40. Ricoeur is referring his comments to Greek tragedy.

112. Ibid.

113. Émélie Desrochers-Turgeon, "North," M.Arch. thesis, McGill University, School of Architecture, 2014.

114. Paz, *The Bow and the Lyre*, 7.

115. I am paraphrasing Northop Frye writing about poetry, cited in Ricoeur, *The Rule of Metaphor*, 229.

116. Ibid.

117. Nelson Goodman, *Languages of Art: An Approach to a Theory of Symbols* (Indianapolis: Hackett, 1976), 248.

118. Ibid., 245.

119. Ibid., 244.

120. I have discussed the importance of desire as a qualifier of architectural space in *Built upon Love*, 9–65.

Chapter 7

Portions of the present chapter are paraphrased from a previously published essay: Alberto Pérez-Gómez and Angeliki Sioli, "Drawing *with/in* and Drawing *out*: A Redefinition of Architectural Drawing through Edward S. Casey's Meditations on Mapping," in Azucena Cruz-Pierre and Donald A. Landes, eds., *Exploring the Work of Edward S. Casey* (London: Bloomsbury, 2013), 153–161.

1. Klaske Havik recently published an important book proposing specific strategies for the use of literary language in this direction. See *Urban Literacy: Reading and Writing Architecture* (Rotterdam: nai101, 2014). See also Angeliki Sioli, "The Re-writing Hi-story Project, or Running a Studio for a History Course," in ATINER, Conference Paper Series ARC2013–0730, http://www.atiner.gr/papers/ARC2013-0730.pdf, accessed September 19, 2014.

2. See, for example, Jacques Ferrier, *La possibilité d'une ville* (Paris: Arlea, 2013).

3. See Alberto Pérez-Gómez, "The Historical Context of Contemporary Architectural Representation," in Phil Ayres, ed., *Persistent Modelling: Extending the Role of Architectural Representation* (London: Routledge, 2012), 13–25.

4. Autodesk Revit product description (2004), http://www.autodesk.com/products/revit-family/overview.

5. This analogy has been evoked in recent times by architects of the most diverse formal persuasions, such as Greg Lynn and the firm of Kierantimberlake.

6. See Vilém Flusser, *Toward a Philosophy of Photography* (London: Reaktion, 2007); *Into the Universe of Technical Images* (Minneapolis: University of Minnesota Press, 2011); and http://mandptheory.wordpress.com/2009/03/01/vilem-flusser-the-technical-image/.

7. Alberto Pérez-Gómez and Louise Pelletier, *Architectural Representation and the Perspective Hinge* (Cambridge, MA: MIT Press, 1997), 298–307.

8. Maurice Merleau-Ponty, "Cézanne's Doubt" and "Eye and Mind," in *The Merleau-Ponty Aesthetics Reader*, ed. G. A. Johnson (Evanston: Northwestern University Press, 1996), 59–75, 121–149.

9. Maurice Merleau-Ponty, "The Indirect Language and the Voices of Silence," in *The Prose of the World*, trans. John O'Neill (Evanston: Northwestern University Press, 1991), 51.

10. Ibid., 52.

11. Ibid., 53.

12. Alva Noë, *Action in Perception* (Cambridge, MA: MIT Press, 2004), ch. 2, and Evan Thompson, *Mind in Life* (Cambridge, MA: Harvard University Press, 2007), ch. 10.

13. Thompson, *Mind in Life*, 278–279.

14. Ibid.

15. Ibid.

16. Ibid., 54.

17. Ibid., 65.

18. This is largely the topic of *Architectural Representation and the Perspective Hinge*.

19. Paul Ricoeur, *The Rule of Metaphor*, trans. Robert Czerny et al. (London: Routledge and Kegan Paul, 1977), 240.

20. Owen Barfield, *Saving Appearances*, cited in Arthur Zajonc, *Catching the Light: The Entwined History of Light and Mind* (Oxford: Oxford University Press, 1993), 35.

21. Alva Noë, *Varieties of Presence* (Cambridge, MA: Harvard University Press, 2012), 96–98.

22. Ibid., 100.

23. Ibid.

24. Claude-Nicolas Ledoux, *L'architecture considerée sous le rapport de l'art, des moeurs et de la législation* (1804; repr., Munich: UHL Verlag, 1981).

25. Paul Holmquist, a Ph.D. candidate at McGill University working under my supervision, is in the process of completing a dissertation devoted to unpacking the relationships between Rousseau and Ledoux: "Educating the Desire for the City: Nature, Institution, and Language in Claude-Nicolas Ledoux's Ideal City of Chaux."

26. See Paul Holmquist, "'More Powerful than Love': Imagination and Language in the Oikéma of Claude-Nicolas Ledoux," in A. Pérez-Gómez and S. Parcell, eds., *Chora: Intervals in the Philosophy of Architecture*, vol. 7 (Montreal: McGill-Queen's University Press, forthcoming). In his essay, Holmquist offers the first convincing interpretation of this project.

27. Zubin Kishore Singh, a Ph.D. candidate at McGill University working under my supervision, is in the process of completing a dissertation on this topic. His work has been very illuminating for my own.

28. Vitruvius, *Ten Books on Architecture*, ed. Ingrid D. Rowland and Thomas Noble Howe (Cambridge: Cambridge University Press, 2002), book 1, 28–32.

29. John Hejduk, *The Lancaster/Hanover Masque* (London: Architectural Association; Montreal: Canadian Centre for Architecture, 1992), 13.

30. Ibid.

31. Ibid.

32. Ibid., 73.

33. Susan Kozel, *Closer: Performance, Technologies, Phenomenology* (Cambridge, MA: MIT Press, 2007), 33–34.

34. Ibid., 92–103.

35. Cited in Hubert Dreyfus, "Why the Mood *in* a Room and the Mood *of* a Room Should Be Important to Architects," in *From the Things Themselves: Architecture and Phenomenology* (Kyoto: Kyoto University Press, 2012), 32.

36. See http://www.themachinetobeanother.org/.

37. Dreyfus, "Why the Mood *in* a Room," 34.

38. See http://usa.autodesk.com/maya/,accessed October 17, 2012.

39. Under my supervision, the project ran between 2007 and 2010. It was entitled "CAD Ballet" and culminated with the multimedia interactive installation and performance *MXT*. Jason Crow, now at Louisiana State University, coordinated the project. I owe him much in the writing of these paragraphs.

Chapter 8

1. See Hans-Georg Gadamer, *The Relevance of the Beautiful and Other Essays*, trans. Nicholas Walker (Cambridge: Cambridge University Press, 1986); and Alberto Pérez-Gómez, *Built upon Love* (Cambridge, MA: MIT Press, 2006).

2. Juhani Pallasmaa's prolific recent contributions in this regard must be recognized, in his collections of essays, such as *Encounters* (Helsinki: Rakennustieto, 2005), and book-length monographs like *The Architecture of Image: Existential Space in Cinema* (Helsinki: Rakennustieto, 2001).

3. Octavio Paz, *The Bow and the Lyre* (Austin: University of Texas Press, 1991), 12.

4. I am grateful to Dr. Lisa Landrum for these references.

5. Available at http://www.perseus.tufts.edu/hopper/text?doc=Perseus:text:2008.01.0392:section=47&highlight=a%29tmoi%3Ds.

6. I am referring to the remarkable Richmond Hill Hindu Temple, the largest in North America, built on the basis of totally traditional formal principles and iconography and inaugurated in 2002.

7. Roberto Calasso, *Literature and the Gods* (New York: Vintage, 2001), 21–22.

8. Kate Rigby, "Gernot Böhme's Ecological Aesthetics of Atmosphere," in Axel Goodbody and Kate Rigby, eds., *Ecocritical Theory: New European Approaches* (Charlottesville: University of Virginia Press, 2011).

9. Hans Ulrich Gumbrecht, *Atmosphere, Mood, Stimmung: On a Hidden Potential of Literature* (Stanford: Stanford University Press, 2012), 81.

10. Calasso, *Literature and the Gods*, 31.

11. Ibid., 112.

12. Claude-Nicolas Ledoux, *L'architecture considerée sous le rapport de l'art, des moeurs et de la législation*, 2 vols. (Paris, 1806; 1846).

13. Werner Heisenberg, *Physics and Philosophy* (New York: Harper and Row, 1958).

14. Hans-Georg Gadamer, *Reason in the Age of Science*, trans. Frederick G. Lawrence (Cambridge, MA: MIT Press, 1981), 146.

15. Giorgio Agamben, *Homo Sacer: Sovereign Power and Bare Life*, trans. Daniel Heller-Roazen (Stanford: Stanford University Press, 1998).

16. Daniel Smail, *On Deep History and the Brain* (Berkeley: University of California Press, 2008), 187.

17. Ibid.

18. Ibid., 188.

19. Michel Houellebecq, *The Possibility of an Island* (New York: Vintage, 2005), 260.

20. Ibid., 332.

21. Ibid., 337.

22. Patrik Schumacher, *The Autopoiesis of Architecture: A New Framework for Architecture* (Chichester, UK: John Wiley, 2011).

23. See Maurice Merleau-Ponty, "The Phenomenology of Language," in *Signs* (Evanston: Northwestern University Press, 1964), 84–97.

24. Antonio Damasio, *Self Comes to Mind: Constructing the Conscious Brain* (New York: Pantheon, 2010), 284ff.

25. Heidegger, cited in Gumbrecht, *Atmosphere, Mood, Stimmung*, 81.

26. Gadamer, *The Relevance of the Beautiful*, 3–53.

27. Evan Thompson, *Mind in Life* (Cambridge, MA: Harvard University Press, 2007), 356–357.

28. Cited in Nick Crossley, *The Social Body* (London: Sage, 2001), 58–60.

29. George Lakoff and Mark Johnson, *Philosophy in the Flesh: The Embodied Mind and Its Challenge to Western Thought* (New York: Basic Books, 1999), 564ff.

30. Ibid., 565–566.

31. Ibid., 567, citing E. Borg.

32. Calasso, *Literature and the Gods*, 31ff.

33. Ibid.

34. I am paraphrasing a description of "magic" in David Abram, *Becoming Animal* (New York: Vintage, 2011), 224.

35. Calasso, *Literature and the Gods*, 5.

36. Ibid.

37. Ibid., 5–6.

38. Ibid., 6.

39. Ibid., 35.

40. Lakoff and Johnson, *Philosophy in the Flesh*, 555.

41. Ibid., 567.

42. Paul Ricoeur, *The Rule of Metaphor*, trans. Robert Czerny et al. (London: Routledge and Kegan Paul, 1977), 43.

43. Francisco Varela, Evan Thompson, and Eleanor Rauch, *The Embodied Mind* (Cambridge, MA: MIT Press, 1991), 220–226.

44. Ibid., 221, citing Nargajuna, *Stanzas of the Middle Way*.

45. Ibid., 223.

46. Ibid., 224.

47. Crossley, *The Social Body*, 55–56.

48. Ledoux, *L'architecture* (1806).

49. Gernot Böhme, "Atmosphere as Mindful Physical Presence in Space," *OASE: Journal for Architecture*, no. 91 (2013): 21–32.

Index

Aalto, Alvar, 198
Abram, David, 17, 23, 110, 171–172, 228
absence, 150
Académie Royale d'Architecture, 67
Académie Royale des Sciences, 66
acoustics, 90, 153, 171–173
Acropolis, 115
action
  architectural mimesis of, 192–193
  ethical dimension of, 42
  habits shaped by, 158, 192
  mind shaped by, 227–228
  moods and, 25–26, 29
  and perception, 108, 126, 146–147, 159, 166, 186, 192–193, 203–204
  sexuality and, 207
  traces following, 193
  will as cause of, 231–232
Aeneid (Virgil), 194
Aeschylus, 217
aesthetics
  atmosphere and, 17–23
  of emotions, 20
  innovation, 177
  meaning of, 17, 72–73
  modern, 72
  philosophical, 36, 125
  science of, 72
  sublime and beautiful, 72, 75, 107, 123
  values, 24–25
affect
  consciousness and, 28

  music and, 58, 73
  sensations producing, 19
affection, 155
Agamben, Giorgio, 93, 135, 163, 221
agency, 147
air (breath), 17, 109, 161, 217
aisthésis (aesthetics). *See* aesthetics
Alberti, Leon Battista, 37, 49–50, 52–53, 162
ambiance, 16–20
Ambrose, Saint, 45
analogy, musical, 33, 45, 48–49, 63–68
anatomy, 113
Anaximander, 110, 112, 131
Andersen, Michael Asgaard, 22
androgyny, 95
angels, dances of, 45
animals, 9–10, 30, 89, 91, 144, 155, 159
anthropology, 87–89
apéiron, 110
apocalypse, 46–47
Apollo (myth), 37
  temples of, 115
appropriateness
  character theory and, 78
  cultural, 73, 108, 189
  of form to setting, 43, 207
  poetic language expressing, 105
  postmodernity, seeking, 187
Aratus, 229
architects, 3, 25, 42, 177, 181–195

Architectural Atmospheres (Borch, ed.), 22
architecture
  affinities, 6–7, 128–129, 153
  allure of, 155
  animal, 9
  for architects, 25, 177
  biomorphic, 19, 76
  as calling, 92, 100, 226–227
  comprehensibility of, 159
  crisis of, 6, 83, 177
  cultural value of, 120, 122
  as discipline, 109
  elements essential to, 22–23
  good versus great, 3, 20, 24, 42, 60–61, 229
  historical, 4–5, 9
  intelligent, 20, 225
  living, 20
  mimetic intention, 114
  nineteenth-century, 5–6, 133–134
  as objectified writing, 171
  objectives of, 40, 163, 180, 232
  parametric, 19
  poetic, 25, 123
  possibilities offered by, 174–175
  purpose of, 7, 216–217, 222
  theory, 15, 40–41
  twenty-first-century, 7–8
  urban, 44, 205–206
  visual nature, 80
  work of, 98–100
"Architecture and Narrative" (Ricoeur), 190
Architecture civile (Lequeu), 98
L'architecture considérée sous le rapport de l'art, des moeurs et de la législation (Ledoux), 98, 205–206
architecture parlante, 18, 123, 127, 179
Architettura civile (Guarini), 60
Archytas of Tarentum, 39
Arendt, Hannah, 30, 192
Aristotle, 2, 9, 14, 29, 41, 45, 53, 55, 65, 81, 91, 112–114, 117, 119, 139, 162, 181–183, 186, 192, 195, 222, 225, 232

armonía, cosmic, 44
Ars poetica (Horace), 79
art
  constructed space in place of, 134
  feeling in, 141
  romantic, 97
art history, 125
artifacts
  architectural, 43–44, 110
  beauty found in, 9
  divine in, 96
  drawings as, 98, 101, 213
  human, 38, 117, 148
  metaphor and, 183–184
  religious, 47
  visual, 110
arts
  and crafts, 42
  origin of, 39
  plastic, 216
  role in society, 6
  and sciences, 79
associationism, 144
Athena (myth), 115
atman, 217, 232
atmós. *See* atmosphere
atmosphere
  acoustic character of, 171–173
  aesthetics and, 17–23
  architectural, 17, 20, 31, 44, 135, 152–153, 160, 170, 195
  atman and, 217, 232
  attuned, 104, 163
  of classical architecture, 74
  communicative space of architecture as, 82–83
  configuration for focal actions, 154
  creation of, 31–32, 161
  defined, 16
  digital simulation of, 211–214
  harmonious, 38–39, 123
  literary invocations of, 218–219
  meaningful, constructing, 97
  meteorological, 16–17
  musical, 33–34, 48–51, 57–62
  perception and, 21
  poetic, 83–84, 94–95, 101–105

Index 267

psychic, 19
of sacred spaces, 119
as thing-like and subject-like, 16–17
transforming experience, 175
Atmosphere, Mood, Stimmung (Gumbrecht), 218
Atmospheres (Zumthor), 21
attraction
  magnetic, 58
  sexual, 43
attunement
  architectural, 97–98, 101, 162
  beauty and, 9
  body and soul, 44
  of *Dasein*, 232–233
  discordant harmony, accomplishing, 75
  embodied consciousness, 51
  environmental, 156–157
  Heidegger on, 28–29
  media of, 95
  music and, 65, 92
  necessity of, 83–84
  object and subject, 209–210
Augustine of Hippo, Saint, 45–46, 59, 72
Aurélia, Life, and the Dream (Nerval), 101
AutoCAD, 199
autonomy, 98–100, 177
autopoiesis, 225
avant-garde, 7, 102, 122, 141, 178
awareness, 17, 171
axonometry, 133, 135

Bachelard, Gaston, 185–186, 188, 216
Ballard, J. G., 20
Balzac, Honoré de, 8
Barbaro, Daniele, 53, 113
Barfield, Owen, 202
baroque music, 58–62
Barragán, Luis, 198
Barrières (Ledoux), 205
Baudrillard, Jean, 7
Baukunst (Rivius), 44

Baumgarten, Alexander Gottlieb, 72–73, 79, 129
BeAnotherLab, 212–213
beauty
  absolute, as self-evident, 76
  aesthetics and, 129
  architecture and, 7, 49–50, 77, 80
  attunement and, 9
  convulsive, 86
  defined, 49–50
  dispassionate, 140
  existence of, 80
  harmony and, 43, 49–50
  health and, 9
  judging, 75
  meaning and, 9
  of music, 73
  Nature and, 49, 75, 77, 80
  Nothingness and, 178, 219
  ornament and, 50
  poetic, 171
  proportion and, 50–51
  relevance of, 215
  sources of, 67, 75
  and the sublime, 72, 75, 107, 123–124
  understanding, 36, 86
Beckman, Isaac, 58
Beethoven, Ludwig van, 99–100
behavioral psychology, 144
Being
  great chain of, 112
  presence of, 148
being
  and becoming, 117–118
  place of, 93, 112
  roots of, 144
  without ground, 232
Being and Time (Heidegger), 93
being-in-the-world, 143
being present, 30
Belli, Sylvio, 53, 113
belonging, 92, 105, 108, 159
Benedetti, Giovanni Battista, 58
Benjamin, Walter, 102, 133, 160
biomimetism, 104, 155, 222
Blondel, François, 63, 67

body
  the absent, 141
  brain and, 212
  consciousness and, 91, 144–145,
    152–153, 157
  ecstatic, 141
  environment and, 160
  groundedness of, 141
  knowledge, sensorimotor, 144, 146,
    158, 201
  metaphor and, 186
  and mind, 88, 139, 227–228, 230
  motor intentionality, 148, 154, 158,
    167–168, 170
  movement, and language, 162,
    167–168
  and orthogonal dimensions of space,
    125–126
  phantom nature of, 212
  prereflective, 147–148
  sexual, 148
  soul and, 44, 65, 72, 114, 140, 157,
    159, 227
  virtual interactions with, 211–
    212
Boethius, Anicius Manlius Severinus,
  46, 55
Boffrand, Germain, 79–80
Böhme, Gernot, 16–17, 22
Borch, Christian, 22
Borromini, Francesco, 64
Boullée, Étienne-Louis, 18, 83, 85, 97,
  122–124, 127, 179, 205
The Bow and the Lyre (Paz), 166
brain
  body constructed by, 212
  development of, 155
  mind shaped by, 227–228
  mirror neurons, 27
  plasticity of, 145
  soul and, 141
breath (air), 109, 161, 217
Breton, André, 10, 86, 102
bridges, 14
Briseux, Charles-Étienne, 63, 80–82
Bruno, Giordano, 96–97, 103
Buddhism, 230–233

buildings
  and drawings, 101, 120–121, 210
  ecologically responsible, 232
  as frozen gestures, 170
  harmonic proportionality in, 53–54,
    113–114
  intelligent, 225
  meaning of, 141
  perception of, 109–110
  and spoken word, 198
  traces in, 193
built environment, 5, 129, 210. *See
  also* cities
Burke, Edmund, 75

Calasso, Roberto, 94, 178, 218
Campidoglio, Michelangelo's design
  for, 49
Il cannocchiale aristotelico (Tesauro),
  183–184
capitalism, 223
Caramuel de Lobkowitz, Juan, 99
Carceri (Piranesi), 97, 100, 121–123,
  204
caretaker's house (Ledoux), 206–207
caritas, 45
Carson, Anne, 110, 114
Cartesianism. *See* Descartes
Carus, Karl Gustav, 91
Casey, Edward, 131
Castel, Père, 82
catharsis, 29
celestial mechanics, 125
cemeteries, 14, 207–208
Cenotaph to Newton (Boullée), 127
Cézanne, Paul, 122, 134, 136, 211
cháos, 228–229
character, 63, 85, 91, 103
character theory, 77–79, 81–82, 130
Chaux, Salines project (Ledoux), 205–
  207, 219
children, 30, 116, 145–146, 156
Choisy, Auguste, 134
chóra, 111–115, 117–118, 226
Christ, 45–46, 48, 53, 62, 180
Christianity, 39, 52, 56
churches, 47–49, 117

Cicero, Marcus Tullius, 36, 40–41, 109, 162, 192
cinematography, 215, 218
cities
　ecological, alternatives to, 232–233
　eighteenth-century, 13–14
　as frozen habit, 158
　impoverishment, 210
　occulted places of, 138
　planned, 13–14, 19, 176
　quality of life in, 160
　space of, 3–4, 44, 134, 229
　surveillance and control in, 5
　sustainable, 232–233
　in a technological world, 129
　traces in, 193
City of God, 46–47
civil community, 74
clients, as architects, 99, 198
climate, 36, 40, 90
codependence theory, 231
cognition, 146, 163
　aesthetic, 23
　emotions and, 24, 186, 195
　enactive understanding, 143–144
　perception and, 17, 20
　prereflective, 89
　sensuous, 124
cognitive science, 88, 132–133, 142, 230
Colbert, Jean-Baptiste, 66
colors, and music, 63, 81–82
columns, proportions of, 50, 76
commodification, 102, 157, 221
common sense, 119, 187, 222
communication
　architectural, 76–77, 82–83, 115, 155–156, 175
　artistic, *Stimmung* and, 15
　elements shaping, 171
　embodied, 24, 228
　emotional, 75
　gestural, 162
　with God, 116
　moods and, 24
　space of, 114, 208–209
　universality of, 169
　verbal, 111
compassion, 232
composition, mechanism of, 116, 127, 181, 198–200
computer-generated architectural documents, 99–101, 133–134, 199, 203
concord, 37
　concordant discord, 47, 90, 93
Condillac, Étienne Bonnot de, 69, 71, 74, 82, 92
configuration, 190, 192
congruity (*concinnitas*), 50
conscience, embodied, 147
consciousness
　animal vs. human, 9, 91, 144
　bodily, 91, 144–145, 152–153, 157
　brain-centered, 27, 64–65, 141, 144
　conceptual and perceptual, 131–132
　in Descartes, 140
　emotion and, 1–2, 109
　enactive understanding of, 169
　environment and, 1–2, 15, 228
　evolution of, 171
　Gemüt and, 86, 88–89, 92
　linguistic, 173, 226
　mind-body-world continuum, 96
　movement and, 193
　nature and, 219
　origin of, 5
　the Other's, 30, 145–146
　perception and, 140–141
　in Perrault, 140
　prereflective and reflective, 155, 169
　retention and protention, 154
　of the self, 8, 30, 45, 49, 145, 147, 152, 155, 228, 232
consciousness, embodied
　architectural meaning manifest through, 120
　attunement of, 51
　engaging, 104
　metaphor and, 183
　origin of language in, 168
　self-awareness, 8
　sexual, 226
　space for, 4

consonance, 63
　and dissonance, 73–74, 90
Constant (Constant Nieuwenhuys), 19
Constantine (emperor), 117
constructivism, 165–166
consumer societies, 15
Coop Himmelb(l)au, 20
Copernicus, Nicolaus, 24, 49, 56–57, 60
Corinthian order, 76–77
correalism, 105
correctness, ornament and, 42–43
cosmology, 39–40, 56, 66, 117
cosmos
　Bruno, 97
　creation story, 56
　harmony, elements of, 57
　mimesis of, 23–24, 43, 74, 110, 176
　origins and order of, 39, 45, 63
　of poetics, 57
counterpoint, 51
Court House project (Hejduk), 208–209
crafts, 47–48, 52–53, 120, 210
creation, Christian, 56, 180
crisis of meaning in architecture, 6, 83, 177
Crossley, Nick, 27, 30, 159
Crow, Jason, 47–48
CryEngine (Crytek), 213–214
Crytek, 213–214
cults, 217–218, 221
culture
　cognition and, 155–156
　creative genius substituted for, 120
　dance (chorós) of, 113
　digital, 201
　habit in, 60, 62, 97, 104, 160, 193
　linguistic nature of, 171, 198
　Nature and, 75–76
　value of architecture to, 120, 122, 217–218

Daedalus (myth), 111
Daidalos, 16
Damasio, Antonio, 24, 28, 195, 226
dance, 39, 42–45, 48, 111–113

Dante Alighieri, 59
Dasein, 93, 227, 232–233
De anima (*On the Soul*, Aristotle), 2, 91
death
　emptiness of, 207–208
　forgetfulness of, 223
　of God, 8, 94
　memory of, 14
　openness to, 30, 93, 156
　technology of writing and, 173
Debord, Guy, 19
décor, 19, 42–43, 175
decorum, 64, 78–79
Dee, John, 118
Deleuze, Gilles, 22
Della pittura (Alberti), 52
Demiurge, 33, 39, 41, 117
Democritus, 38–40
depth, 121–122, 135, 150–151, 213
De re aedificatoria (Alberti), 49–50
Derrida, Jacques, 19, 147
Descartes, René, 2, 24, 34, 56, 58, 60–61, 64–67, 71, 75, 80–81, 86, 119, 139, 140–141, 143, 149, 155, 221
Description of Greece (Pausanias), 217
design
　digital, 99–101, 133–134, 199, 203, 213–214
　experimental research through, 121
　geometry in, 61
　harmonic proportion, 54, 127
　imagination and, 107
　through *lineamenta*, 49
　poetic language in, 11, 165
　processes, 84, 176
　and production, 134
　urban, 13–16, 19
desire
　commodification of, 157
　for desire, 9–10, 30
　and fulfillment, 10
　meaning and, 207
　for the Other, 30
　pain and pleasure of, 8
　protention manifested as, 154
　sexual, 29–30

space of, 30, 86, 101, 130, 226
unity and, 43
determinism, 231–232
Dewey, John, 142
diatonic scale, 63
Diderot, Denis, 84
digital revolution, 181
Dilthey, Wilhelm, 95
dimensionality, harmonic, 92–93
Dionysus (myth), 94
Dioptrics (Descartes), 149
discord, 233
 discordant concord, 47, 75, 115
discourse, 41, 176, 182–186, 194, 209, 220, 230
disharmony, music and, 51
"Dissertation" (Kant), 124
Divina proportione (Pacioli), 52
divine, 96, 114, 122, 178
 divine mind, 119
 divine world soul, 39
 in literature, 94
Doric order, 76
drawings
 atmospheric, 18–19
 axonometric, 133–134
 computer-generated, 99–101, 133–134, 198–200, 203
 dimension and, 80–81
 embodied translation of, 101, 120–121, 210
 future of, 101
 historical, 110–111
 institutionalization of, 99
 literary language, relation to, 208–209
 three-dimensional objects, 128
 as tools of production, 100
 writing and, 173
Dream of Scipio (Cicero), 40
Dreyfus, Hubert, 7, 25, 27, 29, 213
dualism, 71–72, 125, 128, 132, 141–142, 228–229
Du Bos, Charles, 90
Dubos, Jean-Baptiste, 75, 78–79, 141
Duchamp, Marcel, 97, 103, 134, 226
Dufrenne, Mikel, 179

Durand, Jean-Nicolas-Louis, 18, 24, 68, 101, 127–131, 133, 176, 181, 199–200, 221–222
Dwelling, 117
 empathic spaces of, 230
 gift of, 193
 human, 3, 7, 29, 31, 84, 103, 107, 161, 171
 poetic, 85, 191–192
 secular, 54
 symbolic, 103
dynamicism, embodied, 142–143

École des Beaux-Arts, 99–100, 128, 153
École Polytechnique, 99, 128, 129
ecology, crisis in, 221
ego, 5, 64–65
ego cogito, 71, 86, 141, 231–232
Einstein, Albert, 132
Eisenman, Peter, 24–25, 180, 191
Eliade, Mircea, 219
Eliasson, Olafur, 22
The Embodied Mind (Rauch), 142–143
emotion
 aesthetics of, 20, 32, 195
 architectural meaning conveying, 22, 78, 105
 cognition and, 24, 186, 195
 consciousness and, 1–2, 109
 convertibility to rules, 141
 environment and, 24, 109, 154
 existence and, 90–91
 harmonic proportions and, 81
 intentionality and, 154
 interior, 83
 language and, 27, 156, 162
 location of, 162–163
 origin of, 16, 71
 prelinguistic understanding, 156
 as a property of the object, 179
 proportion and, 63, 67
 protention and, 154
 provoking, 43, 128
 sexual desire and, 29–30
 subjectivity and interiority of, 71–72
 transformed into mythos, 195

empathy, 125, 145, 156, 228–229
Empedocles, 40, 109–110
emptiness, 119, 131–132, 174, 207–208, 231–232
Endell, August, 125
Endless House (Kiesler), 103–105
engineering, architecture's affinity with, 129
Enlightenment, 75
Ennemoser, Joseph, 89
environment
  adapting through material culture, 158–159
  attuned, 156–157
  behavior and, 146
  consciousness and, 1–2, 228
  emotions and, 24, 109, 154
  engaging with, 210
  importance of, 1–2
  mind and, 155–156
  technologically induced, 15
  tools for designing, 210–211
Epicurus, 40
Erigena, John Scotus, 47
Eros, 30, 109
L'Esprit nouveau, 134
Essai (Laugier), 64
Essais (Schelling), 87–88
Essais de physique (Perrault), 67
Essai sur l'art (Boullée), 97
Étant donnés (Duchamp), 134
eternity, 87
ethics, 24, 42, 157, 194
Euclid, 38, 71, 112–113
Eumenides (Aeschylus), 217
Euripides, 229
everyday, space of, 119, 191
evolutionary traits, biological, 159
existentialism, 96
Exodus, 117
experience
  aesthetic, 8–9, 72, 153
  atmosphere transforming, 175
  chaosmic, 91
  geometry without, 200–201
  of harmony, 39, 43, 140
  knowledge and, 60, 87

  of the lived world, 102–103
  meaninglessness in, 180
  place and, 109
  of proportion, 78
  reason and, 74–75
  sensuous, 59–60
  synesthetic, 112, 144
  temporality of, 226

fabrication, digital, 128
facades, 49–50, 132
face, human, 49
Facebook, 210
feelings. *See* emotion
Fermiers Généraux, 205
Ficino, Marsilio, 44, 50–51, 72
fiction, narrative, 189, 197–198
Filarete (Antonio di Pietro Averlino), 99, 198
film, 215, 218
fine arts, 128, 153
flâneur, 14–15, 132–133
flesh of the world, 167, 211–212
flow, 152
Fludd, Robert, 58
Flusser, Vilém, 200–201
focal actions, 193
form
  appropriateness to setting, 43, 207
  poetic, 93–94
  primary determinants of, 129
formalism, 53, 179
forms (Aristotle), 113–114
Foucault, Michel, 5, 222
Frankfurt School, 197
freedom, 5, 159
Freemasonry, 63
free will, 5, 49, 221
French Revolution, 177, 221–222
Frézier, Amédée-François, 76–77, 80
friendship, 45
Frye, Northrop, 178–179
Fukuyama, Francis, 223
functionalism, 18, 103, 129–130, 133–134, 177, 222
Fundamentals (Koolhaas), 193–194
Funkenstein, Amos, 56

Index

Gadamer, Hans-Georg, 6, 9, 96, 157, 215, 220, 227
Galilei, Galileo, 24, 56–58, 64, 96, 118–119, 132
Galilei, Vincenzo, 46, 55–56
Gallagher, Shaun, 145–146, 157, 159
garden design, 58–59, 64
Garnier, Charles, 133
Gaudí, Antoni, 22
The Gay Science (Nietzsche), 219
Gelassenheit, 232–233
Geminus of Rhodes, 40, 114
Gemüt, 86–92
Le génie de l'architecture (Le Camus de Mézières), 82–84
genius, 120, 182
geometry
  of architecture, 61–62
  bypassing experience, 200–201
  Cartesian, 118, 133–134
  descriptive, 127–128, 133–134
  of design, 61, 116
  differential, 132–133
  Euclidian, 132
  God and, 57, 61, 85, 115–116
  of the heavens, 206
  of infinity, 59–60
  language of, 60
  meaning through, 176–177
  metaphorical function of, 185
  nature originating, 206–207
  non-Euclidean, 176
  perspectival, 61
  projective, 61, 200
  Pythagorean, 52
  reality of, 114
  sensuous experience and, 59
  space of, 56–57, 116, 118–120, 123–125, 132
gesture, 162–163, 167–170, 218
gnomon, 43–44, 110
God
  as architect, 46
  communication with, 116
  creator, 38, 49, 56, 180
  death of, 8, 94
  as designer, 206
  encountering, 47
  geometry and, 57, 61, 85, 116–117
  incarnate, 48, 53, 180
  intuiting, 45
  luminescence of, 62
  mathematical, 75
  necessity of, 125, 220
  physical residence on earth, 117
  presence of, revealing, 59
  third face of, 51
  transcendence and immanence, 45, 228
gods, embodiment in literature, 218
Goehr, Lydia, 99
Goethe, Johann Wolfgang von, 33, 92, 158
Göhme, Gernot, 218
Golden Section, 52
Goodman, Nelson, 195
Google, 210
Gothic churches, 47–49
Grains de pollen (Novalis), 88
grammatical style, architecture as, 180–181
Grassi, Ernesto, 157, 162, 171
gravitation, universal, 63, 75, 119, 123–124
great chain of Being, 112
Greek epic, 28–29
Gris, Juan, 136
groundlessness, 231
Guarini, Guarino, 60–62, 64, 67, 151
Guérin, Maurice de, 88
Gumbrecht, Hans Ulrich, 218

H_2O Pavilion (NOX/Lars Spuybroeck), 19
habits
  acknowledging and reframing, 159–160
  actions shaping, 137, 158, 192
  agency and, 147
  architecture's effect on, 104–105, 146–147, 154
  becoming rules, 192
  classical architecture and, 44
  cultural, 60, 62, 97, 104, 160, 193

habits (cont.)
  disordered, ordering, 48
  framing, 194–195
  functionalism and, 103
  gestural, 161–162
  Kiesler on, 104
  linguistic, 161–162
  moods and, 24
  physical environment marked by, 193
  plastic, 193
  words and, 137
happiness, 15, 38, 205
Harmonice mundi (Kepler), 57
Harmonic Institutions (Zarlino), 55
harmonic potential, 84
harmony. *See also* world harmony
  atmospheres and moods in, 123
  attainment of, 39
  beauty and, 43, 49–50
  Boullée and, 85
  concentus, 65
  cosmic, 57
  discovery of, 46–47
  divine, 57
  experience of, 39, 43
  expressions of, 9–10
  geometric approach to, 52
  happiness and, 38
  hearing and vision in, 63, 81–82, 140
  kinesthetic experience of, 140
  mathematical, 39, 41–42, 52
  moral and psychic, 36, 40, 90
  musical, 42
  proportion, 52, 78, 81, 127, 171–172
  Pythagorean, in Vitruvius, 49–50, 55
  reestablishing, 92
  scientific conception of, 57
  of the spheres, 39–40
  Stimmung and, 34–38, 40, 90
  within strife, 43
  superlunary world, embodying, 42
  of symmetry, 45
  temperance and, 39–40, 49–50, 54–55
  terms expressing, 39–40
  tonality, 81
  of volumes, 53
health. *See also* well-being
  architecture supporting, 2–3, 7, 24, 53–54, 105
  beauty and, 9
  memory and, 136–137
  music and, 44, 51, 66
  participation and, 136–137
  psychosomatic, 5–9, 13–16, 172, 217, 228, 232
  temperance and, 54
hearing and vision
  conflating, 67–68
  in harmony, 63, 81–82, 140
hedonism, 130–131, 222–225
Hegel, Georg Wilhelm Friedrich, 128
Heidegger, Martin, 3, 6, 11, 27–29, 93, 95, 108, 160–162, 183, 188, 193, 195, 206, 228–229, 232–233
Heisenberg, Werner, 220
Hejduk, John, 22, 98, 135–138, 204, 208–210, 216
Helen (Euripides), 229
Helen of Troy, 28
Heller-Roazen, Daniel, 15, 58
Heraclitus, 37, 40
Hesiod, 39
Hinduism, 217
Hippocrates, 40
Hölderlin, Friedrich, 94, 228
Holl, Steven, 22
Holy Shroud chapel (Turin), 62
home, 3, 6–7, 24
Homer, 29, 72, 79, 171, 194
Hopper, Edward, 209
Horace (Quintus Horatius Flaccus), 79
Houellebecq, Michel, 223–225
houses, 20, 84, 103–105
Hugh of St. Victor, 47–48
Hugo, Victor, 101
human nature, 157–158, 172
human rights, 221
Hume, David, 87, 92
humors, 2, 40, 44, 91

Husserl, Edmund, 34, 87, 93, 127, 142–144, 146, 151–152, 154–155, 201, 227
hymns, Christian, 45
Hypnerotomachia Poliphili, 50

I. *See* ego; self
ideal, Platonic, 112
idealism, 16, 124
ideas, 110, 173, 175
identity, 27, 190
Iliad (Homer), 79
Illich, Ivan, 102
illness, 44, 51
illusionism, perspectival, 61
images, poetic
  architecture and, 95, 103–104, 154, 160, 216
  atmospheres becoming, 20
  creation of, 175
  form contributing, 154
  generating, 137, 174
  language and, 186, 216
  literature communicating, 218
  metaphor disclosing, 88
  space as metaphor for, 103–104
  in storytelling, 85
  universality of, 216
imagination
  design and, 107
  knowledge and, 102
  linguistic, 181–182, 187–189, 194, 197, 211–213
  material, 185, 188
  poetic, 188, 194
  space as production of, 128
  time and space refigured, 189
  visual perception and, 186
imaginative universals, 181
impersonality, anthropology of, 87–88
impression-retention-protention, 152
in-between, 108, 116
indeterminacy theory, 220
"Indirect Language and the Voices of Silence" (Merleau-Ponty), 168
individuality, 178

Industrial Revolution, 71, 127–128, 177
inertia, 56–57, 118
infinity, 59–60, 96, 103–105, 124
Ingres, Jean-Auguste-Dominique, 97
innovation, 158–159, 177, 187–188, 192–194, 210
Inside the Endless House (Kiesler), 103
inspiration, creative, 89
instinct, 158–159
instrumentalism, 64, 221, 232
instruments, tuning, 36, 44, 90
intelligence, 159
intelligibility, 91, 95
intemperies, 35, 44
intentionality
  of the body, 146, 148, 154, 158, 167–170
  emotion and, 154
  empathy as, 156
  Paz on, 166
  poetic, 84–85, 105
interior and exterior, coincidence of, 27, 88, 90–91, 105
intervals, harmonic, 54–55
intuition, 75, 91, 124, 132
Inuit, 193–194
Invalides (Paris), 82
Ionic order, 76
irrationalism, 96
isometry, 133

Jacobi, Friedrich, 97
James, William, 142, 152
Jesuits, 59, 61
John of Patmos, 46
Johnson, Mark, 142, 183, 228, 230
Joseph, Saint, 116
Judaism, 117
judgment
  aesthetic, 153
  artistic, 141
justice, 7

Kafka, Franz, 136
Kahn, Louis, 227

Kant, Immanuel, 75, 94, 121, 124, 128, 131, 220
Kearney, Richard, 189
Keats, John, 180
Kelly, Sean, 7
Kepler, Johannes, 49, 56–57, 59, 64, 66–67, 97, 201
Kerenyi, Karl, 229
Kiesler, Frederick, 22, 103–105, 198
kinesthesia, 140, 144, 156
Kircher, Athanasius, 58–59, 64
know-how, 157–158
knowledge
 art as form of, 95
 bodily, 144, 146, 154, 158, 201
 experience and, 60, 87
 imagination as instrument of, 102
 knowing without knowing, 158
 lived knowledge of life, 93, 222
 logical, 41
 mathematical and divine, 60
 practical, 41
 for salvation, 48
 sensuous experience and, 59–60
 writing and, 111
Kojève, Alexandre, 30
Koolhaas, Rem, 24, 191, 193–194
Koyré, Alexandre, 118
Kozel, Susan, 211–212

Lakoff, George, 183, 228, 230
Lambert, Johann Heinrich, 121, 129
Lancaster/Hanover Masque (Hejduk), 208
landscapes, 92
language
 acquisition, 155–156, 162
 Adamic, 179–180
 algorithmic and natural, 177–178
 analogues, 74, 166
 constructivist, 165–166
 drawing, relation to, 208–209
 and embodiment, 184
 emergent or prereflective, 160–162, 165–166, 171, 225–226
 emotion and, 27, 156, 162
 empirical vs. creative, 168–169
 everything as, 169–170
 expressivity and uniformity, 168
 of geometry, 60
 as habits, 160–161
 imagination and, 181–182, 187–189, 194, 197, 211–213
 innovation in, 193–194
 instrumentalizing of, 180
 Inuit, 193–194
 literary, 84, 169, 181, 205–209
 mathematics and, 175–176
 meaning and, 169
 metaphoric, 163, 181–186
 movement and, 162, 167–168
 musical, 166
 of *mythos*, 163
 natural, 175–176, 211, 222
 original, 167, 168
 phenomenology of, 165–172, 187
 plastic, 166, 185
 reality and, 183–184
 self-referentiality, 168
 Stimmung and, 93, 135, 163, 222
 technological, 179–180
 thought and, 168–169
language, poetic
 architectural project as, 189–195
 for attunement, 101
 in design, 11, 165
 innovation in, 184
 intentionality, 84–85, 105
 metaphoric, 181, 197
 nature of, 167
 as paradigm for architecture, 130, 135–136
 paradox of, 169
 truth through, 122
Laplace, Pierre-Simon de, 124–125, 132, 220
Large Glass (Duchamp), 134
Last Nights of Paris (Soupault), 185
Laugier, Marc-Antoine, 64, 77
Lautréamont, Comte de (Isidore-Lucien Ducasse), 94
Leatherbarrow, David, 22–23
Le Brun, Charles, 91

Le Camus de Mézières, Nicolas, 28, 82–86, 91, 104, 205
Le Corbusier (Charles-Édouard Jeanneret), 18–19, 22, 53, 134–135, 198
Leder, Drew, 141
Ledoux, Claude-Nicolas, 84–85, 97–98, 204–208, 219, 232
Legeay, Jean-Laurent, 99, 123
Leibniz, Gottfried Wilhelm von, 73–74, 79
Leicht, Harmann, 116
Lequeu, Jean-Jacques, 98
letters, phonetic, 172
Lewerentz, Sigurd, 22
Libeskind, Daniel, 98
Libro architettonico (Filarete), 99
life
  biological and political interwoven, 208–209
  bios, 9
  everyday, 119, 219
  future, 7–8
  lived knowledge of, 93, 222
  meaningful, 207–208, 232
  narrative nature of, 190
  reality of, 223–225
  value of, 51, 93
  worth living, 8–9
  zóon, 9, 93, 135, 163, 222
life expectancy, 6
lifeworld, 143
light
  colors and tones in correspondence, 63, 81–82
  life celebrated with, 207–208
  music and, 51
  of reason, 122
  soul associated with, 39
  space as, 116, 119
limits, 85, 151, 206, 225–226
literature. *See also* narrative; novel; poetry
  divinities in, 94, 218–219
  Greek epic, 28–29, 72
  language of emotion in, 156

lived experience, 34, 87, 97, 110, 161, 166, 184, 203
lived space, 53, 103–104
living present, 17, 152–154, 157, 166
Livre d'architecture (Boffrand), 79
Locke, John, 71, 74, 88, 92
Loos, Adolf, 20
Louis XIV, 66, 74, 221
Louvre, 82
love, 8, 45, 63, 150–151, 207, 224–225, 229
Lynn, Greg, 104

Machado, Antonio, 4, 154
machines, 43, 110, 128
"The Machine to Be Another" (BeAnotherLab), 212–213
madness, inspired, 94
Magic Flute (Mozart), 63
Maine de Biran, Marie-François-Pierre, 142, 154
La maison du pauvre (Ledoux), 84
Malebranche, Nicolas, 60, 68
Mallarmé, Stéphane, 25, 98, 169, 177–178, 189, 200, 219, 232
Malpas, Jeff, 131
maps, early creators of, 110
Marion, Jean-Luc, 30
Mars, 91
Mary, Saint, 116
"Masques" (Hejduk), 208–209
materialism, poetic, 188
Mathematical Principles of Natural Philosophy (Newton), 124
mathematical sciences, 112
mathematics
  arts and sciences, 79
  beauty of Nature and, 75
  of design, 176
  harmony and, 42, 52
  intuition and, 132
  music and, 39, 46–47, 73–74, 81
  natural language and, 175–176
  of painting, 52
  the soul and, 112
  of sound, 58
  sublunary space and matter, 119

mathematics (cont.)
  transition to science, 176
  types of, 40–41
Maturana, Humberto, 154, 225
Maya, 213
meaning
  beauty and, 9
  in coincidence of opposites, 227
  constructing, 120–121
  desire and, 207
  foundation of, 148
  language and, 169
  as pleasure, 130
  as presence, 147
  world of, 166
meaning, architectural
  beauty and, 50
  character theory and, 78
  conditions of, 77
  constitutive elements, 80
  conveying, 148–149
  crafts as manifesting, 53
  diminishing possibilities of, 127
  emotion and, 20, 22, 78, 105
  language, relation to, 21–22
  music and, 153
  ornament and, 50
  participatory understanding of, 86
  perceptual depth in, 121–122
  Perrault on, 66–69
  production of, 83
  proportion expressing, 80
  site in, 115
  space of desire in, 86
  as visible presence, 78
meaninglessness, 180
measurement, importance of, 148
mechanical devices, 59
medicine, 6, 40, 44, 93
medieval architecture and music, 48–51, 57–58
meditation, 4, 17, 148, 228
memory, 14, 152, 154, 173, 207
  and forgetting, 136–137
Menelaus, 28
Merleau-Ponty, Maurice, 11, 22, 27–30, 69, 122, 126, 131, 134, 142–144, 146–147, 149, 151, 154, 156, 158–159, 161–162, 167–170, 174, 176, 179, 187, 201, 211, 227–228
Mersenne, Marin, 58–59
metaphor, 115, 163, 181–186, 193, 202–203, 230
metaphysics, 47
Michelangelo Buonarroti, 9, 49, 188, 198, 216
Mies van der Rohe, Ludwig, 22, 135
mímesis, 42, 73, 78, 111, 192, 195, 220
mind
  body and, 88, 139, 227–228, 230
  cognitive potentiality, shaping, 155–156
  construction of meaning, 120–121
  dualistic, 74
  embodied experience in understanding, 143
  enculturation of, 155–156
  environment and, 155–156
  first person, 86
  life of, 157
  perception and, 139
  properties of, 227–228
  restlessness of, 178
  science of, 88, 142
  unfeeling, 15
mind-body-world continuum, 142–143
miracles, 75, 115–116
models, 202–203
modernity, 5–6, 175
  autonomy in, 100
  body-soul dichotomy, 65
  poetry, 177–179, 189
  spirituality for, 228
Mondrian, Piet, 136
Monge, Gaspard, 127–128
monochord, 80
monotheism, 94, 172, 219
Mont Sainte-Victoire (Cézanne), 134, 211
mood
  actions and, 25–26, 29
  ambivalent nature of, 28

Index

appropriate, creating, 99, 172, 195
Cartesian model of, 27
communicative nature of, 24
digital simulation, 211–214
habits and, 24
harmonic proportions and, 81
intercorporeality of, 27
interiority, 71–72, 212
lived experience and, 26–30
lyric mythos, 195
as mimetic of nature, 105, 123
music and, 81
participation, facilitating, 179
phenomenological root of, 23–25
poetry and, 85
prelinguistic understanding of, 156
proportion and, 50, 63
of rooms, 15, 26, 28, 84
sacred power of, 29
semantic nature of, 179
shared, 29
morality, 81, 206
Moses, 117
motion, 56–57, 59, 118
mourning, 15
movement, 126, 142, 144, 162, 167–168, 193
Mozart, Wolfgang Amadeus, 63, 216
multimedia/multisensory experience, 19
multitudes and magnitudes, 46, 52, 56, 78
music
 ancient, 67
 architecture and, 53–54, 153
 attunement and, 65, 92
 beauty of, 73
 centrality of, 38, 66
 character and, 81
 crafts manifesting, 52–53
 emotional affect, 58, 73
 harmonic intervals, 55
 illness and, 44, 51
 incarnation of, 45
 light and, 51
 love and, 45, 63
 magical power of, 63
 mathematics and, 39, 46–47, 73–74, 81
 musical structure in painting, 52
 mystery of, 46
 performances, 29, 39, 45, 62–63, 66, 92
 as poetry, 185, 216
 ratios and, 54–55
 scale, 78
 sensuality of, 51
 temperament of, tuning for, 36, 45
 tonal, 57, 74, 81
 totality of the world symbolized, 46
 in the visual world, 63, 81–82
music theory, 34, 35, 55, 57, 66, 81
Musurgia universalis (Kircher), 58
Muybridge, Eadweard, 153
mystery plays, 48
mythology, 94–95, 115, 156
mythos, 195

Nagarjuna, 230–231
Napoleon Bonaparte, 220
narrative
 architecture and, 177–179, 189–191, 197–198
 poetic images, generating, 137
 referential power of, 189
natural resources, 219
Nature
 architectural mimesis of, 31, 76–79, 123
 beauty and, 49, 75, 77
 communication with, 76
 culture and, 75–76
 four elements of, 14, 39–40, 104, 109
 geometrization of, 59
 mathematics and, 55
 moods of, 23, 75
 nineteenth-century, 219
 speech in, 172
 truth and, 75
neoclassicism, 77
Neoplatonism, 39, 50
Nerval, Gérard de, 101
Neumann, Balthasar, 116

neurobiology, 159
neurophenomenology, 142–143
New Babylon (Constant), 19
Newton, Isaac, 63–64, 74–75, 77, 81–82, 85, 118–119, 123–124, 132, 219–220
Nicholas of Cusa, 85
Nietzsche, Friedrich, 94–95, 97, 172, 219, 232
nihilism, 96–97, 210, 232
Noë, Alva, 27, 142, 144–145, 149–150, 158, 161, 179, 201, 203
no-place, 15, 26, 118
Nothingness and the Beautiful, 178, 219
Novalis (Georg Philipp Friedrich Freiherr von Hardenberg), 65, 88–89, 92, 153, 188
novel, 94, 191–192, 218, 220
novelty, 25, 157, 159–160, 177, 210
NOX/Lars Spuybroeck, 19
numbers, 55–57, 58, 76
nymphs, 219

object and subject, 16, 23, 209–210, 211
observer, 43, 111, 127, 132–133, 209
Odyssey (Homer), 171, 194
Oikéma (Ledoux), 207
Olds, Sharon, 9
Old Testament, 117
Ong, Walter, 171
"On the Drawings" (Hejduk), 209
opera, 62–63
opposites, coincidence of, 27, 88, 91, 105, 183, 227
optical accuracy, 100, 129
optical correction, 68, 79–80, 120, 149
optical perception, 149–151, 186–188, 201–203
Opticks (Newton), 63, 81–82
optics, 61–62, 91–92, 114, 186
orality in culture, 171. *See also* speech
order (*dispositio*), 42, 44
Oresme, Nicolas, 46
orgasm, 95

ornament, 42–43, 50, 77, 127
Ortega y Gasset, José, 93
Other, 30, 145–146, 156, 228
Ouvrard, René, 63, 82
Oxvig, Henrik, 22

Pacioli, Luca, 52
pagan sites, 116
painting, 52, 134, 149–151
Palestrina, Giovanni Pierluigi da, 53
Palladio, Andrea, 53–55, 113–114
Pallasmaa, Juhani, 22, 134, 227
panentheism, 228–230
Paradoxes of Appearing (Andersen and Oxvig), 22
parametricism, 134
Paris Opera House, 133
participation, 75, 111, 136–137, 179, 221
Parts of Animals (Aristotle), 113
passions, 91
passivity, 155
Patočka, Jan, 154
Patte, Pierre, 13–14
Paul, Saint, 225
Pausanias, 217
Paz, Octavio, 6, 11, 122, 166–167, 174–175, 178, 185, 194, 208, 216
peace, projects celebrating, 207
Pelletier, Louise, 86
perception
  and action, 108, 126, 146–147, 159, 166, 186, 192–193, 203–204
  atmosphere and, 21
  Cartesian, 68–69
  cognition and, 17, 20
  consciousness and, 140–141
  embodied, 126, 143–144, 149, 185, 211–213
  enactive theory of, 144, 203–204, 230–231
  enigmatic nature, 148
  erotic, 29–30
  intermodality, 145
  kinesthetic, 144
  language of, 156

as meaningful, 172
optical, 149–150
passive, 65, 68–69
phenomenology of (Merleau-Ponty), 29, 131, 144, 147, 149
spatial, 126–127
synesthetic, 20, 50, 68, 71–72
visual, 91–92, 140, 149–151, 186–188, 201–203
walking and, 4
Perec, Georges, 150
perfection, 38, 97
performance
architectural, 98–99
musical, 29, 45, 62–63, 66, 99
prereflective, 167
Perrault, Claude, 34, 66–69, 74, 78, 80, 120–122, 127, 129–130, 139–140
Perronet, Jean-Rodolphe, 14
perspectiva artificialis, 112–113
perspective, 52, 61, 97, 121–122, 128, 134, 201. *See also* vision: perspectival
phantom of the body, 212
phenomenology, 96, 102, 134, 142, 170, 187, 231
"The Phenomenology of Language" (Merleau-Ponty), 169
Phenomenology of Perception (Merleau-Ponty), 29, 131, 144, 147, 149
Phillips Pavilion (Le Corbusier), 19
Philo of Alexandria (Philo Judaeus), 117
philosophy
contemplative, 115
music in, 34, 35, 55, 57, 66, 81
natural, 75, 123
origin of, 39
phenomenology and, 170
practical (*phrónesis*), 41, 43, 80, 94, 157, 162
romantic, 15, 86–92, 101–103, 142
scientific, 162
photography, 100, 129
phrónesis
authority of, 220

truth as, 162
wisdom in action, 41
physicians, *théoria* of, 113–114
physics, 56–57, 96, 118–119
Physics (Aristotle), 114
Piaget, Jean, 130
Picon, Antoine, 201
picture
architecture as, 128
as model, 203
visual perception as, 149–151, 186, 201, 203
Piero della Francesca, 52
Pietà (Michelangelo), 216
Piranesi, Giovanni Battista, 97, 99–100, 104, 121–122, 204, 208, 216
place. *See also* space
of being, 93, 112
of cities, 13–14
emotions bound to, 1
experience and, 109
in-between, 83–84, 101–103
infinite, lived space and, 84–85
intersubjective, 31, 84, 131, 146, 156
of miracles and saints, 115–116
occultation of, 107, 119–120, 129, 131, 138
qualitative perception of, 83, 108–109, 112
place making, architectural, 84–85
Placita philosophica (Guarini), 60
planets, motion of, 57
plasticity, 158, 166, 184–185, 192
Plato, 23, 32–34, 38–41, 45, 54, 56, 94, 110–113, 117–118, 131, 172, 192, 225–226, 228–229
Platonism, 56
Pliny (Gaius Plinius Secundus), 38
plot, 191–192
poetics
of architecture, 123, 148, 174
of the cosmos, 57
material imagination of, 188
and reality, 89
Poetics (Aristotle), 182, 192
poetic utterance, 162–163

poetry, 178–179, 185–186, 194, 216
  conditions of, 185–186, 216
  demiurgic nature of, 188
  form, 93–94
  function, 180
  Gemüt and, 89, 92
  lyric, 195
  modern, 177–179, 189
  mythology and, 94–95
  reality and, 189
  translatability of, 181
  uniqueness of poems, 194
poiésis is *mímesis*, 192
Poincaré, Henri, 132
political institutions, legitimacy of, 5
polyphony, 52–53, 57, 67
Poncelet, Jean-Victor, 200
pornographic impulse, 157
Poseidon (myth), 115
Posidonius, 38, 114
positivism, 2, 127
The Possibility of an Island (Houellebecq), 223–225
power
  architectural, 217
  of mood, 29
Pozzo, Andrea, 129
pragmatism, 142
prayer, 172
prefiguration, 190, 193, 195
prejudices, language destroying, 174
presence
  in architecture, 216
  of Being, 148
  meaning as, 147
present (time), 30, 103–104, 227
  existence of, 227
  living present, 17, 152–154, 157, 166
projection, orthogonal, 121
Prolegomena to Any Future Metaphysics (Kant), 94, 220
promises, ethical, 161
proportion
  analogy to sensation, 82–83
  appropriate, 76
  basis of, 74

  beauty and, 50–51
  divine, 52
  emotion and, 67
  experienced, 78
  in facades, 49–50
  moods and, 50, 63
  science of, 80
  sensation and, 81
  sequence of, 53
  statics and, 76
  temperance and, 79
prose, 178
Proust, Marcel, 178
Pseudo-Dionysus, 47
psychopathologies, 15, 109
psychotropy, civilization as illusion of, 223
Purgatorial City of Man, 46
purposefulness, 9
purposelessness, 221
Pythagoras, 39–40, 46, 55, 57, 81, 111

quadrattura, 59, 61
quality, architectural, 20–22
Quattro libri (Palladio), 53–54
Quintilian (Marcus Fabius Quintilianus), 184

rainbows, 63, 81–82
Ramachandran, V. S., 212
Rameau, Jean-Philippe, 57, 63, 66, 74, 81
rationality
  geometric, 63
  instrumental, 71
ratios, 53–55, 58, 67
Rauch, Eleanor, 142–143
reading, 171–173, 218
Real as Act, 230
reality
  animal, 148
  codependent origin of, 231
  delusion of technology as, 101
  distancing from, 195
  dualistic structure of, 27, 223, 227
  experienced vs. visual perception of, 150, 201–202

language and access to, 183–184
of life, 223–225
models and, 202–203
poetry and, 89, 94, 189
truth of, 220
virtual, 212–213
reason
egocentric, 2
experience and, 74–75
feelings separated from, 72
mathematical, 220
nature as a source of, 75 (*see also* truth)
positive, 219–220
in romantic philosophy, 93
scientific, 220–221
reasoning
computers as a model for, 157
foundation of, 60
receptivity, 155
refiguration, 190, 195
reflection, 147, 161–162
regionalism, 193
Reil, Johann Christian, 88
religion, 217–218, 221
Renaissance architecture, 77
theory of, 49–51, 57–58
representation
architectural, 202–204
of time, 153
of the world, 154
Republic (Plato), 38
Revelation, 46
Revit (Autodesk), 199, 203
Rhetoric (Aristotle), 182
Rhetoric as Philosophy (Grassi), 162
Ricoeur, Paul, 11, 96, 181–192, 195, 202, 209, 230
Riegl, Alois, 125–126
Rigby, Kate, 218
rights, universal, 221
Rilke, Rainer Maria, 88
rituals, 117, 131–132, 193, 221, 230
Rivius, Walther, 44
Robbe-Grillet, Alain, 136–137
Rondelet, Jean, 68, 200
Rooms, and mood, 15, 26, 28, 85

Rousseau, Jean-Jacques, 87, 205
Rowe, Colin, 53
The Rule of Metaphor (Ricoeur), 181–182
Ruskin, John, 21
Ryle, Gilbert, 27, 228

sacred, 148
profane and, 219
sacred places, 59, 85, 115–117, 119
sadness, poetic, 179
Saint Denis, abbey, 47
saints, martyrdom of, 116
Salines. *See* Chaux
salvation, 45, 47–48
Sappho, 226
Sartre, Jean-Paul, 28, 228
Saturn, 91
Saussure, Ferdinand de, 183
Scarry, Elaine, 189
Scharoun, Hans, 29
Schelling, Friedrich, 87–88
Schlegel, Friedrich von, 89, 94–95
Schleiermacher, Friedrich, 95
Schmarsow, August, 125–126
Schmidt, Siegfried, 229
Schmitz, Hermann, 16
Schubert, Franz, 177
Schumacher, Patrik, 104, 225
science
of aesthetics, 72
art and, 79
geometry and, 176
homogeneous space of, 83
mathematics and, 176
of the mind, 88, 142
modern, 55
of proportion, 80
of the soul, 112
subjective, 220
science fiction, architecture and, 20
"Second Meditation" (Descartes), 140
secular world, architecture in, 217–218
self, 87, 142–143, 161, 217, 231
self-awareness, 8, 147, 152
self-concealment, 141

self-consciousness, 30, 45, 155
self-effacement, 141
self-examination, 232
self-knowledge, 228
self-referentiality, 25, 168, 178–180
self-understanding, 49, 145
Semper, Gottfried, 126
Sennett, Richard, 78
sensations, 58, 75, 82–84
senses, 19, 65, 109, 120, 145, 149
sensing as thinking, 140
sensitive soul, 91
sensuality, 51, 58–60, 124
sentence, 182
sentiment in art, 141
Sermon, Paul, 211
sewer systems, 13–14
sexuality, 29–30, 43, 148, 207, 226
Shaftesbury, Anthony Ashley Cooper, 3rd Earl of, 86–87
Shrine of the Book (Kiesler), 103
sight, 51, 149–150
significance, architectural, 127
signifier and signified, 183, 185
silence, 168, 174
simulations, digital, 211–214
singing, 52
Sioli, Angeliki, 104
sites, 107–108, 115–117, 193. *See also tópos* (natural place)
situationism, 19
Skype, 228
Slaves (Michelangelo), 188
Smail, Daniel L., 222–223
smell, sense of, 13–14
Snell, Bruno, 114
social media, 210
social reality, 24
social world, 159
society, 3, 5–7, 27, 77–78, 178, 118, 223
Socrates, 219
software, architectural, 108, 198–200, 210
solipsism, 177
Sorbonne (church, Paris), 82
soul
  acoustics of, 90, 153
  animal, 232
  belief in, 72
  body and, 44, 65, 72, 114, 140, 157, 159, 227
  brain identified with, 141
  defined, 139–140
  emotion and, 71
  friendship and tuning of, 45
  light associated with, 39
  and mathematical sciences, 112
  in search for order, 39
  state of, 195
sound
  acoustic atmosphere, 171–173
  acoustics of the soul, 90, 153
  mathematics of, 58
  physicality of, 59
Soupault, Philippe, 185
sovereign, 221–222
space. *See also* place
  of appearance, 30, 42, 77–78, 84, 105, 192, 206
  architectural, 83–84, 108, 111
  Cartesian, 112, 120–122, 151, 204
  church and, 116
  of cities, 3–4, 44, 134, 229
  of communication, 208–209
  communicative, 114
  conceptualized, historically, 108, 132
  configuration of, 194
  constructed, 134
  of contemplation, 117–118
  cultural, 112, 115
  of desire, 30, 86, 101, 130, 226
  digital, 108
  of dreams, 114
  empty, 119, 131–132
  endless, 103
  erotic, 104, 114–115
  Euclidian, 38, 56–57, 112
  of everyday life, 97, 119, 191
  of existence, 226
  existence of, 112, 131–132
  geometric, 56–57, 116, 118–120, 123–125, 132
  homogeneous, 14–15

Index 285

human experience of, 126, 151
interior, 84–85
Kantian, 124
as light, 116, 119
as limits, 151
living, 104
of meditation, 4
of metaphor, 115
Newtonian, 132
organizing, 190
in painting, 52
perspectival, 134
private, 105
public, 13–14, 49, 105
refiguring, 189–190
sacred, 59, 85, 115–117, 119
scientific concept of, 109
of seduction, 122
sublunary, 112–114, 119
tectonic, 134
theorization of, 125
between things, 109
three-dimensional, 125–128
and time, 18, 85–86, 110, 131–132, 151
spectators, 19, 32
speech
  architecture as a form of, 179
  figures of, 184
  and gesture, 162
  as poetic utterance, 163
  prayer as, 172
  primacy of, 161, 171, 173
  and signification, 170
The Spell of the Senses (Abram), 17
spiritual destiny, 91
spirituality, 90, 217–218, 227–230
spiritual wholeness, attaining, 228–229
Spitzer, Leo, 10, 34–37, 45, 65–66
spoken word, 110, 198
stage sets, design of, 84, 102–103
starchitecture, 19
star dance, 39, 42–45
statics, 76
Steiner, George, 92

Stimmung
  artistic communication and, 15
  crystallization of, 66
  effective operation, requirements for, 135
  etymons, 34–35, 90
  harmony and concert, 34–38, 90
  hedonism vs., 130–131
  intellectual connotation, 34
  between living (*zóon*) and language (*lógos*), 93, 135, 163, 222
  meaning of, 90, 93
  musical connotation, 34
  opening design to, 18
  the place of being, 93, 112
  romantic, 15, 71, 86–92, 122, 153
  spiritual dimension, 90
  synesthesia recovered, 124
  translations of, 34, 90, 96
  well-tempered mixture (*temperies*), 34–38, 44, 90
stimuli, proprioceptive, 19
Stoicism, 40, 114, 117
storytelling, 41, 43, 115, 117, 161–162, 190, 193
Sturm und Drang, 87
style, 22, 178
subjectivity, 24
sublime and beautiful, 72, 75, 107, 123
Suger, abbot, 47–48
surrealism, 10, 101–103
surveillance in cities, 5
sustainability, cultural, 232
symbols, linguistic, 155–156
symmetry, harmony of, 45
sympathies, fundamental, 91
Symposium (Plato), 225
synesthesia, 88, 112, 144. *See also* colors, and music
  baroque, 58
  forced, 19–20
  perception and, 20, 50, 71–72
  phenomenological, 88
  primacy of, 71–72, 74, 82, 88, 145
  the sensuous and, 58
  Stimmung and, 135

taste, 75, 80
techné-poiésis-mímesis, 111
technique and creation, 194
technological world
  architectural meaning for, 127
  built environment in, 129
  Cartesian dualism, 141
  and natural world, 110–111
  perception in, 109
  place in, 131
  possibility in, 118
  sensorimotor skills and, 210
  telecommunications, 18
telecommunications, challenges to, 18
Telemann, Georg Philipp, 82
Telematic Dreaming (Sermon), 211
temperaments, 91
temperance, 39–40, 44, 49–50, 54–55, 65, 79, 94
temperies (well-tempered mixture), 34–38, 44, 90
temptations, 223
Ten Books on Architecture (Vitruvius), 2, 53, 74
Tesauro, Emmanuele, 183–184
tetrachord, 39–40
theater, 28–29, 172
  stage design, 84, 102–103
theology, secular, 56
Theory of Colors (Goethe), 92
thinking, 41, 140, 157
thinking subject, 2
Thompson, Evan, 133, 142–143, 147, 149–150, 152, 154, 201
thought, 157, 160–163, 168–169
3ds Max, 213
three-dimensional space, 125–128
thresholds, 86
Timaeus (Plato), 32–33, 39, 41, 114, 117, 228–229
time
  defined, 36
  empty, 119
  eternal, 87
  living present, 17, 152–154, 157, 166
  out of time, 227
  refiguring, 189
  representation of, 153
  scientific, 153
  and space, 18, 85–86, 110, 131–132, 151
  time consciousness, 151–152, 227
Time and Narrative (Ricoeur), 189–190
"The Time-Keeper's Place" (Hejduk), 209
tones and colors in correspondence, 63, 81–82
Topography of Terror museum, 136
tópos (natural place). *See also* sites
  chóra vs., 111, 117, 226
  cultural space vs., 112
  geometric figures inscribed into, 115
  geometric space displacing, 120
  sublunary, 118
traces, 98, 158, 189, 193
tradition and innovation, 187–188
traffic, vehicular, 14
Traité du beau essentiel dans les arts (Briseux), 80
transcendence, 228
Trinity, 52
truth. *See also* reason
  absolute, 231
  geometry and, 61
  metaphor and, 183–185
  mimetical and empirical, 114
  mythology and, 95
  nature as a source of, 75
  perspective and, 61
  phenomenal, 231
  as *phronesis*, 162
  poetic, 122
  relative, 231
  transcendental, 129
  as unveiling, 95
Turner, John, 21

Uccello, Paolo, 132
understanding
  emotional, 89
  metaphor and, 182
  models of, 149

Ungrund (positive nothingness), 97
Unity3D (Crytek), 213–214
universal rights, 221
urban architecture, 44, 205–206
urban design, 13–16, 19
urban life, medieval, 48

vaghezza, 62
Val-de-Grâce (Paris), 82
Varela, Francisco, 133, 142, 154, 225
Varieties of Presence (Noë), 203
Vattimo, Gianni, 180
Venus (myth), 122
Venus (planet), 114
venustas, 43, 86, 114, 129, 140
Vesely, Dalibor, 160
Vico, Giambattista, 122, 162–163, 181, 216
Victims (Hejduk), 136–138, 208
video games, 212
Viel de Saint-Maux, Jean-Louis, 83
Vierzehnheiligen (church), 116, 119
Viollet-le-Duc, Eugène-Emmanuel, 133
Virgil (Publius Vergilius Maro), 194, 229
virtual reality, 200, 211–212
virtue, projects celebrating, 207
vision
　constructing, 119
　and hearing, 63, 67–68, 81–82, 140
　kinesthetic, 201
　perspectival, 68, 121, 133–134, 140, 199
vitalism, 93
Vitruvius Pollio, Marcus, 2–3, 9, 16, 33, 36, 39–44, 49–50, 53, 55, 60–61, 74, 79, 86, 109–110, 113–115, 122, 153, 161, 171–173, 175, 185, 192, 194, 209
voices (*Stimme*) of architecture, 166
void, 232
"Void" (Hejduk), 208–209
Voltaire (François-Marie Arouet), 124

walking, 4
Wallis, John, 56

water, 14, 206–207
Watt, Douglas, 1
well-being, 7, 45, 50, 160. *See also* health
wholeness, 29, 88, 95, 102, 228–229
Wigley, Mark, 16, 19
will-to-power, 221
Wilson, Frank, 145, 166
wind, 44
wisdom
　in action (*phrónesis*), 41
　crafts manifesting, 120
　ethical (*phrónesis*), 122
　practical (*sollertia*), 68, 94
　prudent, 162
　psychomotor, 192
　theoretical, 41
Wölfflin, Heinrich, 125–126
wordlessness, 130–131
words, function of, 162
world
　as artifact of God, 57
　beauty of, 51
　flesh of, 167, 211–212
　music and, 58–62
　visual experience of, 201–202
world harmony, 45–47, 52, 62–63
world soul, 40, 45
Wright, Frank Lloyd, 18, 135
writing, 110–111, 136–138, 166, 172–173

Xenakis, Iannis, 19

Zarlino, Gioseffo, 55
Zeki, Semir, 8
Zeus (myth), 94, 229
Zevi, Bruno, 108
zoe and *bios*, 9
Zumthor, Peter, 20–22, 136